Religion and Politics in the United States

THIRD EDITION

Religion and Politics in the United States

THIRD EDITION

Kenneth D. Wald

University of Florida, Gainesville

A Division of Congressional Quarterly Inc.

Washington, D.C.

To Robin, Dara, and Jaina

Copyright © 1997 Congressional Quarterly Inc.
1414 22nd Street, N.W., Washington, D.C. 20037

Cover design: Naylor Design Inc.

Printed in the United States of America

Library of Congress Cataloging-in-Publication Data

Wald, Kenneth D.
     Religion and politics in the United States / Kenneth D. Wald—
3rd ed.
     p. cm.
     Includes bibliographical references and index.
     ISBN 1-56802-157-7
     1. Religion and politics—United States—History—20th century.
     2. United States—Religion—1960– 3. United States—Politics
     and government—1981–1989. I. Title.
BL2525.W35   1996
322'.1'097309049—dc20   96-38169

Contents

Tables, Figures, and Boxes   ix
Preface   xi

1. **A Secular Society?**   1

   The Puzzle of Religious Vitality   3
   Possible Explanations   16
   Why the United States?   19

2. **Religion and Politics: Points of Contact**   25

   Incentives: The Causes of Religious Intervention
     in Politics   27
   Opportunity: How Government Structure
     Encourages Political Action by Churches   32
   Religion as a Political Resource   35
   Limits on Religious Influence in Politics   38

3. **Religion and American Political Culture**   42

   The Puritan Imprint on Colonial Thought   43
   Covenant Theology and the Right to Revolt   46
   Puritanism and Democracy: A Qualification   50
   "Total Depravity" and Institutional Restraint   53
   One Nation Under God: A Civil Religion   59
   Civil Religion as a Double-Edged Sword   66
   One of Many Influences   68

4. **Religion and the State**   73

   The Genesis of Church-State Conflict   74
   Principles of Church-State Relations   77
   The Founders and Religion   82

How Far Can Government Go?   87
The Wall of Separation Grows Higher   92
Religious Expression in the Public Schools   97
Making Sense of the Establishment Clause   101
Extending Free-Exercise Claims   105
A Free-Exercise Standard   108
The Politics of Church-State Relations   111
Assaults on the New Order: Loosening the
  Establishment Clause   115
The Fall and Rise of Free Exercise   118
Can We Do Better?   120

5. Religion and American Public Policy   124

Interest Group Activities   125
Organizing for Political Action   139
The Question of Representation   143
Paths of Influence   145
The Judiciary   149
The President's Religion   153
Religious Values and Government Activities   157
Limitations on Religious Influence   162
Religious Activism in Politics: Costs and Benefits   166

**6. The Religious Dimension of
   American Political Behavior**   169

Patterns of Religious Affiliation   170
Political Identity   176
Political Issues   179
The "Social Issue"   184
The "Culture War" Thesis   188
Religious Differences and Social Standing   191
Religion and Political Values   197
Religion and Group Interests   206
The Role of Social Integration   210

**7. The Political Mobilization of Evangelical
   Protestants**   217

The Political Background   218

Roots of the "New Christian Right"   223
Building a National Movement   225
Evangelical Political Action in the 1980s   228
The Next Generation   230
Theories of Evangelical Mobilization   237
The New Christian Right as a Mass Movement   244
A Fractious Family   249
The Electoral Dimension of the NCR   252
A Republican Dilemma?   257
The Consequences for Public Policy   261

8. **Continuity and Change Outside the**
   Evangelical Camp   267

Catholicism: The Conservative Political Heritage   268
The Transformation of Catholic Attitudes   272
Abortion: The Catholic Response   281
Abortion: A Catholic Issue?   285
The Political Traditions of Mainline Protestants   293
Mainline Activism: Sources and Reactions   297
Retrenchment   300
African American Protestants: The Perpetuation
   of Liberalism   301
The Infrastructure of African American Politics   303
Jews and U.S. Political Trends   310

9. **Religion and American Political Life**   319

The Case Against Religious Influence in Politics   320
Assessing the Evidence   327
The Case for Religion in Politics   334

References   347
Index   389

Tables, Figures, and Boxes

Tables

4.1   Significant Supreme Court Decisions on Church
and State Questions   94

6.1   Support for U.S. Government Efforts to
Assist African Americans, by Religious Group   182

6.2   Support for Restrictive Abortion Law, by
Religious Group   185

6.3   Position on Women's Rights Scale, by
Religious Group and Church Attendance   186

6.4   Support for Policies to Prohibit Discrimination
Against Homosexuals, by Religious Group   187

7.1   Christian Right Organizations and
Their Opponents   234

7.2   Public Agreement on Issues of Government
and Morality   245

Figures

1.1   Effect of Economic Development on Belief in God   10

1.2   Frequency of Churchgoing in the United States   11

1.3   Religiosity in the United States   12

4.1   General Views on Church/State Separation   80

4.2   Specific Views on Church/State Separation   81

5.1   Percentage of Congregants Hearing Clergy
      Discuss Political Issues   132

6.1   Religious Traditions   173

6.2   Political Partisanship by Religious Group   176

6.3   Ideology by Religious Group   177

6.4   Presidential Preference in 1992 by Religious Group   178

6.5   Support for Government Activity by Religious Group   180

6.6   Welfare-Spending Attitudes by Religious Group   181

6.7   Educational Attainment by Religious Group   192

6.8   Democratic Partisanship by Religious Group
      and Education   193

6.9   School-Funding Preferences by Religious Group   207

8.1   Catholic Versus Protestant Attitudes on
      Defense Spending, 1983   278

Boxes

3.1   Civil Religious Sentiment in the United States   62

7.1   Christian Voice's "Report Card" on Key
      1984 Presidential Candidates   232

Preface

S ince the first edition of this book was published, I have occasionally wondered if the subject might have become obsolete. As with most scholars who explore the role of religion in public life, my attention was sharply focused on the topic by two developments in the late 1970s: the Islamic Revolution in Iran and the political uprising of conservative American Christians. Events in Iran destroyed the notion that modernizing societies would inevitably develop "secular" political systems, while the emergence of organizations such as Moral Majority suggested the durability of religious forces in the politics of advanced industrial societies. To my students, these events now seem like ancient history. Perhaps the death of Ayatollah Khomeini, the guiding spirit of the Iranian revolution, and the collapse of the organizations that first mobilized American fundamentalists signal that these forces have finally run their course.

Just when I start thinking like that, reality intrudes to remind me that religion remains a global political force. Whatever the fate of the Iranian revolution, the Islamic movement has gained great influence in Arab states like Algeria and Egypt and among the Palestinian resistance to Israel. In Israel itself, Prime Minister Yitzhak Rabin was assassinated by a zealot who believed Rabin was betraying God's promise to the Jewish people by surrendering land to the Palestinians. In Europe, the bloody and protracted conflict in the former Yugoslavia was fueled by tensions among the Bosnian adherents of Islam, the Serb Orthodox Christians, and the Croatian Roman Catholics.

Closer to home, Americans have witnessed the alarming growth of a native terrorist movement—an antigovernment paramilitary crusade steeped in the doctrines of "Christian Identity." In the more sedate world of conventional politics, the sentiments embodied by the late

Moral Majority remain very much alive. Throughout the 1996 presidential campaign, the abortion issue bedeviled both major parties. Among Democrats, the allegiance of some social conservatives was tested by President Bill Clinton's veto of a ban on one form of late-term abortion. Several "pro-choice" Republican leaders unleashed a firestorm among religious conservatives in their ranks by calling on the party to change its uncompromising platform pledge against legalized abortion. In contemporary American politics, religious and political loyalties seem to draw ever closer together.

If the subject is not obsolete, as these developments attest, neither are the two themes that constitute this book's central premise: Religion is more important in American politics than most Americans realize but in different ways from those they commonly imagine. The first theme simply restates my belief that the content and conduct of American political life are strongly influenced by religious beliefs and traditions. The second theme calls attention to the surprising diversity of political positions associated with different religions. Far from being a predictable political force, religion is a social factor that takes many different political forms in a variety of circumstances. Despite this general premise, the book is not intended to argue that religion is somehow the central animating force of American political life. Thus, just as I attempt to identify the conditions that enhance religious influence on government and politics, I also note circumstances that limit the political impact of religious forces.

Classroom experience makes me vividly aware that people reach different verdicts about the connection between religion and politics. Some people applaud it as necessary and proper; others denounce it as the root of mischief and evil. In this book I have tried to inform readers about both the noble and the notorious sides of the religious element in politics. In the intellectual minefield that is religion and politics, no one book can satisfy everyone, nor would it be of much value if it did. This book is offered on the principle that good teaching prompts believers to question a faith and encourages skeptics to appreciate its value. In that sense, I hope to subvert the states of mind expressed epigrammatically as follows: "For believers there are no questions, and for unbelievers no answers."

The reader should also know that this text takes a social scientific perspective on the subject of religion and politics. After trying to explain that thought in many different ways, I find I cannot improve on the words of a scholar who began a book on the same topic this warning: "To be a historian is to seek to explain in human terms. If God speaks, it is not through him. If He speaks to others, the historian cannot vouch for it. In this sense the historian is necessarily secularist" (Strout 1974, xiv). In other words, the social scientific approach refuses to explain religion in terms of supernatural forces, insisting instead on finding human causes for patterns of human behavior. Likewise, most social scientists resist the opposite tendency to reduce religion to a biological or genetic trait. Supernaturalists may explain the survival of religion as God's will, while some natural scientists might attribute the persistence of religion in society to the sound dietary principles and healthy lifestyles of believers (see National Research Council 1982). Although both these explanations may be true and useful, the social scientist prefers to emphasize the operation of human consciousness and choice. Thus chapter 1 invokes neither the hand of God nor the principles of evolution to explain why religion prospers in America. Instead, consistent with the social scientific outlook, it calls attention to cognitive factors—people's apparent need to reduce uncertainty about their place in the universe—and elements of the social and political structure that encourage religious observance. The rest of the book follows suit.

The book begins with two chapters that establish the framework for studying the relationship between religion and politics in the United States. Chapter 1 demonstrates the continuing significance of religion in American life, and chapter 2 identifies the features of religion and the American political system that promote regular interaction between the two spheres. In ensuing chapters, I examine the potential political impact of religion on different levels of political life. Separate chapters are devoted to the influence of religion on fundamental American beliefs about politics and governance (chapter 3) and views about church/state relations (chapter 4). I then explore the role of religion in the policy-making process (chapter 5) and, in chapter 6, its contribution to mass partisan and ideological orientations. The next two chapters explain the often puzzling changes that have taken place in the political behavior of major religious groups in the United States: chapter 7 explores the theologically conservative Protestant churches, and chapter 8 similarly analyzes the other major religious traditions, groups whose interesting patterns of stability and change have sometimes been lost in the glare of publicity devoted to the evangelical Protestants. I conclude with a chapter that weighs the positive and negative contributions of religion to politics and governance in the United States.

Because religion's role in politics is the subject of strong feeling, readers may want to know something more about the author's background and beliefs. As the child of Holocaust survivors and the grandchild of Holocaust victims, I have long taken an interest in the topic being examined and have a keen appreciation for the potential political consequences of religious belief. It may also account for my belief that religion should speak to public affairs. Though well aware that churches perform an important spiritual mission that might suffer from excessive political involvement, I nonetheless believe that religious institutions have a responsibility to remind the state of its ethical obligations. Accordingly, I am more comfortable when churches challenge the government than when they vest the state with a holy aura. Readers of different backgrounds may spot other assumptions that seem natural to me but perhaps are contentious to them.

Although I cannot be certain of all the ways my personal background has influenced the book, it is easy to identify persons in the foreground who helped prepare me to write it. I owe a great debt to scholars who paved the way for this project with pioneering studies of religion and politics, and to contemporary investigators scattered among various academic disciplines. (Thanks to the efficient Inter-Library Loan Office at the Smathers Library at the University of Florida, I was able to locate and read these important publications.) My friends and colleagues in the Section on Religion and Politics of the American Political Science Association have constantly prodded me with their insightful questions and observations. Some of the thoughts expressed here were forged in the heat of collaborative teaching with colleagues at the University of Memphis and University of Florida. Dave Leege of the University of Notre Dame, my collaborator on other projects, has been generous with his time, intellect, and friendship. This manuscript benefited especially from the detailed comments of M. Richard Cramer of the University of North Carolina at Chapel Hill, Elizabeth G. King of St. Norbert College, and Donald Pienkos of the University of Wisconsin—Milwaukee. Once again, I was astonished that the entire staff of CQ Press managed to treat me as though I were the only author on its list. Thanks especially to Brenda Carter, Julie Rovesti, Gwenda Larsen, Talia Greenberg, and others who helped me put my best foot forward. Kristen C. Stoever, an extraordinary copy editor, deserves special credit for helping me to keep that foot out of my mouth!

On the home front, I continue to receive a sublime mixture of encouragement and distraction from the members of my family and am happy to rededicate the volume to them.

1. A Secular Society?

When you introduce religion into politics, you're playing with fire.
—Senator Lowell P. Weicker Jr. *New York Times,* 21 March 1984

Religion and politics are necessarily related.
—President Ronald W. Reagan, *Church & State*

Everyone knows that it is impolite to argue religion or politics with strangers and dangerous to do so with friends. These topics are treated with such delicacy because they evoke strong passions; men and women have been known to discuss, debate, argue, organize, demonstrate, resist, fight, and kill—or be killed—on behalf of their religious or political beliefs. What, then, could possibly justify violating both taboos by writing a book about religion and politics?

The answer is simply that religion remains an important political factor in the United States. The election of a Catholic president by a predominantly Protestant electorate in 1960 was widely celebrated as marking the end of sectarian appeals in American politics. As the 1992 presidential campaign showed, that conclusion was premature. At the 1992 GOP national convention in Houston, Republican delegates applauded Pat Buchanan's call for the campaign to be a "religious war" for the soul of America. Voters could pick the Republican nominee, "a champion of the Judeo-Christian values and beliefs upon which this America was founded," or endorse a challenger who embraced such irreligious causes as "unrestricted abortion on demand," the "raw sewage of pornography," gay rights, and contempt for marriage and family (Buchanan 1992). In addition to attacking his issue positions, conservative Republicans also claimed that Bill Clinton was not morally fit to assume the presidency. Not willing to be painted in such unflattering strokes, the Democrats responded by portraying their nominee

1

as a staunch advocate of traditional American values who drew deeply on his own religious heritage. Clinton himself often presented his policy proposals steeped in biblical language.[1] Though the Democrats won the election of 1992, the "religious war" strategy continued. During the first two years of his presidency, Clinton found himself embroiled in controversy over his attempt to repeal the military's ban on gays and well-publicized charges that he had engaged in extramarital affairs and pushed unwanted sexual attention on female state employees in Arkansas. Doubts about the president's soundness on "God and gays" helped the Republicans seize a number of Senate and House seats in their 1994 election victory. In America's single most important political ritual, the national election, the religious emphasis has been plain to see.

In recent years, moreover, the national agenda has included a host of controversial domestic questions that touch upon deeply held religious beliefs and outlooks—issues such as abortion, women's role in society, pornography, homosexuality, and similar disputes that recall the passions aroused by the temperance movement and the teaching of evolution in the schools. Contemporary controversies about prayer and religious clubs in public schools and government recognition of religious holidays exemplify the continuing debate over church-state relations. Even economic questions of taxing and spending, traditionally deemed beyond the sphere of religion, are increasingly discussed from a "moral" perspective (Pasquariello 1985). As an example, some Republicans cited the need to protect the biblically ordained institution of the family as a reason to cut welfare benefits to unmarried and underaged women with children but to give larger tax benefits to married couples with children. At the other end of the political spectrum, environmentalists have tried to enlist supporters with religiously grounded appeals (Fowler 1995).

The growth of religious controversy around the globe has also reverberated in American political life. In response to a powerful resurgence of Islamic fundamentalism during the 1980s, the United States was held hostage in Iran, tried to act as peacekeeper in Lebanon, and supplied weapons to Moslem rebels in Afghanistan. The collapse of European communism in the 1990s, often stimulated by the uprisings of religious groups, left a number of dangerous ethnic and religious conflicts that prompted calls by some churches for U.S. intervention.

The role of religious forces in these global conflicts was not always well understood by American policymakers (Rubin 1994). For their part, American churches that used to cooperate in overseas humanitarian relief found themselves increasingly divided by political issues. While many churches developed a preoccupation with human rights abuses—pressing the government to negotiate reductions in nuclear weapons, to admit more political refugees from Central America, and to cut economic ties with the apartheid government of South Africa—other, more conservative churches raised funds to combat left-wing movements in Latin America and elsewhere. During the Gulf War in 1991, spokespersons for some religious organizations echoed President George Bush's claim that the allied cause was godly while other groups condemned the war as incompatible with Judeo-Christian values.

We may applaud it, deplore it, be repelled or fascinated by it—but our first imperative is to understand how and why religion so animates American politics. Despite evidence of the persistence of religious vitality in the United States, scholars and citizens alike have been slow to recognize the political impact of religion in the United States. This underestimation stemmed in large part from a mistaken belief in the inevitable "secularization" of modern life. As the next section shows, the widespread belief that religion was destined to recede from the mind of humankind prepared observers to discount religious influences in the political realm.

The Puzzle of Religious Vitality

Textbooks on American government send a message that "religion is not and never has been a significant factor either in the development of our political institutions or in their operations" (Carey 1982, 7).[2] Critics blame this "secular" prejudice on authors' supposed indifference or outright hostility toward religion. For the most part, however, the neglect of religion as a political force stems from widespread acceptance of certain social theories that guide academic research away from religion. A novelist who wrote that "a man's eyes can only see what they're learnt to see" understood well that expectations can become blinders, prompting us to overlook important information and developments. In the case of religion, most scholars "learnt to see" secularization, broadly understood as the decline of religious influence in advanced industrial societies, and that expectation drew their attention away from the presence of religion in the political realm.

The concept of secularization encompasses a variety of processes as complex as the phenomenon of religion itself (Wallis and Bruce 1992). In its most neutral sense, secularization refers only to changes in religion as society develops. One process, *differentiation,* means the development of religion as a specialized institution with its own sphere of competence. When religion is differentiated, it retreats from a privileged position in such fields as the law, education, and medicine and restricts its operations to other realms. In most of the realms "cleansed" of religion by the differentiation process, government assumes responsibility and conducts business without recourse to religious values. This leaves religion in modern society with the unique task of providing individuals with consolation and moral guidance. Under modern conditions, religion also experiences *privatization.* That term refers to the evolution of religion into a matter of personal judgment and choice that exerts its profoundest impact on individuals, what some have called "internal secularization." A privatized faith is reluctant to tell society how it ought to behave. A third process associated with secularization, *desacralization,* refers to changes in thought rather than to the transformation of religious organizations. Desacralization is the tendency to explain the everyday world in terms of material reality rather than supernatural forces. Modern societies often treat as ordinary what more traditional civilizations may imbue with a divine character. Finally, secularization is often equated with *liberalization* of religious doctrine, the lowering of barriers between religious groups and the relaxation of orthodoxy. Together, these processes constitute a neutral definition of secularization.

If secularization is understood simply as religious change, it leaves room for religion—modified, adapted, and adjusted to new circumstances—as a significant force in contemporary society. None of the trends described above would necessarily remove religion from the political universe, and some might even strengthen its relevance to political conflict. But many scholars have made secularization into an iron law that boldly predicts the virtual extinction of organized religion and points to the consequent elimination of religious influences in contemporary culture. This particular understanding of secularization, the "naive" version that predicts diminishing significance for religion in politics, is associated with two of the most influential theories of social change, the *modernization* approach and the *class conflict* model.

The modernization approach predicts transformations in life and thought because of the rapid growth of cities; the rise of factory production; the spread of education, communication, and technology; and the emergence of vast administrative apparatuses, or bureaucracies. Sociological observers of the late nineteenth and early twentieth centuries believed these developments, which define what we mean by "modern," had wrought massive changes in the place of religion in society. Before the onset of modernization, most people lived in small, geographically isolated settlements and were preoccupied by the daily task of producing life's necessities. With limited exposure to external influences, people living in the settlements shared a stable set of beliefs, customs, and traditions. Subject to forces beyond their control, particularly weather and disease, people were receptive to supernatural outlooks. The myths and folk religions of primitive cultures are commonly thought to have originated in fear of the unknown, in dread and awe (Goodenough 1972). This description may conjure up images of a Stone Age pygmy tribe in a rain forest, but the portrait would be just as appropriate for the Irish villages, Norwegian communes, and East European *shtetls* whose migrants eventually populated much of the United States.

According to modernization theory, the forces of modernity shatter such cultures. Migration to a city in search of work removes the villagers from traditional influences and brings them into regular contact with persons from different backgrounds. When the villages are penetrated by new means of communication, even those who stay put are subject to new influences. Traditional values, particularly the emphasis on fate and the supernatural, are undermined by the doctrine of scientific cause-and-effect taught in school, factory, and mass media (Inkeles 1983). When held up to scientific standards of proof and evidence, religious claims and, therefore, religious faith may falter. The discovery that other people worship different gods may further reduce unshakable confidence in the "one true faith" to a weaker "religious preference." The institutions that arise in modernity—large societies, complex enterprises, extensive governments—treat people impersonally, without regard for their religious identities. Accordingly, behavior formerly governed by deference and obedience, perhaps even as sacred obligation, gives way to exchange, bargaining, and negotiation.[3] As a consequence, people come to define their personal identity and political interests not in terms of religion but as a function of their standing in the marketplace—as owners, workers, proprietors of small business-es, and so forth.

According to the predictions of modernization theory, societies that have been fully exposed to the currents of modern life will accord religion a minor role. Except among the elderly, raised in a more devout age, and the residents of cultural backwaters, the practice of religion will diminish. The institutions of religion will suffer a similar fate unless they are transformed into agencies of social welfare and service centers—and even then churches must compete with the state to perform these tasks. An even more telling sign of religious decay is the erosion of religious thought:

> Men act less and less in response to religious motivation: they assess the world in empirical and rational terms, and find themselves involved in rational orga-nizations and rationally determined roles which allow small scope for such reli-gious predilections as they might privately entertain. Even if . . . non-logical behaviour continues in unabated measure in human society, then at least the terms of non-rationality have changed. It is no longer the dogmas of the Christian Church which dictate behaviour, but other quite irrational and arbi-trary assumptions about life, society and the laws which govern the physical universe. (B. Wilson 1966, 10)

The change in the terms of thought, from a God-centered to a human-centered world, is the most dramatic testament to the victory of secu-larization in the modern world. This understanding of modern society leaves little room for religion as a social or political factor.

The forecast of religious decline in the modern world has been rein-forced by another influential theory of social change—Marxism. Like modernization theorists, Karl Marx and Friedrich Engels believed reli-gious sentiments reflected a human response to forces that defied understanding and that faith in the supernatural was likely to be a casualty of economic development (Aptheker 1968). Writing in the mid-nineteenth century, Marx began with the paradox that the human conquest of nature, which ought to have put an end to hunger and oppression, seemed instead to have intensified them. The sources of wealth, differing from one era to the next, had always been monopo-lized by and used to enrich the few at the expense of the many. But with the coming of industrialization and factory-based economies, he argued, the process of exploitation became more severe. Once subordinate to the forces of nature, workers now found themselves subordinate to economic elites. Unemployment replaced natural calamity as the scourge of human existence.

In this setting, Marx suggested, religion appealed most strongly to the oppressed who desperately needed some explanation for their plight. Christianity found its pioneers among slave populations because it promised them the solace of a better life to come; psychologically, the Christian religion was a balm, a salve for despair. Subsequently, the growth of Christianity was encouraged by the dominant groups in society because it might teach the "lower orders"—be they slaves, serfs, or industrial workers—to accept their condition as God's will and to look for solace in the afterlife. In this way, Marx argued in a famous passage, religion became the "opiate" of the people.

In Marx's view, a society built on exploitation could not long endure because the oppressed majority would eventually recognize its exploitation. As conditions worsened, the working class would realize the inequity of prevailing economic arrangements and their source in man-made doctrines and practices. When this occurred, Marx expected an uprising, the seizure of power on behalf of the previously oppressed majority and the creation of a new, more just and humane social order. In this new world, humankind would reclaim its proper place as the maker of its own destiny, and all the artificial doctrines developed to support the dethroned system—including religion—would be consigned to the "dustbin of history." Religion, which had persisted because of intolerable social conditions, would simply evaporate with these social transformations.

Bolstered by theories that confidently forecast the demise of religion, many students of politics predicted that religious controversy would eventually disappear from the political agenda. Although it would still be available as a basis for defending traditional cultures threatened by social change, religion is likely to lose its political relevance, displaced by disputes rooted primarily in economics. Students of political behavior similarly anticipated a shift in the basis of political loyalty from "premodern" factors such as religion, ethnicity, and region to more modern factors like social class, occupational standing, and socioeconomic status (Epstein 1967, 88). In "mature" political systems, it was said, political campaigns no longer resembled emotional religious crusades but instead took on the flavor of slick exercises in public relations; sober appeals to self-interest replaced passionate calls for national salvation. What most political observers never expected to find was an advanced industrial society in which religion exercised a tenacious hold on the public mind and strongly influenced the conduct of political life. Yet that is precisely what we find in the contemporary United States.

The Persistence of Religion

By most conventional yardsticks, the United States was one of the first nations to have undergone modernization, and it continues to lead the way in many aspects of social development. If modernization leads inevitably to the decline of religious institutions, practices, and feelings—what I have called the "naive" understanding of secularization—then the erosion of religion ought to show up first in such a mobile, affluent, urban, and expansive society. Yet American religion, like Mark Twain, has obstinately refused to comply with reports of its demise.

American religion has certainly experienced the processes associated with the neutral definition of secularization. Religion is a specialized institution with a limited public role and religious affiliation is a matter of personal choice. Consistent with the experience of desacralization, Americans generally interpret events from a scientific and naturalist perspective. Many orthodox doctrines and forms of devotion have been abandoned or modified by church authorities. But these changes do not add up to the global decline in faith predicted by naive secularization theory. It cannot be denied that some religions have lost intensity, esteem, and membership or that many Americans are indifferent or antagonistic toward religion. Yet even these elements of decline have been offset by spectacular growth in some religions, the flowering of new faiths, periodic revivals of religious enthusiasm, and the spread of religious sentiment to some of the most "secularized" segments of the population (Hastings and Hoge 1986; Hadden 1987). The naive model of secularization cannot withstand the facts.

Just how poorly modernization and Marxist theories of religion fit the United States is demonstrated in figure 1.1, which reflects information from a dozen countries in the early 1990s. The diagonal line shows the underlying relationship between level of economic development and the proportion of a representative national sample in each country who told interviewers they were certain of God's existence.[4] The downward slope of the line as the level of "modernization" increases generally confirms the prediction that economic development goes hand in hand with a decline in traditional religious sentiment. The United States is a conspicuous exception, however, to the generalization. With the second-highest score on the index of economic development, it was also one of the most "religious" of countries as shown by the answers its citizens gave to interviewers. The magnitude of American "exceptionalism" can best be gauged by comparing the proportion of Americans who had no doubts about God—63 percent—to the 34 percent expressing no doubts predicted by the pattern in other countries. To highlight the figure another way, Americans were three times as likely as Norwegians to report belief in God, despite the economic similarity between the two countries, and were similar in religious belief to the Irish, who live in a country with about half the American per capita GNP.

By all the normal yardsticks of religious commitment—the strength of religious institutions, practices, and belief—the United States has resisted the pressures toward secularity. Institutionally, churches are probably the most vital voluntary organization in a country that puts a premium on "joining up." There are between 255,000 and 300,000 churches in the United States with a total membership of about 137 million (Bradley et al. 1992; Hodgkinson, Weitzman, and Kirsch 1988). Depending on how "membership" is defined, the church members amount to somewhere between three-fifths and three-fourths of the adult population. Despite all the talk about "decline," the proportion of church members among persons aged fifteen and older is virtually the same today as it was in 1950 and, with due allowance for the raggedness of historical data, actually seems to be higher now than throughout most of American history (Finke and Stark 1992). High as it is, the proportion of church membership may understate the full extent of American religious consciousness. Even if they are not affiliated with any religious organization, nine out of ten Americans typically claim to identify with some religious group or tradition (Kosmin and Lachman 1993).

Support for organized religion shows up in other ways. In annual surveys about confidence in major institutions, churches and organized reli-

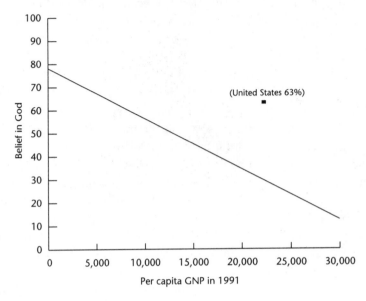

Figure 1.1 Effect of Economic Development on Belief in God (Source: Calculated by the author from International Social Survey Program, 1991)

gion have consistently been ranked at or near the top of the list (Newport and Saad 1994). Along the same lines, the clergy has regularly outdistanced almost all other occupational groups in public estimates of honesty and ethical standards (McAneny and Moore 1994). This vote of confidence has been backed up by perhaps the ultimate expression of commitment—the pocketbook. In 1986, for example, Americans contributed more than $40 billion to religious institutions, making churches by far the most favored recipient of philanthropy. Congregations devoted a significant share of that income to education, human service, health and hospitals, community development, the arts, and environmental protection (Hodgkinson, Weitzman, and Kirsch 1988). With its $1.5 billion annual budget, Catholic Charities is second only to the U.S. government in welfare activities, and the number of Americans working abroad for Christian organizations dwarfs the number of civilian U.S. government employees stationed abroad (McDonough 1994; Nichols 1988, 21).

Surveys of church practice, another presumed casualty of the modern age, show an equally high level of attachment to religion. What

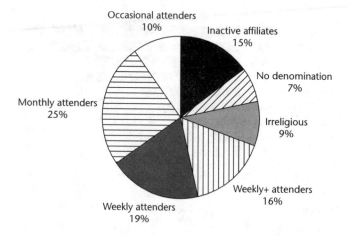

Figure 1.2 Frequency of Churchgoing in the United States (Source: Calculated by the author from the 1989 pilot study, American National Election Study, Center for Political Studies)

anthropologists call "rites of passage" (formal celebrations of an individual's progress through life, such as naming ceremonies, attainment of adulthood, marriage, and funerals) are still monopolized by the churches in the United States, as they are in many other cultures. But as national data reveal, devotion is hardly limited to such occasions (see fig. 1.2). At one extreme, about one-third of the population claims never to attend church outside of weddings and funerals. The "unchurched" comprise the self-defined irreligious (9 percent of the entire population), another 7 percent who consider themselves religious but who have no denominational commitment, and the remaining 15 percent who identify personally with a religious group but do not participate. Slightly more than one-third of the population maintains a moderate association with churches. Though the moderate category includes those who attend church only a few times a year (10 percent), most people in this category (25 percent) attend at least once a month. The most intensely religious third of the population includes people who are in church every week (19 percent) and those who attend even more than once a week (16 percent).

Churchgoing is but one form of religious behavior; Americans engage in a wide range of other public and private devotional acts (see

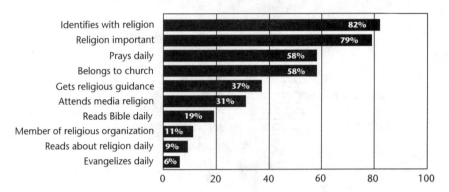

Figure 1.3 Religiosity in the United States (Source: Calculated by the author from the 1989 pilot study, American National Election Study, Center for Political Studies)

fig. 1.3). More than three-quarters of all Americans identify with a religion and consider it important in their lives. Substantial majorities report formal membership in a church and daily prayers. Approximately one-third of the population claims to get a "great deal" of daily guidance from religion and to monitor religious television and radio programs weekly. Almost 20 percent say they read the Bible on a daily basis. One in ten claims membership in independent religious organizations and daily reading about religion in newspapers and magazines. About one in twenty report attempting to convince someone else to accept their faith each day. Based on questions from the same survey, religious involvement appears far more widespread than many forms of political participation. More Americans identify with a denomination than a political party, and the typical citizen is much more likely to attend church than a political meeting. The proportion of citizens who claim to evangelize on behalf of their faith exceeds the percentage who report having tried to influence another person's vote.

But do these findings refer merely to the shell of religion and mask weaknesses in the power exerted by religious values? Certainly the American people believe religion is losing influence in society, and external critics regard the statistics as superficial, a tribute more to habit and conformity than to deep-seated faith. In truth, it is much more challenging to prove the persistence of religious feeling. Precisely that aspect of religion—its capacity to keep people's minds focused on questions of ultimate value, on heaven, hell, right, wrong, judgment, justice—should have declined with the triumph of modern culture. Because feelings of any sort are notoriously slippery things to measure, perhaps the best that can be done here is to note that major studies of contemporary values have repeatedly asserted the underlying importance of religion. For example, a major life insurance company commissioned a report to assess what Americans believed and how those beliefs were related to factors such as age, social standing, place of residence, and so forth. Despite this secular orientation, the authors found that the religious factor emerged as a kind of superstar among all the other pieces of information: "In investigating major aspects of American life—community involvement, political and moral beliefs, personal relationships, and work—time and again, systematic analysis led to the one factor that consistently and dramatically affects the values and behavior of Americans. This factor is level of religious commitment. The initial intention of this study was not to prepare a report on the impact of religion on American life, but the pattern of responses was compelling" (Research and Forecasts 1981, 6).

Detailed findings from a host of surveys have borne out this conclusion. By overwhelming majorities, Americans have continued to endorse the core assumptions of Christianity—the existence of God, the divinity of Jesus, the reality of an afterlife—and to insist on the importance of these values in their own lives (Gallup and Castelli 1989; Greeley 1989). Most Americans believe in the divine origins of humankind and nearly a majority accept a literal interpretation of the Genesis story (Newport 1993). When Americans think about God, they conceive of a creator and healer; the image of heaven carried in the minds of modern Americans depicts a place of union with God and reunion with loved ones (Harley and Firebaugh 1993). "Two centuries after the intellectual world has said that these kinds of things do not happen," reported a scholar who interviewed two thousand small-town Midwesterners, "many people reported mystical experiences such as visions, prophetic dreams, voices from heaven, and visits from spirits." [5] Despite all the publicity accorded the "New Age" movement, Americans are much more likely to perceive a spirit world of angels and devils than to believe in crystals and channeling (Gallup and Castelli 1989, 75–76) and may in fact be less disposed today to believe in magic and astrology than they were centuries ago (Butler 1990).

To the extent that such things can be measured, religious feeling, like religious institutions and practices, has survived intact in probably the most "modern" society known in history. Statistics have been used to make the point because numbers are the currency of argument in a scientific culture. But because national statistics often have a numbing effect, they should be supplemented with a local example. The stability of a religious texture in American life has been demonstrated forcefully by a continuing study of a small industrial town in eastern Indiana. In the 1920s a pair of gifted social observers decided to put "Middletown," a pseudonym for Muncie, under the microscope of social analysis (Lynd and Lynd 1929). Curious about the changes wrought by the passage of fifty years, a team of social scientists set out in the 1970s to repeat the study of Muncie (Caplow, Bahr, and Chadwick 1983). In the half-century since the first study, Muncie had experienced all the changes that are supposed to encourage secularization—rapid population growth, relentless technological advance, the spread of education, increasing bureaucracy, the penetration of mass media, an expanded governmental presence. Could the vibrant religious tradition of the town possibly survive the corrosive effects of these changes?

Despite the odds against it, traditional religion was found to be doing quite nicely in modern Muncie. In the words of the most recent study of the town, "The Reverend Rip Van Winkle, Methodist minister, awakening in Middletown after a 60-year sleep, would hardly know he had been away" (ibid., 280). He might be surprised by the growth of tolerance among religious groups, but little else had changed since the 1920s. The "Middletown" residents of the 1970s seemed every bit as pious as their grandparents and great-grandparents. Most people still subscribed to the core beliefs of Christianity and, whether measured by the numbers of clergy and buildings, by financial contributions, or by attendance at worship, the churches flourished. But surely, it may be argued, the survival of religion was purchased at a high price—by sacrificing the traditional emphasis on the emotional and spiritual for a more modern style stressing reason and social reform. This plausible suggestion collapses under the evidence of growth in the most theologically conservative churches, a renewed emphasis on emotional forms of worship in all denominations, and the continuing priority placed by the clergy on the spiritual well-being of their flocks. Against all expectations, the most recent study of Muncie uncovered a community with reverence for the sacred and faith in religion as a source of strength and guidance.

Because I have been trying to counter the widespread myth that religion is dead or declining in the United States, I have deployed the arguments for persistence in the starkest possible way. Critics of this approach deploy their own trinity of counterarguments, maintaining (1) that contemporary religious commitment is exaggerated—being wide but not deep, (2) that some degree of religious decline has in fact occurred, and (3) that American religion has purchased its longevity by selling its soul to secular culture. There is some truth to each of these claims. In the same way that Americans exaggerate their level of voting, giving charity, or performing other good deeds, they massively inflate their church attendance. Perhaps only half the people who tell pollsters they were in church actually do attend in any given week (Hadaway, Marler, and Chaves 1993). Presumptuous though it is to assume we can determine when religious commitment is superficial as opposed to authentic, it is striking how little Americans know about the essentials of their declared faiths and how readily they switch from one denomination to another (cf. Gallup and Castelli 1989). The critics can also score points by pointing to evidence of religious decline. Consistent with the desacralization hypothesis, religious belief has declined among the best-educated segment of the population and the appeal of the "old time" religion remains strongest among groups with the least exposure to modernization: housewives, the elderly, inhabitants of rural areas and small towns, Southerners, and persons with low levels of education. People deeply embedded in such major institutions of modernization as the marketplace, cities, industry, and schools are less likely to have maintained religious orthodoxy.

Although all these facts can be accommodated as qualifications to the persistence interpretation, the claim of religious continuity is most seriously challenged by the argument that American religion has become much more "secular" than sacred. Consider the way God has been recast. What is left of the forbidding and wrathful deity from the Hebrew Bible in contemporary religious writing that portrays God as a therapist, economic adviser, athletic trainer, and friend, the source of stable families, financial prosperity, mental and physical health, and sexual satisfaction (Hunter 1983, chaps. 4, 6)? We seem to hear more about God's forgiving nature and much less about divine punishment or demands for repentance (Witten 1993).[6] As an institution, religion also seems to be grasped less for its truth than its usefulness. Congregations evolve from holy assemblies to community centers that provide good opportunities for networking and recreation. As the tools of marketing research are brought into the quest for church growth, church planners emphasize comfortable surroundings rather than divine truth as the key to attracting new congregants. If the critics are to be believed, the quest for religious revival is transformed under modern conditions from a crusade for souls to a battle for market share. In the "divine supermarket" of the contemporary United States, people are solicited to spend some of their precious disposable time and income in this rather than that church (Ruthven 1989).

It is one thing to acknowledge these changes, quite another to over-interpret them as signs of the imminent extinction of religious senti-ment in American life. Religion has certainly been touched and influ-enced by the modern world, but it is more accurate to speak of secu-larization as adjustment and adaptation than to employ the image of decline and fall. Many of the trends cited as evidence of changes are actually longstanding traits of American religious life. It is not at all clear that Americans are any less pious or serious about faith today than they were in some distant past (Butler 1990). Nor is the "selling" of religion as a product something new even if modern techniques are more sophisticated and visible (R. Moore 1994). The United States has managed to modernize without casting off religion in the process. As we shall see throughout the remainder of the book, religious change has not meant that religious concerns have disappeared from the pub-lic agenda. In some instances, secularization has enhanced the rele-vance of religion to political life.

Possible Explanations

Where did modernization theorists and Marxists go wrong in pre-dicting that religion would disappear from the highly developed United States? Both social theories appear to have underestimated both the need for religion, even in the most advanced societies, and the capacity of American religious institutions to adapt to changing circumstances.

Some students of religion cite the durability of religious beliefs as proof that religion meets a basic human need, much like food and shelter (Bell 1977; Greeley and Baum 1973; Prozesky 1984; Stark and Bainbridge 1985). Alone among creatures on Earth, human beings possess the ability to think in a sophisticated way about their place in the universe. They wonder about the meaning of life, the reality of death, the basis of ethical behavior and human cooperation. They ask, among other questions, why some people commit evil; why the good and innocent should suffer from it; and how, apart from instinct, they can even think to know what is good and what is evil. To answer these questions about life—to give meaning to human existence—they develop systems of belief that include religion. So long as the world requires some explanation, it is argued, human beings will create faiths to live by. Nothing about this notion would bother most modernization theorists or Marxists. They would argue merely that the need for a system of meaning will eventually be satisfied fully by science or by a comprehensive body of political ideas, making religion unnecessary.

Science seems inadequate, however, as a religious substitute. The assumption that scientific understanding eliminates a need for religious explanation falters because of persistent questions about life on this planet that no scientific advance can ever settle. It is hard to see how familiarity with, for example, the third law of thermodynamics could ever comfort troubled or grieving individuals or improve on religious faith in enabling them to cope with their inevitable mortality.[7] Science is simply irrelevant to such questions. In other cases, the progress of science may reinforce concern for spirituality. The more Albert Einstein learned about the beauty and symmetry of nature, the more he appreciated what he saw as God's hidden hand; he is not the only scientist to have been so moved (Tracy 1973). Finally, science may actually intensify concern about questions of value. The spectacular growth of medical technology has raised agonizing moral dilemmas about the nature and conditions of life, dilemmas that appear on the political agenda in the form of issues such as abortion, euthanasia, organ transplantation, in vitro fertilization, genetic engineering, embryo experimentation, life extension, and "living wills." Progress in weapons development has underlined dramatically the problem of human evil and the necessity for cooperation. To the extent science liberates us from misery and economic insecurity, it gives us freedom to ponder questions of ultimate value.

In advanced technological societies, paradoxically, there has been a striking loss of faith in reason as a solution to all human problems. Consider this assessment of the current mood: "These are gloomy times. People are fatalistic and death possessed. There is a conviction that we have been collectively asleep at the wheel, that the path of so-called reason has taken us far along the road to hell, probably past the point of no return. More and more, the feeling is taking hold that we are on the edge of a volcano that is about to explode" (Frankel 1984, 162).

This comment, all the more remarkable because its author is a man described as "a business consultant who specializes in information and telecommunications technologies," illustrates how a society built on science may generate profound discontent with the consequences of scientific activity. For some people, the reaction to a technological society apparently run amok is a return to spirituality, a renewed respect for the religious values that science once seemed to render unnecessary. The loss of confidence in modernity also breeds more extreme social reactions, such as the militia movement, which justify acts of violence against society in the name of "higher" spiritual values.

If not science, will politics perhaps substitute for religious faith? The quest for justice through political movements may well take on the form of a religious crusade. But in the end, when political movements have triumphed, the perennial problems remain, and the perennial solutions, including religion, offer themselves. Well before the collapse of Communist regimes in Eastern Europe, some Marxist intellectuals were prompted by the abuses and inadequacies of the system to consider traditional religious dogma as a source of reform (Machovec 1976). More fundamentally, the efforts of many of these regimes to replace religious faith with a new "Socialist consciousness" must now be regarded as spectacular failures. Poland is only the most vivid illustration of how Marxism was no match for the power of religious orthodoxy (Szajkowski 1983).

In the United States political faith has not yet managed to supplant religious commitment. While some political activists discard their religious faith as an impediment to social change, others see no need to choose between them. When religious and political loyalties do appear to collide, the choice may actually favor the former. During the turbulent late 1960s and early 1970s, the extremes of the American political spectrum were represented by Eldridge Cleaver, an eloquent and angry spokesman for black nationalism, and his opposite number, a conservative political operative named Charles Colson, who once boasted that he would have sacrificed his own grandmother to gain political advantage. In the 1980s, disillusioned with the consequences of their political activism, these two firebrands shared public platforms to preach for a return to biblical Christianity. With less publicity, other intellectuals have traveled the same path from political activism to religious commitment (Schumer 1984). A few conversions may not indicate a social trend, but they do illustrate that politics may prove to be an ineffective alternative to religion.

Why the United States?

The inadequacy of science and politics to address basic human needs only partly explains the persistence of religion in the United States. Theories about intrinsic human needs and failed alternatives are global concepts that do not resolve questions about why the United States, in particular, has remained so much more deeply tied to religion than other modern societies. American exceptionalism in religion (see fig. 1.1) has usually been attributed to cultural compatibility, a need for social identity, the independence of religion from the state, and a competitive religious environment.

Cultural Compatibility

Early American churches emphasized self-government for congregations and voluntary affiliation for individuals, thus encouraging Americans to value their autonomy and to distrust hierarchy (Lipset 1967, 180–192). To this day, Americans find religion "comfortable" because it fits in well with deep-seated cultural values about freedom of choice and individual initiative. Religion may also reinforce the larger culture by supplying what individuals find lacking in society. Robert Booth Fowler (1989) argues that churches thrive in the United States because they provide an antidote to the extremes of individualism and relativism. People join churches, he argues, because they want a sense of community—a sense that is absent from other parts of their lives.

They also turn to religion for rules and guidelines, something sorely missing from a society that makes every individual the arbiter of right and wrong.

Social Identity

Religion has also flourished because it meets a continuing need for social identity that is particularly important in the United States. Physical mobility, economic change, and immigration have constantly threatened people with a loss of roots—the loss of a sense that they belong to any meaningful group or tradition. Confronted with chaos, individuals find much-needed stability in religion. In what John F. Kennedy called "a nation of immigrants," the church helped newcomers adjust to life in a new and confusing environment. Churches still fill that role for newcomers who migrate from abroad or simply move around frequently from place to place.

Political Independence

The "wall of separation" between church and state—Thomas Jefferson's metaphor for the independence of churches from government support and patronage— may well have strengthened the position of religion in the United States (Caplow 1985; Tong 1992). Many advocates of state support for religion believed that churches could not prosper lacking financial and legal support from government. Ironically, just the opposite may be true. In the long run, churches closely associated with worldly power risk guilt by association. If a repressive regime endorses a state religion, the church may be perceived as a barrier to justice. Marx had expected religion to collapse when the workers recognized it as a prop of capitalism, justifying exploitation as God's will and conveniently postponing justice until the next life. In truth, state religions have often defended corrupt governments in order to maintain a privileged position. Equally dangerous, the state might become identified with a certain religion or group, prompting enemies of that faith or group to embrace the banner of irreligion.

But American religion has not always served the purpose of the dominant economic powers. Slaveowners found support for servitude in the Bible, but the slaves could and did read the Old Testament as a call to resistance and revolt. The religious impulse that could be used to justify the worst abuses of capitalism could also fuel movements against the oppression of industrial workers. Even today, when many Roman Catholics have joined the ranks of the wealthy and powerful, their church continues to speak out against poverty and to remind Americans about the plight of the oppressed. Hardly the "opiate" derided by Marx, religion in the United States is more fittingly characterized as an amphetamine (Finke and Stark 1992, 251).

Unlike the churches in many other societies, those in the United States appear to have avoided an exclusive association with any particular political affiliation. As a rule, particularly in countries with a tradition of state-supported religion, surveys reveal moderately strong statistical associations between individual religiosity and political ideology (Heath, Taylor, and Toka 1993; McDonough, Barnes, and Pina 1984, 661–663). Political conflict frequently pits a "secular" left wing against a "religious" right. In the United States, by contrast, a much weaker relationship is found between personal religious attachment and self-described ideological position. The 1991 World Values Survey showed the United States to be virtually the only one of fifteen countries where vote in national elections was essentially unrelated to the measure of belief in God (see fig. 1.1).[8] This suggests that the tie between religion and ideology is not natural but rooted in history. By remaining independent of the state, reserving the right to pass judgment, American religion has avoided becoming an adjunct of the political system and, so, can remain unscathed when the political system itself is in disrepute. The high regard for churches in the United States may owe something to their avoidance of too close an identification with any political party or administration.

Religious Pluralism

Signifying the remarkable diversity of denominations in the country, religious pluralism contributes to the persistence of religion in the United States (Salisbury 1983). The early settlers subscribed to a variety of faiths, and Americans have since taken advantage of the freedom of religion to found literally hundreds of new sects (M. Marty 1984). The diversity among the early settlers was compounded by the importation of new faiths through the global population migration to America. To an extent possibly unparalleled in the modern world, the American citizen is confronted with a vast range of denominational options. As a result, no single denomination today comprises more than about 40 percent of the church membership (Bradley et al. 1992); thus, it is correct to say that all Americans belong to minority religions. This conclusion holds at the local level: nearly half the U.S. population resides in counties in which no single denomination has majority status (Salisbury, Sprague, and Weiher 1984).

Pluralism has forced the churches to compete for members and, so, encouraged them to adapt to new social realities. In religion, as in politics and economics, competition in an open market has stimulated church leaders to bid for support with all manner of incentives. Denominations have had to master the very latest techniques in persuasion and recruitment as they reach out to potential "consumers"— hence, the churches' use of sophisticated means of communication, marketing skills, and information technology (McDaniel 1989; Stewart 1989). The emphasis on attracting members from the religious marketplace has also prompted the churches to offer attractive benefit packages and services that in other countries might be provided by government.[9]

As noted above, even the message of religion has been tailored to modern times, through an emphasis on the relevance of religion to worldly pursuits as diverse as sports, the stock market, and mental health. In countries lacking religious diversity, churches may well remain attached to symbols, rituals, and patterns of behavior that cannot withstand the social forces that promote secularity. Not having the luxury of a monopoly, the American churches have deliberately cultivated skills and qualities that almost certainly have contributed to the persistence of religious attachment.

I have gone to such lengths to stress the staying power of religion for a reason. Religious conflict in politics is commonly treated as a throwback, an interesting diversion from the "real" issues of the modern era. But if religion remains a vital force in this day and age, then one cannot claim to understand the contemporary era without appreciating the role played by religion, especially in the realm of politics. The remainder of the book delineates the many ways religion intersects political life in the United States.

NOTES

Lowell Weicker's observation, quoted in the chapter epigraph, appeared in the *New York Times*, 21 March 1984. Ronald Reagan's quotation is taken from p. 9 of his article "Religion and Politics Are Necessarily Related," which appeared in *Church and State* 37 (October 1984): 9–11.

1. Gustav Niebuhr, "Books on Faith Are a Comfort, President Says," *New York Times*, 4 October 1994, 1.

2. In slighting religion, political science resembles public education (Shriver 1988), psychology (Lehr and Spilka 1989), and television (Skill et al. 1994).

3. In *Habits of the Heart*, Robert Bellah and his coauthors (1985) demonstrate how the language of contract and the philosophy of individualism have robbed many Americans of the capacity to offer moral justification for even their most intimate ties to other family members.

4. Belief in God was measured by the percentage of respondents who selected "I know God really exists and I have no doubts about it" in response to question 14 in the 1991 World Values Study (International Social Survey Program 1994). The 1991 per capita GNP for all countries except Northern Ireland was obtained from the World Bank (1994). Following T. Wilson (1990), the Northern Ireland figure was set to two-thirds of the U.K. total. This approach was first suggested by Walter Dean Burnham.

5. "Mystical Experiences Abound in Culture That Spurns Them, Studies Say," *Tallahassee Democrat*, 14 February 1987, 1-D.

6. The authoritarian and wrathful Old Testament God is a caricature that neglects the Hebrew Bible's portrayal of a loving and reasonable sovereign, willing to intercede and open to negotiation.

7. For a fascinating account of how religious values may fill a void where science appears to fail, see the *Manchester Guardian* story on a British hospice ("In the Midst of Death We Are in Life," 4 March 1984, 4). It reports: "Religion plays a central part in the life of St. Christopher's. It is not compulsory, nor is it thrust upon patients. 'But I don't think anyone could work here for long without the support of some faith', she [the founder] says firmly. The pressure and intensity of the work, the great demands of the dying and their relatives means that those who work there need answers, or at least partial answers, in order to sustain themselves."

8. In the American sample, the rank-order correlation between belief in God and vote choice (Variable 103) was virtually zero and statistically insignificant. In all other countries but Poland, which lacked most cases on the partisanship variable, the relationship was large, significant, and consistent with the pattern of religiosity encouraging a vote or preference for right-wing parties.

9. One anecdote may illustrate how the churches outperform "secular" authorities. A Gainesville, Florida, newspaper reports that after a storm blew a tree onto an elderly woman's property, cutting off electricity, she contacted the

local utility to restore service. Because the damage occurred on private property to equipment that was legally the responsibility of the woman, the company had no authority to fix the problem. Over the course of the next day and a half, the woman's problem was brought to the attention of a dispatcher for the utility company, a representative from the Older Americans Council, several officials from the local office of the responsible state agency, a citizen advocate, and her church. By the time the public officials had begun to investigate the situation, the church had sent over volunteers to repair the damage and to look after the woman until family members could arrive to help. Theologians used to refer to a "God of the gaps," a deity invoked when other resources had failed; this example illustrates how a "church of the gaps" can act when secular authorities fail.

2. Religion and Politics: Points of Contact

The prophet had assembled his followers and instructed them to remain aloof from the corrupt society that surrounded them. Together, they would await God's return to earth and promise of deliverance. The members were indoctrinated with the warning that the federal government was plotting to attack them with force, murder their leader, and destroy their religion. To outsiders, they appeared less like a religious group than a dangerous cult of fanatics with a mentally unbalanced leader who suffered delusions of divinity and persecution. Reacting to rumors that the group planned violent attacks against outsiders and was stockpiling weapons for use in an insurrection, the federal government eventually sent agents to search for illegal weapons. Although it remains unclear who fired the first shot, an unlucky band of men, women, and children died in the crossfire between the two sides.

With thousands of their coreligionists dead, the survivors fled across the Atlantic to the United States. Despite the distance, they did not forget the events that had made them refugees. To enlist the American government on behalf of an independent homeland for their persecuted brethren, they organized powerful national associations, raised enormous amounts of money, and tried to pressure public officials by threats of electoral retaliation. Having gained special strength and influence in New York and the Democratic party, the group managed to create a national consensus on support for the beleaguered new nation. Though the cause continues to enjoy considerable sympathy among Americans, the group's single-mindedness occasionally draws the charge that members put the well-being of the foreign homeland above the broader interests of the United States.

A small group of men and women, motivated by an intense Christian faith, call on the United States to mend its evil ways. They are outraged by national policies that deny legal standing to other human beings—policies upheld by the U.S. Supreme Court. Although some members are willing to try changing the law through normal political activities, others on the fringe of the movement resort to violence and murder. To their critics, these crusaders for public moral- ity appear narrow-minded, intolerant, and uncompromising. The group responds to such accusations by insisting that America return to the religious values that have long sustained the republic.

Another group of American Christians sees the arms race as the paramount threat to world peace and human survival. Persuaded that nations will use weapons if they are available, these activists call on their government to stop its weapons buildup and negotiate treaties of arbitration with its military adver- saries. They are also worried about America's growing military involvement in Latin America and urge the government to send teachers, medical supplies, and economic assistance instead of troops.

These four vignettes describe real religious-political events in the United States. The attentive citizen should have no difficulty attaching names to the groups described in these passages. The cult is obviously the Branch Davidian movement of David Koresh, which ended with a televised conflagration in Waco, Texas, in 1993. The second vignette, of course, describes the efforts of the American Zionist movement to build public and governmental support for a Jewish homeland in the Middle East. For forty-some years, Zionist leaders have helped to persuade Congress and various presidents to provide strong military and diplo- matic assistance to Israel. The third group is immediately recognizable as the "New Christian/Religious Right," a label for religious conserva- tives who have challenged the liberalization of abortion rights, changes in long-established sex roles, and other policies regarded as departures from traditional moral values. The final passage clearly deals with the growing support for nuclear disarmament in the Roman Catholic church and other denominations. Or so it may seem!

As closely as the labels appear to fit the facts of each case, the four vignettes actually refer to earlier episodes in American history where religious enthusiasm fused with political action: the founding of the Mormon settlement in Utah in the mid-nineteenth century, national- ist political agitation by Irish-American Catholics, the abolitionist cru- sade against slavery, and the Christian pacifism of William Jennings

Bryan.[1] As these examples from the nineteenth and early twentieth centuries make clear, religious activity in politics is neither new nor unprecedented in American experience. To the contrary: a close look at American history reveals a durable tradition of interaction between religious and political activity, arising from and strengthened by several factors.

If church and state are kept separate in the United States, as most Americans believe they should be, how can we explain the frequency with which religion becomes a political factor? What does religion have to do with politics? To understand why religion and politics are so frequently tied together in this country, it is necessary to examine the *incentives* for political activism by religiously committed people and groups, the *opportunities* for involvement, and, finally, the *resources* that enable the religious to participate effectively. Any coherent explanation of the persistent linkage of religion and politics in the United States depends on close examination of all three factors.

Incentives: The Causes of Religious Intervention in Politics

Visitors to the United States are often struck by the readiness of Americans to enter the political arena in pursuit of moral causes and to interpret complicated public issues in terms of good versus evil (Brogan 1960, chap. 5). Although moral crusades are not unique to the United States, they seem to occur more frequently here than elsewhere. In most other advanced industrial societies, political conflict commonly centers on questions about the distribution of economic resources and burdens. Such issues are not unknown in American political life, but they must share the national agenda with controversies that touch more directly on moral values and religious doctrine. The passion that suffuses such issues as abortion rights, school prayer, equal rights, pornography, and other moral concerns seems notably lacking when Americans confront questions such as tax rates, national health insurance, labor union rights, or tariff protection. Moreover, at a time when the politics of religious concern seems to be weakening in other advanced societies, it has gained a renewed foothold in American politics.

Why should religion become an element in political controversy in the first place? Part of the answer to this question lies in those forces within religion that encourage political activism. All three aspects, or "faces," of religion are capable of promoting an interest in politics—creed, institution, and social/cultural group (Wald 1983, chap. 5). Although these three elements may not constitute the essence of religion, they do represent the major "manner and form in which religious phenomena appear in human experience" (Capps 1972, 135), and each provides an incentive for religious groups to enter the political arena.[2] As used here, *creed* refers to the fundamental beliefs, ideas, ethical codes, and symbols associated with a religious tradition, including what others call a theology or belief system. The emphasis here is on the content of religious teachings and the values that the tradition encourages. As comprehensive systems of belief, religious traditions may provide guidance for believers about appropriate behavior in secular realms, such as politics.

Churches differ in the degree to which they assert a connection between religious faith and political principles. Some, such as the Mennonite congregations, are quite explicit about the political lessons of their faith, announcing that the church is committed to nonviolence, separation of church and state, and mutual service. Other churches transmit political messages through posters and wall hangings, the choice of hymns, the content of sermons and homilies, bumper stickers affixed to the minister's car, announcements during worship services, and articles in the church bulletin. In most churches, however, the political orientation has to be inferred from the beliefs and ethical codes of the religious tradition. When a church lacks an authoritative statement of political principles, its members may disagree about how (or even whether) the faith applies to political questions. Whether the cues are direct or indirect, religious belief systems may send messages that influence political outlook and behavior.

Religious communities are represented in concrete form by specialized *institutions*, the second face of religion pertinent to political activism. The organizations associated with religion may provide a link to politics through the tie of interest. As institutions devoted to worship and evangelism, religious organizations automatically acquire an immediate interest in preserving their freedom of operation. When the government or private agencies seem to threaten church autonomy, religious interests are quick to respond. The tax advantages enjoyed by religious organizations—the direct exemption of church income from federal and most other forms of taxation and the indirect subsidy provided to church operation by the deduction of individual charitable and religious contributions—may also encourage political involvement. Beyond these matters of survival, religious organizations have other reasons to contemplate political involvement. In the United States, churches are not merely buildings that provide places for worship; rather, they have become multipurpose agencies providing an astonishing array of services, including formal education, social welfare, pastoral counseling, publishing, charitable fund-raising, recreational facilities, medical care, cemeteries, libraries, and summer camps. Several of the largest churches have become the hubs for worldwide operations, complete with the organizational complexity of a major corporation. Ties to a common denomination and to interchurch movements of various kinds have further enmeshed the churches in a web of formal institutions.

As a result of these extensive responsibilities and activities, churches often acquire a strong and immediate interest in policies determined by the government. A church day school, for example, is subject to governmental regulations on zoning, taxation, health and public safety, professional standards, wages and working conditions, racial integration, curriculum, accreditation, and standardized testing. If it cannot afford to provide separate schooling, a religious group may nevertheless work to safeguard the rights of its children in public schools or to guarantee that church members are free to educate their own children as they see fit. Religious broadcasting, like its secular counterpart, is regulated by the Federal Communications Commission. A church that offers counseling services or engages heavily in charitable fund-raising may unwittingly expose itself to legal action.

Because of the potential impact of governmental decisions on their many activities and interests, religious groups frequently find it valuable—or necessary—to take an active role in the political process. We should not forget that the traffic between religion and politics in the United States runs two ways. Religious groups may take the initiative in political action, but they may also react to the decisions of government and other political actors. Roman Catholic doctrine on abortion did not draw the church into political activity until the Supreme Court struck down most legal restrictions on the availability of abortion. The politically conservative pastors of the New Christian Right have characterized their entry into politics largely as a response to government actions that left traditional churches aggrieved. Such a reactive posture by the churches may well be more common today because of changes in the scope of governmental authority. The state now claims more regulatory power than it used to—power that may be used to establish policies that affect the major functions of religious groups. If there truly is greater political involvement by religious institutions, that situation may reflect a defensive reaction to an expanded government rather than any desire to impose religious values on a reluctant society.

Religion also denotes a *social group*, a subculture or community of believers. The members of a congregation may share regular social interaction, a common status, and a distinctive way of life. Out of these experiences, a common culture may emerge. Adherents may come to develop a similar way of looking at the world, what is sometimes called a "group mind." Of course, churches differ in the demands they place on members and in the degree to which they constitute genuine communities, as opposed to casual associations. Nonetheless, the communal nature of religion may induce a particular pattern of political activity by members of a congregation. If a church attracts people who experience similar conditions of life, whether poverty or affluence, that shared status may lead congregants to develop a common outlook on politics and social issues. Underlying political tendencies can be brought to the surface by messages from the pulpit and reinforced by continued social interaction with like-minded church members. In some cases— the black churches, for example—political solidarity is virtually imposed on the group members by the hostility of outsiders. The larger the role played by the church in defining the lives of its members, the greater the church's potential impact on their political activities.

A revealing example of how all these incentives can affect the level of political involvement is that of the U.S. Roman Catholic church, which has repeatedly attempted to relate Catholic religious thought to important issues on the national political agenda. Through homilies, sermons, pastoral letters, and the dissemination of papal encyclicals, church leaders have attempted to educate Catholics about how to apply the principles of the faith to diverse public problems such as abortion, national defense, economic policy, and the position of women in society. The church has also taken a strong public stand on issues that affect the immediate welfare of its institutions. To ease the financial burden of the church's comprehensive system of religious day schools, Catholic leaders have sought public assistance in the form of textbook sharing, public transportation, and tuition tax credit or vouchers. As individuals, Catholic laypersons have shown a traditional attachment to the Democratic party. This link was formed at the turn of the century, when the predominantly immigrant and working-class Catholic population found Democrats far more receptive than Republicans to their needs and aspirations. The historical memory of how the Democratic party provided a path of upward mobility for ambitious young Catholics kept the alliance intact even after many Catholics had moved into the social and economic mainstream.

Creed, institutional interest, and social standing have also been responsible for the political actions of other religious groups in American life. To some extent, the Catholic church has only followed in the footsteps of other religious groups (Handy 1984). During the nineteenth century many Protestant churches took public stands on such vital issues as slavery, tariffs, and imperialism, justifying their preferences as an outgrowth of their beliefs. In the attempt to defend institutions or public practices that supported Protestant interests, moreover, the churches frequently intervened in the legislative process—trying, for example, to mandate the holy character of the Sunday sabbath or to adjust immigration quotas so as to encourage migration from Protestant nations. Like the Catholics, the Protestants have tended to form alliances with political groups that represent their social and economic interests. For Protestants, no less than for Catholics, creed, institutional self-interest, and social bonds have encouraged political involvement and shaped its form.

In the current period, new or revitalized religious groups have been drawn into political action by the same incentives that have motivated the well-established churches. The forces that encourage an intersection of religion and politics are numerous and diverse. The Mormon church has urged its membership to follow church doctrine in public disputes over abortion, school prayer, pornography, and the like. Evangelical Protestant churches, many of which have become imposing organizations that sponsor broadcast networks, school systems, and major publishing houses, have entered politics to safeguard these institutions from governmental regulation. Because an increasing proportion of the American Roman Catholic community comprises poor and deprived

Hispanic immigrants, the Catholic church has become far more aggressive in advocating government spending to address social problems.

Opportunity: How Government Structure Encourages Political Action by Churches

In order for churches to act on the incentives just described, the political system must be open to them. At a minimum, this requires opportunities for participation without legal restriction. Whereas even some democratic societies severely limit the political activities of churches and religious leaders, the United States has historically given religious groups relatively free rein to participate in public affairs.[3] The federal tax code does require churches to refrain from endorsing candidates if they want to retain their exemption from the income tax, but this provision has not been strictly enforced. The political system is thus open to U.S. churches in the sense that few formal barriers keep them from political activity.

In another sense, the U.S. political system actually encourages organized groups like churches to compete for influence over public policy (Truman 1962). As political scientists have long recognized, the complex structure of the U.S. government encourages groups to undertake political activity. In this regard, religious groups are no different from the many other organizations that attempt to influence public policy at all levels of society.

Decentralization is fundamental to U.S. political life. Rather than concentrate power in the hands of one institution, the founders of the nation divided political authority among three autonomous branches of government. Advocates of any particular policy thus have three separate routes open to them: through legislation, litigation, or the administrative process. Because political power is further subdivided among at least three separate levels of government (national, state, and local), a group with political goals has additional freedom to choose the ground on which to fight. Governmental fragmentation, accordingly, gives groups multiple points of access to the policy-making process. Such a complex governmental structure may or may not be conducive to good policy making, quick reaction to pressing problems, or clear direction, but it certainly keeps the decision-making process remarkably open to causes that can find an effective advocate.

Decentralization is reinforced by a tradition of popular sovereignty that limits the authority of national party leaders. The American system of political recruitment puts the effective power of nomination in the hands of citizens rather than political parties. Under this system, the elected official must always attend first to the wishes of the constituents, who hold the power to deny nomination. When those citizens are agitated by an issue or problem, the official must pay heed. Responsiveness to the wishes of the voters, even if they conflict with the party platform or the pledges of its leaders, is the highest priority. This cultural pattern reflects and reinforces the structural qualities that enhance group involvement.

The way in which this structure makes a difference for religious groups can be seen in the contrasting history of antiabortion movements in the United States and Canada (Schwartz 1981). In Canada, as in the United States, penalties for abortion were reduced or eliminated in the late 1960s to early 1970s. In both countries, liberalization brought forth vociferous objections from Catholics and conservative Protestants. But there the similarities end. The Canadian policy shift has been sustained while liberalized abortion has been significantly curtailed in the United States. The differences are partly due to the religious composition of the two countries, but they mainly reflect differences in political structure that allowed American opponents of abortion more scope to pursue their agenda.

The different outcome of the abortion debate in the United States, where antiabortionists have won a number of significant victories, testifies to the many avenues of attack provided by the complex and multifaceted U.S. system of government. When national abortion policy was liberalized through the *Roe v. Wade* decision handed down by the Supreme Court in 1973, critics sought to use the amending power of the Constitution to restore restrictive policies. Failing in that and in attempts to remove abortion from the Court's jurisdiction, they proceeded to chip away at the decision in several other arenas. Congress has been persuaded to reduce or eliminate federal payments for abortion under various programs of health insurance and foreign assistance. Using ordinances, some of which were initiated by petition and approved in public referendums, some states and localities have invoked zoning, the regulation of public health, and parental rights to restrict access to abortion facilities, and several such restrictions have been sustained by the Supreme Court. In 1989, by upholding a Missouri law that placed numerous restrictions on abortion, the Supreme Court conceded to state legislatures much authority to control abortion policy. All the while, abortion opponents have also challenged *Roe* on the ground, so to speak, by organizing demonstrations, parades, pickets, rallies, and other forms of public protest guaranteed by the Bill of Rights. The Supreme Court may yet overturn its 1973 ruling and restore the limits on abortion in effect before *Roe*. Even falling short of that, it is clear that the opponents of abortion have capitalized on the separation of powers and on the federal structure of government to partially offset the Supreme Court's 1973 ruling.

Most of these options were not available to the religiously motivated opponents of abortion in Canada. Organized on the British parliamentary model, the Canadian governmental system offered the opponents of liberalized abortion few opportunities to challenge official policy. Because the criminal code was the exclusive responsibility of the national government, the provincial authorities and local governments could do little to restrict the availability of abortion services. At the national level, the governing Liberal party easily defeated antiabortion efforts originating in the courts or in the Parliament. Political leaders who might have disagreed with the decision to relax restrictions on abortion largely toed the line, lest they endanger their careers in a system that rewards loyalty to party. Thus, despite strong objections from a large Catholic population, the Canadian government was able to persevere in its policy of making abortion more widely available to the population.

Similar barriers have faced antiabortion movements in countries where the policy decisions of a national government are not routinely subject to review by an outside agency, nor where they can be overturned by appeal to a higher law as embodied in a constitution. Citizens usually lack the tools of direct legislation—the initiative and referendum—which can be used to circumvent the decisions of legislative assemblies. In most circumstances the party in government has a relatively free hand to shape legislation without competition from other national institutions. Similarly, because of concentration of lawmaking authority and administrative power in the central government, provinces and localities are powerless to block the implementation of national policy.

The cultural tradition of popular sovereignty also encourages some American politicians to join, or at least endorse, the antiabortion crusades sponsored by religious groups. As noted above, candidates for public office in the United States are required to develop personal electoral organizations, raise most of their own campaign resources, and emphasize whatever issues resonate most powerfully in the constituency. Once in office, they enjoy considerable leeway vis-à-vis the party line and the freedom to engage in moral advocacy. Where nomination to office, campaign finance, and promotion to higher office depend on the party, as in Canada, ambitious politicians have strong reasons to conform to the party line. The absence of these weapons in American political parties helps to explain why public officials feel free to take up moral causes if they judge that such issues will advance their political standing.

Religion as a Political Resource

Many groups, not just those motivated by religion, have incentives and opportunities to pursue their goals through political action. Religious groups, however, have resources that make them especially likely to participate effectively. That is, religiously motivated activists are valuable political allies. Their resources grow out of the three faces of religion already examined in this chapter: creed, institution, and social/cultural groups.

Religious ideas are potentially powerful sources of commitment and motivation. As history has repeatedly taught, individuals will make enormous sacrifices if they believe themselves to be driven by a divine force. When the power of the churches is applied to a political issue, the message is likely to exert substantial influence over parishioners. Until quite recently, the major American churches largely restricted their political preaching to questions involving personal behavior. The "social" message from the pulpit tended to stress public solutions for individual problems such as drinking, gambling, drug use, and licentious sexual behavior. It is precisely on such issues that the attitudes of churchgoers differ most substantially from those of persons who do not regularly encounter church preaching on politics (Hoge and Zulueta 1984).

The potential political strength of religious ideas has been displayed repeatedly in conflicts over pornography, homosexual rights ordinances, the Equal Rights Amendment, liberalized abortion laws, and other policies regarding changing social practices. The ability of these issues to ignite political action was nicely demonstrated in a study conducted by political scientists Paul Allen Beck and Suzanne Parker (1985). In interviewing a group of adult Floridians in 1981 and again in 1982, they found that many people shifted their positions on political issues from one interview to the next. This high degree of inconsistency suggested that citizens do not have firm or deep convictions about many of the issues that dominate political conflict. Beck and Parker did find three exceptions to this generalization, all of which involved issues touching on moral values. The members of the sample were most consistent in their views about abortion, school prayer, and the Equal Rights Amendment. A similar pattern emerged from a study that tracked delegates to state party conventions in Virginia and Iowa from 1980 to 1988 (Stone 1991). Over that time, delegates were most consistent in their attitudes toward abortion and the Equal Rights Amendment. Because these issues apparently tap into opinions of great intensity and durability, it is not surprising that the issues have generated sustained political action.

Conflicts over abortion, school prayer, and other "social regulatory" issues differ from many items on the political agenda; they center on "community values, moral practices, and norms of interpersonal conduct" rather than on allocation of federal funds, redistribution of national resources, or economic regulation (Tatalovich and Daynes 1988, 1). Throughout American history, moral controversies and cultural debates have frequently overshadowed economic conflicts (Noll 1990). Although it was once thought that the advent of modernity had shifted political debate away from moral concerns to questions about economics, we now recognize the continuing potency of cultural values as a basis for political mobilization. In large measure, moral controversies fit the profile of what Carmines and Stimson (1980) have described as "easy" issues—political questions that are symbolic rather than technical, concerned more with ends than means, and have a long history on the political agenda. Such qualities make it easy for politicians to deploy moral controversies as a way of engaging the attention of the electorate. In turn, the public uses them as a means of deciding which candidate to choose. Because moral debates associated with religion clearly fit the profile of an "easy" issue, astute politicians have often crafted political campaigns around appeals to deep-seated cultural values rooted in religion (J. White 1990). During the 1988 presidential campaign, the Republican campaign succeeded in making the Pledge of Allegiance such an issue. Precisely because values and moral practices are their currency, religious groups seem drawn to issues of this nature.

In addition to what might be called their intellectual resources—the capacity to motivate people to action on behalf of moral values— churches also enjoy substantial organizational advantages. Success in politics depends in part on the ability to mobilize citizens behind a common goal, for which purpose it helps greatly to have public credibility, access to citizens, and a means of communicating ideas. The churches, with precisely these traits, are natural political organizations. As observed in the previous chapter, the churches are held in very high esteem in American society—a level of prestige that can yield political credibility. Moreover, churches are powerful organizations with formal membership, headquarters, regularly scheduled group meetings, publications, and full-time professional leadership. Because of patterns of association in American society, the church is often the only such well-organized group to which a citizen is likely to belong. If the church wants to transmit political messages, it has the apparatus to do so with great efficiency.

As a social system or subculture, the church has yet other resources that can contribute to a powerful political role. By virtue of participating in a social network, the church member may encounter messages about political issues and interact with fellow members who adhere to the church's line. A person surrounded by church members who participate actively in a campaign is likely to learn about the issues from a religious point of view, to receive encouragement about joining in the activity, and to observe and acquire social skills that may promote political success. Though not intended for that purpose, congregational organizations may serve as leadership-training institutes for people who lack other means of exposure to organizational skills.

These social factors help to explain the positive relationship many observers have found between church attendance and voter participation in local and presidential elections (Hougland and Christenson 1983; Hughes and Peek 1986; Macaluso and Wanat 1979; Martinson and Wilkening 1987; Rosenstone and Hansen 1993). These studies infer a connection between religious and political involvement by comparing the attitudes and behavior of people with different levels of exposure to church influence. To explain why frequent church attenders are more active politically, scholars have cited the capacity of religious teaching to impart a sacred character to civic obligations (Macaluso and Wanat 1979), the correlation between religious affiliation and a high level of community attachment and concern (Strate et al. 1989), and the "spillover" effect that results when churchgoers apply to community affairs the democratic decision-making experiences learned in the local congregation (Peterson 1992). From the resource perspective, churches may stimulate political involvement largely as a by-product of the participation skills they provide members. Participation in associations of any kind promotes "the social contacts and organizational skills necessary to understand political action and to exert effective influence"(Hougland and Christenson 1983, 406). This assumption has been powerfully supported in recent studies showing that political participation is significantly associated with the acquisition in church of such civic skills as letter-writing, group decision making, running meetings, and making oral presentations (Verba et al. 1993; Leege 1988). Whatever the exact factors involved, the churches serve as social networks that seem to draw participants into public affairs.

Limits on Religious Influence in Politics

Although churches possess imposing political resources and the opportunity to participate in politics combined with the incentive to do so, there are four potential limits on religious group activism. To begin with, certain types of faith actually depress political involvement. Some religious traditions regard politics as irrelevant or harmful to their primary task of saving souls (Jelen 1994a). Government persecution has conditioned some churches to keep their distance from government or political involvement (Dudley and Hernandez 1992). A belief about the futility of political action can also be a potent deterrent to political participation (Quinney 1964). Other religious groups have gone even further, insisting that members separate themselves from the corrupting influence of secular institutions and activities. Even if a church does not discourage political participation, it might make such heavy demands on the members' time, energy, and resources that congregants have nothing left to devote to political action. Studies of the impact of religious involvement on a variety of forms of political participation—not just voting—have found no evidence that churchgoing encourages more active forms of political involvement, such as campaign contributions, volunteer work for candidates, or communication with local government officials (Hougland and Christenson 1983; Martinson and Wilkening 1987; Stark 1964; Cheal 1975; Bean 1991). There is also evidence from a variety of studies that heavily religious environments discourage women from political careers (Medoff 1986) and generally retard the level of membership in trade unions (Christiano 1988). Hence, the link between religion and participation seems to be restricted to the least demanding form of political action— casting a vote.

Another limitation on church political activity is the fear that political clout will be purchased at the expense of spiritual influence. It has long been suspected that churches enjoy such a positive image in the United States because they are regarded as places apart, a refuge from the corruption of other secular institutions. According to polling data, the public generally prefers the churches to remain "above" politics and reacts negatively to clergy who become agents of a particular party or candidate. If the church enters the political world as an active participant, it risks losing some of the prestige and social influence that makes it such a respected institution. That outcome is particularly likely when a church or religious group takes a political position that alienates members who might otherwise remain loyal.

The experience of "liberal" churches in the 1960s, when social activism often produced intense conflict among members, suggests that political involvement inevitably undermines congregational harmony. That conclusion needs to be qualified by recognizing conditions that encourage congregational support for political involvement. Strange as it sounds, support for political involvement may depend on portraying that activism as nonpolitical. That is, church members are likely to accept the legitimacy of political action when it defends religious values or the interests of congregants. In such cases, politics is perceived as an extension of religion rather than as an alien force grafted onto it. That distinction helps to explain how the leader of the American Family Association, an interest group that opposes pornography, abortion, televised sex and violence, and sex education, could blithely attribute the success of his organization to its scrupulous avoidance of politics (People for the American Way 1989, 22). It may also account for the overwhelming level of support that African Americans give to their ministers as political spokespersons. These two examples should serve as a warning not to overestimate the barriers to political activism by churches.

The role of religion in politics may also be limited by the nature of politics itself. In the United States, the realm of government is formally separated from the religious sphere, and participants in political debate customarily use the secular language of bargaining, negotiation, and compromise. Overt religious appeals do not go down well with a sizable portion of the electorate. This poses a daunting problem for people who enter politics motivated by religious enthusiasm (S. Carter 1993). To be effective, religious groups that enter the public realm must speak the language of public interest rather than religious particularism and adopt a cool tone that does not offend people who subscribe to a different religious worldview. Yet people who are fired by faith and passion, convinced of their own purity and the inherent corruption of their opponents, may have trouble maintaining political involvement if they cannot "be themselves" in the public square. If they do not adapt their style to the reigning secular fashion, they may well be rendered politically marginal.

Finally, it is important to remember that churches do not enjoy a monopoly on political resources. Other associations—labor unions, professional groups, service clubs, business networks—possess communications and mobilization capacities and instill the same politically relevant skills as religious organizations. If church impact is greater than that of other similarly advantaged organizations, that is because church affiliation is so much more widespread than membership in other kinds of associations.

The combination of incentives, opportunities, and resources serves to draw churches into politics at several different levels. Religion may play a role in forming the fundamental assumptions and outlooks that channel public thinking about government and politics. When it operates to affect such basic orientations about politics, religion has an impact on "political culture." At a second level, religion may contribute to political identity and partisan loyalties. The traditional tie between Catholics and the Democratic party illustrates this effect. The third level at which religion interacts with politics involves specific policy debates. The remainder of the book will examine religious influences in those spheres.

NOTES

1. For information about these movements, consult the accounts in Brooks 1962; F. Carroll 1978; Clements 1982; and Wise 1976. There are also striking parallels between the Back to Africa movement of Marcus Garvey and the Peoples Temple led by Jim Jones (cf. Burkett 1978).

2. By focusing on those aspects of religion that are apparent in the form of beliefs, subcultures, and institutions, I have tried to sidestep the perennial debate between substantive and functional definitions of religion. As such, I accept the useful definition of religion as "actions, beliefs, and institutions predicated upon the assumption of the existence of either supernatural entities with powers of agency or impersonal powers or processes possessed of moral purpose, which have the capacity to set the conditions of, or to intervene in, human affairs" (Wallis and Bruce 1992, 10–11).

3. Many nations prohibit members of the clergy from holding public office. In Mexico, where the church was identified with the losing side in a civil war, political parties are forbidden to use religious labels and the public role of the church is strictly limited. Trying to keep the lid on simmering religious conflict, Egyptian authorities have even banned bumper stickers with any religious references.

3. Religion and American Political Culture

> People act politically, economically, and socially in keeping with their ultimate beliefs. Their values, mores, and actions, whether in the polling booth, on the job, or at home, are an outgrowth of the god or gods they hold at the center of their being.
> —Robert Swierenga

In hunting for evidence of religious influence in American political life, most observers examine church-state controversies or search for indications that religious groups vote in solid blocs. Another kind of religious influence is not quite so apparent. As William Lee Miller recognized, religion may contribute to the basic political values that citizens share.

There is also a still more important, if less measurable, *indirect* and long-term effect of the religious tradition upon the nation's politics. This is the impact of ways of thinking, believing, and acting in religious matters upon the shape of the mind, which . . . affects the way other fields, like politics, are understood. Such effects, seeping down into the national character, may be discernible not only in clergymen and church people but in members of the society at large. (1961, 83)

By forming an important strand in American culture, religion has helped to define the context of American political life. This chapter will trace connections between the religious ideas and practices prevalent in the American colonies and in subsequent American thought about important political questions.

To assert that religion contributed to the development of national political ideals is not to claim a monopoly for it. In the development of something as complex as a national political creed, secular thought and material interests of many kinds also play vital roles. The modern era has taught us to doubt the purity of motives, especially when they are expressed in terms of idealism, and to look for self-interest as the source of most human action.[1] Recognition that human beings undertake activity for diverse reasons, however, should not mislead one to disregard the impact on social conduct of abstract forces such as religion. Religious creeds, institutions, and communities exerted a major impact on colonial life and work. These spilled over quite naturally into politics. Because the contribution of religion to American political culture covers such important beliefs as obedience, the design of government, and the national mission, the religious roots of American political culture merit close investigation.

The Puritan Imprint on Colonial Thought

Although Americans often think of their country as a "new nation," its history and development largely untouched by the rest of the world, much that appears unique about American culture can be traced to the European heritage of the colonial settlers. For American political thought, the critical element of that heritage was the commitment of the settlers and their descendants to the particular form of Christianity that emerged from the Protestant Reformation (Bercovitch 1975; Niebuhr 1959).

Throughout sixteenth- and seventeenth-century Europe, dissatisfaction with the established churches fueled revolts against ecclesiastical authorities and the civil officials who sustained them. The leaders of the revolt in England—recognized today as the inspiration for American Protestantism—regarded themselves as nothing less than God's agents, engaged in a desperate struggle to liberate the church from "centuries of superstition and error" (A. Simpson 1955, 17). For its part, the Church of England regarded its Puritan critics as dangerous heretics, to be suppressed by any means necessary, including torture and execution. Eventually convinced that they could not reform or replace the state church, many Dissenters (as critics of the Church of England became known) chose to separate themselves from "an unregenerate government which persisted in maintaining a corrupt church" (ibid., 14–15), leaving England for places where they could practice a religion consistent with their faith. Driven by the impulse to create societies that would honor God in what they saw as the one true Christian fashion, the Puritan settlers crossed the Atlantic to found the

American colonies. In America, they were free to build a culture in which the Protestant images of God, humanity, and the church became the core assumptions of everyday thought.

The influence of the Puritan outlook on American thought did not depend solely on the weight of numbers. The denominations most closely identified with the Puritan wing of the Protestant Reformation, the Congregationalists and Presbyterians, were dominant only in New England. The Church of England, though a minority faith in most of the settlements, enjoyed official status at one time or another in the southern colonies of Virginia, Georgia, and North and South Carolina. Roman Catholicism was a force to be reckoned with in Maryland. The Middle Atlantic colonies were settled principally by members of the Dutch Reformed church, the Quakers, and adherents of several German Protestant traditions. Even in New England, the dominance of Puritan congregations was soon challenged by the strength of newer sects like the Baptists and the Methodists and weakened by internal conflicts over questions of theology and politics. Despite this religious diversity, few modern historians would contest the early nineteenth-century judgment of Alexis de Tocqueville (1945, 32) that the Puritan vision suffused the whole of the colonies.

As difficult as it may be for the late-twentieth-century mind to comprehend a contemporary, the challenge is compounded many times over when the task involves understanding a seventeenth-century mind. Yet the task is essential if one is to arrive at any understanding of the perspectives that shaped the early American political thought. In the century and a half that elapsed between the establishment of the first permanent English settlements on the North American continent and the founding of the Republic, the theology of the Reformation was continually adapted to the American situation. The specifically religious impulse may have waned over time—its preeminence challenged by new intellectual currents and commercial considerations—but periodic revivals kept it very much alive in the American mind.

Early American politics bore the imprint of this religiosity. For example, the Puritans were voracious readers of Scripture. Under the doctrine that ordinary people needed no intermediary between themselves and the word of God, and indeed God Himself, Puritanism encouraged individuals to look for divine guidance in the Scriptures. Up to the time of the Revolution and perhaps for some time thereafter, the Bible was the book most familiar to the typical inhabitant of America. A study by Donald Lutz (1984) suggests that the biblical tradition seems also to have greatly influenced those who led the Revolution and wrote the Constitution. In an intensive study of nearly one thousand political documents issued to the public from 1760 through 1805, Lutz found that the Bible was the single most frequently cited work in these documents. Though this hardly supports Thornton's claim that the Bible was "the textbook of the fathers of the Republic" (quoted in Sandoz 1990, 142), it at least suggests an environment of intense scriptural literacy and consciousness and explains why political argument was usually couched in biblical language and why biblical analogies were employed to explain the political situation.

Further illustrating the impact of religion, preaching and worship styles were quickly transplanted to political realm. Political campaigning adopted the techniques of mass persuasion seen during the "Great Awakenings," those periodic outbursts of intense religious enthusiasm that swept across the continent. Candidates rallied supporters with torchlight parades, tent meetings, door-to-door canvassing, and public declarations of faith, the same methods pioneered by evangelists seeking religious converts (Jensen 1980). Campaigns appropriated religious hymns for political use or else commissioned campaign songs that drew on sacred music. Daniel Walker Howe (1990, 124–125) traces a prominent American political innovation, the national nominating convention, to the national meetings pioneered by religious associations.

In addition to its impact on the language and techniques of politics, the religious environment was also an important factor in developing national unity among the colonists. In response to the outbreak of hostilities in 1776, an astonished Englishman reported, "From one end of North America to the other, they are FASTING and PRAYING" (quoted in Sandoz 1990, 141). Throughout the Revolutionary War, the Protestant clergy built support for the cause by emphasizing the religious nature of the conflict. In a typical sermon preached in 1777, the Rev. Nicholas Street (Cherry 1972) reminded congregants that the people of Israel had grown restive and fearful when led from the security of Egyptian slavery into the unpredictable freedom of the wilderness. In the same manner, he argued, the colonists had thrown off a tyrant only to find themselves apprehensive about the future. They must confront their fears, he said, by recognizing that "God frequently brings his own people into a state of peculiar trials, to discover to them and others what there is in their hearts." In the case at hand, the minister said, God was looking for signs of genuine piety and repentance before delivering the colonies from the hands of their enemies. In addition to providing aid and comfort to the colonial army, the minister advised his audience that it would render a signal duty to the war effort by confessing its wickedness and endeavoring to avoid sin. Some ministers went well beyond this measured tone to equate Britain with the anti-Christ and to treat the republican cause as the pure expression of Christian values (Bloch 1990, 49–52; Noll 1988, chap. 3). Popular support for the Revolutionary War owed something to the way the Revolution was "preached to the masses as a religious revival" (Perry Miller quoted in Sandoz 1990, 135).

The imprint of Protestant Christianity on the era of the Founders and, through time, on contemporary U.S. political life is apparent in several respects. From the body of Puritan thought come three elements that proved especially important for subsequent American political practice: covenant theology, the emphasis on the total depravity of humankind, and the concept of a chosen people. Each of these doctrines was applied by the Puritan thinkers and their successors to the earthly realm of politics. Covenant theology helped Americans decide under what conditions governments required obedience. The Puritan image of human sinfulness provided clues about the best design for maintaining stable government. And the idea of "chosenness" encouraged Americans to think about their nation in missionary terms. Despite the passage of two centuries, these ideas continue to cast a long shadow over the conduct of American political life.

Covenant Theology and the Right to Revolt

Most Americans take it for granted that citizens owe allegiance to governments that respect their "inalienable" rights and liberties; they also seem to accept without question the assertion in the Declaration of Independence that citizens have a right to revolt against governments that deny fundamental freedoms. The idea of conditional allegiance, of a "contract" between citizens and rulers that can be voided when the government misbehaves, is a cornerstone of American political thought.

This concept of government as a covenant gained such ready acceptance among colonial Americans because it bore a close resemblance to
a central element in Puritan theology, the covenant. Puritan thinkers
gave considerable warrant to this model of association, which appears
at several different points in the Bible (Elazar 1980, 12–20). In the
most influential of the biblical covenants, Abraham and God were
joined together by bonds of mutual obligation as Abraham accepted
the promise of God's blessing for himself; his heirs, the people of Israel,
in turn pledged to do God's work in the wilderness (Gen. 12:3). This
obligation was imposed on Abraham not by fiat but by a "conscious
contract with God" whereby Abraham "promised to do certain things
for God in return for which God pledged Himself to recompense
Abraham" (P. Miller 1956, 119). As the Puritans understood it, the
defining characteristic of a covenant was that of a voluntary agreement, sanctified by God, in which individuals freely surrendered
autonomy in exchange for something of greater value. God hovered
over covenants either as a partner or, in the case of contracts among
individuals, as the sanctifier and guarantor in whose name the agreement was forged.

This model of social organization was applied by the Puritans to all
manner of human associations. Under the image of the covenant, the
"church" was redefined: rather than an institution with authority in a
particular geographical area, it was seen as a community of the elect, a
gathering of those who received the promise of eternal salvation in
exchange for accepting a mission to act as God's agents in this world.
Extended to civil societies, the covenant provided a basis for human
governance. In crossing the Atlantic, the Puritans envisioned themselves as a latter-day people of Israel, recreating the Hebrew covenant
in their pilgrimage to the New World. The most famous reenactment of
the covenant ritual was the Mayflower Compact, in which the Pilgrims
(a Puritan congregation) aboard the ship pledged to create a holy,
Bible-based commonwealth in the wilderness in exchange for God's
blessing. This ceremony was repeated after landfall in the famous
Plymouth Compact. The settlements that spread throughout the New
England colonies during the seventeenth century were founded on
similar compacts (Lutz 1994).

The political implications of the covenant idea became especially
important when Americans sought to justify their decision to cut all

legal ties with Great Britain. The crucial link was forged when the idea of a covenant was extended to encompass an entire nation. If the relationship between colonist and king was a contract sealed by the authority of God—in other words, a covenant—then the terms of that contract bore divine authority. The citizens owed allegiance to the ruler, and the ruler, in turn, was committed to honor the contract by acting within its limits. In the view of the colonists, "Rulers who violate the agreed-upon forms are usurpers and so are to be legitimately resisted" (P. Miller 1967, 98).

The implications of this type of reasoning were revolutionary. Whereas others interpreted the Bible as saying that God ordained obedience to government, a view that promoted absolutist rule, the Puritans understood the relationship between people and government as one of mutual obligation. The basis for this revised interpretation was the model of the biblical covenants. Through agreements with Adam, Noah, Abraham, and others, God had entered into binding contracts with human beings. Though surely not the equal of the mortals in these partnerships, God nonetheless promised to behave in accordance with the terms of the contract, acting as a kind of constitutional monarch in the universe. If God had agreed to be bound in this manner, how could any earthly monarch presume to be exempt from limits or obligations?

Fortified by biblical precedent, the colonists insisted that the monarch respect their universal rights as creations of God, along with the specific rights due to them as citizens of the British Empire.[2] Because obedience was conditioned on the ruler behaving in conformity with agreed-upon standards, it could justly be withdrawn whenever the standards were violated. Thus, when King George III clearly abridged the rights to which the colonists felt entitled, they claimed that the colonies no longer owed him loyalty. Resistance to a government that violated God's law could even be seen as a religious obligation.

The colonists repeatedly invoked the covenant tradition to justify the breaking of their bonds with Great Britain. Almost a year to the day before the Declaration of Independence was made public, the Continental Congress called on Americans to observe a day of national confession, marked by "publick humiliation, fasting, and prayer." After promising this confession and pledging repentance, the colonists asked God for help in persuading the British to respect the terms of the compact that bound the colonies to the mother country (P. Miller 1967, 90–91). When the British proved resistant to these prayers, the colonists once again stressed that a broken covenant justified revolt. The Declaration of Independence begins with the assertion that the colonists deserved independence under "the Laws of Nature and Nature's God." Consistent with covenant theory, the colonists asserted that the bond between rulers and ruled was dependent on the ruler's respect for those rights that God granted to men. Once the terms of the compact had been violated by a despotic King George (as the colonists sought to demonstrate in great detail), the people of America could claim a divine mandate to dissolve their ties. The Declaration concludes with the submission of the purity of the rebels' claim to "the Supreme Judge of the World."

The breaking of the covenant not only entitled the people to withdraw authority from a corrupt government, but also, as the Declaration emphasizes, authorized them to form a new system of rule. Once independence was secured, the colonists went about the task of building a new state on the promise that a new covenant was required. After a false start, they settled on what is sometimes called the American national covenant—the Constitution of the United States. Although the Constitution does not explicitly recognize God as a partner or invoke divine blessing—a sign of its secular purpose—the document bears the mark of covenant thinking in a number of important respects (Hughey 1984).

Following the original Hebrew concept of covenant as a voluntary undertaking, the Constitution was a contract freely entered into by the people of the thirteen states. It was presented to them as a document that they were free to accept or reject. The biblical covenant created a "people" who, if they accepted the agreement, were promised God's blessings; similarly, the Constitution was presented in the name of the "People of the United States" to achieve for them such beneficent ends as justice, order, welfare, and liberty. Covenants, as the Puritans understood them, routinely set limits on the power of authorities. The privileges of power were legitimate only insofar as they were carried out with respect for the God-given rights of the contracting parties. Commentators have called attention to the corresponding emphasis on limits in the U.S. Constitution. The document is replete with provisions spelling out what government may not do and holding government subject to strict rules and standards in the performance of its duties.

Americans continue to live under the Constitution, of course, but do they ascribe any religious significance to it? Some commentators suggest that the Constitution is enveloped in an virtual aura of holiness. The document enjoys the status of a holy relic, encased in a shrine to which citizens make pilgrimages, its authors revered as saints or demigods, and its meaning entrusted to an elite group of judges (i.e., Supreme Court justices) that strikingly resembles "a priesthood which sits in a temple" (Rountree 1990, 204). If not a full-fledged religion, the Constitution supplies U.S. citizens with a national identity, sacred civic values, and comforting rituals (Levinson 1988; Rountree 1990, 204–207). If they needed reminding of the covenantal roots of American political thought, the American people received it during the 1992 presidential election. At the nominating convention, during the campaign, in his inaugural address, and thereafter, Bill Clinton (1992) repeatedly invoked the covenant theme and called his agenda the "New Covenant." He challenged Americans to remember that government's responsibility to promote opportunity is balanced by the citizens' obligation to act responsibly. By stressing the concept of mutual obligation and giving it a sacred character, Clinton both appealed to religious traditionalists and underlined the vitality of this cornerstone of American political thought (Barnes 1992).

Puritanism and Democracy: A Qualification

Associating Puritanism with democracy sounds strange in an age that views Puritans as "insufferable, self-righteous precisionists with narrow minds and blue noses, authoritarian, clericalist, intolerant, and antidemocratic" (Ahlstrom 1965, 95). Historians remind us that Puritan settlements were motivated not by an abstract commitment to religious liberty, which they routinely denied to dissenters in their midst, but rather by the desire to protect their own religious practices. They succeeded magnificently in this objective, imposing on the colonies "a narrower band of religious choices than fellow subjects enjoyed in England" (Murrin 1990, 21). Reflecting "a narrow, sectarian spirit" (Tocqueville 1945, 41), their legal codes mandated church attendance, forbade worship in alien faiths, and "constantly invaded the domain of conscience" by exacting criminal penalties for every imaginable sin. How could such people possibly lay the foundations of a democracy?

Tocqueville supplied one answer when he credited Puritanism with a "spirit of democracy" that sustained freedom and liberty as cultural values (Kessler 1992). This spirit came first from the egalitarian New Testament vision of the church as an association open to all humanity. It was reinforced by the distinctly Protestant view of individuals as capable of discovering religious truth through their own efforts. Both arguments, deployed against the territorial and hierarchical Church of England, mandated that individuals be granted religious choice. Choice was not to be construed, however, as freedom to run riot but rather as a divine gift of "liberty for that only which is just and good" (Tocqueville 1945, 44). Paradoxically, Puritan citizens used freedom to impose on themselves "fantastic and oppressive laws" supposedly in accord with God's plan for humankind. But the potent ideal of liberty, once proclaimed, could not be effectively restricted to the narrow channel approved by Puritan orthodoxy. It eventually challenged the very idea of an "official" religion and undermined any special claims to authority by a religious elite. In the political sphere, the assumption that individuals will discover truth by exercising liberty imparted a sacredness to majority opinion. If the Puritans neither embraced nor practiced democracy as we know it, they nonetheless paved the way for it.

The democratic elements in the Puritan creed were reinforced by institutional interest and the social practices of Protestant Christianity in the New World. The "interest" that first drew Puritans to the New World, a desire to escape the entrenched Church of England, was increasingly threatened by the efforts of the British government to assert greater control over the colonies. Even the transplanted Anglican establishments in the southern colonies had grown accustomed to remarkable autonomy from the mother church in England (Mead 1976, 25–27). In the 1760s, colonists were particularly agitated by plans to appoint Anglican bishops in America. To persons steeped in a tradition of congregational autonomy and religious pluralism, a system in which religious leaders enjoyed minimal civil authority, the prospect of a centralized system of church government seemed to be the opening wedge in a campaign to undo the legacy of their Puritan forebears. As Carl Bridenbaugh (1962) demonstrated in a convincing analysis of the continuing conflict between the Church of England and the colonies, fear of losing religious liberty played a major role in the development of American nationalism and helped to stimulate the drive for independence from Britain.

Viewed as a social force, religion taught the colonists themselves much about the actual practice of democracy. In most of Europe, local churches were held accountable to centralized national hierarchies that prescribed a code of belief, determined acceptable forms of worship, and provided ministers to ensure that local practice conformed to national standards. Membership in the church, determined solely by place of residence, was essentially a matter of passive acceptance rather than active involvement. Colonial religious life, in contrast, developed on the principles of voluntary affiliation and congregational independence. After "planting" a church in the wilderness, the founders could prescribe conditions of membership, formulate their own code of belief and practice, and select a minister who served at the pleasure of the congregants. Membership in a church was an option, rather than an automatic status, and carried with it an obligation to participate actively in the running of the congregation.

The tradition of self-rule that developed in the churches before and after the Revolution encouraged the corresponding growth of a vigorous democratic spirit in the political realm (Hatch 1990). These habits and attitudes eventually spread far beyond New England and the Puritans, encompassing most of the religious traditions that claimed the loyalties of colonists (Bonomi 1994; Calhoon 1994). In the judgment of the historian Sydney Ahlstrom (1975, 424), membership in self-governing churches "prepared men to regard the social compact as the proper basis of government." Modern research supports this logic by demonstrating that democratic experience in the home, school, and workplace "spills over" into politics, promoting democratic dispositions (Lipsitz 1964; Renshon 1975). Ahlstrom's conclusion gains further support from the simultaneous development in New England of the congregational principle in church governance and democratic practices in civil life. To a degree unparalleled at that time (though restricted by today's standards), the New England colonies achieved high levels of suffrage, powerful representative institutions, respect for the rule of law, and social policies that encouraged the spread of education, science, culture, and charitable activity (Shipton 1947).

The link between democracy and religion thus turned on all three dimensions of religion. If the creed of Protestant Christianity was ambiguous about democracy as a system of government, the fear of English assaults on the reformed churches and the training in self-government provided by autonomous congregations tipped the scales in favor of the revolutionary cause. For these institutional and social contributions, as much as covenantal theology, the heirs of the Protestant Reformation deserve recognition as precursors of the democratic spirit in America.

"Total Depravity" and Institutional Restraint

Another aspect of Puritanism shaped the political system adopted after the Revolution. The Puritan emphasis on the inherent sinfulness of humankind (a strong theme in Protestant thought) provided principles of governance that the Founders observed in constructing their constitutional alternative to the colonial framework. Though we are apt to think of their creation, the Constitution, as a neutral set of institutional arrangements, the system they fashioned is infused with a moral architecture that still guides the conduct of American political life.

The American governmental system was designed by political architects who assumed that human beings could not be trusted with power. To keep government safely under control, they divided authority among three separate branches, giving each leverage to use against the others, and they added additional safeguards such as powerful territorial governments (the states). As a consequence of that framework, the great challenge to any U.S. political leader is to overcome the inherent division of authority by mobilizing all institutions and levels of government on behalf of a common purpose. Compromise, delay, and deadlock are the characteristics of normal political life, to the frustration of advocates of rapid change.

The ultimate explanation for this aspect of U.S. political life lies in the concept of humanity that guided some of the Founders in their deliberations at Philadelphia. Far from adoring "the people," many of the Founders appraised them with a cold eye and found more to say about the defects of popular will than about its virtues. In emphasizing their suspicions about humanity, the Founders repeated a theme found in Reformation theology. For the Puritans, the fate of mortals was symbolized by the story of Adam. In sinning against God, Adam forfeited eternal happiness for a life of toil and sorrow that would end in death. Puritans saw this story as illustrative of the inherent depravity of human beings who, given a choice between good and evil, would often choose the latter. Unlike Catholic doctrine, which taught that the church could offer believers an escape from damnation, or the religions that held out some hope for redemption through good behavior, Puritan theology grimly promised that only a few (the "elect") would enjoy the light of God's grace and that the rest would know only sinfulness on Earth and eternal torment thereafter.

This perspective led to two important political conclusions. First, because governments were the creations of fallible mortals, no government could be expected to act with rectitude. Quite the contrary, a government that reflected the sinfulness of its human creators would be prone to exceed its rightful authority. Under those circumstances, prudence dictated that the power of government be limited, or, in the words of one Protestant clergyman, that "we should leave nothing to human virtue that can be provided for by law or constitution" (Strout 1974, 61). Second, because God was the only source of redemption, it was not the task of governments to make people good. The highest aspiration for government should be merely to subdue the most blatant excesses of human behavior. Puritan thought acknowledged that these rules could be softened if those who constructed and ran the government happened to be members of God's elect. But even then, it would be wise to put restraints on government lest it fall into the hands of the unregenerate. And even a government of saints, unlikely as that would be, could do no more than promote the conditions under which men and women might have the opportunity to live righteously.

These assumptions weighed heavily in the deliberations of the Constitutional Convention and were offered to justify the document that emerged from that conclave. Although revered as the foundation of a democratic republic, the Constitution was crafted by politicians who made no secret of their faith in the Puritan doctrine of human sinfulness (Wright 1949). In a series of newspaper articles written to encourage ratification by the states and now regarded as the authoritative reflection of the Founders' intentions, Alexander Hamilton, John Jay, and James Madison outdid one another in trumpeting their belief that human beings should not be trusted with unlimited power. The authors of what came to be known as the *Federalist Papers* presented countless historical examples to show that people were inherently prone to choose evil over good, self-interest over the public good, and immediate gratification over prudent delay. Previous attempts at republican government had foundered because organized groups destroyed the institutions of representation in their single-minded pursuit of power and wealth. With its wealth of examples of past failures, the *Federalist Papers* reads like a catalog of human imperfections. This jaundiced (or, to some, realistic) assessment of humankind was accepted as a basic condition, rooted in human nature, revealed in history, and impervious to changing social conditions.

Like the early Puritan settlers, the Founders identified the innate corruption of humankind as the root problem of government and the great challenge to stable democracy. The task of the Constitution they crafted was to permit republican government in spite of human tendencies to destroy liberty. To accomplish this, the Founders broke with traditional political thought by viewing human depravity both as a barrier to liberty and, under the right circumstances, as a republican asset. The problem, they agreed, was to secure a government capable of providing order yet limited enough to maintain a large degree of freedom. In practical terms, this meant that the national or central government must be given greater power than it had been allowed in the aftermath of the Revolution. The question was how to harness and control the power a strong central government would require.

The Founders' principal solution to this problem was to partition the major powers of government by embedding them in distinct and separate institutions. Given an independent base of power, the Founders thought, the three branches of government could be expected to resist encroachments by each other. They would pool their authority to achieve a common goal only when it was clearly in the national interest. By dividing power in this way, John Adams had written earlier, "the efforts in human nature toward tyranny can alone be checked and restrained, and any freedom preserved in the Constitution" (quoted in Wright 1949, 9). In dividing government roles among different institutions and embracing such doctrines as election of public officials, fixed terms of office, geographical decentralization, and strict limits on government authority, the Founders of the late eighteenth century appropriated the very methods that Puritans of the early seventeenth century had developed to restrict local religious and government officials (Witte 1990).

Paradoxically, then, the weaknesses of humankind were called on to fuel the engine of free government. The human shortcomings that other theorists had perceived as the stumbling block to any plan for durable republican government were enlisted by the Founders as the bulwark against tyranny. What would keep the branches independent of one another, the framers predicted, were precisely those less-than-noble qualities that reposed in typical human beings: ambition, envy, greed, lust for power, and so on. Jealous to preserve its own power and status, Congress would never cede to the president the absolute authority of a monarch. Recognizing that their perpetuation depended on preserving the Constitution, the state governments would use the veto power over amendments to retain their role. Judges and executive branch officials would be restrained by the recognition that they could lose their exalted status by impeachment. All in all, as one scholar has written (Diggins 1984, 53), the Founders believed "that the Republic would be preserved by the 'machinery of government,' not the morality of men."

Considering that the Constitution had to be submitted to the people for their evaluation, it may seem remarkable that the Founders were so explicit in denouncing the trustworthiness of human behavior. In one of the most important letters of the *Federalist Papers,* no. 51, James Madison did little to flatter the citizens whose votes he sought. To control the government, he wrote, it was not enough to rely on the best instincts of the people; it required "auxiliary provisions" such as the various limiting mechanisms of the Constitution. The great hope for the preservation of liberty was to equip each branch of the new government with "the necessary constitutional means and personal motives to resist encroachments of the others." Then, in a phrase that nicely encapsulated the Federalist philosophy of humankind, he reiterated the principal rationale for the various devices that controlled the exercise of governmental authority: "It may be a reflection on human nature that such devices should be necessary to control the abuses of government. But what is government itself but the greatest of all reflections on human nature? If men were angels, no government would be necessary. If angels were to govern men, neither external nor internal controls on government would be necessary" (Rossiter 1961, 322). Precisely because mortals fell short of angelic standards and angels did not deign to rule, prudence demanded that government be restrained from acting on its worst impulses.

That the framers felt free to defend the Constitution in those terms suggests that their understanding of human depravity was widely shared by the American people. In the fight over ratification, the most effective opposition came from critics who accepted the Puritan diagnosis but doubted that the proposed remedies for it were strong enough to control the weaknesses of human nature (Kenyon 1955). The antifederalists, for example, believed that the framers of the Constitution were naive to imagine that any strong, centralized government could withstand the depredation of the greedy and ambitious. Whatever the differences between the proponents and the enemies of the new governmental framework, however, the important point is that the entire debate was conducted within the bounds defined by the Puritan vision of human sinfulness.

Skepticism, rooted in the Puritan worldview, also led the Founders to a negative view of government that is still widely shared by American citizens. For all their veneration of the American way of life, Americans are quite cynical about politics and tend to hold its practitioners in low regard. There is a pronounced distrust of the motivations of politicians and an enduring yearning to purify politics by bestowing leadership on persons who have achieved eminence in other fields— astronauts, generals, business leaders, soldiers, engineers, farmers, and the like. These people, untainted by contact with a corrupting system, must be prevailed upon to relinquish the pleasures of life and to enter the sordid world of political combat. There they are supposed to save the citizenry from "politics" by restoring a measure of sanity and common sense to political life.

The traditional American view of politics as a sordid endeavor derives in part from the Founders. As we have just seen, they perceived government as a necessary evil, an institution that had to exist to preserve order but was not a good thing in itself. By embracing so wholeheartedly the Puritan concept of humanity, emphasizing human bellicosity as the constant threat to liberty, they essentially reduced government to the status of a nightwatchman. Believing that government could just as easily threaten liberty as safeguard it, they called for as little governmental authority as was necessary to prevent society from collapsing into disarray. As for the higher task of cultivating human virtue, that was to be left to private institutions, such as the church, and did not belong in the government's sphere of responsibility (Diamond 1977).

The Founders' concept of government would have astounded the ancient political thinkers, to whom politics, which Aristotle called "the master science," was the highest expression of human capacity (Will 1983). To the ancients, the state was a moral tutor, whose task was to promote certain virtues among its citizens. According to this conception, politics was the realm in which people could overcome narrow self-interest by searching for the best interests of the community. "Citizenship" was not a term denoting a dry legal status, but a title of honor reserved for those who cared deeply about the community and cultivated the public good. A republican form of government could not survive unless it inculcated such virtuous qualities in its inhabitants. According to classical republican thought, the very maintenance of the state depended on its commitment to elevate, to ennoble, to advance the interests of the community by promoting exemplary behavior. To accomplish those ambitious goals, the state had to possess substantial means, even the ability to coerce recalcitrant people to conform to what the community defined as acceptable conduct. Participation in that enterprise was seen as important and honorable.

Nothing could be further from the American conception, which equates good government with limited government. Most Americans operate from the assumption that the inherent rights of individual citizens normally take precedence over the claims of the state or those of any broader social purpose. Because such individual rights can be threatened by an overbearing government, Americans put a premium on protecting individuals from the heavy hand of the state. Following the Founders, Americans have routinely denied government the right or authority to regulate belief or to limit most forms of conduct. Outside a very limited sphere, "personal virtue" is simply not seen as the proper concern of government.

Such a negative view of authority has affected the image of politicians. Those who are most deeply involved in conducting the business of the state, it has commonly been assumed, do so in pursuit of nothing more than self-interest. The vocation of politics, perceived in the classical tradition as the pursuit of public welfare, appears to the modern age as merely a struggle for power and personal advantage. Indeed, there is a widespread suspicion that politics attracts people because, as careers go, it is a fairly good way to make a living.

Limitations on government power can certainly be defended by reference to the terrible damages inflicted by governments that saw themselves as agents of God or history, charged with remaking humanity in a new image. Just as certainly, it presents problems when government tries to persuade the citizenry to undertake actions that contribute in the long run to the public good but run against immediate self-interest. As Robert Horwitz asked, "How can a republic based solely on the principle of individual self-interest continue to defend itself against its external enemies if its citizenry has not an iota of patriotism, public spirit, or any element of that sense of duty that leads men to make sacrifices in defense of their country?" (1977, 333). By teaching that government is a threat to the liberty of free-born citizens, that it is a necessity born of human imperfection, the Founders unwittingly made it difficult for their successors to motivate behavior in the public interest.

One Nation Under God: A Civil Religion

Yet another aspect of American political life, a pronounced tendency to approach political issues in moral terms, owes much to the Puritan legacy. Commentators have long noted that American political rhetoric is infused with religious symbols and references and that debates about contending policy choices are frequently couched in terms of competing moral values. According to some scholars, this constant recourse to religious images and symbols in American political culture provides evidence of the existence of what has variously been called a public theology, a political religion, a religion of democracy, a public philosophy or, most commonly today, a civil religion.

At the core of the rich and subtle concept of civil religion is the idea that a nation tries to understand its historical experience and national purpose in religious terms (Bellah 1975; Bellah and Hammond 1980; Richey and Jones 1974). In the same way that religion may endow the life of an individual with a greater meaning than mere existence, so a civil religion reflects an attempt by citizens to imbue their nation with a transcendent value.[3] The nation is recognized as a secular institution, yet one that is somehow touched by the hand of God. British author G. K. Chesterton recognized this tendency in the United States, which he referred to as "a nation with the soul of a church."

The term civil religion does not refer to any formal code of beliefs that is fully developed and authoritatively encapsulated by a single written document. Because there is no formal statement of it, the content of a civil religion has to be inferred from the speeches and writings of political leaders. It lacks the status of a state religion, so citizens are not obliged to assent to it. A civil religion is neither the religion of a particular church nor, at the other extreme, a fully articulated religion that competes with existing denominations. Rather, it is a code subscribed to, in varying degrees, by all religions in the nation. Accordingly, it closely resembles one anthropologist's definition of a creed: "A constellation of ideas and standards that gives people a sense of belonging together and of being different from those of other nations and cultures" (cited in Mead 1974, 45–46). By imparting a sacred character to the nation, civil religion enables people of diverse faiths to harmonize their religious and political beliefs.

In thinking about the transcendent purpose of their nation, Americans have traditionally been drawn to the biblical metaphor of the "chosen people" (Cherry 1972). As noted in the section on covenant theology, the Puritan colonists were prone to interpret their passage to the New World as a reenactment of God's covenant with Abraham and his descendants. Like the ancient Jews, the Puritans felt they had been selected by God for the purpose of bringing redemption to humankind. If they succeeded in establishing Christian communities in the wilderness, creating "God's New Israel," the rest of the world would see how the faithful were rewarded with good fortune. Although the settlements themselves strayed far from the Christian models that motivated their founding, the Puritans were constantly reminded that their success or failure had implications for all humankind. That the existence of the United States is still viewed as part of a divine plan shows up in the "Pledge of Allegiance" in the phrase, "one nation under God"—which was added only in the 1950s.

Ever since the concept of a civil religion was first suggested, in the late 1960s, its existence has been the subject of a sustained debate among scholars of American society (see Gehrig 1979 for a good summary). Some observers have discounted civil religion as nothing more than religious nationalism, the common tendency among nations to endow themselves with divine favor.[4] Robert Bellah, the sociologist who has done more than anyone else to popularize the concept, has argued that the national traumas of the 1960s and 1970s largely eroded American faith in the nation's higher purpose (1975). Against this backdrop, social scientists have tested for the existence of civil religious sentiments with a variety of research tools. Although the findings have not been entirely consistent, most studies have detected in public attitudes something very much like civil religion.[5] A content analysis of the national magazine published by the Masonic fraternal organization identified a large number of statements emphasizing the nation's divine purpose (Joliceur and Knowles 1978). Using questions listed in the box on the following page, Ronald Wimberly and his colleagues have been able to demonstrate a high level of public assent to statements that seem consistent with the civil religion theme (Christenson and Wimberly 1978; Wimberly 1976; Wimberly 1979). Responses to these questions, which have been asked of divergent audiences, do not simply reflect commitment to general religious values or any other background factors. Rather, just as predicted by the scholars who first called attention to an American civil religion, civil religious feelings have been widely diffused among the persons interviewed in the polls. A similar survey among elementary-school children in the Midwest yielded comparable support for the civil religion hypothesis (Smidt 1980). These findings are not surprising in view of the many ways that public schools inculcate the beliefs, display the symbols, and act out the rituals associated with the creed of Americanism (Gamoran 1990). On the basis of these studies, it does appear that Americans expect their nation to fill a spiritual purpose.

The presidency appears to play a crucial symbolic role in American civil religion, an observation brought home in an unexpected way by public reaction to the assassination of John F. Kennedy in 1963. Sociological investigators noted a marked increase in prayer, worship, and other forms of religious activity. Despite the formal secularization of the governmental system and President Kennedy's membership in a minority faith (Roman Catholicism), many Americans reacted to the assassination by expressing intense religious commitment. To the political scientist Sidney Verba (1965, 354), the public response revealed that "political commitment in the United States contains a prime component

Civil Religious Sentiment in the United States

The existence of an American civil religion has been inferred from the responses of American citizens to the following statements:

1. It is a mistake to think that America is God's chosen nation today.
2. I consider holidays like the Fourth of July religious as well as patriotic.
3. We need more laws on morals.
4. We should respect a president's authority since his authority is from God.
5. National leaders should affirm their belief in God.
6. Good patriots are not necessarily religious people.
7. Social justice cannot be based on laws; it must also come from religion.
8. To me, the flag of the United States is sacred.
9. God can be known through the experience of the American people.
10. If the American government does not support religion, the government cannot uphold morality.

Source: Ronald C. Wimberly, "Testing the Religious Hypothesis," *Sociological Analysis,* 37:341–352.

Note: Positive responses to items 2–5 and 7–10 indicate a civil religious orientation, as does disagreement with items 1 and 6.

of primordial religious commitment." In mourning the slain president, Americans were honoring a sacred symbol. The discovery that a political leader could take on a religious significance for the public provided further evidence that the nation is viewed in transcendent terms.

Civil religion has also reinforced the "deep-rooted belief in American culture that political and personal virtue should be inseparable" (Sennett 1987, 42). In the 1988 presidential campaign, southern voters told pollsters they believed a candidate's moral behavior in private life foretold success in office and cited previous drug use, extramarital affairs, and lying as behavior they would weigh against a candidate.[6] Accordingly, one candidate was driven from the race for the nomination by allegations of marital infidelity, another was forced out in response to charges of plagiarism, and two had to endure criticism when they admitted having smoked marijuana in their youth. This was neither the first nor last example of such moral transgressions affecting political standing. Evidence that he had lied about his knowledge of the Watergate burglary drove Richard Nixon from the White House in 1974. By admitting past use of marijuana, a 1987 nominee for the Supreme Court raised grave questions about his fitness for the post. Questions about Bill Clinton's marital fidelity, drug use, and personal honesty were prominent features of the 1992 presidential campaign. There is less room for leeway when a public official is also a religious symbol (Fairbanks 1981).

The concept of civil religion stimulates two contrasting impulses, both of which can be discerned in Puritan rhetoric (Hutchison 1993, 5). When they described themselves as embarking on an "errand into the wilderness," the first settlers seemingly accepted the responsibility of spreading the Puritan model to the rest of humanity. The alternative description of their settlement as a "city on a hill" implied the task of building a just society worthy of emulation. The first metaphor suggests an active mission to impose a system whose virtue is assumed, while the latter image assigns more priority to setting an example. In much the same way, the civil religion of the United States has encouraged citizens both to celebrate the glory of the nation and to hold it to account.

In what social scientists call "legitimation," or its "priestly" aspect, civil religion helps to cement loyalty to the nation. God blesses the nation because it serves a sacred purpose. So long as the nation conducts its affairs according to some higher purpose, it warrants allegiance from its citizens on grounds other than mere self-interest. By giving the nation a mission to which citizens are emotionally attached, civil religion may thus counter the tendencies to elevate self-interest into the only basis for loyalty and obedience. The "legitimation" function of civil religion has been evident in the attitudes of children who link a religious or spiritual view of the nation with very positive images of political authority (Smidt 1982; Funderburk 1986).

Civil religion also provides standards by which to judge a nation's behavior. It suggests that there are things higher than the nation and that it is permissible to criticize the nation for its departures from moral codes. As the New Testament taught, a nation "under God" is deemed responsible to God and will be held to a high standard of behavior. Because transgressors suffer severe punishment from a just God, citizens have an incentive to keep the nation firmly on the path of righteousness. This is the ethical or prophetic function of civil religion, as may be seen in the comments of two very different social critics, Sidney Schanberg and Phyllis Schlafly:

It is true that, by and large, the press in Indochina wrote stories critical of the American policy there. But it was not because reporters were unpatriotic. It was, rather, because reporters saw America slipping toward the habits of total-itarian powers whose activities we deem as less than moral.

What we did was to hold this country to a greater standard. Since our Government says that it stands on higher moral ground than the Communist powers, that it is different, it must behave differently, not just say so. That is the standard by which the press measured its country. (Sidney Schanberg, *New York Times*, 23 April 1985, op-ed)

Q.   Whose side *is* God on?
A.   Well, I think He's on the side of Right, Justice, and Goodness—all those things. And I think the side anti-ERA is on.
Q.   Is God American?
A.   No, but He certainly blessed America more than any other country. And with that goes the responsibility to do the right thing and assume that leadership. If America abandons that responsibility, it could face a terri-ble destruction.
Q.   Who is God against? Who's on the other side?
A.   The Devil.
Q.   Represented by whom?
A.   . . . . The Devil is a very intelligent creature, who appears in a lot of forms. I do think he's in the Kremlin, among other places. (Phyllis Schlafly, interview with *Ms.* magazine, January 1982, 92)

Critics of U.S. policy, whether protesting slavery, economic oppression, or the Vietnam War (like the journalist Sidney Schanberg, quoted here), have usually invoked the prophetic side of civil religion by call-ing America to honor its own aspirations and standards (Williams and Alexander 1994). When he admonished American Christians to chal-lenge racial segregation, the Rev. Martin Luther King Jr. imagined what St. Paul would have said to them:

You have a dual citizenry. You live both in time and eternity. Your highest loy-alty is to God, and not to the mores or the folkways, the state or the nation, or any man-made institution. If any earthly institution or custom conflicts with God's will, it is your Christian duty to oppose it. You must never allow the tran-sitory, evanescent demands of man-made institutions to take precedence over the eternal demands of the Almighty God. (1963, 128)

The deep hold this prophetic concept has had on the American mind is evidenced by its recurrence among those who have resisted the changes sought by King. In their indictment of American policies, conservative critics like Schlafly have stressed that God's blessing on the United States is contingent on the country's adherence to biblical morality. Although they are more prone than King to cite biblical passages that appear to anoint the political system with divine sanction, right-wing leaders such as Schlafly have reserved the right to disobedience when they see human law in conflict with divine law.

No American politician expressed the priestly and prophetic themes of civil religion more eloquently than Abraham Lincoln (Morgenthau and Hein 1983). Although relatively untouched by "church religion," Lincoln saw the United States as a nation with a divine purpose that had been most clearly revealed in the noble principles of the Declaration of Independence. For Lincoln, the commitment to secure free government, which had been sanctified by the sacrifices of the Revolutionary generation, was the higher purpose that the United States represented. He told Congress in 1862 that, by adhering to the principles of the Declaration, the nation was nothing less than "the last, best hope of earth." Because the Union was the concrete embodiment of that continuing commitment to liberty, Lincoln made its maintenance and eventual restoration his highest priority. At Gettysburg, he interpreted the deaths of Union soldiers in transcendent terms, saying their sacrifice in the cause of liberty had reaffirmed the sacredness of the American mission. He then asked Americans to respond with "increased devotion" to the cause for which the soldiers have given the "last full measure of devotion" (1959a).

If Lincoln enunciated civil religious themes to sanctify the Union, he was equally willing to call down the wrath of God on the nation when he thought it had strayed from the path of righteousness. Although favoring moderate solutions to slavery, he clearly regarded the maintenance of the institution as a great national sin—perhaps the American equivalent of Adam's fall from God's grace. In his second inaugural address, delivered only a month before his assassination, Lincoln (1959b) chided Northerners and Southerners alike who claimed God's support for their cause. Quoting from Scripture, he noted that God punished those who committed offenses in the world. Those responsible for the "offense" of American slavery included all Americans, both

the Southerners who kept slaves and the Northerners who had acqui-
esced in slavery's continued existence. He saw the bloodshed and violence of the war as God's retribution: "He gives to both North and
South this terrible war as the woe due to those by whom the offense
came." Rejecting complacency and self-righteousness, Lincoln called
on the nation to accept its punishment and then to rededicate itself to
the principles of the Declaration.

Lincoln was far from alone in his invocation of civil religion; in fact,
students of political rhetoric have demonstrated its recurrence in the
public statements of nearly all American presidents (R. Hart 1977). In
a systematic content analysis of inaugural addresses delivered from
George Washington to Ronald Reagan, Cynthia Toolin (1983) found
the speeches replete with reference to the nation's divine origin and its
corresponding moral obligation to light the way for the remainder of
the earth. To judge from the utterances of two recent occupants of the
office, the priestly and prophetic strains of civil religion have retained
potency. Jimmy Carter's first speech as president encouraged
Americans to develop "full faith" in their country—wording that signi-
fies dedication to a transcendent force—and contained numerous references to the country in clearly religious terms (Hahn 1984). Carter
also emphasized the prophetic side of civil religion in enjoining the
nation "to do justly, and to love mercy, and to walk humbly with thy
God," quoting Micah 6:8. In declaring at his inauguration that "I
believe God intended for us to be free," Ronald Reagan made an even
more explicit statement of belief in a civil religion (1981a, 4; also W.
Shannon 1982). The prophetic side of Reagan's faith can be inferred
from his frequent suggestions that the United States has strayed from
the intentions of the Founders in asking government to do too much
(1981a, 3). Though he did not say directly that God had punished
Americans by sending an economic recession, that line of reasoning
would be consistent with the view that violations of a sacred covenant
bring retribution to transgressors.

Civil Religion as a Double-Edged Sword

To be a constructive force in political life, civil religion must balance
the priestly and prophetic impulses. In that condition, it can ennoble a
people by prompting generous instincts and a resolute commitment to

the nation's principles. Yet the two streams of civil religion—legitimation and prophecy—can also be vulgarized. Attributing a sacred purpose to the nation can degenerate all too easily into idolatrous worship of the state. The belief that a nation embodies God's will can inhibit the skepticism and self-criticism that is so important to democratic politics (Lipsitz 1968). Similarly, in holding the nation to high standards of conduct, the civil religious tradition may produce a frame of mind that disdains the kind of compromises necessary for an orderly political life. If the standards are rigid and unbending, the system one of moral absolutes, then all deviations are equally reprehensible—a view that does not encourage a sense of proportion.

The dangers of imbalance have been most visible in American interactions with the rest of the world (Tiryakian 1982). Barely concealing his irritation, a Canadian described American foreign policy as "a determined ideological and evangelical offensive to redeem the rest of the world from its backward, sinful self" (Rawlyk 1990, 254).[7] Such critics contend that Americans are so certain of their nation's virtue that they view international politics as a clash of moral opposites, assuming without thought that God has blessed their endeavors. Consider how this sense of righteousness may have distorted the U.S. government's behavior toward international communism in the tense period following World War II. When the wartime alliance between the United States and the Soviet Union broke down in the aftermath of victory, American policy reverted to a position of unrelenting hostility. Whatever the real and considerable provocations in Soviet behavior, the U.S. foreign policy leadership was prone to treat the Soviet Union as a moral leper that had to be isolated from the world community (Hoopes 1973). Many thoughtful critics who harbored no illusions about Soviet intentions have noted that the moralistic approach prevented American policymakers from recognizing and exploiting the split in the late 1950s between the Soviet Union and the People's Republic of China and may have prompted the United States to enter military conflicts that could have been avoided. As George Kennan (1951) charged, stigmatizing opponents as the embodiment of evil breeds a "total war" mentality, impedes compromise, and thus exacerbates international tension.

The alternative, perceiving the United States solely in terms of its failings, is no more constructive than viewing the country as the embodiment of virtue. Nations do have interests and those interests may occasionally, tragically, require a resort to force. Critics of Allied behavior during World War I helped leave the nation ill-equipped for combat when the next global war broke out just two decades later. A loss of faith in America's mission, the product of the Vietnam War experience, left many citizens persuaded that their country could not be trusted to act righteously in foreign policy. Short of providing humanitarian assistance to poor countries, these critics essentially advised the United States to withdraw from world affairs. By undermining confidence in the nation's legitimacy and purpose, the prophetic impulse may simply paralyze national will.

The sociologist Robert Wuthnow fears that large sections of the American religious community have succumbed to these extreme manifestations of civil religion (1988, chap. 10). He notes the emergence of a "conservative" version of civil religion that endows the nation with holiness and puts the government and economic system beyond the reach of criticism. This position, which appeals to many members of the more evangelical and fundamentalist denominations, may account for the greater hawkishness displayed by religious conservatives in U.S. military engagements from Korea to the Gulf War (Hero 1973; Wald 1994; Jelen 1994b). Wuthnow also detects a "liberal" version of civil religion that casts doubt on the moral legitimacy of the nation-state itself. Many liberal church leaders in the grip of this critical stance, finding "no conceivable circumstances in which United States military force could ever be justified," automatically condemned U.S. actions in the Gulf War (Hertzke 1991, 60). Instead of imparting an independent perspective to foreign policy deliberations, religious conservatives invariably sanctify American behavior and religious liberals predictably denounce it. The loss of balance between the priestly and prophetic roles has robbed religion of a distinctive voice and made it a source of conflict rather than consensus (Nichols 1988).

One of Many Influences

It would surely be an exaggeration to state flatly that religion alone caused important political attitudes—including the social contract, limited government, and American destiny—to take hold of the American imagination. The path connecting sixteenth-century religious thinkers and eighteenth-century political activists is tangled and meandering. Religion, in its various guises, should be recognized as only one of the forces operating in the development of American political culture.

At least two other influences shaped the American political system in its formative period—a new intellectual force and the lure of economic advantage. The foremost intellectual rival to the ideology of the Protestant Reformation was the Enlightenment, a body of thought developed in seventeenth- and eighteenth-century Europe (May 1976).[8] This movement, characterized above all by a belief in human progress through the systematic application of reason, supplied a heavy dose of optimism to counterbalance the Puritans' stern view of humanity. Without some sense that humans could engage in reasonable conduct under the proper institutional arrangements, the Founders could not have contemplated constructing a democratic political system. Their attempt to create a written constitution alone bespeaks a tremendous confidence in human ability to discover eternal truths by reflection and debate. The influence of the Age of Reason, as the Enlightenment era has been called, was apparent in the thought and behavior of political activists throughout the revolutionary period and during the early history of the nation.

In addition to the sway of intellectual currents from Europe, the colonists were also moved by material forces. Clearly key elements of the political culture served to advance the economic interests of powerful groups in early American society. As generations of schoolchildren have learned, a major incentive to break with Great Britain was economic: the colonists had serious grievances about taxation and other matters. The Founders' commitment to the idea of limited government may have also been the product of economic self-interest, for a government with limited authority was a government incapable of redistributing income from the wealthy to the poor. The Founders generally came from the more affluent stratum of colonial society, and material interests may well have disposed them to want governmental authority tightly reined in. Similarly, the missionary impulse in American political culture permitted the nation to fuel its economic expansion by the constant acquisition of new land, raw materials, sources of labor, and markets.

Given the many factors at work in forming the American political culture, the more appropriate conclusion is that certain patterns of religious thought, habitual ways of reasoning about God and humankind, made it easier for some political ideas to take root in American society. Accustomed to thinking about God and mortals in contractual terms, Americans were receptive to a political theory that treated government in a similar fashion. The widespread belief that humans behave sinfully disposed the colonists to accept the doctrine of limited government. Trained by their religion to see God at work in the daily lives of men and women, Americans could easily imagine a divine hand guiding the destiny of their country. In this view, religion was one of the factors that facilitated the development of a common political outlook.

Recognizing religion as one among several sources of the founding of America should provide a perspective on the debate about the nation's path since the Revolution. Among some intellectual heirs of the Puritans, recent American history is often described in terms of decline and fall. Such historical treatments begin with the assumption that the United States "emerged from the generally Christian actions of generally Christian people [who] . . . bequeathed Christian values, and a Christian heritage, to later American history" (Noll, Hatch, and Marsden 1983). By loosening legal constraints on items as diverse as abortion, school discipline, sexual behavior, drug use, and sex roles, it is charged, the government has betrayed its heritage and abandoned its Christian foundations. But if Christianity certainly played a prominent role in the American founding, the evidence presented herein does not sustain the claim that colonial America was exclusively influenced by Christian values.[9] Whether early America was morally superior to present-day society will continue to be debated; but presupposing a golden age, a one-time "Christian America," is a dubious starting point.

The political concepts of social contract, limited government, and American destiny remain integral elements of American political culture even if they have lost most of their religious grounding. The next chapter explores the formal role of religion in the American system of government. For many foreign observers of the United States in its formative period, the most original and arresting feature of the young nation was the revolutionary divorce of religion and government. While most Americans continue to believe in the wisdom of that principle, there is no such harmony on how to apply that philosophy to many practical issues of church and state.

NOTES

The chapter epigraph quoting Robert Swierenga is taken from his chapter, "Ethnoreligious Political Behavior in the Mid-Nineteenth Century: Voting, Values, Culture," in *Religion and American Politics,* ed. Mark Noll (New York: Oxford University Press, 1990), 154.

1. As a student once remarked to me, perfectly revealing the cynicism of the age, "People are rich or poor before they are anything else."

2. The development of contract thought among the colonists has traditionally been credited to the "secular" influence of English philosopher John Locke. But as Winthrop Hudson (1965) argued, Locke drew on the ideas of the Puritans to formulate the doctrine of government by consent of the governed.

3. In a review of the civil religion concept, Richey and Jones (1974, 14–18) identify five overlapping uses of the term. I have adopted the definition of civil religion as a sense of national transcendence because that is the manner in which the "chosen people" metaphor has entered the political culture.

4. The degree to which this type of civil religion is the unique property of American culture or a more universal phenomenon has yet to be fully addressed. Michael Walzer (1985) has found the Exodus metaphor throughout political history. For some suggestive thoughts on civil religion in comparative perspective, see Coleman (1970) and Bellah and Hammond (1980, chaps. 2–4).

5. The exceptions include Thomas and Flippen (1972), who found few references to any divine plan for the United States in newspaper editorials published during "Honor America" week. In interviews that Benson and Williams (1982) conducted with members of the U.S. Congress, most legislators proved unwilling to endorse statements that interpreted the nation's destiny in transcendent terms.

6. "A Candidate's Morals Matter, and Lying Is the Cardinal Sin," *Atlanta Journal and Constitution,* 31 January 1988.

7. In a similar vein, Fatima Mernissi (1992, 102) reported Arab outrage at President Bush's frequent use of religious language during the Gulf War. Invoking God on behalf of American troops created the impression "that the satellites themselves were the objects of spiritual machinations" and that liberating Kuwait from Iraq was merely a pretext to cloak "a religious war, a global conspiracy to destroy Islam and win victory for another religion, the religion of arrogant, capitalist America." Language intended to reassure Americans of the moral worth of a military campaign may inspire quite the opposite reaction among others.

8. Because the Christianity of the Protestant Reformation was skeptical about the capacity for human regeneration and emphasized revelation as the key to understanding, it may be tempting to portray religion and rationalist thought as incompatible. In practice, the two traditions at times found common ground and at times competed for influence—often within the mind of the same individual.

9. Noll, Hatch, and Marsden (1983) have made a strong case that a "Christian culture" is generally unlikely and that colonial America was a considerable distance away from a scripturally based commonwealth. They also raise doubts that the Christian influence in early America was uniformly positive.

4. Religion and the State

When Caesar, having exacted what is Caesar's, demands still more insistently that we render unto him what is God's—that is a sacrifice we dare not make.

—Alexander Solzhenitsyn

It may not be easy, in every possible case, to trace the line of separation between the rights of religion and the Civil authority with such distinctiveness as to avoid collisions and doubts on unessential points.

—James Madison

The subject of the previous chapter, the religious sources of early American political thought, leads naturally to questions about the official role of religion in the government of the United States. Some Americans believe that religion contributed so profoundly to the early Republic that the Constitution should be understood as the fusion of the "precepts of Christianity, civil government and Christ." [1] To this way of thinking, the Founders of the United States intended to give religion a privileged place in the new nation, and subsequent generations have departed from that plan by artificially separating religion from government. With equal fervor, other commentators acknowledge the importance of religious thinking at the time of the nation's founding but draw radically different conclusions about the intended role of religion. In this perspective, the framers are frequently described as deists and freethinkers who were highly skeptical about traditional forms of religion and who therefore wrote a Constitution to create an impeccably secular state. Only by imposing a high and impregnable "wall of separation" between church and state, it is argued from this point of view, does the Supreme Court faithfully implement the mandate of the Founders.

This chapter explores the interactions between government and religion that often come to mind with the phrase "church and state." I attempt to provide some guidance for readers who may be puzzled by the reasons for church-state tension, the conflicting claims about "the intentions of the Founders," and how the Supreme Court has interpreted the Constitution on this subject.[2] Because government policy on church and state is not etched in stone, we also explore the possibility that the United States may have entered a new phase in the relationship between religion and government.

The Genesis of Church-State Conflict

The relationship between church and state presents two sets of problems for democratic governments. On the most fundamental level, governments must decide what legal status to grant to religious forces. Should government take account of religious sentiments, treat churches as just another type of institution, or try to regulate and control religious activity? The problem is particularly severe when, as in the United States, many types of churches compete for the loyalty of the citizens. In such a situation, "taking account" of the public's religious sentiment may inflame members of religious minorities and persons who are not religious. Yet by ignoring religion or limiting its public role in the interest of preserving harmony, the government runs the risk of alienating citizens for whom religion is an important source of personal identity.

The second type of church-state problem stems from possible conflicts between religious motivation and behavior in the secular realm. Religions provide guidance about how people should live their lives. In some cases, religious beliefs may counsel individuals to undertake actions that violate the duly established laws of the state. Government may demand behavior that a church forbids or may prohibit actions that the church requires. In either case, the citizen is forced to choose between loyalty to the public law and loyalty to religious faith. What should be done when church and state provide conflicting guidance about appropriate or permissible behavior?

Because it involves the rights and privileges of two different institutions, the question of the legal status granted to churches is known as the "boundary" problem, or, from the phrase made famous by Thomas Jefferson, that of the "wall of separation" between church and state.[3] The second type of church-state problem, collision between the teachings of church and state, is usually described as the "free exercise" controversy—a label that recognizes that the free exercise of religious belief may run afoul of limits established by secular law. Both types of problem have repeatedly found their way onto the American political agenda. From any number of possible examples, two incidents will be used to illustrate each type of church-state problem.

Two court cases raised in the starkest possible way the religious basis of disobedience to secular law (Zlatos 1984).[4] On February 16, 1984, an Indiana infant named Joel David Hall died of pneumonia. Less than four months later, in a neighboring town, nine-month-old Allyson Bergmann died of bacterial meningitis. The parents of both children had refused to seek medical care because of their religious convictions. The Hall and Bergmann families belonged to Faith Assembly Church, a large congregation in northern Indiana that preaches, among other things, faith in God as an alternative to medical care. Believing that God will conquer disease and pain if souls are pure, church members regard illness as a sign of defective spiritual commitment by individuals and their families. They also believe that any resort to professional medical care will only hasten death because God will interpret it as evidence of diminished faith. Consistent with their understanding of life as a divine gift dependent on intense spiritual devotion, the church members avoid hospitals, reject medical devices such as eyeglasses and hearing aids, refuse immunizations, and do not maintain life insurance or use seatbelts. For failing to seek timely medical care, the parents of the two infants were charged under Indiana laws with reckless homicide and child neglect, convicted in jury trials, and sentenced to prison terms. Similar charges are frequently filed against Christian Scientists who may refuse on religious grounds to obtain conventional medical treatment for children.

These cases represent, in extreme form, the free-exercise basis of church-state conflict. Government and religion came into conflict because each claimed the authority to set standards for human behavior. The right of government to limit what citizens may do is widely accepted by most modern societies. The authority of government is recognized in codes of law that state the types of behavior that are unacceptable and define the penalties for disobedience. Religions also take positions on what behavior is permissible, and their beliefs are spelled out in sacred documents and religious codes. Recognizing the authority of government in most spheres, churches frequently urge the state to make religious morality the basis for determining what behavior is to be encouraged or forbidden. But when the laws do not agree with church doctrine, the religious claim the right to follow what they see as God's "higher law." That was the premise of Martin Luther King Jr. when he openly defied laws on racial segregation as incompatible with Christianity; that was also the premise of the parents of Allyson Bergmann and Joel David Hall for not seeking medical care.[5]

In the Faith Assembly cases, government demanded one standard of behavior and the church another. Based on the widespread belief that government should protect children, who usually cannot defend themselves, the state of Indiana invoked laws calling for heavy fines and jail terms for parents who do not seek timely medical care for sick children. In moving against the parents of the Bergmann and Hall infants, the state was particularly alarmed by evidence that infant mortality rates among Faith Assembly members were three times the state average, even though church members could have afforded medical treatment. According to the prosecutor, the substitution of prayer for effective medical care constituted "negligence and criminally reckless conduct" under secular law. On their part, the Halls and Bergmanns claimed that faith healing was a legitimate exercise of their religion and that the state of Indiana had no legal basis for forcing them to act against their beliefs by calling in a physician. The bedrock of their defense, however, was the claim of moral superiority for church doctrine over the state laws. Asked by the judge if she would ever seek medical treatment for her children, the mother of the Hall infant declared, "On the basis of my convictions, and of my fear of God almighty, I could not provide medical care." What the state required as evidence of reasonable behavior by a parent, the church denounced as a form of blasphemy. In such a case, the parents asserted the right to follow their conscience.

The boundary problem does not usually appear in so dramatic a form, but it probably occurs more frequently than the free-exercise cases. In 1992 it arose when the student government at the University of Virginia denied funding to a student group that published a Christian magazine. Like most institutions of higher learning, the university requires students to pay an activity fee that supports a wide range of student-initiated organizations, speakers, and events.[6] Wide Awake Productions, a student group, applied for $6,000 from these funds to defray printing costs for a magazine devoted to a Christian perspective on community and university life. The student council refused the request, citing a regulation that prohibited the university, as an agency of government, from funding activities with an explicit religious purpose. With crosses adorning each page and an editorial goal of encouraging students to develop a personal relationship with Jesus, the magazine made clear its commitment to promoting a particular religious orientation. To provide state funding for printing costs, the university contended, would put it in the position of using compulsory fees for the purpose of promoting a particular religious faith and thus of violating the Constitution's ban on government actions to "establish" religion. To deny funding to an otherwise eligible organization solely because it took a religious perspective, the magazine's editors contended, amounted to denying constitutional freedoms of speech, press, religion, and equal protection of the law. This conflict was not resolved until 1995 when the U.S. Supreme Court ruled on the lawsuit filed against the University of Virginia by Wide Awake Publications.

In focusing on these two major types of church-state conflict, I do not mean to suggest that the two institutions are permanently locked in a battle for supremacy. Though conflicts occur, not all church-state interaction is marked by hostility. Churches may receive various types of public aid when they perform social services. As corporate institutions, churches are entitled to the protection of government in matters of property and security. Government may also be asked to help individuals secure religious liberty from threats posed by other, nongovernmental, institutions. For example, the federal courts have been petitioned to require businesses to recognize the conscience of employees whose faith does not permit them to work on certain days of the week or to perform certain responsibilities. But in most cases, and particularly in those that draw headlines, controversies arise over where to draw the proper line between the institutions (boundary) and the moral authority (free exercise) of church and state. The sources of controversy may be as seemingly trivial as a $6,000 printing bill for a religious newspaper or as significant as a parent's decision to withhold medical care from a critically ill child.

Principles of Church-State Relations

The American approach to the boundary and free-exercise problems is governed by the famous phrase from the First Amendment of the Constitution: "Congress shall make no law respecting an establishment of religion, or prohibiting the free exercise thereof." That statement and a prohibition on "religious tests" for holding public office in Article 6 are the only formal references to religion in the Constitution. This brevity has inspired continuing debate over what kinds of government action toward religion are permitted and how far individuals may go in claiming religion as justification for violating secular law. The constitutional language on religion, like that on so many other subjects, has been interpreted differently from one generation to the next. The debate over the precise meaning of the words in different circumstances, a source of passionate controversy and fierce argument, is examined in later sections. Despite its intensity, however, that debate should not disguise what has been a strong American consensus on the role of religion in the state.

The American pattern rejects the two extreme options embraced in totalitarian political systems, subordinating the government to the authority of the church through a *theocracy* as in Iran or, conversely, adopting the *Erastian* model that treats churches as departments under government authority and control (Francis 1992). Rather, the United States has pursued what might best be described as a "partial" separation of church and state. There has been virtually unanimous agreement that the establishment clause ("Congress shall make no law respecting an establishment of religion") forbids the government to grant preference to any particular religion. Together with the corresponding free-exercise clause ("or prohibiting the free exercise thereof"), it also seems clearly to rule out the possibility of the government imposing one religion as the official faith or prosecuting members of another because their beliefs are repugnant. But if "separation of church and state" is interpreted to mean that government should make no allowances for religion or belief, then the United States is a long way from complete separationism. In numerous ways, the government has recognized the strong religious beliefs held by many citizens and made it clear that separation does not require state hostility to religious influence (Kirby 1977).

The currency, national seal, "Pledge of Allegiance," national anthem, legislative prayers, and oaths sworn in federal courts all make explicit reference to belief in God. Most of these practices have been upheld in court challenges. In such political events as a presidential inauguration, the religious motif is readily apparent through the Bible on which the oath is sworn and the prominent participation of clergy in the ceremony. In addition, the churches on occasion have been asked to participate in the formation of public policy. Until the Supreme Court broadened the grounds for "conscientious objection" to military participation, it was customary for members of the clergy to sit in judgment on the moral sincerity of persons who applied for exemption from military service. Even today, the clergy may be sought out to review public policies that raise moral issues.

Choosing neither theocracy nor subordination of religion to government, Americans must still resolve what Madison described as "collisions and doubts" vis-à-vis church and state issues. In so doing, they choose among two major, competing interpretations of the Constitution's religious language.[7] Favoring Jefferson's "high wall," advocates of separation believe "government and religion will better achieve their ends if they remain independent of each other" (Adams 1986, 69). This doctrine takes a dim view of any government aid or support for religion but is generally sympathetic when individuals seek exemption from laws on religious grounds. The separationist viewpoint was most forcefully expressed by Justice Hugo Black in a 1947 Supreme Court decision:

The "establishment of religion" clause of the First Amendment means at least this: Neither a state nor the Federal Government can set up a church. Neither can pass laws which aid one religion, aid all religions, or prefer one religion over another. Neither can force nor influence a person to go to or to remain away from church against his will or force him to profess a belief or disbelief in any religion. No person can be punished for entertaining or professing religious beliefs or disbeliefs, for church attendance or non-attendance. No tax in any amount, large or small, can be levied to support any religious activities or institutions, whatever they may be called, or whatever form they may adopt to teach or practice religion. Neither a state nor the Federal Government can, openly or secretly, participate in the affairs of any religious organizations or groups and vice versa. (*U.S. Reports*, 330 U.S. 15 [1947])[8]

In sharp distinction, the doctrine of *accommodation*, sometimes known as "benevolent neutrality," or nonpreferentialism, urges government to protect the nation's Judeo-Christian heritage. Accommodationists believe government may extend benefits to religion in a nondiscriminatory manner. The clarion call for accommodation was sounded by Justice William O. Douglas in 1952:

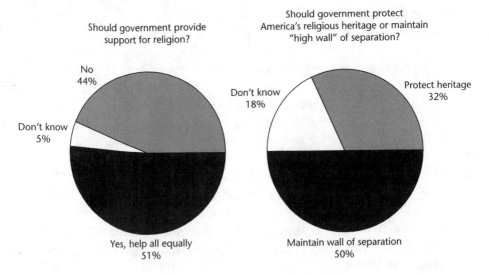

Figure 4.1 General Views on Church-State Separation (Source: Williamsburg Charter Foundation, 1988, Washington, D.C.)

We are a religious people whose institutions presuppose a Supreme Being. We guarantee the freedom to worship as one chooses. We make room for as wide a variety of beliefs and creeds as the spiritual needs of man deem necessary. We sponsor an attitude on the part of government that shows no partiality to any one group and that lets each flourish according to the zeal of its adherents and the appeal of its dogma. When the state encourages religious instruction and cooperates with religious authorities by adjusting the schedule of public events to sectarian needs, it follows the best of our traditions. For it then respects the religious nature of our people and accommodates the public service to their spiritual needs. (*U.S. Reports,* 343 U.S. 310 [1952])

The doctrines of accommodation and separation pit "those who think that government should accommodate and encourage the sort of religion that they see as a foundation of our culture" against "those who think that the government should not extend aid or support to religion in any way" (J. Wilson and Drakeman 1987, xviii). The American public partakes to some degree of both doctrines (see fig. 4.1). When asked whether government should provide no support to any religion or should support all religions equally, a narrow majority opts for the accommodationist perspective by selecting the latter option. But when the issue is phrased another way, the majority shifts

paration in the First Amendment reflected a compromise between
ose who disagreed about the political value of religion. Rather than fit
atly into the categories of religious supporters or opponents, most of
e Founders recognized religion as a force with the potential both to
hance and to undermine political stability. Hence the particular
rangement of church-state relations in the United States constitutes
ither a wholehearted endorsement of religious influence on govern-
ent nor unremitting hostility to it. To appreciate the American solu-
n to the boundary and free-exercise problems, it is essential to exam-
e the circumstances under which it evolved.

e Founders and Religion

When the Founders prohibited "religious tests" for holding federal
ice, they were reacting against both their understanding of British
tory and common practices in the colonies. From the Reformation,
ich had inspired the settlement of America, they acquired the belief
t alliances between a powerful church and an absolute state would
rupt both institutions. More immediately, they observed how some
he North American colonies appeared to court that same danger by
viding religion with the sanction of government in the form of reli-
us requirements for public office, the establishment of an official
h, and denial of religious freedom to members of minority religions.
Many colonies demanded that public office be filled only by persons
could pass some test of acceptable faith. Even where a relatively
e range of religions was recognized, as a rule, Christianity was the
s for these religious tests. Pennsylvania reserved public office for
ons who would swear, "I do acknowledge the Scriptures of the old
New testament [sic] to be given by divine inspiration" (Schappes
, 68). Belief in God was not sufficient in Maryland; although one
e most tolerant colonies, it further demanded that officeholders
pt the concept of the Holy Trinity (Kirwin 1959, 24–29). North
lina also went one step further than Pennsylvania, excluding not
Jews but also Catholics from holding executive or judicial office
appes 1971, 598).

addition to such religious tests, most of the colonies formally
wed certain religions with official status—the core of what was
vn as the "establishment" of religion. Under this system, citizens

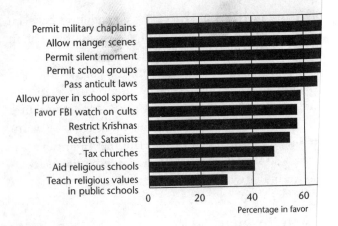

Figure 4.2 Specific Views on Church-State Separation (Sou
Charter Foundation, 1988, Washington, D.C.)

to something closer to the separationist perspectiv
question, individuals were asked whether governn
special steps to protect the Judeo-Christian herita;
States or, rather, if there should be a "high wall" of se
church and state. The majority supports Jefferson's v

Public reaction to specific church-state relationsh
fig. 4.2). Accommodationists could point to majority
al types of government recognition of religion—pra
tary chaplains, religious displays on public property,
religious groups in high schools, and prayers at the
school sporting events. To prove that public opinio
wall between church and state, separationists c
emphatic rejection of aid to religious schools and th
public schools emphasize Judeo-Christian values. (
such as "moment of silence" laws allowing private
the public appears to take a strong stand in favo
rights. Yet to judge from the number of individ
restrictions on religious cults and minority faiths,
want to extend such rights in a nondiscriminatory

Each doctrine of church-state relations claims h
So, what did the American Founders say and do a
gion in government? As we shall see, the scheme o

could be obliged to attend services at a church of the favored denomination and were taxed to provide revenue for the dominant religion. Besides enjoying material support from the government, the clergy of the established church were often granted legal privileges such as exemption from certain types of civil laws. Competing faiths were put at a further disadvantage by laws making worship the privilege of the established church. As an example, the charter for New York colony limited the right of public worship to all "who profess faith in God by Jesus Christ" (cited in ibid., 18–19).

The degree to which legal support of one church hampered the free exercise of other faiths was apparent in several restrictive features of colonial law. In some colonies, conformity to the official faith was a condition of residence and dissent the grounds for expulsion or worse. The "worse" in Massachusetts was death. According to that colony's charter of 1641 (cited in Dunn 1984, 22), "If any man after legal conviction shall have or worship any other god, but the lord god, he shall be put to death." What it meant to "have any other god" was spelled out by another law that warranted the death penalty for anyone who cursed or blasphemed "the name of God, the father, Son or Holy ghost." This law was invoked in 1660 to hang a Quaker woman who had refused repeated orders to stay out of Massachusetts. For denying the divinity of Jesus, the doctrine of the Resurrection, and the occurrence of miracles, a Jewish resident of Maryland faced the possibility of death and the loss of property (Schappes 1971, 13–15). Under these conditions, the free exercise of religion applied only to the established religion of the colony.

Although differing over how far the government might go in recognizing religion, the men who most influenced the Constitution and operated the new system of government in its first years were virtually unanimous in rejecting state support for a national faith. Such support was deemed bad for the state because it promoted false values, undermined respect for the law, and introduced an unhealthy fanaticism to public affairs. As men of strong if unorthodox faith, the Founders also shared a belief that establishment of a national religion or government support for religions would do religion more harm than good. Because each of these objections is relevant to current debate over church-state relationships in the United States, the Founders' logic demands careful review.

For some of the Founders, notably Thomas Jefferson and John Adams, organized religion deserved no government support because, among other reasons, it was thought to pervert the true meaning of religion. Their extended correspondence shows that the architects of the Declaration of Independence and Washington's successors to the presidency both agreed that true religion consisted of benevolent conduct toward one's fellow human beings. They outdid one another in denouncing the "irrelevance" and "superstition" of dogma that obscured the simplicity and beauty of religion's moral content (Cousins 1958, 85, 139, 283; see also the comments of Ben Franklin, 25–26). All that was important in Christianity and the other religions, Adams wrote (ibid., 81, 281), could be found in the Sermon on the Mount and the Ten Commandments. Jefferson agreed heartily: years before, he had tried to rewrite the Scriptures by pruning away all the doctrines he saw as unnecessary—including the divinity of Jesus, the Holy Trinity, and the structure of the church (ibid., 173–216). Precisely because formal religion appeared to give more attention to such mystical concepts than to emphasize the essential truths of the Golden Rule, it evoked little enthusiasm from Adams and Jefferson. Hence, they believed organized religion would not contribute to the public good if it enjoyed the patronage of government. Government needed protection from such religion.

Establishment was also considered unwise by some of the Founders because it seemed likely to bring the law into low esteem. As deeply held matters of personal belief, religious views could move people to take extreme actions in defense of conscience. History seemed to demonstrate that government attempts to impose a uniform faith would inevitably unleash passion and violence. With so many different religious groups in the colonies, each offering its own distinct version of the truth, any national establishment would be certain to offend many citizens who subscribed to different faiths. Under these circumstances, a law commanding support for an established church could not realistically be enforced. According to Madison, an unenforceable law would result in a striking demonstration of the government's impotence and a reproach to its authority (ibid., 108). In the absence of consensus, he thought, it would be better to pass no law at all than one certain to elicit widespread disobedience.

The final political problem connected with establishment was the Founders' firm belief that a state church would inevitably degenerate into a system of religious tyranny. The experience of the colonies suggested to them that although establishment might begin as a benign preference for one church, the privileges of governmental support would almost certainly encourage attempts to suppress alternate views. John Adams, whose skepticism of the churches earned him an unwarranted reputation for irreligion, asked rhetorically, "When or where had existed a Protestant or dissenting sect who would tolerate a free inquiry?" Answering his own question, he noted that the clergy would accept all manner of brutality and ignorance in the name of preserving the one true faith. "But," he wrote from personal experience, "touch a solemn truth in collision with a dogma of a sect, though capable of the clearest proof, and you will soon find you have disturbed a nest, and the hornets will swarm about your legs and hands and fly into your face and eyes." Having experienced similar condemnation for his attempt to reduce all religions to a common core of moral commands, Jefferson echoed Adams's appraisal of the tendency of churches to persecute those who did not fully accept their doctrines. To give such an institution access to the full powers of the state, they agreed, would create a powerful engine of oppression.

The harmful political consequences of a national religion were not the only reasons the Founders rejected establishment. They also argued that political support would make for bad religion. Hence, religion needed protection from government. As Jefferson observed, a government that compelled religious exercises could dictate other terms to a church, reducing it to a servant of power (ibid., 137). More fundamentally, the Founders concurred that religion was meaningful only when it was a sincere expression from the heart and mind of a free people. Second to none in his admiration of religion as a spur to upright conduct, George Washington repeatedly emphasized the need to keep religion a matter of personal conscience, free of government intervention. To do otherwise, Washington argued, was to put human beings in God's role as the judge of other people's conscience (ibid., 49). Jefferson advised his nephew to "question with boldness" even the existence of God because, if a Supreme Being existed "he must more approve of the homage of reason than that of blindfolded fear" (ibid., 128–129). Although the government could force people to swear loyalty to a public faith, it could not make their hearts pure or their behavior any better. From this evidence, it seems clear that resistance to establishment did not grow out of hostility to faith. Even Tom Paine, the Founder most widely regarded as an enemy of Christianity, believed the practice of true religion would improve if churches were separated from the state.

All these supposed defects of establishment would be turned into benefits if government refrained from endorsing a religion or from trying in any way to regulate acceptable belief. Freed from state support, political leaders in the early Republic predicted, the false churches would collapse as humanity returned to the essentials of religion (ibid., 320). Instead of undermining respect for the law by insulting the conscience of dissenters, a government that respected religious freedom would enjoy widespread popular support and obedience in the legitimate exercise of its power. In fact, citizens watchful of their religious freedom would be equally sensitive to safeguard their other fundamental and natural liberties. Finally, in the absence of attempts to enforce a single faith, the Founders expected an even greater number and diversity of churches. In religion, as in politics, they thought that diversity would make tyranny less likely, and so they welcomed the prospect of the growth in the number of denominations. On top of these political benefits, of course, rested a firm belief that religion would be purified as its practice was freed from compulsion and hypocrisy.

The constitutional framework governing church-state relations is thus the product, in part, of the Founders' Enlightenment perspective. So long as it was "universal, noninstitutional, and uncoerced" (Diggins 1984, 80), religion could contribute to good government by teaching restraint and instilling a commitment to good works. It was that kind of faith that was endorsed when, for example, Washington in his farewell address referred to the importance of religion to morality. In that sense, religion was a factor with the potential to stabilize republican government. Yet the Founders remained aware that religion in a particular, institutional, and coerced form could do enormous damage to the stability and reputation of republican government (Cousins 1958, 67). Beyond simply forbidding the state from aiding churches or giving them legal privileges, those Founders influenced by the Enlightenment insisted that government "could give no symbolic endorsement, expression, or acknowledgment of religion" and should not "pass laws or policies on religious grounds or religious arguments" (Witte 1991, 495). This perspective inspires contemporary separationism.

The First Amendment religion clauses would not have passed without an alliance between this elite group of Founders and the "free churches" that grew so explosively in the Great Awakening of the pre-Revolutionary period. Baptists, Methodists, and other new religious movements, offering "palatable spiritual food for the hungry souls of the common folk," challenged the dominance of legally established churches (Mead 1976, 29). These "evangelical separatists" shared the goal of liberating religion from the state, wanting the freedom to perform their religious mission without facing restrictions imposed by established churches. Together with the Founders, the Protestant advocates of religious liberty helped persuade the first Congress to adopt the religion clauses of the First Amendment and, in a campaign that lasted until the 1830s, to disestablish the churches in every state of the union. Their support for disestablishment, conditioned on a level playing field, did not extend to the goal of keeping the state free from all religious influence. Unlike the Enlightenment separatists, these Protestant separationists wanted government "to accommodate and aid all churches without conditions or controls and to foster a climate conducive to the cultivation of a plurality of religions" (Witte 1991, 494). We can recognize the origins of the doctrine of accommodation in this religious movement.

How Far Can Government Go?

For different reasons, the Founders and the numerous Protestant sects that soon dominated the religious landscape agreed that the national government created by the Constitution should not prefer any one religion or faith over another. Beyond that central postulate, there is considerable disagreement today about what the government is or is not allowed to do regarding religious values and institutions. This is a seemingly inevitable result of the dual heritage of the First Amendment's religion clauses. The Founders, moved primarily by Enlightenment separationism, acted fairly consistently to limit religious influence on the state, while the Protestants influenced by the Great Awakening saw government as a legitimate instrument for spreading a religious message. When we look at the actions taken by individuals and governments during the early Republic, we see that the law bears traces of both these impulses.

None of the Founders appeared to believe government must ignore religious feeling in its official actions. Thinking God's blessings would be important in the outcome of the Revolutionary War, Washington ordered officers and soldiers in the Continental Army to maintain "punctual attendance" at worship services (Cousins 1958, 50). Samuel Adams, the least reluctant of the founding generation to limit religious expression, used his position as governor of Massachusetts to issue religious proclamations (ibid., 355–356); Washington did the same when he called for the first day of "thanksgiving" by the new nation (ibid., 71–72). Even Jefferson, who provided the momentous interpretation of the First Amendment as building "a wall of separation" between church and state, had no objection to the use of municipal buildings for worship by the different congregations in his village (ibid., 163). Though he steadfastly recommended against paying for religious instruction at the state university he founded in Charlottesville, Jefferson advised the Virginia legislature to encourage the denominations to fund professorships of their own (ibid., 164). By accommodating the claims of different churches in this manner, he thought the university could counter the false impression that it stood "against all religion." James Madison, usually portrayed as the strictest separationist among the founding generation, also appears to have conceded religion an important public role (P. Weber 1982b).

Does this mean, as accommodationists argue, that the Founders understood the Constitution to permit nondiscriminatory support for religion in general? In a frontal assault on this accommodationist interpretation, Leonard Levy (1986) contends that the Founders meant the First Amendment expressly to prohibit any form of government assistance to any and all churches. He points out that the colonial establishments deviated from the European pattern of a single official religious faith. When the First Amendment was framed, "all state establishments that existed in America were general or multiple establishments of all the churches of each state, something unknown in the Europe familiar to Americans" (ibid., 9). If "establishment" meant that all churches were eligible to be supported by tax revenue, as Levy argues, then the First Amendment's prohibition against establishment must be read as a separationist mandate against any government support for religion—even if that support is neutral vis-à-vis competing denominations.

Many Founders appeared to have doubts about the very idea of governmental aid to religion, even if it were to be allocated on a nondiscriminatory basis by state governments. Washington objected on principle to a bill introduced in the Virginia legislature to pay religious teachers from tax revenue. Rather than rankle the consciences of dissenters and so "convulse the State" with religious conflict, he much preferred a scheme like Jefferson's compromise on religious instruction at the state university. In a letter to a political friend, Washington expressed himself as favoring the obligation of all religions—Christianity no less than Islam or Judaism—to pay for their own religious instruction (Cousins 1958, 64–65). "I wish an assessment had never been agitated," he wrote, "and . . . that the Bill could die an early death." Madison, the most relentless critic of public aid to religion, responded with vehemence the same year to a proposal in Congress that would set aside a section of the Northwest Territories to support the church favored by a majority of the inhabitants. He denounced the proposal as "unjust" and "hurtful," a bill "smelling so strongly of an antiquated Bigotry" that it would reduce international respect for the country" (ibid., 306–307). Although neither Washington nor Madison might have considered such proposals as unconstitutional under the terms of the First Amendment, they did declare them to be unwise.

The strongest evidence that the Founders did not favor even nondiscriminatory aid or noncoercive state recognition lay in their expressed sensitivity to the feelings of religious minorities. Their apparent awareness of how state recognition might injure the feelings of religious minorities can be interpreted to support preference for governmental aloofness to any religious expression, however bland and noncontroversial. A deeply religious man who served several terms as president of the American Bible Society, John Jay of New York objected to opening the sessions of the Continental Congress with a prayer. Citing the diversity of belief and custom among the delegates, he doubted that a prayer could be found that would not offend some member of the assembly.

As president, George Washington showed the same sympathy to the religious groups that suffered the brunt of exclusion under state laws of establishment. He told a general meeting of Quakers that he believed that "the conscientious scruples of all men should be treated with great delicacy and tenderness" and wrote to the Jewish community in

Newport, Rhode Island, of his belief that religious freedom was a "natural right," not a mere "indulgence" of toleration to minority faiths that the majority could grant or withdraw at will (ibid., 60–61). Jefferson provided the clearest display of sensitivity to the implications of state recognition of religion when, as president, he was asked to proclaim a religious holiday (ibid., 136–137). Reluctant to assume an authority that was, if it existed at all, reserved for state governments, he refused to issue a watered-down proclamation encouraging national prayer with nothing more than the force of public opinion behind it. Challenging the proponent of such a plan, he asked: "Does the change in the nature of the penalty make the recommendation less a *law* of conduct for those to whom it is directed?" Jefferson doubted the Constitution gave the president "the authority to direct the religious exercises of his constituents" even if such "direction" was nothing more than bland verbal encouragement.

The government should avoid recognizing any denomination, even something as broad as Christianity, lest it offend the sentiments of nonbelievers. The religious authority of the government extended solely to prohibiting conduct that impelled believers to "disturb the peace, the happiness, or safety of Society" (ibid., 301). In his *Notes on the State of Virginia*, Jefferson made the point very clearly:

The legitimate powers of government extend to such acts only as are injurious to others. But it does me no injury for my neighbor to say there are twenty Gods, or no God. It neither picks my pocket nor breaks my leg. If it be said his testimony in a court of law cannot be relied on, reject it then, and be the stigma on him. Constraint may make him worse by making him a hypocrite, but it will never make him a truer man. It may fix him obstinately in his errors, but will not cure them. (ibid., 123)

On this reading, the Founders appear to have been as eager to keep the state from limiting individual religious expression as they were to keep the government from promoting it.

The separationist view also predominated in an instructive controversy that began in the early years of the nineteenth century (Blakeley 1970; John 1990). Since the founding of the nation, the government had always permitted the mail to be transported between communities on Sunday, the Christian Sabbath. In 1810 Congress enacted a law requiring post offices that received Sunday mail to stay open on that day and directing postmasters to make deliveries the same day they received shipments. Despite numerous protests from Christian organizations over defamation of the Lord's Day, Congress not only repeatedly refused requests to repeal the law but also extended it on several occasions. Early reports from the House committee with jurisdiction over the Post Office stressed that suspension of Sunday mail would impede the efficient performance of a major and legitimate government function. But as the protests mounted, the committee increasingly cited separationist considerations as the basis for refusal to end Sunday delivery of posts.

The language of a report issued in 1830 made the case for continued Sunday delivery in terms that would probably have pleased the founding generation. By acceding to requests to end mail delivery on Sunday, it was argued, Congress would effectively be granting official recognition to the Christian Sabbath. Withholding the mail on Sunday would force non-Christians to respect a holiday that they did not recognize in their hearts. In strong language, the House committee reminded the petitioners that the Constitution gave religious equality to all people by denying privileges to any—even if the faith in question was shared by the vast majority of the population. Echoing the fear of the Founders that even slight concessions to one faith might open up a wedge for greater government regulation in the future, they wrote:

The conclusion is inevitable, that the line cannot be too strongly drawn between Church and State. If a solemn act of legislation shall, in *one* point, define the law of God, or point out to the citizen one religious duty, it may, with equal propriety, proceed to define *every* part of divine revelation; and enforce *every* religious obligation, even to the forms and ceremonies of worship; the endowment of the church, and the support of the clergy. (Committee on Post Offices and Post Roads 1830, 1)

Rather than coerce individuals by using the authority of government, the committee recommended that petitioners try to "instruct the public mind" on the evils of the practice that they condemned. If all men and women truly came to believe in the evil of Sunday mail, the practice would wither instantly; so long as people did not unanimously share the views enunciated by critics of Sunday mail, governmental intervention could only inflame religious passions. Although this view was not unanimously accepted, as indicated by dissents from the 1830 report and by language in earlier committee documents, the ideas of the Founders were interpreted as supporting the "wall of separation" that Thomas Jefferson sought between the institutions of government and the churches.

These examples underscore the danger of ascribing accommodationist motives to the political leaders who dominated the early Republic (Cord 1982). It is equally wrong to overlook the numerous ways that the culture of Protestantism was incorporated in the earliest actions of government (Witte 1991). From government chaplains, official prayers and proclamations, the institution of religious holidays, and religious symbols on government documents, it was clear that government acknowledged the religious heritage of the United States. In various ways, governmental agencies channeled direct assistance to religious enterprises. Even more fundamentally, many of the laws and institutions created by government were animated by religious values. By attaching criminal penalties to conduct like prostitution, gambling, blasphemy, and sacrilege, the social values of Protestantism were given the force of law. These efforts were commonest at the state level, where the First Amendment did not apply, but were not unknown at the national level. Even at the state level, where establishment was permitted under the Constitution, separationists occasionally succeeded in passing legislation that limited the public role of clergymen and reduced the opportunities for government assistance to religious institutions. The current tension between separationists and accommodationists is built into the Constitution by the conflicting motives of the architects of the First Amendment.

The Wall of Separation Grows Higher

Despite the constant potential for controversy, neither the boundary problem nor the free-exercise concept excited much national attention in the first 150 years under the Constitution. Over that span of time, the controversy over Sunday delivery of mail was one of the few church-state items to engage Congress. At the state level, fierce battles were fought over proposals to drop establishment and to soften other forms of official support for religion. Although denominational competition and conflict remained important elements of political controversy, the constitutional status of religious institutions and belief was simply not a pressing item on the national agenda.

The relatively small volume of "religious" cases decided during the first century and a half of American history set some broad outlines for the relationship between religion and government. In *Reynolds v. U.S.* (1879) the Supreme Court put an important limit on the free exercise of religion by upholding a congressional ban on the practice of plural marriage. By making polygamy a crime in the Utah Territory, Congress had seemingly intruded on the religious values of the Mormon population who accepted polygamy as a religious duty. Nonetheless, the Court argued, Congress could restrict *behavior* motivated by religion provided it did not prescribe or proscribe certain religious *beliefs*. Mormons were free to believe that God intended plural marriages but they could be prohibited from acting on the belief because the government had a legitimate reason to regulate marriage. If the *Reynolds* decision gave the government authority to limit certain religious practices, the *Pierce* decision in 1925 limited the reach of such authority. The Court struck down an Oregon statute forbidding students from attending private schools. In practice, this law was aimed at Catholic schools, and the Supreme Court concluded that Oregon had usurped the rightful authority of churches to operate schools and of parents to educate children according to their own religious beliefs.

Church-state relations became a major topic of political discussion only in the 1940s, when the Supreme Court began to reinterpret the First Amendment's language on religion. Since that period of reappraisal began in the mid-1940s, the Court has decided more than fifty church-state cases (summarized in table 4.1). The decisions of the past fifty years have provided a legal framework that departed from previous church-state doctrine in three important respects. First, it abandoned the traditional distinction between national and state action toward churches. Whatever the First Amendment forbade or required the national government to do about religion, the Court now held, also applied to the state and local levels of government. The different treatment of religion by nation and state was first rejected in principle by a 1940 Supreme Court decision; eight years later, a policy developed by an Illinois school board became the first state or local regulation actually struck down by the Supreme Court as being in conflict with the establishment clause.

Second, the Court attempted to fortify the boundary between church and state by broadening the list of government actions that constituted an impermissible establishment of religion. Formerly understood to for-

Table 4.1 Significant Supreme Court Decisions on Church and State Questions

Case	Year	Issue	Outcome
West Virginia Board of Education v. Barnette	1943	flag salute	separationist
Everson v. Board of Education	1947	school transportation	accommodationist
McCollum v. Board of Education	1948	school time-release program	separationist
Zorach v. Clausen	1952	school time-release program	accommodationist
McGowan v. Maryland	1961	Sunday closing law	accommodationist
Torcaso v. Watson	1961	religious oaths	separationist
Engel v. Vitale	1962	school prayer	separationist
Abington School District v. Schempp	1963	school prayer	separationist
Sherbert v. Verner	1963	unemployment benefits	separationist
United States v. Seeger	1965	draft exemption	separationist
Epperson v. Arkansas	1968	teaching evolution	separationist
Board of Education v. Allen	1968	textbook loans to parochial schools	accommodationist
Walz v. Tax Commissioner of the City of New York	1971	tax exemptions for church lands	accommodationist
Lemon v. Kurtzman	1971	state aid to parochial schools	separationist
Tilton v. Richardson	1971	state aid to sectarian colleges	accommodationist
Wisconsin v. Yoder	1972	compulsory education	separationist
Committee for Public Education v. Nyquist	1973	state aid to parochial schools	separationist
Meek v. Pittenger	1975	state aid to parochial schools	mixed
Roemer v. Maryland	1976	state grants to sectarian colleges	accommodationist
Wolman v. Walter	1977	state aid to parochial schools	mixed
McDaniel v. Paty	1978	religious tests for public office	separationist
CPERL v. Regan	1980	money for education	accommodationist
Stone v. Graham	1980	school prayer	separationist

Case	Year	Issue	Classification
Widmar v. Vincent	1981	religious meetings in college	accommodationist
Valley Forge Christian College v. Americans United	1982	money for college	accommodationist
Larson v. Valente	1982	regulating solicitation	separationist
United States v. Lee	1982	social security tax exemption	accommodationist
Larkin v. Grendel's Den	1982	zoning around churches	separationist
Bob Jones University v. United States	1983	tax exemption for sectarian colleges	accommodationist
Mueller v. Allen	1983	tax credit for parochial schools	accommodationist
Marsh v. Chambers	1983	legislative chaplains	accommodationist
Lynch v. Donnelly	1984	Christmas displays on public land	accommodationist
Alamo Federation v. Secretary of Labor	1985	minimum wage	accommodationist
Wallace v. Jaffree	1985	school prayer	separationist
Thorton v. Caldor	1985	Sabbath exemption	separationist
Grand Rapids v. Ball	1985	funding for parochial schools	separationist
Aguilar v. Felton	1985	funding for parochial schools	separationist
Witters v. Washington	1986	funding for sectarian colleges	accommodationist
Bowen v. Roy	1986	social security numbers	accommodationist
Goldman v. Weinberger	1986	military dress codes	accommodationist
Edwards v. Aguillard	1987	school prayer	separationist
Corp. of Presiding Bishop v. Amos	1988	employment discrimination	accommodationist
Bowen v. Kendrick	1988	birth control	accommodationist
Texas Monthly v. Bullock	1989	tax on religious publications	separationist
Hernandez v. Commissioner of Internal Revenue	1989	taxes	accommodationist
Heffron v. International Society for Krishna Consciousness	1989	religious activity on public land	separationist

Continued on next page

Table 4.1 *Continued*

Case	Year	Issue	Outcome
County of Allegheny v. ACLU	1989	religious symbols on public lands	mixed
Employment Division of Oregon v. Smith	1990	drug use	accommodationist
Swaggart Ministries v. California	1990	sales tax exemption for religious items	accommodationist
Board of Education v. Mergens	1990	school prayer	accommodationist
Lee v. Weisman	1992	school prayer	separationist
Lambs Chapel v. Center Moriches Union Free School District	1993	access to school buildings	accommodationist
Zobrest v. Catalina Foothills School District	1993	services for parochial school students	accommodationist
Church of the Lukumi Babalu Aye v. Hialeah	1993	prohibition of animal sacrifice	separationist
Kiryas Joel School District v. Grumet	1994	separate school board for religious group	separationist
Rosenberger v. University of Virginia	1995	state funding for religious publications	accommodationist

Source: Adapted, revised, and updated by the author from Joseph F. Kobylka, "The Mysterious Case of Establishment Clause Litigation: How Organized Litigations Foiled Legal Change," in *Contemplating Courts*, ed. Lee Epstein (Washington, D.C.: CQ Press, 1995), 96, 102–103.

bid only actions that treated religious groups unequally, establishment was now seen to encompass many activities that appeared to favor religion in general. Finally, the Court became much more sensitive to claims that government rules and regulations unconstitutionally interfered with the free exercise of religion. Before this period, the justices had tended to strike down only those practices that seemed to force individuals to endorse religious beliefs that might be contrary to their own. Now, however, they began to identify a wide range of actions that produced the same effect and either prohibited their enforcement or required government to exempt persons from certain practices on grounds of conscience.

Religious Expression in the Public Schools

In moving toward a more separationist definition of what the Constitution had meant by "establishment," the Supreme Court dealt mostly with cases involving schools—the limits of religious expression in public schools and the extent of governmental assistance to private religious schools. The Court has been particularly sensitive to religious exercises in the public school, insisting on the need to maintain a sharp boundary between religion and government in that setting. Because children are thought to be especially open to influence, are required by law to attend school, and do so mostly in educational institutions paid for by tax revenue, any apparent favoritism toward a creed can appear to constitute government endorsement of religion. Putting the government's weight behind religion, the Court has ruled, is particularly inappropriate in such an environment. The same issue of apparent governmental favoritism also arises when the state provides financial assistance to schools run by religious organizations. The threat of endorsement seems less severe in schools for older students who attend voluntarily, persuading the Court to grant much freer reign to religious expression and assistance in institutions of higher learning. Even in such environments, the Court has wrestled with the question of which state actions are essentially neutral and which forms of assistance forge an unacceptable link between government and religious schools.

In 1947 the Court decided a case that was to herald a flood of litigation about the modern meaning of First Amendment prohibitions "respecting an establishment of religion." In *Everson v. Board of Education,* the justices ruled that New Jersey could constitutionally compensate the parents of all children, including those attending religious schools, for the expenses of bus transportation to and from school. Defraying the cost the parents incurred for sending their children to religious schools, the Court held, did not involve an excessive degree of state support for religion. Even though this ruling appeared on the surface as a victory for advocates of government aid to religious education, the language of the majority opinion made it clear that breaches of the wall of separation would be tolerated only under the narrowest of circumstances. Consistent with that warning, in *McCollum v. Board of Education* (1948), the Court said that the school board in Champaign, Illinois, could not allow students in public schools to receive religious instruction on the premises even though attendance at such classes was voluntary and paid for privately. Opening up the school building to religious training while other classes were in session struck the Court as virtual endorsement of religion by the local government, an action that fell within the meaning of the establishment clause. But suppose that instead of inviting religious teachers to offer voluntary instruction in the school building, the state simply allowed students to travel off-campus for that purpose during the school day? In a 1952 decision, *Zorach v. Clausen,* the justices ruled that a New York City law releasing students from normal classes to attend religious classes somewhere else did not offend the establishment clause. This pattern of ruling first to permit some action, then to deny others, has persisted to the present day.

Rulings about how far the state could go in helping students receive religious training did not settle the issue of what the public schools could do about religious ideas. The two decisions that spoke clearly to that issue rank among the most unpopular rulings in the history of the Supreme Court. The 1962 case of *Engel v. Vitale* challenged the prayer that New York State required teachers to read at the beginning of the day. Because a government agency composed the prayer and insisted it be read aloud by state employees as part of the daily routine, six justices declared that the New York practice illustrated precisely the type of action that the First Amendment forbids as an establishment of religion. A year later in *Abington School District v. Schempp,* the Court extended the ban on state-mandated religious ceremonies to cover a Pennsylvania law requiring the reading of Bible verses and recitation of the Lord's Prayer at the beginning of the school day. By these two decisions, the Court seemed to say that "establishment" included any celebration of religion conducted or promoted by an agency of the government.

Since those decisions, the Court has consistently struck down laws that, in its view, use the power of the public schools, a governmental institution, to promote religion or religious ideas. One such initiative, state laws permitting a "moment of silence" at the beginning of the school day, was declared unconstitutional in 1985 because it was intended to encourage student prayer. As recently as 1992 in *Lee v. Weisman*, the Court cited the *Engel* and *Schempp* precedents to prohibit collective prayers at high school graduation ceremonies. The Court has been equally vigilant in guarding against efforts to teach religious doctrine through the curriculum. Thus it rejected as unconstitutional infringements of the establishment clause an Arkansas law that prohibited the teaching of evolution in public schools (*Epperson v. Arkansas*, 1968), Kentucky's requirement that the Ten Commandments be posted in every public school classroom (*Stone v. Graham*, 1980), and a Louisiana law that mandated teaching the religiously inspired theory of divine origin (*Edwards v. Aguillard*, 1987).

To some critics, it seemed that these cases went beyond the goal of making public schools neutral toward religion—the professed goal of the Supreme Court—and created an atmosphere of outright hostility to traditional religious values. In one counterattack using a novel legal strategy, parent groups in two states charged that certain public school textbooks promoted what amounted to a religion of secular humanism—the doctrine that humanity, not God, was supreme. Though the effort to ban these books on establishment grounds failed, it raised anew the question of what public schools could do regarding religion. According to guidelines issued by the U.S. Department of Education (Riley 1995), the Court decisions leave room for students to pray individually or in groups, discuss their religious beliefs with others, read and distribute religious literature, express religious beliefs through schoolwork and slogans on clothing, and to form religious clubs. School authorities may neither encourage these activities nor discourage participation. School officials are not allowed to participate in student religious events and may regulate them only as necessary to ensure order and without putting special restrictions on religious activity. These rights belong to students only. The school itself may teach objectively about religion and must permit religious groups to meet on the premises if it offers that option to nonreligious groups.

The debate over the church-state boundary in education also entails government action vis-à-vis religious schools. On the one hand, precisely because such schools inculcate religious values, the Court has worried about the degree to which state support favors religion and sends a religious message in violation of the establishment clause. On the other, the Court has wanted to leave room for the state to further secular educational goals by working through parochial schools. As we saw in *Everson,* states may help transport pupils to private schools. In *Board of Education v. Allen* (1968), the Court decided that New York State could lend parochial school students the same textbooks provided free of charge to students in the public schools. In subsequent decisions, governments have also been permitted to administer standardized tests to private school students, provide them with diagnostic services, and allow parochial students to participate in therapy offered on "neutral sites" outside private schools (Flowers 1994, 70–74). Most states have taken advantage of these rulings to provide the permitted services (and other forms of assistance that are probably not permitted) to private religious schools (Abraham 1987, 18). In a 1993 case from Arizona, the Court further authorized states to pay for interpreters who assist deaf students attending religious schools. The Court reasoned that the interpreter was more like a hearing aid, something the government can legitimately supply regardless where it is used, than an unconstitutional symbol of state support for religious education.

Beyond these services, the Court has largely prohibited various forms of state assistance to religious schools. In a string of cases decided during the 1970s the Court ruled that the boundary was violated if states contributed to the salary of parochial school teachers to cover their "nonreligious" responsibilities (*Lemon v. Kurtzman,* 1971), allowed church schools to finance the upkeep of their buildings with tax money (*Committee for Public Education v. Nyquist,* 1973), reimbursed parents for the costs of private school tuition (same case), paid religious schools for the cost of educational testing required by state law (*Levitt v. Committee for Public Education,* 1973), or lent instructional materials other than textbooks to schools supported by religious institutions (*Meek v. Pittenger,* 1975). Continuing the restrictive trend in two 1985 decisions

(*Grand Rapids v. Ball; Aguilar v. Felton*), the Court forbade public funding of even part-time or remedial teaching in religious schools. When
New York recently tried to draw a public school district so its boundaries encapsulated only a distinctive Jewish sect (*Kiryas Joel v. Grumet,*
1994), effectively turning over control of public education to the sect's
religious leaders, six of the nine Supreme Court justices decided the act
was an unacceptable fusion of state and religion.

Making Sense of the Establishment Clause

Critics of the Court's establishment clause jurisprudence wonder
aloud how the Court could possibly find it acceptable for the government to pay for textbooks loaned to private schools but unconstitutional for that same government to supply those same schools with
educational materials like maps, globes, and film projectors. Some of
the apparent inconsistency from case to case stemmed from the division of the Court into factions with different interpretations of the
meaning of the First Amendment's language (Pritchett 1984, 158).
Because these groupings were fluid and relatively evenly balanced,
changes in circumstances from one case to another could swing
enough votes to produce apparent contradictions between decisions. In
making distinctions among permitted and prohibited action, the Court
also drew on a general rule. Stated most fully by Chief Justice Warren
Burger in the 1971 *Lemon* decision (R. Miller and Flowers 1987,
480–498), the Court's standard required that a law must pass three
tests before it could be deemed compatible with the antiestablishment
language of the First Amendment: a primarily secular purpose, primarily secular consequences, and no excessive entanglement of church
and state.

To pass the first test, a law's major purpose must be to further some
secular mission of government. Though it may touch on religion in so
doing, that cannot be its principal intention. Thus, compensation for
bus transportation was valid because New Jersey wanted *primarily* to
get all children safely to and from school—a perfectly reasonable state
policy not connected to religion. Because of this legitimate secular purpose, the law was acceptable even though it indirectly helped religious
schools by marginally reducing the transportation costs that would
otherwise have been borne by the parents. The Court could find no

legitimate secular purpose in teaching the "creationist" view of human origins or mandating a "moment of silence" each school day.

The second test set up by the Court applies the same standard of secularity to primary *effects*. Because lending textbooks to all students, in private and public schools alike, would principally expand knowledge in secular subjects, New York was authorized to keep its law on distribution. As long as the undeniable benefit to religion was not the principal outcome of the legislation, the law fell within the Supreme Court's view of legitimate public policy. But the New York law that permitted parents to receive tax credits for private school tuition had the primary effect of supporting instruction for religious purposes. Children would certainly benefit from attending schools with greater resources, but that was not deemed to be the primary consequence of the state law. Hence the tuition tax credit was rejected for breaching the boundary. On the other hand, the Court approved a Minnesota tax deduction available to all parents facing educational expenses (*Mueller v. Allen*, 1968).

Even if a law is deemed principally nonreligious in purpose and result, it must still satisfy the requirement that it does not "excessively entangle" the church and government. That means a law should neither bring the government too deeply into the affairs of religion nor encourage religious groups to enter the political process as religious groups. The first type of entanglement was cited when the Court ruled that paying parochial school teachers for secular instruction imposed on government a responsibility to see that the teachers did not let their religious values intrude on that portion of their work supported by tax revenue. To enforce such a provision, the justices decided, the government would have to monitor teaching in church schools and so involve itself deeply in matters best left free from state action. The other entanglement the Court wanted to avoid was the encouragement of continuous political activism by churches as corporate bodies. If local school boards had the discretion to give certain types of assistance to private religious schools, the justices thought, school board elections would inevitably become transformed into conflicts among churches and candidates would be judged primarily by their religious affiliations. Acknowledging that church members could and should get involved in politics as individuals, the Court sought to discourage the evolution of churches into political parties.

What kind of state action could survive scrutiny on this entanglement rule? The Court pointed with approval to a New York law that exempted churches and church-related institutions from property tax. In *Walz v. Tax Commissioner of the City of New York* (1971), it upheld the state's decision to keep religious property and the holdings of other nonprofit institutions off the tax rolls. Reasoning that taxation of churches would require local governments to assign a monetary value to church property and might even lead the state to put liens on the property or foreclose if taxes were not paid, the Court preferred exemption as much the lesser evil. Once certified as a nonprofit institution, exempt from the taxing authority of government, the church would be relatively free from the excessive entanglement that threatened the wall of separation. For that reason, among others, the Court's majority sustained tax exemption for property held by religious bodies. So, "entanglement" prohibited programs that might enable the church to draw on the resources of the government, as in the case of salary supplements for parochial school teachers, or policies of taxation that gave government potential power to interfere with the mission of religious bodies. Whatever the effect, too much intermingling of church and state made government action unconstitutional.

The *Lemon* test did not shield churches from any sort of contact with the state. Early in 1990, the Supreme Court upheld California's right to tax sales of religious material by a televised ministry. In *Swaggart Ministries v. California,* the Court concluded that the general sales tax had an undeniable secular purpose—raising revenues—and no significant effect on religion. Even though the tax satisfied the first two prongs of the *Lemon* standard, the ministry argued that it "excessively entangled" church with state because of the administrative burden of complying with the law and possibility of a state audit of its records. The Court rejected the entanglement claim principally because the California tax did "not require the State to inquire into the religious content of the items sold or the religious motivation for selling or purchasing the items." This suggests that governments have the right to tax or to exempt religion so long as churches are treated the same way as other organizations.

Under the Court's three-part rule, statutes involving religion were presumed to violate the establishment clause unless they could be shown to meet all three requirements. Challengers had to demonstrate only one failing for the law to be declared invalid. With such a demanding set of conditions, it is hardly surprising that the advocates of a high wall of separation won most of the critical Supreme Court cases and generally succeeded in church-state litigation when cases were decided by lower courts (see Sorauf 1976).

The *Lemon* standard has been criticized as rigid, unworkable, and misguided. The difficulty of applying it consistently is most evident in cases involving government sponsorship of religious symbols, most prominently the so-called December Wars fought over Christmas displays on public property (Menendez 1993). In the 1984 case of *Lynch v. Donnelly,* a divided Court ruled that the city of Pawtucket, Rhode Island, could constitutionally erect a Christmas nativity display without violating the establishment clause (Swanson 1990). Acknowledging the Christian origin of the crèche, the Court nonetheless found that it was a "passive" endorsement of religion. Placed among holiday symbols such as Christmas trees, carolers, candy-striped poles, and a Santa Claus sleigh pulled by reindeer, the crèche was adjudged to be primarily a cultural and historical symbol, part of a legitimate government effort to engender "a friendly community spirit of good will in keeping with the season" (R. Miller and Flowers 1987, 363). Five years later, in *County of Allegheny v. ACLU,* the Court followed this somewhat tortuous logic by upholding the constitutionality of a large Chanukah menorah placed outside one government building in Pittsburgh while simultaneously ruling against a Christmas crèche displayed on a staircase in a nearby courthouse. The menorah was acceptable, despite its religious significance in Judaism, because it was deemed to include cultural and historical references and because it was placed among other holiday symbols. By standing alone as an unadorned symbol of Christianity, a seeming endorsement of a particular faith, the crèche violated the establishment clause.[9] These decisions appear to permit government to host religious displays in public space providing the display is not monopolized by a single religious tradition—a decision consistent with the accommodationist interpretation of the First Amendment—and is open to nonreligious displays—a requirement closer to separationist doctrine. By this logic, the Court ruled in a 1995 case from Ohio, the Ku Klux Klan could not be forbidden from erecting a large cross on a state-owned plaza that had been festooned with a Christmas tree and a menorah.

The *Lemon* test is a kind of measuring device, not a binding precedent, and the Supreme Court has sometimes ignored it and occasionally threatened to replace it altogether. The leading candidate to replace it, a more accommodationist test, would strike down only governmental actions that coerced people to accept particular religious doctrines. Not many of the contested practices ruled unconstitutional under *Lemon* would be forbidden under the coercion rule. Perhaps for that reason, the Court has yet to abandon the *Lemon* test altogether.

Extending Free-Exercise Claims

Even as it was broadening the meaning of establishment and thus restricting the scope of state action to encourage religion, the Supreme Court was growing markedly more receptive to individuals who challenged governmental actions as barriers to the practice of their faith. The same justices who demonstrated a concern to protect individuals from unwanted religious influences emanating from the government also showed a willingness to defend worship and other forms of religious activity from interference on the part of public authorities. The Court's concern was particularly likely to surface in cases where the faith was unconventional and the restrictive government regulation may have reflected hostility to the minority religion by better-established religious groups.

The Court's initial concern in this regard was to ensure that religious groups enjoyed full freedom to practice their faith and to undertake activities related to it. For religions outside the mainstream, such as the Jehovah's Witnesses and Seventh-Day Adventists, the practice of religion involved public activities that might run afoul of local and state ordinances regulating access to public facilities or limiting door-to-door soliciting. Given its propensity to support speech and other forms of public expression about political ideas, the Court had little difficulty offering the same support to religious ideas.

Many of the critical decisions in this area asserted that religious minorities should enjoy the same basic freedoms extended to unpopular political movements and causes (Pritchett 1984, 133–134). As early as 1938 the Court cited freedom of the press in allowing Jehovah's Witnesses to sell literature door-to-door without first having to obtain a municipal permit. The same rationale was cited in a 1943 ruling that exempted Jehovah's Witnesses from a Pennsylvania municipal license fee required of all door-to-door commercial solicitors. The free-speech clause of the First Amendment provided the basis for a 1948 decision upholding the right of a preacher from the same sect to broadcast his sermons in a public park. In a Maryland case decided in 1951, the justices overturned the conviction of some Witnesses who had preached in a public park in defiance of municipal ordinances prohibiting such activity. Noting that the ordinance was enforced against the Witnesses but had not been used when mainstream religious groups held prayer services in the same location, the Court decided that the law was enforced unequally—a violation of the Fourteenth Amendment's requirement that all must enjoy the equal protection of the laws.

The Supreme Court also moved to defend religious freedom by explicit reference to the free-exercise clause. The majority opinion in *Cantwell v. Connecticut* (1940) was the first to enshrine the principle of free exercise on its own terms and became a powerful precedent. The case arose when three ministers from Jehovah's Witnesses were convicted of several offenses against municipal ordinances in New Haven, Connecticut. The key conviction of soliciting without a license was overturned on the grounds that the law unconstitutionally allowed the state government to determine if the ministers' actions were motivated by genuinely religious convictions. For the government to screen religions in this manner, Justice Robert Jackson wrote, would "lay a forbidden burden upon the exercise of [religious] liberty protected by the Constitution" (R. Miller and Flowers 1987, 62). In subsequent cases, the Court struck down a number of laws, regulations, ordinances, and administrative practices for interfering with religious exercise or preaching. Even when respect for free-exercise rights might prove burdensome in some way, the Supreme Court generally insisted they take precedence. For example, prison authorities have been required to extend a number of privileges to inmates who practice Muslim, Buddhist, and Native American religions.

Worship and preaching clearly fall under the scope of free exercise. But what happens when the exercise of religion appears to be inconsistent with an obligation that government imposes on citizens? Following the antipolygamy *Reynolds* case in the late nineteenth century, the Court had normally permitted government to compel or forbid action that might violate religious belief. In the 1934 case of *Hamilton v. Regents of the University of California,* for example, the Court permitted California to require all able-bodied male college students to take mili-

tary training. Even though this would force members of pacifist churches to engage in activity forbidden by their faith, the paramount need for
military preparedness was seen as taking precedence over religiously
grounded objections to participation in military activity.

Shortly thereafter, the Court began to offer more support to religious dissenters who chose faith over law. In 1943 a Seventh-Day
Adventist from Canada was refused American citizenship because he
said religious beliefs would prevent him from taking up arms to defend
the United States. Like other members of his faith who had served as
noncombatants in the military and contributed in nonviolent ways to
the war effort, the applicant was willing to support the nation by other
means. Hence, Justice William O. Douglas argued for the majority in
Girouard v. United States (1946), any attempt to demand the willingness
to fight as a condition for citizenship contravened religious scruples for
no good purpose. The right to seek noncombatant status, which
Congress had granted to persons with religious scruples, was upheld
when the Court ordered a draft board to grant conscientious-objector
status to a member of Jehovah's Witnesses (*Sicurella v. U.S.*, 1955).

The Jehovah's Witnesses also figured in the pivotal case that covered
exemptions to secular law under the free-exercise clause (Manwaring
1962). Inspired by the wartime atmosphere, West Virginia's Board of
Education had demanded that public school students salute the
American flag or face punishment for insubordination. The state
claimed that forcing students to honor the flag was justified as a way
to promote the patriotism and national unity essential for preserving
liberty. Members of the Jehovah's Witnesses had sued on the grounds
that salutes conflicted with the biblical injunction against worshiping a
"graven image," a practice apparently forbidden by a literal reading of
some passages in the Book of Exodus (20:4–5). The Supreme Court's
ruling in the case of *West Virginia State Board of Education v. Barnette*
(1943) sided with the Witnesses against the state. The flag was a symbol of state, comparable to the banner of a fraternal organization or the
cross of a church, and the salute meant nothing more than a gesture of
respect. As such, it was an expression of opinion that could not be
forced on a person who was unwilling, for any reason, to endorse the
sentiment. As the majority opinion stated, the constitutional provision
that "guards the individual's right to speak his own mind" did not give
government the authority "to compel him to utter what is not in his

mind" (R. Miller and Flowers 1987, 88). Ever since that landmark decision, the courts have generally supported religious minorities seeking
the protection of the First Amendment against different types of
required patriotic expression, such as reciting the "Pledge of
Allegiance," standing during the national anthem, or displaying mottos
on license plates.

Beyond simply enlarging the scope of actions covered by the free-
exercise clause, the Court also broadened its definition of "religion" to
permit other types of belief systems to enjoy First Amendment protection. In essence, the Court has recognized faith motivated by "conscience" rather than traditional religion (Hammond and Mazur 1995).
The principal case in this realm, the 1965 decision in *United States v.
Seeger,* ordered local draft boards to treat applications for conscientious-
objector status with the same respect whether the individual cited nontraditional forms of belief in a Supreme Being or orthodox ideas of God
as the basis for exemption.

A Free-Exercise Standard

The Supreme Court's formal standard for determining violations of
the establishment clause, the so-called *Lemon* test, emerged after a
string of decisions that hinted at the new direction. Similarly, the Court
did not announce a parallel test to identify free-exercise violations until
after it had signaled its intention to grant priority to religious conscience. The free-exercise standard was first announced in the 1963
case of *Sherbert v. Verner* (R. Miller and Flowers 1987, 59). When confronted with charges that a secular law or custom unconstitutionally
limits the right of free exercise, the Supreme Court asked if the policy
places a burden on the exercise of religion by individuals or groups. If
so, the government, first, must demonstrate that it has a compelling
interest in the law or policy and, second, that its goal cannot be
achieved without hindering religious observance. This test means that
government must have a very strong reason to force people to act
against religious conscience. Unless the government could show that
exemption would do severe damage to some important national or
state function, the Court insisted that free exercise of conscience had
priority. In the words of a 1972 opinion, assigning a "preferred position" to the First Amendment rights meant that "only those interests of

the highest order not otherwise served can overbalance legitimate claims to the free exercise of religion" (ibid., 1987, 202).

The *Sherbert* standard originated in a dispute about unemployment discrimination and was widely used to prohibit state governments from denying unemployment benefits to persons whose religious beliefs kept them out of a job. Though the original case involved a Sabbatarian, a person who was religiously obligated to observe a day of rest, the Court expanded the protection to people who refused particular kinds of work on religious grounds and to individuals who belonged to faiths that did not mandate a day of rest. Perhaps the most dramatic application of the *Sherbert* rule was in education. In *Wisconsin v. Yoder* (1972), the Court upheld the right of Amish parents to keep their children out of public school after the age of fourteen. As the state could not convince the justices that an additional year or two of schooling was critical for any social purpose, the Court was more impressed by Amish fears that exposure to additional secular instruction might undermine the children's commitment to their community's values. By decisions such as these, free exercise was extended to support mandatory exemption from a variety of obligations imposed on American citizens.

As noted above, the Court defined "free exercise" for individuals both as religious activity and as conscientious objection to selected government policies. But the Court also moved more aggressively to extend to churches as collective institutions "a right to be left alone by government so that they may freely exercise religion" (Laycock 1986, 37). The doctrine emerged slowly from a variety of specific decisions. As much as possible, the Court took itself out of the business of resolving internal church disputes over property, recommending that the judiciary generally defer to the decision of the supreme authority in the church. The Court has also upheld the right of churches to impose religious requirements on employees of its "nonreligious" enterprises. The churches have been shielded from lawsuits alleging malpractice by members of the clergy, and given protection against outside attempts to monitor church political activity. Communication between clergy and church members, like that between doctor and patient, is still deemed confidential. Although advocates of this type of free exercise worry about government intrusion in several realms, the trend since the 1940s has been toward greater autonomy.

The *Sherbert* test always had its limits. Recognizing the state's interest in protecting public health and safety, the Court has approved compulsory vaccination and other medical procedures, especially those involving children, and permitted government to ban religious practices that might endanger the participants. The Supreme Court has also upheld the constitutionality of the so-called blue laws, state statutes that compel businesses to close on Sunday. Originally passed as part of the Protestant campaign to give legal support to the Sabbath—clearly a religious purpose—they were upheld by the Court because they had become a species of welfare legislation, serving the interests of public safety and employee health by stopping business activity on one day of the week. Over the protests of some Orthodox Jewish merchants, for whom the law meant another day of shutdown after the Jewish Sabbath, the Court adjudged the laws reasonable and saw no alternative to achieve a valid public purpose. Similarly, the Court has declared that employers need only make a reasonable effort to accommodate the religious beliefs of their workers; there is no legal obligation to incur financial hardship.

The Court's tendency to support religious objections to secular law inspired a substantial growth in the filing of such cases and a dramatic increase in the success of such suits. A study by Way and Burt (1983) illustrates the magnitude of the trend away from the presumption favoring government. During the first decade covered by their study, 1946–1956, the state and federal courts decided thirty-four cases in which minority religions—groups outside the Protestant, Catholic, and Jewish faiths—claimed free-exercise rights. Although the courts sustained the claims in only 20 percent of the cases, the significance of the decisions apparently stimulated more litigation. Between 1970 and 1980, the number of such cases more than quadrupled to 145. Over that period "marginal" religious groups won slightly more than half of the cases they brought; in contrast, victories resulted in only about one-third of the lawsuits involving mainstream religions. The minority religious groups were more likely to succeed in legal challenges to laws or practices that limited efforts to spread the faith and in suits brought to extend rights of practice to prisoners. They broke even in cases related to employment and taxation and lost more attempts to gain exemptions from secular laws governing schools or to refuse medical care for minors.

Thanks to almost forty years of intense judicial activity, both the free-exercise and establishment clauses of the First Amendment took on new and broader meanings. In the process, the actions of the courts raised new issues and fueled compelling debates about the place of religion in American society.

The Politics of Church-State Relations

In the majesty of their surroundings and the dignity of their procedures, the courts often appear isolated from the normal processes of political conflict. Despite the exalted image of the judiciary, its behavior is permeated by the same types of political influences that affect other arenas of government. Any discussion of church-state relationships must therefore take into account the larger political context in which the judicial decisions are made. An investigation of the politics of church-state interaction is necessary to understand why the issue became so important when it did and how the religious community reacted to the crucial court decisions.

The Supreme Court's radical transformation of church-state doctrine did not occur in isolation. As noted above, one source of revision was the general tendency of the justices to extend the First Amendment to cover the actions of state and local governments. In that sense, the new limitations on government action toward religion were a by-product of a broader tendency to nationalize the Bill of Rights. But beyond this general shift in the constitutional interpretation, another factor was involved in the Court's specific rulings about religion. As is often the case in political and legal change, the consciousness of the Court was shaped by intensive grassroots political activity that raised the church-state issue to a high place on the national agenda (Morgan 1968; Sorauf 1976). Throughout the era of judicial activism on the church-state question, the churches, allied groups of laypersons, and interfaith organizations functioned much as classic interest groups—designing legislation, raising public support in well-orchestrated campaigns for public opinion, lobbying legislatures and courts, and bringing and defending lawsuits. This description fits both the coalition that opposed the Court's separationist stance and those who sought a more accommodationist perspective.

Many of the state aid laws evaluated by the Supreme Court in the decades after World War II were inspired by religious groups as a means of supporting church-affiliated schools, whose financial health had been seriously impaired by a combination of social changes. As most of these schools were Roman Catholic, the principal groups defending aid to parochial schools were Catholic organizations, such as the Education Division of the United States Catholic Conference, the National Catholic Educational Association, the Catholic League for Religious and Civil Rights, and the Knights of Columbus. They were joined by several organizations representing non-Catholic private schools: Citizens for Educational Freedom, the National Association for Hebrew Day Schools, the National Jewish Commission on Law and Public Affairs, and others. Ranged on the other side were liberal Protestant groups in the National Council of Churches, those conservative Christian denominations that feared state aid as the opening wedge in a government drive to take over the schools (e.g., the Baptist Joint Committee on Public Affairs), secular groups such as the American Civil Liberties Union, American Association of Humanists, and Americans United for Separation of Church and State, and the major umbrella organizations for the American Jewish community. The lineup was similar but not identical on questions involving religious expression in the public schools. Because they believed that any such public religion would invariably reflect the values of the predominantly Christian population, Jewish groups were the most consistent force in the separationist camp (N. Cohen 1992; Ivers 1995). The conservative Protestants who opposed state aid as a Catholic subsidy generally allied with Catholic organizations in pressing for greater religious content in public schools. Although some of the opponents of state aid and religious expression were motivated by hostility to religion in general, the debate also split many religious communities internally and cannot be reduced to a single dimension such as religion versus irreligion.

Even though most of the court cases were won by separationists, limiting both state aid and public religious expressions, the Court's decisions inspired much discontent. Public opinion polls have consistently revealed that a clear majority of Americans—possibly as many as two-thirds of the population—favors some sort of organized prayer in public schools. The apparent public support for restoration of school prayer has made it politically appealing to challenge the *Engel* and *Schempp* rulings. When Court rulings strike an exposed nerve, those most affected will sometimes attempt to get around them by interpreting the decision narrowly, by evading them, or, those options having failed, by trying to override the

Court by changing the Constitution. In the case of the school prayer decisions, critics of the Court rulings tried each of these strategies.

Following the first strategy, the courts were besieged with new state laws attempting to alter this or that feature of a school prayer policy that had previously been struck down. Perhaps if the government got out of the business of selecting and ordering prayers, merely facilitating it instead, the Court would accept voluntary religious expression. However, the Court consistently ruled against the constitutionality of governmental efforts to celebrate religion in public schools. Undaunted, supporters of religious observance then tried to undermine the prayer decisions with "silent meditation" laws. Passed by more than half the states, these statutes typically provided for a moment of silence or meditation during the school day. The Supreme Court subsequently ended most doubts about the constitutionality of this newest form of school-prayer law when it struck down Alabama's silent meditation statute in *Wallace v. Jaffree* (1985).

Rather than petition the courts for an allowable practice short of organized prayer, some authorities attempted to evade the rulings. Because control over school religious practices effectively rests with thousands of local school districts and tens of thousands of classroom teachers, the prayer and Bible-reading decisions offered great opportunities for noncompliance (Patric 1957; Katz 1965; Sorauf 1959). In a study of Tennessee reactions to the Court's prohibition of Bible reading, Robert Birkby (1966) discovered that all but one school district had allowed the forbidden practice to continue, leaving the question of religious ceremonies in the classroom to the discretion of the teacher. Even though the Court had ruled that voluntary religious activity was no more constitutional than coerced worship, many local school boards adopted it unless they were faced with legal challenges. Although more than thirty years have passed since the Court issued its blanket prohibition on state-directed school prayer, many school districts continue to promote compulsory religious observance until ordered to cease and desist by federal courts.[10]

The widespread adoption of the teacher discretion policy throughout the United States did not prevent a substantial decline in formal religious observance in the classroom. A nationwide survey of public school teachers during the 1964–1965 school year found that the incidence of morning prayers declined from 60 percent before the *Engel* decision to 28 percent after, and that Bible reading, a regular practice in the classrooms of 48 percent of the teachers before *Schempp*, survived in only 22 percent after the case was decided (Way 1968, 191; see also Dierenfeld 1967). Reported compliance was lowest in the southern states, where nearly three-fifths of the teachers continued reading the Bible and just under two-thirds maintained the practice of morning prayers. Studies of compliance patterns in local communities by Muir (1967), Johnson (1967), and Dolbeare and Hammond (1977) have suggested that the degree of conformity to the Court's will depended on a variety of factors—the religious composition of the area, the prestige of the Supreme Court, the willingness of individuals to demand implementation, and the position taken by political elites. Depending on the mix of circumstances in the local environment, the Court decisions were either implemented in full, accepted in a half-hearted manner, or treated as a dead letter.

Other critics have mounted a frontal attack on the Court's rulings, without much success (Alley 1994). The favorite instrument, a constitutional amendment to overturn *Engel* and *Schempp*, failed repeatedly to obtain the required two-thirds majority in the House and Senate. (Unless they receive that extraordinary majority in both houses of Congress, amendments cannot be submitted to the states for approval.) In 1984 a proposed constitutional amendment to permit vocal prayer by individuals or groups in public institutions, schools included, fell short of the required two-thirds vote in the U.S. Senate.[11] The diversity of both the support for and the opposition to the proposal underlines how such church-state issues split normal coalitions in American politics. Supporters of the proposed amendment included liberals and conservatives (e.g., Sen. William Proxmire of Wisconsin and Sen. Jesse Helms of North Carolina), Jews and Mormons (Sen. Edward Zorinsky of Nebraska and Sen. Orrin Hatch of Utah), and representatives of both the mainline and evangelical wings of Protestantism. The Senate opponents of organized school prayer included some of the most conservative members of that body (Barry Goldwater of Arizona), its only clergyman (John Danforth of Missouri, an ordained Episcopal priest), and one of its most prominent evangelical spokesmen (Mark Hatfield of Oregon).

Following the defeat of the prayer amendment in 1984, Congress gave tangible support to religious observance by passing an "equal access" law. Under its provisions, high schools that allow noncurricular student groups to meet on campus before or after classes must extend the same privileges to students who want to form religious associations. This apparent concession to the advocates of school prayer was qualified in several respects. For one thing, it applies only to high school students, whereas many prayer advocates regard elementary school students as especially in need of moral guidance. Also, in recognition of the Court's insistence on governmental neutrality, the law stipulates that no teachers or other school personnel may participate actively or supervise worship. Even more significantly, the equal access law appears to give administrators several openings for evasion. By prohibiting the government from denying or withholding education funds from noncomplying school districts, Congress reduced the incentive for compliance. Furthermore, the requirement that religious groups enjoy the same access to facilities as other noncurricular groups may have undermined the law's intent by giving school boards a basis for refusing facilities to all groups. Largely on free-speech grounds, the Supreme Court upheld the constitutionality of the equal access law in 1990.

Assaults on the New Order: Loosening the Establishment Clause

Advocates of accommodation—the doctrine that smiles on general government support for religion—never approved of the Supreme Court's post–World War II movement toward separationism. To these critics, the Court disregarded both the intentions of the Founders and the predominant body of constitutional interpretation by interfering with state actions and broadening the meaning of "establishment" (Cord 1982; R. Morgan 1984). Court decisions—especially those limiting state aid to parochial schools—have also been denounced for their allegedly adverse policy consequences. Isolating the churches behind a wall of separation, it is charged, prevents the state from cooperating with institutions that could advance the quality of national education (Berger and Neuhaus 1977). By issuing decisions that fly in the face of public support for religion, it has also been claimed, the Court diminishes the public esteem for the rule of law and reduces the likelihood of compliance with its rulings. (Note that these are precisely the consequences that Madison cited to argue against establishment.)

The Court's separationist defenders argue that it has correctly read the Constitution and intelligently adapted the ambiguous phrases of "establishment" and "free exercise" to changing social conditions and greater religious diversity (Pfeffer 1967). They have also made use of public opinion polls to dispute the claim that religious rulings have undercut public support for the judiciary. Although the public appears to disagree with a number of Court rulings (see fig. 4.2), studies have suggested only a modest spillover onto the general image of the Court (Kessel 1966; Dolbeare 1967; Caldeira and Gibson 1992). The most useful information was uncovered in a 1966 poll of voting-age American citizens (Murphy, Tanenhaus, and Kastner 1973). Of nearly 1,300 persons surveyed in the study, only about 500 made any responses when asked if there were something they liked or disliked about the recent work of the Supreme Court. If less than 40 percent of the sample felt the need to volunteer any praise or condemnation of the Court just four years after the first decision on school observance, the salience of the issue for the general public must be questioned. It is not clear what to make of the further finding that the school prayer and Bible-reading decisions were the source of 30 percent of the actions that displeased respondents. On the one hand, the fact that no other set of decisions accounted for more criticism suggests that the issue was relatively important. On the other, 70 percent of the critical remarks were directed at different issues. Unhappiness with the Court's religious rulings may reflect general displeasure with the Court's liberal orientation on questions of civil rights, prisoner rights, reapportionment, and other policy areas. To the extent public opinion polls can gauge such matters, the broadening of the establishment clause was not the object of widespread enthusiasm, particularly insofar as it prohibited religious observance as an official part of the school day; but the hostility it engendered should not be overstated, either.

Ever since Richard Nixon assumed the presidency in 1969, inaugurating a long period of Republican dominance, Court watchers have been waiting for a U-turn. Using their control over judicial appointments, Presidents Nixon, Ronald Reagan, and George Bush tried to produce a more accommodationist Court less sensitive about incursions on the establishment clause. The Court has from time to time trimmed back some of its separationist orientation and seemed on the verge of embracing accommodationism wholeheartedly more than once. Nonetheless, the counterrevolution has yet to materialize and the Court never abandoned separationism (Kobylka 1995). Once on the Court, many of the justices appointed by presidents committed to weakening the *Lemon* test have turned out to be far less enthusiastic about that goal. Even when joining decisions that permitted greater public expressions of religion, these Republican appointees have carefully crafted the result to apply in narrow circumstances.

Having given up on the Court, the advocates of accommodation were encouraged by the election of sympathetic Republican majorities in both houses of Congress in 1994. The principal hope for imposing accommodation, a proposed "Religious Equality" amendment to the Constitution, prohibits government from denying to anyone—including public school students—the freedom "to engage in prayer or other religious expression in circumstances in which expression of a nonreligious character would be permitted" (Davis 1995). The proposal also permits government "to give public or ceremonial accommodation to the religious heritage, beliefs, or traditions of its people" and states expressly that such expressions of religion do not constitute an establishment of religion. Advocates contend this amendment will simply restore the original meaning of the First Amendment religion clauses. In practice, the amendment would permit many practices that the Supreme Court has expressly forbidden on establishment clause grounds—prayers at high school graduation and religious displays on public property. Critics see the amendment as the effective repeal of the establishment clause, charging further that it facilitates direct subsidies of religious education and preferential treatment for religious majorities who could impose highly sectarian prayers and practices on minorities.

Despite the Republican majority in the 104th Congress and strong public support for the concept of school prayer, the amendment faced serious challenges (Wells 1995). In the past, the level of support for school prayer was not intense enough to prompt legislative action. The advocates of school prayer have been put at a further disadvantage by the fact that citizens who support such legislation have tended to be less educated and less affluent than supporters of the current policy (Elifson and Hadaway 1985; Woodrum and Hoban 1992). Accordingly, those seeking to overturn the restrictive policy on religious observance in the schools must rely on a constituency that has relatively few political resources. Moreover, the church organizations that might be

expected to lead the effort have divided over the wisdom of challenging the restrictions on school prayer.

The Fall and Rise of Free Exercise

The Court's renewed emphasis on free-exercise rights was subject to
much less criticism than its jurisprudence regarding the establishment
clause. Ironically, then, few accommodationists or separationists
expected the Court to slam the door shut on exemptions motivated by
religious sentiment. Yet that was the outcome of the Court's startling
decision in the 1990 case known as *Employment Division v. Smith*. The
Court upheld Oregon's decision to fire two state workers because they
ingested peyote, a hallucinogenic drug, as part of Native American religious rituals. Under the *Sherbert* standard, the Court could simply have
decided that Oregon had a compelling purpose in prohibiting illegal
drug use and could find no way of accomplishing that purpose without
overriding the religious rights of the two employees. Instead, the
majority opinion abandoned the compelling-interest test altogether. In
the future, the government only had to show that it had some rational
basis for passing the law—not compelling but simply reasonable—and
that the law did not expressly target a religion for hardship. If that was
done, no group could claim its free-exercise rights were abridged. The
requirement of neutrality in the law left some room for free-exercise
claims, as the Court showed in 1993 when it struck down a Florida
municipal statute that banned the animal sacrifice practiced by the
Santeria religion but permitted hunting, slaughtering animals for food,
and euthanasia. But beyond the neutrality requirement, *Smith* left it up
to governments to choose whether or not to exempt religious behavior from laws of general application. If this meant that practitioners of
Native American religions might have to give up peyote in deference
to Oregon's general campaign against drugs, that was the consequence
of democracy. This decision put at risk virtually every exemption that
the Court had previously granted on religious grounds. It also put the
fate of exemptions for minority religions in the hand of political
authorities responsive to a public eager to limit religious practices for
unorthodox and unpopular religious movements (see fig. 4.2).

Whatever their divisions on other issues, virtually all religious traditions and secular civil libertarians condemned the decision and worked

to restore the pre-*Smith* standard. Late in 1993 the Religious Freedom Restoration Act was signed into law. This legislation put the *Sherbert* standard into federal law, stating that government actions that impose a burden on religious believers are permissible only when they serve a compelling public purpose and are the least restrictive means of accomplishing that purpose. Apart from concerns about its constitutionality, critics have emphasized the statute's limitations. The act merely gives the Court a standard to use when it determines whether the religious scruples of some person or group have been burdened by a law or practice. This leaves courts free to judge whether the law imposes a burden, if that burden is legitimate, or could be accomplished by some less restrictive means. Under this standard, the Supreme Court itself once decided that the need for uniformity in military dress permitted the Air Force to forbid its Jewish officers from wearing the unobtrusive head covering required by Jewish law. Nor did the Court stop the U.S. Forest Service from building roads through Native American tribal lands used for sacred ceremonies.

Other governmental agencies, often abetted by courts, have shown no reluctance to impose serious burdens on unorthodox or unpopular religions. Because of the unique qualities of Native American religion, governmental authorities have frequently transgressed on sacred beliefs and inhibited hallowed rituals (Carmody and Carmody 1990, 132–135; Deloria 1992). Hostility rather than ignorance explains the extraordinary persecutions visited upon unconventional religious movements labeled as "cults"—the free-exercise rights of adult members have been forcibly violated through "deprogramming," the collective rights of the churches imperiled by assessments of damages or government investigations of financial practices (Boothby 1986). Some scholars even describe the Waco tragedy of 1993 as a case of religious intolerance. On the assumption that members of the Branch Davidians could not possibly have been rational adults choosing to practice their religious faith, the FBI automatically interpreted the standoff as a "hostage" situation and treated David Koresh's theological arguments as symptoms of mental illness rather than a serious way of understanding the world (Tabor and Gallagher 1995). Had the Mt. Carmel compound been inhabited by Methodists, Catholics, or adherents of other mainline faiths in similar circumstances, these critics argue, law enforcement officials would never even have considered using massive firepower. So the restoration of the *Sherbert* test, while friendlier to religious minorities, still leaves ample opportunity for legal encroachments on the religious autonomy of unconventional groups.

Can We Do Better?

Apart from criticism of its decisions in this or that court case, the whole thrust of Supreme Court reasoning on church-state matters has engendered serious debate. In practice, the Court has treated the two religion clauses of the First Amendment as autonomous, each aiming at a separate goal. In recent years, some critics have claimed that this approach is fundamentally misguided because the two clauses were meant to serve a common goal—to extend the range of religious freedom. This has been the rallying cry of people who urge the Court to judge every challenged government action under the religion clauses by the simple test of whether it advances or limits religious freedom—and to reject practices if and only if they restrict religious liberty.

As much as simplicity is desirable in constitutional doctrine, other commentators doubt that the two clauses can be so happily reconciled. A law that extends Student A's religious liberty by allowing him to lead a prayer at high school graduation infringes the liberty of Student B to escape religious pressure at her official commencement ceremony. In this case, freedom *of* may contradict freedom *from*. No doubt Student A would feel that his religious liberty was circumscribed by the Court's intention to defer in all cases to Student B. Nearly every proposal to reconcile the religion clauses amounts to siding with one or the other provision of the First Amendment (Sherry 1993). The Religious Equality amendment, giving absolute priority to Student A's right to speak religiously in a public setting, means that Student B has less religious freedom as she understands it. The proposal advances the free-exercise rights of the first student by gutting the establishment clause protection enjoyed by the other student. Making the establishment clause absolute by forbidding any governmental concessions to religion would eliminate the free-exercise rights of both religious majorities and minorities.

Faced with this tension, the Supreme Court has searched for an elusive balance. In some cases, it decided that enforcing the establishment clause aggressively had the salutary effect of insuring that religious minorities were not coerced. In other cases, it decided that the establishment clause could be infringed if that was essential to promote religious diversity. Thus in the University of Virginia "boundary" dispute cited earlier, the Court accepted some appearance of state endorsement of religion as the price to pay for robust debate. The narrow 5–4 vote requiring the university to pay for the expenses of the religious newspaper suggests the Court might—or might not—strike down the next government action challenged as a violation of the establishment clause.

Having looked at the ebb and flow of particular cases and controversies, it is worth reminding ourselves that the core of First Amendment religion clauses remains intact. Whatever their unhappiness over the postwar church-state rulings, accommodationists have not forgotten that the United States enjoys an unparalleled level of religious vitality. Separationists, too, recognize that most of the types of accommodation urged on the Court fall far short of the extreme religious persecution of dissenters and nonbelievers that characterized the American colonies. The emphasis on areas of controversy, however intensely felt, should not be allowed to suggest that church and state are perenially engaged in a war of autonomy.

Most of the "religious" issues on the national political agenda do not involve the legal standing of religion. Debates about abortion, gay rights, the state of the family, and "obscene" art have little to do with the types of legal disputes examined in this chapter. We now shift our attention from religion itself as a source and subject of political controversy to examine the ways that religious sentiment is drawn into larger debates over the formation and execution of public policy.

NOTES

James Madison's quotation in the chapter epigraph is taken from Norman Cousins, ed., *In God We Trust: The Religious Beliefs and Ideas of the American Founders* (New York: Harper and Brothers, 1958), 324.

1. These words, spoken on 6 April 1994, during a floor debate in the Florida House of Representatives, were supplied to me by Rep. Steven A. Geller.

2. A "Dear Abby" column illustrates the extent of confusion on this subject. The columnist answered a letter from a woman who was unhappy about her daughter's decision to raise her child outside the family faith. According to the advice columnist, the constitutional guarantee of freedom of religion meant that the letter writer had no right to criticize her daughter's choice in religion. Although the free-exercise clause of the Constitution does prohibit interference with an adult's choice of faith, it does not compel tolerance.

3. The "wall of separation" phrase, first used by Roger Williams, is from Jefferson's 1802 letter to a congregation of Connecticut Baptists. Neither this phrase nor "church and state" appears in the Constitution, persuading some critics that the Supreme Court has read something alien into the national charter. Of course, these same critics have no trouble describing the Constitution as a document based on God and religious values even though there is no mention of God or religious heritage in the document. If Jefferson's words do not appear, it is arguable nonetheless that the sentiment does.

4. "Faith Healers Convicted of Homicide and Child Neglect in Daughter's Death," *Gainesville Sun*, 12 September 1984, 4A; "Faith-Healing Couple Sentenced to Five Years in Death of Infant," *Gainesville Sun*, 21 December 1984, 6B. There is a comprehensive listing of such cases in Kondos (1992) and an interesting discussion of the issues in Bullis (1991).

5. The major difference was that King did not seek to escape punishment for his behavior; indeed, he hoped that the conscience of the nation would be so moved by the example of unjust suffering that the law in question would subsequently lose credibility and be repealed. From the newspaper accounts of the Indiana trials, it seems that the accused parents denied that their behavior constituted a breach of the law.

6. This account of the case is taken from the text of the Supreme Court decision, conveniently reprinted in "U.S. Supreme Court Decision: *Ronald W. Rosenberger et al. v. Rector and Visitors of the University of Virginia et al.*," *Journal of Church and State* 37 (1995): 690–727.

7. A third model, strict neutrality, calls on the government to confer neither benefits nor disabilities on individuals based on religion. In terms of the establishment clause, strict neutrality insists that religious groups be treated no differently from other organizations—neither given exclusive rights nor subjected to any particular limitations. In the same way, individuals would have difficulty claiming exemption from secular laws because of religious beliefs but could challenge laws that imposed burdens on them primarily because of their religious standing. In some formulations, this attempt to harmonize the religious clauses would amount to accommodationism (Monsma 1993). In any case, the person who developed the doctrine of strict neutrality recently pronounced it "a dead letter" in constitutional jurisprudence (Kurland 1995).

8. The full text of the Supreme Court decisions referred to in this chapter can be found in either the *United States Reports* or the privately published *Digest of U.S. Supreme Court Reports*. The major decisions are compiled and updated every five years in the casebook edited by R. Miller and Flowers (1987). For an

inexpensive edited collection of decisions, consult Eastland (1993). Flowers (1994) has written the single most useful overview for general readers, although critics of the separationist orientation might prefer A. Adams and Emmerich (1990). The quarterly *Journal of Church and State* publishes a valuable preview of court cases as well as the full decisions in important cases.

9. Unsure about how many other holiday symbols they would have to add in order to denude the crèche of its religious symbolism, Pittsburgh officials decided to leave it in storage for the next holiday season rather than risk the censure of what one legal scholar cuttingly described as "those interior decorators" on the Supreme Court.

10. On the extent of noncompliance, see "Prayer in Many Schoolrooms Continues Despite '62 Ruling," *New York Times,* 11 March 1984. For recent cases in which federal courts have stopped school district practices, consult Boston (1994) and Peter Applebome, "Court Restricts Religious Activity at Mississippi School," *New York Times* (electronic edition available at http://www.nytimes.com), 4 June 1996.

11. "Amendment Drive on School Prayer Loses Senate Vote," *New York Times,* 21 March 1984.

5. Religion and American Public Policy

The separation of church and state does not mean the segregation of religion from politics. Nonetheless, the American public is divided on the merits of political involvement by religious groups. When asked if the clergy should speak out on public issues in their places of worship, churchgoers are split almost evenly (Welch et al. 1993). For more direct forms of public involvement by religious groups—endorsing candidates for office, spearheading political campaigns—there is outright majority disapproval. While accepting the constitutional right of churches to take positions on public issues, the public is quick to note the potentially divisive consequences (Williamsburg Charter Foundation 1988). Americans tend to look to their religion for solace and meaning, not political direction.

Nevertheless, American religious institutions have been repeatedly drawn into the thick of the political process. On some occasions, as the previous chapter recounted, churches have entered the public realm because they felt that their spiritual mission was endangered by some action of government or of another secular institution. They have also become important participants in public decision making about issues that do not appear to touch on their immediate interests. Religious institutions have taken public stands on issues as narrow as the zoning decisions of local planning boards and as broad as the national economy or global problems of hunger and war.

Religious groups do not always take the initiative in these battles. They are frequently drawn into controversies at the urging of secular political forces. In the perennial debate over revisions of the federal tax code, for example, political leaders have structured their proposals so as to bring certain religious groups into the conflict. To enlist support from conservative religious groups, advocates of cuts in federal income taxes have emphasized increasing exemptions or credits for personal dependents. These proposals are promoted among "profamily" groups on the grounds that they would relieve large families of extra financial burdens; this would presumably reduce incentives for women to enter the labor force and, by making another child less expensive, discourage elective abortion for economic reasons.[1] According to Timothy Byrnes (1991, 3), this pattern of recruitment by secular politicians is the norm rather than the exception. He finds that Roman Catholic leaders "have been actively sought out and drawn into the political process by politicians and political leaders anxious to emphasize new issues and build new electoral coalitions."

Whatever the basis for political involvement—be it a policy affecting the ability of churches to perform religious activities, an issue that addresses the social concerns of church members, or a government action that is seen to challenge church doctrine—religion is a potentially significant factor in the policy-making process. We now turn to the role of religion in forming public policy. The first part of this chapter explores the day-to-day political activity of religious groups and the methods by which they attempt to influence government decision making. We then turn to other avenues through which religious and moral considerations may bear on public issues. The remainder of the chapter is devoted to the difficult task of estimating the impact of religious forces on policy making.

Interest Group Activities

The techniques used by religious groups in attempts to shape public policy are conditioned by the U.S. political process. The diverse political strategies of "religion"—a term that encompasses individuals, congregations, denominations, church-affiliated groups, and interchurch organizations—are dictated by the fragmentation of political influence in the American system. Political decision making takes place in three different spheres of authority—the legislative, judicial, and executive branches of government. Overlying this division of power among the relatively equal branches is a further division of political authority among local, state, and national levels of government. To further complicate matters, many areas of public life are left altogether outside the scope of government action, reserved instead for private associations such as business corporations.

For any group that wants to influence public life, the complexity of the U.S. political structure creates a multitude of opportunities and access points. Churches may try to pursue political goals through statutes, administrative procedures, and/or court cases. Along with a choice of arenas, they can decide to concentrate on influencing local, state, or national authorities or to apply pressure on nongovernmental organizations. The options for involvement also extend to the various stages of the policy process: churches and religious groups can specialize in raising awareness of problems, shaping policy alternatives, trying to influence the content of policies, or monitoring the implementation of government action. Like all interest groups, religious groups can employ strategies that fall into four major categories: direct public action, lobbying the government, campaign-related activities, and what I choose to call "infiltration." Although the strategies differ in levels of risk and likelihood of success, each has at one time or another been adopted by groups and individuals motivated by religious concern.

Direct Action

The strategy of direct action may entail activities as diverse as peaceful demonstrations, public relations campaigns, civil disobedience, and in extreme cases, violence. These techniques have been widely adopted by various religious groups.

Peaceful demonstrations have been particularly attractive to groups motivated by intense and deeply felt commitments but lacking in other resources such as money, political experience, and organization. By holding prayer services in public, religiously motivated demonstrators have tried to add moral weight to their position. In my community, open-air services have been conducted both outside the walls of the state prison, to protest capital punishment, and on the sidewalk outside a medical clinic, to protest abortions performed there. Rather than concentrate on sporadic demonstrations, other religious groups have organized boycotts against institutions that offended their religious principles. Over the past thirty years or so, many clergy have participated in nationwide boycotts of certain agricultural products as a way to force growers to bargain collectively with their workers. The boycott was the weapon favored by an interfaith coalition that convinced international corporations to change their practice of marketing potentially dangerous infant feeding products in poor countries (Ermann and Clements 1984). The American Family Association, led by the Mississippi minister described in chapter 2, has used boycotts against companies for advertising on "immoral" television programs or selling what he regards as "pornographic" reading material (see Swatos 1988).

In an attempt to gain public sympathy for their efforts, religious groups may reach out to a larger audience by using sophisticated public relations techniques. The Church of Scientology has advertised regularly in the pages of the *Washington Post*, seeking public support as it contests several indictments by the federal government. Subscribers to national newspapers and magazines should be familiar with other religiously sponsored advertisements, addressing issues such as abortion, school prayer, and foreign policy. Borrowing a page from family-planning groups, the Roman Catholic bishops have committed several million dollars to a major public relations offensive against abortion.[2] The church uses public opinion studies and marketing research to develop public education campaigns. For groups without the resources to mount such expensive public relations exercises, free publicity can be obtained by letters to the editor, press releases, and guest appearances on local talk shows or news broadcasts. In this way, religious groups can attempt to create a favorable climate of opinion for their causes.

Peaceful demonstrations, boycotts, and public relations campaigns are types of public actions that normally fall within the letter of the law. Sometimes, though, frustrated by the failure of more conventional efforts to influence policy, religiously oriented persons have purposely taken actions that violated the law. Religion has inspired many campaigns of civil disobedience, in which protesters have intentionally challenged laws in the name of higher laws. One such effort, the Sanctuary movement, provided asylum in the 1980s for refugees from civil strife in Central America (Coutin 1993; Cunningham 1995). Defying a U.S. policy limiting immigration from Central America, Sanctuary workers went to prison for smuggling refugees into the

United States and harboring them in churches, religious houses, and private homes. Despite the alleged illegality of the actions, the program was endorsed by national organizations affiliated with a wide range of churches: the American Friends (Quakers), the Conservative wing of Judaism, United Presbyterians, United Methodists, and the American Baptist Association. More than 150 local congregations, including Roman Catholics, Unitarians, ecumenical groups, as well as the denominations mentioned above, supported the movement financially and were willing to offer a place of refuge. Considering that much of the leadership of the movement consists of clergy and other devout believers, it is not surprising that the illegal actions have been defended in the name of moral and ethical premises derived from religious teaching. Under the same claim of conscience, groups morally opposed to nuclear armaments have committed symbolic acts of sabotage and withheld income tax payments.

The most extreme form of public action, calculated acts of violence, has occasionally been undertaken by people who claimed to hear God's command. No modern moral issue can match abortion as a focus of religiously connected violent protest in the United States. The Supreme Court justice who wrote the majority opinion in *Roe v. Wade* (1973)—in which the Court removed many restrictions on the availability of the controversial medical procedure—was apparently the target of an assassination attempt. Between 1993 and 1995, five individuals who provided abortion services were shot dead by antiabortion activists, and others were the target of violence. Hundreds of attacks have been made on medical clinics that performed abortion—incidents ranging from minor vandalism to arson and lethal bombings. In demonstrations outside these clinics, protestors have harassed clinic staff and patients, obstructed physical access, and generally tried to shut down medical procedures—eventually prompting Congress to pass special legislation protecting the clinics. Although violence has been denounced by virtually all leaders of the antiabortion movement, most of the persons convicted of major assaults have cited religious convictions in their defense (Blanchard and Prewitt 1993). (They also claim that attacks on abortion facilities represent a measured response to the much greater violence used against the fetus.) When four young people were accused of bombing two facilities in a Florida city, one Baptist minister even hailed them as "heroes." [3]

As both American history and recent world events should remind us, there is nothing particularly new about the use of violence to advance moral causes. The antislavery movement of the nineteenth century, thoroughly infused by religious passion, decried the "martyrdom" of John Brown, who had killed unarmed civilians in assaults on proslavery settlements and government facilities. Like some of today's antiabortion zealots, Brown portrayed himself as the instrument of God's will, wreaking vengeance in the name of higher law. The same "holy war" mentality appears to characterize the militias and paramilitary cults that have waged war on agents of the U.S. government and were implicated in the 1995 bombing of the Oklahoma City federal building.

Lobbying

Religious groups have also turned to lobbying, a term signifying efforts to influence public officials. With its unsavory connotations of using pressure, bribery, and corruption to advance self-interest, lobbying might seem like a strange activity for groups committed to high moral standards. The very use of the term clearly makes religious interest groups nervous (Zwier 1988). Yet most lobby work is ordinary and morally unobjectionable—monitoring government actions, assembling facts and figures, making public presentations, visiting offices, negotiating the details of legislation and government regulations. These "insider" tactics, available to groups with personal access to government elites, require the resources to support professionals for whom lobbying is a primary responsibility.

Paul Weber and W. Landis Jones (1994) have identified 120 nonprofit organizations that seek to influence policy formulation from a religious perspective.[4] Most maintain permanent advocacy offices in Washington, D.C., representing a significant increase in the scale of religious lobbying (J. Adams 1970; Dexter 1938; Ebersole 1951). Staff members employed by these groups spend their time much like lobbyists for secular organizations, "drafting bill language, offering amendments, forging coalitions behind the scenes, negotiating with opponents over compromise provisions, and providing useful facts and arguments to members during legislative debates" (Hertzke 1988, 70). Even though direct communication with members of the Supreme Court is not deemed appropriate in the American political system, the religious groups lobby justices by submitting "friend of the court" briefs, written arguments about cases under Supreme Court review. In the important case in which the Court first evaluated the constitutionality of affirmative action for disadvantaged minority groups, the flood of briefs sent to the justices included submissions from the National Council of Churches, the Young Women's Christian Association, and the Anti-Defamation League of B'nai B'rith. Issues that touch directly on religious interests bring out appeals from an even broader range of religious groups.

Lobbying may be undertaken to advance the theological, institutional, or communal interests of a religious group. Consider the report of the official lobbyist for the Florida Catholic Conference for one week in 1985, which highlighted three bills under consideration by the state legislature.[5] The church opposed on moral grounds one bill that permitted the withdrawal of intravenous food and fluids from terminally ill patients. Because food and water are necessities of life rather than forms of medical treatment, the official testified, their withdrawal would constitute a type of euthanasia, which church doctrine condemned. A concern for the church's institutional strength was evident in the lobbyist's support for a bill to grant privileged status to communication between clergy and church members in cases involving child and adult abuse. Without the protection of the law, it was argued, the church's counseling programs might be threatened. Finally, the lobbyist expressed grave concern about a bill on the state senate floor to repeal all state and local tax exemptions, including those for the religious, educational, and charitable activities sponsored by churches. Even though the repeal was merely a device designed to permit the legislature to consider each category of tax exemption on the books, the church opposed the bill because it threatened "the freedom of religion, the separation of church and state, and the orderly planning for . . . institutions which provide basic necessary services." It should be pointed out that the Catholic church was not the only participant in lobbying on these bills and that its lobbying failed in two of the three cases. Even more important, although each bill touched a particular facet of the Catholic religion, it would be foolish to claim that one particular motivation was paramount in any one issue. The churches, like other interested actors, may intervene for a variety of religious and secular reasons.

The use of professional advocates is only one prong of the effort to lobby public officials. To a much greater extent than secular interest groups, religious lobbies attempt to reinforce their influence by such classic "outsider" strategies as demonstrations, public relations campaigns, and other efforts at grassroots mobilization (Hofrenning 1995). Such tactics are partly the result of the decision by many religious lobbyists to play a very different role from advocates of secular causes. Unlike secular lobbyists who typically focus on a narrow range of issues and seek only incremental changes, religious lobbyists often take on the mantle of biblical prophets, challenging the political system in the name of sacred values like justice, freedom, and decency. Through outsider tactics, religious groups try to convey the impression that their constituencies stand ready to support officials who go along and to penalize legislators who do not. Because more Americans belong to religious organizations than to any other voluntary association, public officials are disposed to listen.

The views of churchgoers are made known to public officials in several ways. The American tradition of letter-writing campaigns to public officials has been followed by many religious organizations engaged in matters of public controversy. When, for example, President Gerald Ford proposed to sell several sophisticated intelligence-gathering airplanes to Saudi Arabia, several Jewish groups fought the proposal as a threat to Israeli security. In a coordinated campaign to defeat the sale, members of the Jewish community in some cities were sent preprinted postcards addressed to congressional representatives. By flooding Capitol Hill mailbags with messages opposing the sale, the Jewish groups hoped (in vain) that Congress would overturn the president's decision.

Often portrayed as spontaneous outbursts by enraged congregants, mass mobilization usually results from campaigns that are meticulously planned by the Washington office of the religious group. Media-based ministries have effectively used mass mailings, phone banks, computerized telephone messages, and broadcast programs to generate letters, telegrams, personal visits, and telephone calls by their supporters (Hertzke 1988, 50). Less common on the religious left, similar techniques have been used effectively by the peace movement to mount grassroots campaigns against such initiatives as the MX missile or U.S. assistance to the Nicaraguan *contras*. In those campaigns, the appeals

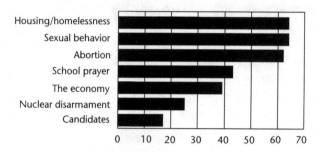

Figure 5.1 Percentage of Congregants Hearing Clergy Discuss Political Issues (Source: Calculated by Welch et al. [1990] from the 1989 pilot study, American National Election Study, Center for Political Studies)

were targeted to the small churches with pacifist traditions, such as Mennonites, as well as to mainline Protestants who were sympathetic to calls for disarmament. The ground for appeals to congregants is planted in the tradition of church guidance on public issues. Churchgoers hear from their leaders on a broad range of public issues (see fig. 5.1), with clear majorities stating that religious leaders have spoken out on homelessness, sexual behavior, and abortion. Sizable minorities report clergy statements on school prayer, the economy, and nuclear disarmament. These issue appeals are far more common than communication about candidates for public office.

Nobody should be surprised to learn that churches were the key players in passing both the Equal Access Act and the Religious Freedom Restoration Act, legislation that covered matters at the center of the religious mission. But it may be more surprising to discover the central role of the organized religious community in passing what many observers regard as the most important piece of domestic legislation since World War II, the Civil Rights Act of 1964 (Findlay 1990). Working through the National Council of Churches, representatives of various churches brought pressure on key members of Congress whose votes might swing a majority on behalf of the bill. The tactics favored by the interfaith coalition included conferences at which theologians urged the moral case for desegregation, sending teams of speakers into pivotal districts, and enlisting parishioners and church members to lobby directly with influential legislators. At the center of the storm in

Washington, D.C., the church personnel played key roles in tracking the fate of the legislation and ensuring constant communication with wavering supporters. Decades later, another interfaith coalition used similar tactics as part of a coordinated effort to change American policy in Central America (Brett 1994).

In the campaigns for civil rights and Central America, the churches were part of broader coalitions that included organized labor, African American groups, and other allies. Likewise, in the world of organized political influence, religiously motivated groups are a very small component that can compete with representatives of major economic interests only as part of a collective effort. Even the best-equipped religious denomination does not begin to match the organizational resources typically available to corporations, trade associations, or labor federations.

Political Campaigning

Lobbying is likely to be especially powerful if the person on the receiving end thinks the lobbyist can affect his or her chances for retaining public office. Hence, some religious groups have become involved in various phases of political campaigning at all levels of the government. The extent of campaigning is limited by federal law. Under the Internal Revenue Service (IRS) Code, charitable organizations such as churches are exempt from taxation and may receive tax-exempt contributions only if they refrain from direct involvement in political campaigns (Davis 1991). Despite its broad powers, the IRS has generally refrained from invoking this law except for the most egregious violations. Churches have been allowed to host political speakers and voter registration drives, lobby for and against referendums, and issue voter guides that provide virtual recommendations to members. They are sometimes warned if they appear to stray too close to becoming adjuncts of a campaign. In 1992 a New York congregation crossed the line when it placed an anti-Clinton advertisement in *USA Today* and the *Washington Times*. By asserting that candidate Clinton's policies represented "rebellion to God's Laws" and that a Clinton vote would therefore be sinful, the church eventually lost its tax-exempt status (Boston 1995). The courts will be asked to decide if limiting public advocacy in this manner constitutes an infringement of the free-exercise clause.

For some religiously affiliated groups, campaign involvement may take the form of merely questioning candidates about issues in which the church takes an interest. That familiar mixture of theological, institutional, and social concern was very much in evidence in the questions sent to the 1984 presidential nominees by the St. Augustine (Florida) diocese of the Roman Catholic church.[6] The candidates were asked if they supported or opposed a constitutional ban on abortion, elimination of capital punishment, cutbacks in the deployment of nuclear weapons, income tax credits for private school tuition, and major new federal programs to combat hunger and increase housing opportunities. In addition to indicating their orientations on human life issues (abortion and capital punishment), state legislative candidates were asked their views on welfare funding, the provision of services to nonpublic schools, ratification of the Equal Rights Amendment, and the broadcasting of "indecent" material on cable television. Having defined each of these concerns as moral issues, the church encouraged its members to consider the candidates' response before casting their ballots. Such questionnaires may help parishioners judge the candidates in terms of the church's policy agenda.

As citizens, clergy enjoy the right to influence the votes of church members provided they stop short of official endorsement. By extolling the moral virtues of one candidate and pointedly refraining from comment about the competition, a minister can clearly indicate a preference without actually recommending a vote from the pulpit. Even that fine line can be breached when ministers explicitly endorse candidates from a platform outside the church. Does ministerial support pay off at the polls? When asked where they turn for political advice and guidance, Americans do not frequently mention the church. That finding may indicate only that Americans feel it is improper for churches to take sides in elections—not that they are unaffected by clergy influence. In the African American community, where the clergy have long wielded authority over political issues, voters certainly seem to respond to cues from the pulpit (Vedlitz, Alston, and Pinkele 1980).

In an age of weak political parties and generally low rates of political participation, the support of religious groups is usually seen as a valuable asset in a political campaign (Berke 1994a). Religiously involved people can supply resources to help favored candidates or, conversely, to defeat unacceptable ones. Simply providing the candidate a forum gives invaluable free publicity and the opportunity to spread a message among attentive audiences. As organizations possessing membership lists and other resources, the churches may even be pressed into action as the core of a candidate's campaign effort. In bidding for presidential nomination in 1988, both Jesse Jackson and Pat Robertson, ordained ministers, relied heavily on sympathetic churches for leadership, funding, platforms, and various support services (Wald 1991). Though major political parties in the United States attempt to draw support from different religious groups, several minor parties have been built almost exclusively on specific religious constituencies. That was true of the antislavery and prohibitionist parties in an earlier age. Since 1978 antiabortion activists in New York have supported the Right-to-Life party, which as of 1984 had more than seventeen thousand enrolled members. Though not formally tied to any church, the leaders and members of the party appear to have been recruited mainly from denominations that favor conservative theology and positions on public issues (Spitzer 1987).

Infiltration

Finally, there is the method called *infiltration*. Reasoning that the most reliable kind of official is the one who shares the group's values, a religious organization may seek to place one of its members in office. If the office is filled by public election, members of a religious group may organize to win the seat for a fellow member. Although the Constitution forbids the government to impose "religious tests" for holding office, it does not restrict citizens from applying such tests when they exercise their right to vote.

Judging by their actions, candidates have recognized the potential electoral power of religious affiliation. In 1982 a candidate with the decidedly non-Jewish name of Larry Smith wanted to indicate his Jewish identity to voters in a Florida congressional district. Concerned that his name would be a handicap in a race against other Jewish candidates in a district with a predominantly Jewish electorate, Smith had his wife introduced to district residents by her maiden name, Sheila Cohen, and distributed campaign literature with pictures of his son's Bar Mitzvah ceremony (Ehrenhalt 1983, 333). Also, in a packet of material sent out to influential leaders and community groups, the candidate called attention to his active membership in a local synagogue and reminded readers that he had helped to found a chapter of B'nai B'rith and been named "Man of the Year" by the local chapter of the Jewish National Fund. Consistent with the tactics that eventually brought victory, Smith's 1984 campaign biography called attention to his membership in the congressional Caucus for Soviet Jewry and an award received for zeal in promoting the sale of Israeli bonds. Quite the opposite problem faced Marc Holtzmann, a Jewish candidate for a Pennsylvania congressional seat with a majority of Roman Catholic voters (Taylor 1985). To offset the potential disadvantage of a Jewish-sounding name, Holtzmann asked the American ambassador to the Vatican to arrange a meeting with Pope John Paul II. Despite blanketing the district with pictures of his meeting with the spiritual leader of the Catholic church, Holtzmann lost.

Do voters actually respond positively to such appeals to vote for "their own kind" of people? Although complex motivations cannot be attributed to any single factor, a candidate's religious affiliation clearly can play a role in voter decision making. The most persuasive evidence leading to this conclusion has been obtained in experiments simulating the electoral process. In a classic study by the psychologist Leon Festinger (1947), a group of female college students was asked to listen to speeches by candidates for the presidency of a college club. On contrived grounds, the first vote (in which the names and religious identities of the candidates were not revealed) was voided. After a suitable interval, during which the participants learned the candidates' religious affiliation, a second ballot was conducted. Festinger interpreted the changes in preference between ballots as evidence that knowledge of a candidate's religious identity inflated support among members of the candidate's religious family. That conclusion has been sustained by studies in which voters have been asked to choose between hypothetical candidates for public office. In these studies the ethnic identity of the candidate, a quality frequently associated with religious affiliation, apparently brought in additional support from members of the same ethnic group (Kamin 1958; Lorinskas, Hawkins, and Edwards 1969—see Pomper 1966 for actual election data). Studies of Catholic voting patterns in 1956 and 1960 showed that Catholic candidates running for national offices against candidates from other faiths earned substantially more support from their coreligionists than party ties could have explained (Campbell et al. 1960, 319–321; Converse 1966).

All other things being equal—and they rarely are in electoral politics—voters usually favor a candidate of their own religion.[7] Religious affiliation is only one element in the voters' image of the candidate, which is, in turn, only one of the three factors that strongly sway electoral choice. The other two factors—partisanship and the issues—may limit or offset the impact of religious affiliation. In two studies that examined the impact of candidates' ethnic and religious traits under partisan conditions, the effect was clearest when the normal party cues were absent (Kamin 1958; Pomper 1966). When a voter has to cross party lines to support a candidate with the same ethnic or religious identity, the religious factor has a much smaller impact. The candidate's stands on the issues may also deter members of his or her religious community from giving additional support. As has been shown by studies of predominantly Jewish districts, Jewish candidates whose political views differed from those of most of their coreligionists have lost badly to non-Jewish candidates whose policies are more closely attuned to public opinion (Leventman and Leventman 1976). These studies have suggested that voters do not attribute quite as much significance to a candidate's personal religious affiliation as candidates seem to imagine.

The religious factor has also played a role in the politics of appointments. When President Ronald Reagan filled an important position in the U.S. Department of Education with an official from the conservative religious group Moral Majority and named a leader of the antiabortion movement to the post of surgeon general, he reenacted the familiar American ritual of awarding patronage to a group that had supported his election (Schuster 1981). Moral Majority undoubtedly welcomed the appointment providing a way to safeguard its growing private school movement and to interject its moral concerns into the decision-making process on education policy. If that case illustrates how religious groups may take the initiative to receive appointments, it is worth remembering that public officials may seek out religious leaders for positions on public bodies. As respected community leaders with considerable prestige, members of the clergy may seem to be perfectly positioned to lend credibility to policies that would otherwise inspire political controversy.

Given the central role of judges in the policy process, it should not be surprising that judicial appointments have also been the subject of intense religious-group activity. Before World War II, when Catholics and Jews were still struggling for political recognition, it was customary to reserve a seat on the U.S. Supreme Court for each group (Perry 1991). Interest now focuses on the specific views of nominees for judgeships. At congressional hearings on the appointment of federal judges, representatives of church groups have testified in favor of or against nominees because of preferences on policy issues. Since 1980 antiabortion groups have repeatedly persuaded the Republican national convention to pledge support for restricting federal judicial nominations to persons who "respected the sanctity of human life." What might sound like routine political rhetoric struck many observers as a commitment to make opposition to abortion a requirement for judicial appointment. Studies of the judicial appointment process in the Reagan and Bush administrations (1981–1993) suggest that the platform pledge was carried out (Goldman 1993). In 1984 the Reagan administration withdrew support from its own nominee for a seat on the District of Columbia Court of Appeals in part because of conservative complaints that he belonged to the National Abortion Rights Action League and Planned Parenthood. In a questionnaire sent by three Republican senators, a nominee for a federal judgeship in New Jersey was asked seven questions about the legalization of abortion and about such religiously based issues as school prayer, the death penalty, the Equal Rights Amendment, and public financing for private schools. And when the Reagan administration was considering the appointment of an outspoken evangelical Protestant to chair the Justice Department committee on judicial selection, fears of religious tests for the judiciary inspired fierce, and ultimately successful, opposition (Kurtz 1985a). Supreme Court nominations were also made very much with an eye toward the likely impact on decisions involving religious claims.

By presenting the various tactics in separate categories, I do not mean to suggest that churches and religious activists must specialize in one or the other type of political activity. Rather, churches resemble secular interest groups in their ability to pick and choose among the methods of political action. Few religious groups have used as many different techniques as the National Conference of Catholic Bishops and United States Catholic Conference, the central organizations of the largest single denomination in the United States (T. Byrnes 1991; D.

Shannon 1993). Representing more than 50 million Americans and possessing a substantial resource base, the church is able to employ a number of full-time lobbyists at its Washington headquarters and to provide them ample legal assistance. The professional lobbying effort is supplemented by a stream of Catholic witnesses at congressional hearings, the filing of legal briefs in critical court cases, and other activities. The top authorities of the church, its bishops, have intervened in presidential politics, and parish clergy have followed that lead by raising Catholic concerns in many local electoral contests. The bishops and clergy have not hesitated to instruct Catholic public officials in their religious duties nor, when circumstances seemed right, to support various types of direct action. Owing to the diversity of Catholic social thought, these efforts have been brought to bear on a wide range of political issues and to support positions both "liberal" and "conservative." Rather than representing a monolithic Catholic position imposed by the Vatican, a charge once commonly voiced by extremist Protestants, the political activities of the church seem to have added to the rich variety of perspectives that inform the American policy process.

Organizing for Political Action

Like American religion itself, the efforts of religious groups in politics are remarkably diverse. In surveying seventy-five groups that maintained offices in the nation's capital in 1981, Paul Weber (1982a) was particularly struck by the diversity of the groups on a number of dimensions. In terms of denominational orientation, there were groups representing the views of Catholics, Jews, mainline and evangelical Protestants, African American Christians, and secularists with a strong interest in church-state relations. Some groups represented single denominations, others broad coalitions with common interests. As organizations, some relied on dues-paying individual members, whereas others were subsidized departments of national church organizations whose very existence might not be known by the church members who supported them financially. The social issues pursued by the groups were in some cases identified by an elaborate system of consultation reaching down to member churches and in others left to the discretion of centrally based leaders of the church organization. Politically, the groups ranged from narrowly conceived single-issue movements that worked alone to organizations with a broad range of concerns that were willing to coalesce with secular groups if that would advance their preferred policies. These differences extended to groups representing the same religious denomination. Thomas O'Hara (1989b) found important policy and strategy differences among Washington lobby groups established by the Catholic church, independent groups representing different orders of the Catholic clergy, and lobbies founded by Catholic laity.

This diversity was strikingly evident in the five-year battle over a key piece of civil rights legislation (O'Hara 1989a). The issue arose from a 1984 U.S. Supreme Court decision that exempted institutions or their programs from penalties for discrimination levied against a subdivision. Under the ruling, federal grants to a university could no longer be cut off if a program within it, such as the athletic department, had discriminated against women. Fearing that this narrow interpretation crippled enforcement efforts against race, sex, and age discrimination, civil rights groups determined to make the entire institution liable for discrimination by any of its programs or divisions. They turned for support to the same religious communities that had promoted the civil rights legislation of 1964.

In contrast to the united front evident in the struggle for the 1964 act, deep divisions among religious groups prevented passage of the bill for five years and limited the scope of the law finally approved in 1989. The struggle for the Civil Rights Restoration Act was supported enthusiastically by most mainline Protestant and Jewish groups, important allies since the 1960s, but encountered serious resistance from other religious interest groups. The remedial legislation was opposed outright by groups that had not been active during the heyday of civil rights—Christian schools associations, various conservative social movements like Moral Majority and Christian Voice, and several major televised ministries. Never known for moderate rhetoric, the Rev. Jerry Falwell expressed his opposition in extreme form when he claimed the proposed act would define sin as a disease or handicap, thereby forcing church-related institutions to accept "active homosexuals, transvestites, alcoholics and drug addicts, among others" (quoted in O'Hara 1989a, 18). The United States Catholic Conference, once an integral part of the civil rights coalition, also opposed the bill. Their representatives expressed fears that the prohibition against sex discrimination might force them to offer abortion coverage in benefit programs for university students and staff and, equally troublesome, render every Catholic institution in a diocese liable for the actions of a single offender.

In the five years it took to resolve these concerns, the religious groups also embraced a variety of strategies. The Catholic Conference worked closely with the congressional committees to revise the language of the bill and to round up support for an amended version. Most of the conservative Protestant opponents never accepted the legislation, first trying to load it down with amendments that would kill the bill, then persuading President Reagan to veto it. When Congress threatened to pass it over the veto, these groups mounted a massive campaign of public mobilization.

Diversity also characterizes the manner in which religious groups formulate their public agenda. In particular, aspects of a denomination's religious tradition, especially its preferred form of organization, may shape the process by which it develops a position on a public issue and lobbies policymakers. For purposes of comparison, the Catholic and Jewish communities provide an excellent contrast (E. Fisher and Polish 1980). Catholicism is organized on a hierarchical basis with centralized decision making; Judaism, in this respect resembling many of the Protestant denominations in the United States, accords individual congregations a very high degree of autonomy.

The American Jewish community is divided into four major theological camps that support a wide range of organizations for both religious and secular purposes. Many organizations function at the local level to secure the immediate interests of the Jewish community. In addition to these local organizations, there are a number of national groups and federations of congregations. Furthermore, the spiritual leaders of Judaism, the rabbis, have traditionally enjoyed wide latitude in making social pronouncements as individuals or as members of rabbinic associations. Each of these groups may take public positions on issues of national and international concern, leading to a chorus of voices singing in different keys.

To date, as Peter Medding (1989, 28) notes, "American Jews remain fiercely united around the principle that no single body speaks for the entire community." Attempts at coordination can be made through the National Jewish Community Relations Advisory Council (NJCRAC), described as "an umbrella body consisting of all national Jewish organizations and 106 local Jewish Community Relations Councils drawn from almost every community in the country containing an organized Jewish community" (Brickner 1980, 9). However, the NJCRAC is merely an advisory body. It has no authority to issue binding pronouncements on questions of public policy. The awkwardly named Conference of Presidents of Major Jewish Organizations has also attempted to speak in the name of the entire Jewish community, but it too enjoys only limited legitimacy. When an authoritative Jewish voice is sought out by the media—as it was, for instance, when President Bush proposed major arms sales to Arab nations following Iraq's invasion of Kuwait—there is no single obvious place to go.

In the Catholic church political decision making follows a more hierarchical pattern.[8] As the apex of the authority pyramid, the pope may issue binding statements about Catholic policy on social issues. These statements of church policy may not persuade all Catholics, but the pope wields enough disciplinary power to enforce some compliance. Within the United States, the Catholic church addresses public issues primarily through the policy statements issued by the bishops through the Catholic Conference. The head of the conference, elected by the bishops, is widely recognized as the authoritative spokesman for the church and may even become a major public figure. The messages issued by the conference represent the teaching authority of the church and legitimacy does not depend on democratic decision making. Within their own domains, the bishops also enjoy power to define the official Catholic position. On this authority, the bishop in one diocese recently ordered parishioners to quit such organizations as Planned Parenthood, Catholics for a Free Choice, and a grassroots church reform group named "Call to Action" or face excommunication.[9]

In terms of direct political action, with the outbreak in 1973 of the Yom Kippur War, the heads of major Jewish organizations lobbied the administration and Congress to provide assistance to Israel and worked to enlist American public opinion on behalf of that country. By all accounts, these efforts at mobilization contributed to Israel's subsequent victory (Elazar 1976, app. A).

But there are limits to organized political activity by religious groups. The American Jewish community, united behind Israel during the Arab-Israeli wars, has split into competing camps on the issue of the Middle East peace process spearheaded by the Clinton administration. These camps will certainly seek to influence U.S. foreign aid policy in the event that Benjamin Netanyahu, Israel's conservative new prime minister, seeks to slow the peace process. Likewise, American Catholics have differed over how to implement their church's formal condemnation of abortion. Proponents of restrictive policies have argued over the best mechanism to achieve their goal, and opponents have insisted that Catholics have no obligation to follow church doctrine. In a telling comment on the limits of church authority, scholars have reported that the contraceptive practices and abortion attitudes of American Catholics do not differ significantly from those followed by persons from other churches (Goldscheider and Mosher 1991; Henshaw and Silverman 1988). In that sense, the bishops' resort to the public relations campaign described above may be an admission that preaching has been ineffective. Religious groups, like other politically organized interests, cannot simply command their members to toe the line.

The Question of Representation

The political intervention of churches and religious groups has been condemned as divisive, politically motivated, naive, unconstitutional, and theologically wrong (Atkins and McConnell 1986). Although some of these complaints probably represent dissatisfaction with the positions taken rather than with the act of advocacy itself, many critics have argued that churches and religious groups are prone to misrepresent the views of their members (Reichley 1985; Hallum 1989). In formulating church statements on public policy, it is charged, religious elites take advantage of their power to foist their own views on denominations, speaking in the name of the church when its members are divided on or even opposed to the church's official stance. This charge, long made against the liberal Washington representatives of the mainline Protestant churches, has recently been lodged against the Roman Catholic bishops in the 1980s for their public opposition to support for the Nicaraguan *contras*, abortion, nuclear weapons, and "supply-side" economic policy. Despite its constituency's deep support for human rights, some Jewish organizations have appeared to lend uncritical support to Israeli actions against Palestinians on the West Bank. Likewise, the conservatives who claim to speak for the white evangelical Protestants have also been charged with misrepresenting the more moderate views of their members on several issues.

The charge of misrepresentation is doubly serious. First, it impugns the religious organizations by suggesting they are out of touch with their members. "Correct" public policy positions may be chosen at the expense of alienating congregants and weakening the church. Second, such charges undermine the effectiveness of church representatives. An advocate who confronts a public official without membership support will have little credibility. In response, religious elites often claim they play a prophetic role. In this view, churches are not democracies that determine policy on the basis of majority votes but proclaimers of the truth that must follow the dictates of conscience and educate their members. If the price of prophecy is dissension in the ranks, they reply, so be it. This response does not deny that official positions may differ from the preferences of the laity; it justifies such deviation in terms of moral imperatives.

American religious elites certainly appear to differ from the citizenry. Leaders of Catholic and mainline Protestantism are much more likely than their parishioners to identify with liberalism, support Democratic candidates for president, and hold liberal views across a range of political and social issues (Lerner, Rothman, and Lichter 1989). But do the church advocacy groups accurately represent their congregants' policy views when they lobby the government? Allen Hertzke's answer (1989, 134; see also 1988, chap. 5), based on comparing lobbying positions with poll data, is mostly yes. Mainline Protestant lobbies diverged from member preferences on social issues, but they agreed with their members on other controversial issues—from environmental protection to food stamps. Almost a mirror image of mainline lobbying, evangelical lobbyists reflect member concerns about social policy while taking a more conservative line on several domestic and foreign policy issues. Both Catholic and Jewish lobbyists were close to member opinion on most issues. Like Hertzke, Daniel Hofrenning (1995) observed that lobby positions were closest to the views of members on the most salient issues, less so on other matters. These studies suggest that religious elites blend a concern for rank-and-file opinion with a prophetic orientation. If not perfectly representative of mass opinion, neither are they consistently out of step.

Paths of Influence

Religious groups have traditionally been viewed as supplicants to power, outsiders trying to influence the policy process. But in fact, religion may influence policy more directly, through the religious views and preferences of policymakers. Religion can become the foundation for public policies in several ways. When laws are decided through public referendums, religious groups may simply vote their preferences into law. That has been the case for evangelical Protestants in voting against referendum proposals relaxing limits on alcohol and gambling or adding sexual orientation to antidiscrimination policy (D. Morgan and Meier 1980; Wasserman 1989; Haider-Markel and Meier 1996). Voting patterns have followed religious lines in other policy areas. Howard Hamilton (1970) noted a peculiar pattern in the relationship between religion and support for "open housing" laws in three referendums conducted during the early 1960s. In two of the contests, voters with no religious preference gave greater support to the proposals than did members of Christian churches, a finding consistent with survey data on the greater racial liberalism of persons with no religious preference. But in a similar referendum in Toledo, Ohio, where all major churches took a strong and active role on behalf of the fair housing ordinance, churchgoers were more likely than nonmembers to endorse antidiscrimination housing legislation. The pattern in Toledo suggests that religious values are most likely to influence voting on questions of public policy only when the church provides unambiguous clues for its membership (see Richardson 1984).

Most laws are enacted, not by a public vote, but by the concerted action of elected officials. Religion can play a role in this process by influencing the values of officeholders. Particularly when they are chosen by public election, government officials are likely to share the dominant religious values of their community. Even if the officials come from another religious tradition, a dependence on public approval for reelection should motivate them to express the preferences of their constituents. In either case, government officials could play a crucial role in translating religious sentiment into public law.

It is important to recognize the limits of the hypothesis, that the behavior of political elites can be shaped by their personal religious orientations. Political scientists continue to debate the relative weight to assign the many factors that influence the behavior of public officials. In deciding how to cast a roll call vote, for example, members of Congress are subject to the pull of party loyalty, regional culture, judgments about constituency preferences, the influence of the president, the flow of national public opinion, staff recommendations, the lobbying efforts of myriad groups, and other personality characteristics. Although the sources of influence might be different, officials in the executive and judicial spheres are similarly buffeted by forces that could override any single personal characteristic. Religion is just one of the factors that might account for an official's decision to favor or oppose a particular course of action on a public problem.

Considering the clear importance of religion in mass voting, it is remarkable to discover how little attention has been devoted to the study of the religious factor in congressional behavior. Most systematic research has simply attempted to establish if members of Congress vote as religious blocs on issues decided by roll call votes. Even with a limited focus on basic denominational differences, the studies have not reached consensus. John Fenton (1960) compared the behavior of Catholic and Protestant members of the House and Senate during the 1959–1960 session of Congress. Fenton found that for the most part, when compared with members from the same party and region, Catholics and Protestants did not differ much in their support for civil rights legislation, foreign aid, or bills affecting organized labor. In contrast, Leroy Rieselbach (1966) showed consistent differences between Catholic and Protestant representatives on foreign aid votes in five Congresses from 1934 to 1964. In most cases, Catholics were more supportive of foreign aid appropriations than their fellow partisans, whether Democratic or Republican, or representatives from urban districts. This difference did not extend, however, to the realm of foreign trade issues, the other dimension of Rieselbach's study. Using roll call votes on those social welfare issues that had elicited policy statements from mainstream Protestant denominations, John Warner Jr. (1968) also observed significant differences among Catholic, Protestant, and Jewish members of the Eighty-ninth Congress. Like other observers, Warner found Protestants to be the most conservative and Jews to be the most liberal, but he also found no significant policy differences between mainstream and evangelical Protestant legislators once party affiliation had been taken into account.

Denominational affiliation might prove to exert a significant impact on legislative voting only when the issue under consideration has been the subject of intense religious controversy. The abortion issue, which has long engaged the attention of many churches, would seem to offer a good test case for this proposition. Two studies of voting on abortion laws in the American West have indeed revealed clear differences in legislative behavior by different religious groups. In a study of legislators from an unnamed state, James Richardson and Sandie Wightman Fox (1972, 1975) sought evidence for the impact of religious affiliation in votes on bills to liberalize abortion policy. Taking into account the urbanization levels of the districts and the legislators' age and party—factors likely to influence votes on moral issues—they found support for more liberal access to abortion among the Protestant and Jewish members of the lower house, and opposition to the proposals from the Catholic representatives. The Mormon legislators switched to the opposition side after their church issued clear statements about the incompatibility of liberalized abortion with Mormon doctrine. Observing a similar battle in another western state, O'Neil (1970) found essentially the same pattern of conflict in the Senate committee that killed a proposal for liberalized abortion. The ill-fated bill was supported by all liberal Protestants and Jewish members of the committee and opposed by every Roman Catholic and conservative Protestant. That pattern also governed early voting on abortion in the U.S. House of Representatives (Daynes and Tatalovich 1984).

The principal weakness of these studies was their failure to sort out systematically the impact of personal religion from either district composition or the other sources of influence on congressional voting. That problem has been addressed in several published studies. In examining roll call voting records for approximately one-fourth of House members in the Ninety-fifth Congress (B. Page et al. 1984), the legislators were ranked according to their attitudes toward social welfare spending, race relations, women's rights, law and order, and, finally, abortion. Using a powerful statistical technique, the researchers then attempted to assess the influence on this ranking of the demographic characteristics of the district, its collective opinions on public issues, the representative's party affiliation, and his or her personal traits (including religious affiliation). On most issues, the investigators found little significance for personal traits. Abortion was an exception. Even taking into account the impact of district characteristics, the religious affiliation of the representatives exerted a significant impact by prompting Catholic members to support restrictive procedures on abortion. Similar research in a variety of legislative settings finds Catholic, Mormon, and evangelical Protestant legislators more likely to support restrictive abortion legislation after taking account of personal qualities such as party and ideology and the influence of the legislators' district (Vinovkis 1979; Gohmann and Ohsfeldt 1990; Granberg 1985b; Tatalovich and Schier 1993; Chresanthis, Gilbert, and Grimes 1991; Witt and Moncrief 1993).

In a comprehensive study on the Ninety-sixth Congress, John Green and James Guth (1991) looked at the overall voting records of the representatives. The study attempted to determine the factors that influenced the score of each member of Congress on a widely used index composed by the Americans for Democratic Action (ADA), a liberal interest group. Controlling for partisanship, the single major contributing factor, the ADA scores also varied significantly with the personal religious identity of the representative and the religious composition of the congressional district. As expected, the greater the concentration of theologically conservative religious groups, the more conservative the voting habits of the district's representative in Congress. Because it looked at voting over a wide range of issues, measured both the religious affiliation of the representative and the constituents, and included a host of other potential influences, this study represents the strongest evidence of religious impact on the legislative process.

As valuable as they are, these statistical investigations of denominational differences in legislative behavior only scratch the surface of possible religious effects on political elites. Much additional light has been shed by a pair of studies that transcended simple denominational classification by interviewing legislators to learn their religious values. Based on her interviews with twenty-five Catholics serving in the U.S. Congress in the period 1973–1974, Mary Hanna (1979) concluded that Catholics did not form a separate bloc and, with a few exceptions on issues such as abortion, were not strongly influenced by their Catholic constituents or the lobbying efforts of the church. Rather, Hanna found, the principal contribution of faith to Catholic legislators' political identity was its influence on their basic political attitudes. Two different streams of Catholicism guided their values, one "that emphasized strict codes of conduct, rules, and guidelines, a rather rigid, puritanical devotion to duty and order; and one which stressed Christian love, compassion, and concern for one's fellow man, especially the poor, the helpless, and the unfortunate" (ibid., 99). Not surprisingly, adherents of the first tradition were conservative Republicans, and legislators who drew from the social reform stream were liberal Democrats.

A similar distinction between religious types was noted by Peter L. Benson and Dorothy L. Williams (1982), who interviewed eighty members of the House of Representatives from a wide range of denominations. Politically conservative and liberal representatives were found in each major American denomination, but members of the two camps tended to stress different aspects of belief. The conservatives conceived of religion as something for the individual, a force that gave them comfort in times of distress, strength of conviction, self-discipline, and the promise of eternal reward. In contrast, political liberals put a great deal of emphasis on the communal aspect of religion. Where conservatives saw religion as a one-to-one relationship between individuals and God, the theology of liberalism stressed the oneness of humanity and the need for social transformation on earth if God's will is to be recognized adequately. These differences showed up in voting on specific types of legislation. "Individualism preserving" religion was correlated with support for free enterprise, private ownership, and military expenditures and with opposition to government spending on social programs. Its opposite, what Benson and Williams labeled "community building" religion, encouraged support for programs of foreign aid, hunger relief, civil liberties, and liberalized abortion rights. These differences in religious style appeared much stronger than the group differences normally observed when legislators are divided into broad families, such as Protestant, Catholic, and Jew, or classified according to denominations. For elites just as the masses, studies using denominational affiliation may underestimate the connection between religious values and legislative behavior.

The Judiciary

If legislators may be influenced by religious backgrounds, the same force could in principle affect the decisions of judges. Some scholars have argued that in the American political system, which gives judges broad discretion to interpret the laws, a complete understanding of judicial decisions requires the use of information about personal and social background. Although this point has by no means been universally accepted by judicial scholars, it has inspired several careful studies that have traced patterns of judicial behavior to the traits of individual judges. The need to be cautious in ascribing religious motives to public acts must once again be recognized. A judge's decision is likely to reflect certain norms of the legal profession—a respect for precedent, the quality of advocacy, views about the proper scope for judicial discretion, and, of course, the facts surrounding any particular case. If religion fits into the equation, it does so merely as one factor among many.

Systematic analysis of religion has been as scarce in research on judicial behavior as in studies of legislative behavior. Probably the best evidence for a religious effect can be found in Sorauf's (1976, chap. 9) analysis of denominational differences in voting on church-state issues by judges on high appellate courts. In analyzing nonunanimous decisions during the 1950s and 1960s, he found that more than 80 percent of Jewish judges favored a strict "separationist" policy that limited government's ability to recognize religion, whereas Roman Catholic judges, by an equally lopsided margin, voted to endorse policies and practices that accommodated religious interests. Protestants, who made up by far the bulk of the judges hearing the church-state issues, split roughly in half between the separationist and accommodationist camps. The historic tension between Protestants and Catholics in the United States was apparent in the tendency of Protestant judges to become more accommodationist when Catholics were not a party to a lawsuit and for Catholics to become decidedly more separationist when non-Catholic groups were involved in the case (ibid., 225). As Sorauf realized, this set of cases was particularly conducive to the operation of a denominational effect because "the religious affiliation of the judge relates in the judicial decision to the direct and immediate interests of his religious group as well as to the social values derived from the religious tradition and its belief system" (ibid., 222). When the interests of specific denominations are not so self-evident, religious affiliation should play a lesser role.

The existing research supports the foregoing conclusion. Analyzing the decisions issued by state and federal supreme court justices in 1955, Stuart Nagel (1962) found statistically significant differences between

Protestants and Catholics in four out of fifteen categories of cases. In three of the types that fit into a conservative-liberal spectrum, the Catholic judges were more liberal: they were more likely than their Protestant colleagues to rule on behalf of convicted criminals appealing a verdict, government agencies engaged in regulating business practices, and employees seeking compensation for injuries. In divorce cases, however, the Catholic judges exhibited a much higher tendency to rule in favor of the wife—perhaps a reflection of the tradition of Catholic conservatism in family matters. Most of the difference between Catholics and Protestants was associated with partisanship rather than religion, however (Nagel 1961). Skepticism about a religious effect on judicial decisions was supported by Goldman's (1966, 1975) studies of decisions issued by the federal courts of appeal during the 1960s. In only two of the ten areas examined by Goldman did significant Protestant/non-Protestant differences surface, and most of the apparently greater conservatism of Protestant judges could be explained by the high proportion of southerners in the Protestant category. S. Sidney Ulmer (1973) extended this type of social background analysis to the U.S. Supreme Court in examining voting patterns on criminal cases from 1947 to 1956. He concluded that Protestants were more likely than non-Protestants to support the government side against appeals by convicted criminals.

Rather than investigate a range of issues, some scholars have concentrated on one particular area of judicial activity—race relations. The courts were the catalyst for racial change in the southern states, and some observers have thought that religious values could have accounted for the willingness of federal judges to challenge the deeply entrenched system of segregation in the South. The guiding hypothesis has been that those judges who were least immersed in the southern culture of segregation, including those who were not affiliated with the numerically dominant evangelical Protestant churches, would be most inclined to rule on behalf of another out-group. Kenneth Vines (1964), the first to check out this expectation with social scientific methods, examined judicial rulings in nearly three hundred civil rights cases decided in southern circuits from 1954 through 1962. On the basis of decisional patterns, thirty-seven federal district judges were classified as segregationist, moderate, or integrationist. As one might expect, there was a demonstrable difference in rulings associated with religious affiliation. The "orthodox Protestants," a term Vines used for denominations defined here as evangelical, were principally found in either the segregationist (45 percent) or moderate (36 percent) camps, leaving less than 20 percent for the integrationist. At the other extreme, the two Catholic judges were classified as integrationists. That left the middle position for judges who were presumed to be mainline Protestants. They were less likely to be integrationist than Catholics (45 percent) but also less likely to issue rulings in favor of segregation (21 percent).

Despite its conformity to prediction, the Vines study suffered from weaknesses of technique. By using religion without any controls for possibly related factors, he exposed himself to a charge of spurious correlation. Furthermore, because the cases differed from circuit to circuit, he may have, in effect, compared apples with oranges. To remedy those defects and to update the findings, Giles and Walker (1975) examined the problem anew. Rather than use dissimilar cases, they used the same measure in each circuit—racial imbalance in public schools. Because all schools were under court order to implement antisegregation policies, Giles and Walker contended, the measure of racial imbalance remaining in 1970 indicated "the district judge's policy decision in implementing the desegregation mandate at the local level" (ibid., 924). Trying to capture the religious factor, the analysis compared judges from what the authors labeled as "fundamentalist Protestantism" with members of all other religious affiliations. Religion, included as a social background factor in an equation that also contained a measure of the racial climate, the judge's connection to the community, and several characteristics of the school district, was not found to exert a substantial influence on the racial imbalance permitted in the district. Whether these conflicting findings can be laid to different techniques or to a real change cannot be determined; on balance, however, the systematic studies examined in this section do not strongly support the notion of a religious effect in judicial decisions.

If analysis of religion in Congress were similarly dependent solely on statistical studies, negative conclusions about religious effects in that branch might also have been reached. A fuller understanding of the legislative arena was possible because members of Congress were available for interviews that could elicit religious beliefs beyond mere denominational affiliation. Because judges rarely submit to such interviews, it has been difficult to find out if more sensitive measures of religious values might account for behavioral differences. Some judicial biographies have speculated about possible religious influences on particular decisions or even judicial style. Late in 1981, when the Equal Rights Amendment (ERA) to the U.S. Constitution was in the waning days of its unsuccessful ratification period, a federal judge from Idaho issued an adverse ruling that further reduced the amendment's slim chances for passage. Because the judge held a position of authority in the Mormon church, which vehemently opposed the ERA, several critics charged that his ruling improperly reflected his religious values. Then, too, in a psychologically oriented analysis of the great Supreme Court justice Felix Frankfurter, H. N. Hirsch (1981) argued that religion influenced the judge's highly combative and aggressive style. Though the point is too complex to summarize easily, Hirsch argued that Frankfurter, the child of Jewish immigrants from Austria, was caught between the attractiveness of the Protestant establishment that dominated the legal profession and his standing as a conspicuous outsider who was reminded powerfully that he did not fit in. Consequently, he developed a personality and style highly conducive to the role of the outsider. That kind of linkage cannot as yet be subjected to systematic testing, but at least it suggests how religion may contribute to judicial behavior by an indirect path.

The President's Religion

Because laws are not self-executing, the administrative agencies of government play an important part in public policy making. Yet, as little as is known about religion in the legislative and judicial branches, even less seems clear about the executive wing. For the political appointees and career civil servants who staff the executive branch and its agencies, only fragmentary evidence about religious values is available. From time to time, for example, we hear about zealous federal prosecutors whose crusades against pornography are reported to be a function of their intense religiosity.

As the official head of the executive branch and the principal focus of American government, the president has a unique opportunity to affect both the substance and tone of public policy. In this area, as in the others examined in the chapter, scholars have disagreed about the

importance of social background factors relative to the many competing influences brought to bear on presidential decision making. The
specific influence of religion has been even harder to assess because all
but one president have come from Protestant backgrounds, usually the
so-called mainline Protestant tradition of Methodists, Episcopalians,
and Presbyterians. Nonetheless, there is at least suggestive evidence
that religious background may affect a president's approach to politics,
if not the specific policies of a chief executive. This can best be demonstrated by comparing three recent occupants of the White House.

To a degree uncommon in the twentieth century, Jimmy Carter
brought questions of religious values and character to the center of his
political campaigns. A devout Southern Baptist, churchgoer, and
"born-again" Christian who was familiar with the work of modern theologians and experienced in missionary work, Carter was a novel factor in the 1976 presidential campaign (Ribuffo 1989). His candidacy
appeared to hearten evangelical Protestants and worry many mainline
Protestants, Catholics, Jews, and the nonaffiliated. Partly because of
unfamiliarity with the Southern Baptist tradition and partly because of
the presumed association of evangelical Christianity with social conservatism and intolerance, many worried that a deeply religious president would try to enforce his "narrow" moral preferences on the
nation or, fortified by a belief in a personal relationship with God,
would reject compromise and negotiation with those who did not see
the world in the same way. Throughout the campaign, Carter attempted to assure voters that he did not see God's hand in every policy proposed in his platform and that he would not use the law to enforce his
own standards of moral rectitude. Rather than prompting an unshakable faith in the rightness of his own preferences, he argued, his religious values had taught him the need to recognize his own fallibility.
And to those who expressed concern about the Baptist social agenda,
Carter emphasized the Social Gospel tradition of religion as a force for
economic and political reform.

In practice, few observers were able to link Carter's major political
tendencies with his personal religiosity. On church-state issues, for
example, he adhered to the traditional Baptist insistence on a sharp
wall of separation, even refusing to hold worship services in the White
House (Flowers 1983). His religious background showed up, however,
in several ways that might not have been apparent to most observers.

According to one analysis, Carter's personal style—marked by enormous self-discipline, a commitment to hard work, orderliness, and fiscal conservatism—bore the unmistakable traces of Puritanism from which his faith had descended (Mazlish and Diamond 1979, 253). In his insistence that other nations respect human rights, a priority often called a "crusade," Carter might have been exhibiting a "typical" evangelical's missionary tendency. So, too, his controversial pardon of draft evaders appeared to be another carryover of religion into politics (J. Baker 1977). Carter issued not an amnesty, which declares that a person did no wrong, but a pardon, which forgives a wrongdoer. Underlying that distinction is the biblical notion of grace, which offers love and forgiveness to the sinner. On another front, Carter might never have taken such risks to promote peace in the Middle East but for his reverence toward the Holy Land.

Unfortunately, the validity of this analysis is anything but certain. The only other Southern Baptist to hold the presidency before Carter, Harry Truman, exhibited few traits in common with his coreligionist. And some presidents from different religious traditions acted in ways similar to Carter. John Kennedy spoke in missionary terms about the nation's world role. Gerald Ford issued an even more controversial pardon (of former president Richard Nixon). Because each of these men was far removed from Carter's religious background, it is clearly dangerous to draw too firm a conclusion about the impact of theology on politics.

Carter's successor, Ronald Reagan, also described himself as a born-again Christian and argued strongly for the relevance of religion to public policy. But unlike Carter, whose theology treated politics as a calling to establish social justice, Reagan saw a need for government only "to restrain the darker impulses of human nature" (Reagan 1981b). Domestically, government should maintain order so that humanity's goodness and creativity could flourish in social and economic pursuits (J. Thomas 1984). In the international arena, where he identified the Soviet Union as the "focus of evil" in the modern world and the United States as the fount of virtue, President Reagan exemplified the "priestly" strain of civil religion. Critics worried less about this orientation than the possible influence of "Armageddon theology" on the president. This stream of thought, supported by certain Bible passages regarding the apocalypse, envisions global turbulence and possibly nuclear war as heralds of the Second Coming. Reagan was raised in the Disciples of Christ, a denomination whose founder was a leading advocate of this millennial perspective. Would this view make Reagan more willing to authorize the use of violence against American enemies and less willing to exploit opportunities for arms reduction? In practice, there was no evidence that the president's interest in prophecies affected his foreign policies.

In 1992 Americans elected another Southern Baptist to the White House. As a "yuppie from Yale" married to a modern career woman, Bill Clinton certainly seemed less a product of traditional religion than Jimmy Carter. Clinton's policies on moral issues—his support for liberalized abortion and for dropping the military's ban on gays and lesbians—were far removed from the official position of the Southern Baptist Convention. Furthermore, Clinton's "style," epitomized by campaign appearances on MTV and the famous stint as a leather-jacketed saxophone player on late-night television, was worlds away from popular notions about "born-again" Baptists. Yet this portrait of Clinton ignores the deep religious influences said to affect his behavior (Painton 1993; Solomon 1993; Casey 1993). Clinton has long been a committed Southern Baptist, well-versed in the Bible and modern theology, who enjoys choir singing and regularly attends Pentecostal revivals. His speaking style recalls the evangelical sermons heard in his youth. In his political theology, Clinton seems to mix the "social gospel" of progressive Baptists and the social teachings of Catholicism he imbibed from the Jesuits while attending college at Georgetown University. How have these influences marked his presidency? Perhaps the focus on education and health care early in his administration reflects the historic emphasis on these missions by both Baptists and Catholics. A deep respect for individual conscience, a major principle of the Baptist tradition, could account for Clinton's support for abortion and gay rights. This "liberal" strain coexists, however, with conservative tendencies that emphasize traditional values. Consistent with that vision, Clinton supports the death penalty, opposes gay marriages, and criticizes the destructive behavior of some welfare recipients.

The impact of religion on presidential behavior might take several different forms (Monsma 1977). In one such model, closest to the Reagan style, the president serves as the "high priest of American civil religion," calling the nation to righteousness through order and obedience (Calhoun 1993). Alternatively, the personal morality model, expressed to some degree by President Carter, expects the president to express religiosity by living up to Christian moral standards in personal conduct. Yet a third option is for the president to pursue policies "molded by basic Christian principles and insights such as justice, healing, man's purpose as an image-bearer of God, and the sinfulness of human nature." This is not a call to theocracy but an insistence that presidents recognize moral imperatives when they act.

Religious Values and Government Activities

Whatever types of influence religious groups may attempt to wield, is the political system responsive to religious values and appeals? Although it is very difficult to sort out the relative importance of all the factors that influence government decisions in any policy area, there is much evidence linking general patterns of public policy to religious factors.

Because American churches have traditionally given major priority to questions of personal conduct, it should not be at all surprising to find a strong link between religious affiliation and government "morality" policies. In a series of studies tracing policy differences between the states to variations in religious composition, scholars have discovered a strong correlation between the proportion of the population belonging to evangelical Protestant churches and the restrictiveness of state statutes affecting gambling, liquor, and drug use (Fairbanks 1977; Meier 1994). The willingness of local governments to extend antidiscrimination law to homosexuals also varies negatively with the presence of a morally traditional religious population (Wald, Button, and Rienzo 1996; Haeberle 1996). Because evangelical churches have usually regarded these "deviant" activities as inconsistent with Christian orthodoxy, it seems reasonable to conclude that state and local laws have reflected community values. Similarly, the clearly expressed resistance of the Catholic church to artificial birth control and divorce probably explains why in the various states, the strictness of contraception and marriage laws has varied directly with the proportion of Catholics in the population (Fairbanks 1979). Because these relationships have survived the application of several environmental factors that might be supposed to underlay them, it appears that the moral values of a state's dominant religious group are somehow conveyed to lawmakers.

In abortion, a policy area heavily laden with moral overtones, religious groups also appear to have played a decisive role in determining how the Supreme Court's decision of 1973 was implemented. In the period before the Court invalidated most state laws on the subject, the restrictiveness of state regulations was directly related to the concentration of Catholics and evangelical Protestants (Mooney and Lee 1995). Since then, the willingness of states to fund abortions under the Medicaid program has been negatively associated with high concentrations of the same two groups (Meier and McFarlane 1993). The religious composition of a community also seems to affect whether hospitals are willing to perform abortions. According to Susan B. Hansen (1980), the enormous differences in abortion rates across the American states in 1976 depended largely on the availability of hospitals willing to offer abortion services. The restrictiveness of hospital policy, in turn, depended on a number of factors, including the state's religious composition. The percentage of Mormons in the population had a negative impact on community tolerance for abortion (as measured by the votes of the states' legislative delegation) and a direct depressive effect on the rate of abortion. Similarly, the greater the Catholic share of the state population, the lower the community support for abortion and the more restricted the availability of facilities offering abortion. In a national survey of hospital administrators in 1979, John R. Bond and Charles A. Johnson (1982) found that individual hospitals were influenced by the religious climate. Along with other factors, high rates of church membership promoted restrictive hospital abortion policy.

Given that churches have often spoken out forcefully on matters of personal conduct, it should not be surprising to discover a correlation between legal restrictions on unorthodox activities and religious geography. But studies of the American states have supplied much evidence that religious composition is related to policy patterns that do not have such an obvious link to theological values. Most such studies have built on the hypothesis that religion contributes in a major degree to the assumptions, values, and habits that may define policy preferences over a wide range of public issues.

In the area of race relations, for example, Fenton and Vines (1967) argued that the level of voter registration of Louisiana blacks depended largely on the religious values of the politically dominant whites in the community. More than a decade after the Supreme Court struck down state laws excluding African Americans from voting in public elections, local communities had found ways to keep more than two-thirds of black adults off the electoral registers. As a rule, the level of African American registration in Louisiana was much higher in the predominantly Catholic parishes (counties) of the southern area of the state than in the northern area, where Protestant groups predominated. Finding that this difference held up in the face of checks for the influence of various nonreligious social, political, and cultural factors, the investigators pointed to differences in social attitudes between Catholics and Protestants:

Permissive attitudes toward Negro registration in French-Catholic parishes seem expressive of the basic value that the Negro is spiritually equal in a Catholic society. Such a view of man's relation to man, a scheme of elementary justice implicit in a Catholic society, some Catholics maintain, is sustained by traditional Catholic theology and actively promoted by the Church in Louisiana. There is little evidence in the Protestant parishes of cultural values assigning the Negro a spiritually equal place in the community or of activity by the church itself toward these values. (ibid., 176)

In addition to possessing a doctrinal basis for racial tolerance, the Catholic church also had institutional and social reasons to discourage ill treatment of African Americans. As a universal church that crosses racial and ethnic boundaries, Catholicism itself would be threatened if all the faithful were not treated on equal terms. Moreover, because the Catholic church was one of the few integrated institutions in the South, its members were given the opportunity to dispel their prejudices. In contrast, the segregated white Protestant churches of northern Louisiana catered to the segregationist values of their members and did little to promote the contact between races that might have fostered mutual tolerance.

Religion may affect an even broader range of policies through its influence on attitudes toward the role of government in society. In chapter 3, I noted that one way religion might shape American political behavior is by its general effect on the national political culture. Along the same lines, a leading authority on American federalism has suggested that the religious and ethnic groups that settled the various American states were the carriers of particular cultural values that have left a mark on contemporary state politics and policy. According to

Daniel Elazar, migrating groups subscribed to different views about the nature and purpose of government, the role of politics in society, and other politically relevant beliefs. For example, he noted the emphasis in Puritan thought on using the power of the state to create a holy commonwealth on earth. In the parts of the country settled by Puritans, their successors, and immigrants with similar religious traditions, this conception of politics as a calling has survived in a highly moralistic approach to politics:

Politics, to the moralistic political culture, is considered one of the great activities of humanity in its search for the good society—a struggle for power, it is true, but also an effort to exercise power for the betterment of the commonwealth. Consequently, in the moralistic political culture both the general public and politicians conceive of politics as a public activity centered on some notion of the public good and properly devoted to the advancement of the public interest. Good government, then, is measured by the degree to which it promotes the public good and in terms of the honesty, selflessness, and commitment to the public welfare of those who govern. (Elazar 1984, 117)

This approach, like those of the individualistic and traditionalistic cultures elsewhere, dictates a particular configuration of values that should affect the scope, nature, and style of political practice. Noting that religious groups with such distinctive political conceptions clustered in different parts of the country, Elazar predicted a correlation between state policy orientations and ethnoreligious settlement patterns.

Although it was developed principally to account for contemporary policy differences, Elazar's theory has been strikingly confirmed by studies of political conflict in the nineteenth-century United States (Hammond 1979; Kleppner 1979). Abolition, Prohibition, and a host of other social reforms were fired by the enthusiasm and crusading mentality of a moralistic culture and resisted on the basis of values that sound remarkably like Elazar's description of the traditionalist culture. What is more, according to the influential ethnocultural school of American history, the basic groupings of voters were defined largely by the type of religious values that Elazar identified as the core of differing political cultures. Whatever its historical value, Elazar's assertion about the policy impact of religiously based value systems has inspired several research projects on contemporary state-level variations in public policy. Although the specific predictions have not always been confirmed, several scholars have detected affinities between the concentration of certain religious groups and particular sets of policies enacted by the states.

Based on statistics of church membership, Hutcheson and Taylor (1973) classified American states in terms of the proportion of the population affiliated with fundamentalist denominations—defined in the study as religious groups who believe the Bible is the literal word of God. The groups in Hutcheson and Taylor's "fundamentalist" category, essentially denominations classified as evangelical Protestant, have been identified by Elazar (1984, 130–131) as carriers of the "traditionalistic" political culture. Precisely as would be expected from a culture that wants government to play a "conservative and custodial" role (ibid., 119), the fundamentalist share of the population was associated with a high teacher-pupil ratio in public schools and a low level of state taxation. Using a similar technique, Charles Johnson (1976) and David Morgan and Sheilah Watson (1991) reported that the concentration of religious groups with a moralistic orientation correlated strongly with high levels of spending for social welfare programs but that the proportion of traditionalistic denominations depressed governmental efforts in that area. Klingman and Lammers (1984) confirmed that conclusion with a different approach. The states were ranked on a scale of "general policy liberalism," in which high scores identified a willingness to utilize government power on behalf of disadvantaged groups. The scale included such diverse components as state efforts to combat racial discrimination, spending for child welfare and social services, ratification of the Equal Rights Amendment, and the level of consumer protection efforts. Although no direct measure of religious concentration was included in the long list of factors tested as possible influences on policy liberalism, the analysis did rank each state by the moralism of its political culture. As it happens, the measure of state political culture turned out to be one of the two strongest predictors of a state's ranking vis-à-vis policy liberalism. The states with the most moralistic political cultures were the most likely to adopt innovative policies designed to improve the status of disadvantaged groups.

In one of the most imaginative studies of its kind, Michael Johnston (1983) managed to demonstrate a connection between religious geography and what Elazar described as the "moralistic approach" to politics. As an expert on political corruption, he wanted to test an explanation for what appears to be very different levels of toleration for illegal acts by public officials. In some communities, official misconduct is accepted as a fact of life, something as inevitable as bad weather; other communities react to governmental malfeasance with shock and horror, deploying the full resources of the law to combat it. On the assumption that communities with high concentrations of moralistic denominations would be especially averse to such misconduct, he included religious affiliation in a model to explain the rate of conviction for public officials. As it did in the other studies conducted in Elazar's framework, the variable that tapped the moralism of political culture exerted a strong influence in the predicted manner. The higher the concentration of denominations that Elazar identified as carriers of a moralistic outlook on politics, the greater the number of successful prosecutions for official lawbreaking.

On the basis of this evidence, it appears that political culture—which Elazar traced specifically to the beliefs and historical experience of religious denominations—affects not only the content of state policy but its style as well. This conclusion could be subjected to the same criticism about spurious relationships that was raised in the discussion of religion as mass political behavior. Surely, a state's level of spending, its social programs, and its record of prosecution for corruption and other actions depend, for the most part, on its governmental capacity and level of economic development. In each of the studies cited above, that possibility was taken into account by the inclusion of variables to represent the social and economic status of the areas under comparison. Although the precise measures differed somewhat, the application of controls for economic development did not eliminate the linkage between religious groups and policy patterns. Religion, which according to the previous chapters has left its mark on American political values, mass political behavior, and the law, apparently has also contributed to the different configurations of public policy pursued by the states.

Limitations on Religious Influence

The influence of a particular religious group in a particular policy area represents only one force in the struggle to shape government action. Because of the complexity of public policy making in the United

States, it is important to appreciate how religion and moral influences compete with other factors for an impact on decisions. The need for a balanced appraisal can best be conveyed through a case study of American policy in the Middle East. Though frequently cited to illustrate the potential impact of religious considerations, this case also points to conditions that limit religious influence on public policy.

Since the state of Israel was founded in 1948, the United States has consistently supported it with vigorous diplomatic action, military aid, and significant amounts of economic assistance. That support has frequently been attributed to a pair of religious factors—namely the Jewish lobby in the United States and the moralistic strain in U.S. foreign policy. American Jews have used their considerable political resources—voting strength, organizational ties, campaign contributions, access to decision makers, media influence—to mount an energetic campaign on behalf of Israeli interests. The campaign has succeeded because a pro-Israel position suits the moralistic style of American foreign policy. Formed in the shadow of the Holocaust, besieged by hostile neighbors, and holding steadfastly to the same democratic political values as the United States, the new state drew on a powerful current of goodwill in postwar American opinion. Zionism appealed especially strongly to American Christians. Liberal Protestants admired Israel for its social and ethical values; conservative Protestants were heartened by Israeli military successes that seemed to confirm biblical prophecies.[10] Responding to a Soviet leader who asked why America was pledged to Israel, Lyndon Johnson said, simply, "We think it's right" (Glick 1982, 106).

Yet it is crucial to put U.S. policy toward Israel into a broader context. A critical element in U.S. support for Israel has been national interest. Reviewing President Harry S. Truman's initial commitment to Israel, Ganin (1979) concluded that the chief motivations were fear of disorder and bloodshed in Palestine, competition with the Soviet Union for Middle East influence, and Truman's desire to assert his primacy over the U.S. State Department. Successive administrations maintained and expanded the U.S. commitment to Israel because it served their overriding foreign policy objectives (Spiegel 1985). The Carter administration, preoccupied with maintaining American access to Middle East oil supplies, valued Israel because it was located near the crucial transportation lanes for petroleum exports. Concerned above all else to contain the Soviets, the Reagan administration saw great benefits in cooperating with Israel, which had the military might to deter Soviet proxies in the region. With the end of the cold war, the Bush administration appeared to assign lower priority to the U.S.-Israeli alliance, refusing to underwrite loans to Israel in protest against Israeli settlements on land claimed by Palestinians. The Clinton administration subsequently threw its weight behind a treaty returning some of those lands to the Arab inhabitants. Hence, although religious factors help to explain the pro-Israel thrust of U.S. Middle East policy, most authorities have given precedence to the United States' overriding strategic objectives and the perceptions of decision makers. When those judgments coincide with the wishes of the Israeli lobby in Washington, the policies invariably carry the day. But that same lobby, despite its reputation of invincibility, loses three-fourths of the battles when its policies conflict with the wishes of the chief executive (Bard 1991; D. Goldberg 1990).

The Israeli case, usually cited to illustrate domestic influence on U.S. foreign policy, shows how many forces have to fall into place to produce a religious impact. Consider as a more typical case the conspicuous failure of Irish Catholics in the United States to build similar levels of American support for a united Ireland (Healy 1989). No doubt, this failure reflects the complex issues at stake in the conflict between the Protestants and Catholics of Northern Ireland. These conditions make it harder to claim that unswerving support for the Catholic minority is consistent with American national interest or the moralistic strain in U.S. foreign policy. Even if that case could be made to the American public, the potency of lobbying by Irish Catholics would be diminished because Irish nationalism is much less salient for American Catholics than is the cause of Israel for American Jews. Since the Six-Day War, Jews have capitalized on the favorable circumstances mentioned above because the state of Israel is perceived as central to their self-preservation (Medding 1989), an important source of "psychological, ethnic, and religious pride" (Glick 1982, 126), and an expression of Jewish social values. By contrast, when "the Troubles" broke out in Ulster in 1968, "the majority of Irish Americans remained apathetic and largely uninterested in Northern Ireland" (Wilson 1995, x). Moreover, were American Catholics to mobilize aggressively on behalf of their brethren in Northern Ireland, they would face intense opposition from

American Protestants who are equally committed to the cause of their coreligionists in Ulster. The American Jewish community has not faced domestic opposition that can match its political sophistication and unity. To the extent that religion has contributed to the United States' pro-Israel policy, then, it has depended on a rare combination of favorable circumstances.

Compared to the secular interests with whom they compete for influence, the religious groups that lobby in Washington have minimal budgets, small staffs, and limited government experience (Hertzke 1988, 70–79; Zwier 1988). This lack of resources can be offset somewhat by the pursuit of a modest strategy that includes, among other things, attempting to influence the early stages of legislation through contacts with key officials and developing expertise and effective communication skills (P. Weber and Stanley 1984). With their highly positive images and substantial social prestige, the religious lobbies have enjoyed some success, particularly in securing religious liberty or other concerns where they supported narrow goals. But when the pursuit of broad goals like social justice or world peace puts them in head-to-head competition with entrenched secular lobbies fortified by ample resources, the religious lobbyists seldom claim policy victories.

Even if they were better endowed with material resources, the religious interest groups would still face the inherent challenge of applying moral standards to items on the public agenda. According to Sen. Paul Simon (D-Ill.), "Practical dilemmas that real-life politicians face do not fit into easily wrapped packages to which moral labels can be attached"(1984, 131). As an example, Simon cites a 1977 congressional debate on a bill to renew a federal program that sent American agricultural products to countries facing food shortages (ibid., 22–23). When a representative introduced an amendment to prohibit the purchase of tobacco for export under the program, Simon faced a moral dilemma. Because tobacco was a significant crop in nearly a hundred House districts, the amendment might endanger support for the program, resulting possibly in the "clearly immoral" denial of food to starving people. Yet without the amendment, the government would spend money that could buy food for 900,000 hungry people on a product with lethal consequences for public health. As Simon asked rhetorically, "What could be a clearer moral issue?" The testimony of other legislators and administrators amplified Simon's conclusion that policy makers normally confront choices between conflicting moral norms, rather than simply between good and evil (J. Anderson 1970; Haughey 1979).

Religious Activism in Politics: Costs and Benefits

From the evidence presented in this chapter, it seems clear that religion can influence political decision making, particularly when issues are narrowly defined, but that it is rarely decisive. Aside from competing interests, the major limits on religious impact are divisions of opinion within and among religious groups and the inherent confusion of the policy-making process.

The decision to enter the political arena, whether taken by a religious group of its own volition or virtually commanded by external authorities, may impose a significant cost. Political conflict is characterized by disagreement, strife, and competition. In associating itself with such a process—or being seen as part of it—the church could lose its reputation as a place apart. Yet, paradoxically, abstention from politics may also diminish the church's stature. If members of the community perceive religious values as relevant to a political issue or under threat from some external actor, they may lose faith in a church that stands idly by. Because religious values are so all-encompassing and couched in a universal language, indifference is not really an option.

At the level where most people experience religion—the individual congregation—religious communities cope with these conflicting pressures in different ways. A survey of congregations in Hartford, Connecticut, revealed four basic positions regarding community life (Roozen, McKinney, and Carroll 1984). "Civic" churches, probably the overwhelming majority of American congregations, generally take a positive view of existing social structures and tend to avoid political confrontation. If members participate in public life, something the church endorses as a worthy activity, they do so as individuals. At the other extreme, "activist" churches define their mission as fighting the injustices said to prevail in contemporary society. All members of the congregation are expected to participate in this endeavor, and the church does not shy away from controversy or conflict. For all their differences, both civic and activist churches tend to regard their communities as a model for human society, consider nearly all religious groups as worthy of respect, and try to educate members about social issues. What of "otherworldly" churches that see salvation as achieved not through social action but through personal rectitude and regard the church's only legitimate task as saving souls? Some churches in this category adopt a "sanctuary" model that sees the congregation as a place of refuge, sheltering members from the immorality of the larger society. Beyond paying taxes, voting, and obeying the law, the member has no political obligations. Other churches embrace an "evangelistic" orientation and seek to share the true faith with others. Only public actions consistent with this mission—such as proselytizing in doorways and running crusades—are worthy of support. Members of the latter two types of churches will occasionally mobilize to oppose sinful behavior, but their political involvement is sporadic. The position of a congregation on this matrix of choices is the product of its environment, the traits of members, and its religious codes and doctrines.

Within very broad limits, the constitutional system of the United States guarantees a wide range of political expression to religious groups. The political system offers numerous avenues for exploiting these rights. The doctrines and interests of religious organizations may encourage them to take advantage of opportunities for political involvement. We shall postpone until the final chapter a consideration of whether a religious presence enhances or diminishes the quality of public life. In understanding why religious groups intervene on particular issues and which positions they embrace, it is necessary to understand the interplay between public opinion and religious commitment. We will now examine how the differences among religious traditions affect mass attitudes on policy and behavior in the voting booth.

NOTES

1. "Substance, Tactics of Tax Revision Cause Conflict Among Administration Hard-Liners, Pragmatists," *Wall Street Journal,* 8 October 1985, 64.

2. "Catholic Bishops Hire Firm to Market Abortion Attack," *New York Times,* 6 April 1990, 10A.

3. "Defense Fund Set Up for Bombing Suspects," *Gainesville Sun,* 19 March 1985, 11A.

4. Under IRS regulations, a nonprofit organization can generally maintain tax-exempt status so long as less than 20 percent of its budget is used to influence the decisions of public authorities (Davis 1991).

5. "Lawmakers Debate Three Critical Issues," *Gainesville Sun*, 21 April 1985.

6. "Candidates' Poll, General Election, 1984," *Gainesville Sun*, 28 October 1984.

7. Before jumping to the conclusion that voters are bigoted and irrational in favoring a candidate of the same religion just because of the common tie of church membership, consider another possibility. Because religion is an important element in influencing the social system, persons from the same religious community may share similar experiences and develop similar views about the issues of the day. These features, not the mere fact of common religious affiliation, can make a candidate attractive to a voter. It is worth keeping in mind that the studies cited on this subject (except for Pomper) used hypothetical candidates in fictitious races; hence, there were few cues other than ethnicity or religion to guide electoral choice. As Donald Granberg (1985a) demonstrated with both survey and experimental data, voters who lack information about a candidate's position on an issue—particularly an issue with religious implications—may infer a position by using religious affiliation as a cue.

8. Using the issue of the Equal Rights Amendment, O. Kendall White Jr. (1984) has shown that the Mormon system for reaching judgments on public issues also follows a very centralized pattern.

9. See the decree in "Extra Synodal Legislation," *Southern Nebraska Register*, 22 March 1996 (available in electronic form at http://www.csn.net/advent/misc/lincoln2.htm). The Lincoln case was exceptional as the bishops have worked harder of late to involve the laity in formulating church positions on public issues.

10. For those Christians who were not moved by either appeal, it might not have escaped notice that the probable alternative to a Jewish state was increased migration of Jewish refugees to the United States.

6. The Religious Dimension of American Political Behavior

> By the side of every religion is to be found a political opinion, which is connected with it by affinity. If the human mind be left to follow its own bent, it will regulate the temporal and spiritual institutions of society in a uniform manner, and man will endeavor . . . to harmonize earth with heaven.
> —Alexis de Tocqueville

Politics is the process by which a nation settles differences and decides national policy. When religious leaders enter this process, pressing for laws that conform to their views of morality and justice, it suggests that different religious traditions promote distinct political priorities. To what extent are Americans politically divided along religious lines? Individuals hold opinions and cast votes, but they do so subject to the tug of group tradition and influence. Global studies have revealed that religion, in concert with such factors as social class, race, ethnicity, and region, has continued to exert a major influence on a variety of political orientations (Lijphart 1971; Rose and Urwin 1969). After reviewing numerous studies of voting patterns in different countries, one leading expert on mass political attitudes was forced to conclude that "religious differentiation intrudes on partisan political alignments in [an] unexpectedly powerful degree wherever it conceivably can" (Converse 1974, 734). The use of the word *unexpectedly* reveals the bias of modern observers surprised that political differences are tied to "primordial" religious cleavages.

In recognition of the importance of religion in contemporary political loyalties, this chapter describes how religious groups agree or disagree on a variety of political orientations and explains major differences among groups by reference to creedal, institutional, and social/cultural characteristics. Of course, American political attitudes

169

bear the imprint of many influences. This chapter will not argue either that other group loyalties are absent from the public agenda or that religion intrudes on every political issue of importance. Rather, by charting the contours of denominational differences and evaluating explanations for the link between religious group membership and mass political behavior, it will explore the religious roots of some contemporary political controversies.

Patterns of Religious Affiliation

A valuable perspective on the contemporary relationship between religion and political attitudes in the United States can be gained through the semiannual public opinion surveys conducted by the Center for Political Studies at the University of Michigan. Known as the American National Election Studies (ANES), these periodic interviews with representative national samples of the adult population contain a broad range of data about social and political attitudes. Because the surveys also identify the religious preferences of the participants, they make it possible to compare religious groups with one another. In the following analysis, we rely on the surveys conducted during the 1992 presidential campaign.[1]

The staggering diversity of American religious identity and the fluidity of individual loyalties make it impossible to develop any classification system that fully represents all varieties of religious expression. Even if we could devise such a system, the practical limits of public opinion research would restrict our capacity to implement it. In a survey that took more than a full year of fieldwork and over 113,000 interviews—many times the normal amount of survey effort—there were simply too few members of numerous religious minorities for reliable subgroup analysis (Kosmin and Lachman 1993, 15–17). That limitation applies even more severely to the polls used for this chapter. Although the 2,500 interviews typically conducted by the ANES provide an accurate overview of the general population and enable us to explore the behavior of major religious groups, we are forced to overlook a number of interesting religious tendencies. There were insufficient numbers of people outside the Judeo-Christian tradition—Muslims, Hindus, Buddhists, Native Americans, as well as the smorgasbord of "New Age" belief systems—to include them in the analysis.

Certain groups that identify with the Christian tradition but depart in significant ways from traditional Christian theology—Mormons, Unitarians, Christian Scientists—were also excluded because too few of them turned up in the ANES random national samples. Persons who call themselves humanists, agnostics, atheists, and freethinkers might differ from one another politically, but we are forced to lump them together to obtain enough nonreligious people for statistical analysis. By virtue of their marginal status in a society that overwhelmingly embraces Judeo-Christian faiths, members of these various excluded groups have often spearheaded the legal battles over religion that were chronicled in chapter 4. While it is unfortunate to lose them for purposes of analysis, the groups remaining in the analysis compose more than 95 percent of the adult population and the vast majority of religious faiths subscribed to by Americans.

These exclusions still leave us the task of reducing the hundreds of religious *denominations*—formal associations of churches with common beliefs and customs—into a more manageable set of religious *traditions*, a term for families of denominations with common histories, similar belief systems, and distinctive racial and ethnic compositions (Kellstedt and Green 1993). Following the lead of this research, I have subdivided the population into six religious categories. The initial distinction between Protestants, Catholics, and Jews, the starting point for any such classification, hardly begins to cover the variety of organized religious expression in the United States (Roof and McKinney 1987). *Roman Catholics* and *Jews* form distinctive religious and political communities, so their separation from Protestants should come as no surprise. In a society that values religion, those who swim against the tide by disclaiming a religious identity might also exhibit unconventional behavior in the political realm. We thus carved out a separate category for *seculars,* people who neither adopt any religious label nor have any involvement with organized religion. Taken together, the three groups outside Protestantism compose approximately 40 percent of the ANES sample.

To those accustomed to thinking of Protestantism as a unified faith with minor denominational differences—"sixty sauces with one flavor" in the sarcastic phrase of a Frenchman—it will be surprising to find the Protestant majority apportioned among three distinct camps. I have carved out a separate category for *African American Protestants*. By virtue of its historical situation, social role, and organizational independence, black Protestantism requires separate treatment. For the remaining Protestants—almost half the adult population—the principal dividing line runs between the *mainline* and *evangelical* camps. Mainline and evangelical Protestants differ in theology, styles of worship, church governance, and views about the role of religion in society. R. Stephen Warner (1988, chap. 2) argues that this "two-party system" is animated primarily by different understandings of Jesus. Mainline groups regard him predominantly "as a moral teacher who told disciples that they could best honor him by helping those in need," while evangelicals treat Jesus principally "as one who offers [personal] salvation to anyone who confesses his name" (ibid., 33–34). This polarization has led to important variations in religious and social practice. Stressing Jesus' role as a prophet of social justice, the mainline tradition sanctifies altruism and regards selfishness as the cardinal sin. In this tradition, which extends membership to all and understands religious duty in terms of sharing abundance, the Bible is treated as a book with deep truths that have to be discerned amidst myth and archaic stories. Consistent with their view of Jesus as personal savior, evangelicals "are obligated above all to share their creed" by bringing others to salvation through a personal embrace of God. The church, a limited community open to those who have attained salvation, sees its principal task as sustaining and extending belief. "Because the Bible is the source of revelation about Jesus," Stephen Warner explains (1988, 34), evangelicals treasure it and credit even its implausible stories. Unlike mainline Protestants who accept many different sources of religious truth, the evangelicals assign religious authority to the Bible alone.

The gap between these two perspectives was captured nicely by two *Newsweek* readers who responded on April 29, 1996, to an Easter-time cover story about the Resurrection of Jesus. In language that no evangelical would ever use, one reader dismissed the debate over whether there was a bodily resurrection: "If he was not the Son of God, then Jesus certainly was the greatest social reformer ever to walk the earth. . . . In the end, it doesn't really matter what happened after he died. It is enough to know that his life, not his death, altered the course of history." But to another reader, steeped in the evangelical worldview about the Risen Christ, any "attempt to reduce the Son of God to social reformer should be labeled for what it is—blasphemy."

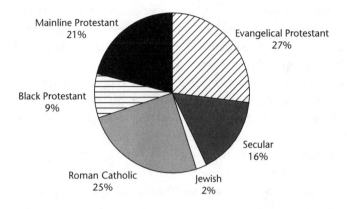

Figure 6.1 Religious Traditions (Source: Calculated by the author from the 1992 American National Election Study, Center for Political Studies)

Applying these subtle and complex outlooks to individuals who participate in attitude surveys is a daunting task.[2] In practice, the evangelical/mainline cleavage often runs through denominations and churches. Other Protestants, particularly in the African American denominations, manage to combine the evangelical emphasis on salvation with the mainline commitment to social action. To further confuse the picture, some Catholics have adopted aspects of the evangelical approach. Nonetheless, there is general consensus among scholars that the evangelical label should be reserved for white Protestants who share core beliefs in the unique authority of the Bible, the divinity of Jesus, and the relevance of his life, death, and resurrection to salvation of the soul (Hunter 1983, 7). Such views are widespread among Protestants variously described as conservative, traditional, fundamentalist, pentecostal, holiness, charismatic, free church, adventist, and reformed. Most evangelicals may be found among Baptists and the southern wings of Methodists and Presbyterians. By contrast, the "mainline" adjective is sometimes used synonymously with labels such as liberal, moderate, historic, and mainstream. As such, it encompasses most Congregationalists, Methodists, Presbyterians, Episcopalians, and Lutherans. We have followed this denominational strategy in assigning white Protestants to either the evangelical or mainline category.[3]

Figure 6.1 shows the distribution of the survey participants among the six basic religious categories. Even after excluding some of the smaller religious groups that add variety to the mix of religious commitment, the size of the slices confirms the extent of religious pluralism in the United States. No single religious group comes close to claiming a majority of the population; and were the groups to be subdivided to reflect their internal diversity on issues of theology, worship, and church organization, the religious fragmentation would be reinforced. Nonetheless, three groups together account for almost three-fourths of the respondents—evangelical Protestants (the single largest religious tradition), Roman Catholics (by far the single largest denomination), and mainline Protestants. The remainder of the adult population is divided among African American Protestants (9 percent of the total), the seculars who claimed no religious attachment (16 percent), and Jews (2 percent).

Previous research has identified some basic political tendencies of these religious groups. American Jews, like their coreligionists in other countries, have long been identified with left-wing political causes (Fuchs 1956; Guysenir 1958; Liebman 1979; Rischin 1962). Black Protestants have usually supported the same liberal policies and candidates as Jews. Since the 1960s, some commentators have professed to see (and others have hoped for) a movement toward more conservative positions in both groups and the uncoupling of their political alliance. Even with these purported changes, most experts still find African American Protestants and Jews to the left of the political spectrum (A. Fisher 1979). Although seculars have not been subject to much research, one clue about their general direction in politics has been the finding that such people tend to be young, mobile, well-educated, and affluent, and to live in urban or metropolitan areas (Edmondson 1995). Because such characteristics are usually associated with unconventional thinking, it has been thought that the nonaffiliated tend to share the liberal political outlook of Jews and African American Protestants.

The white mainline Protestants have been strongly affected by the political and social traumas of recent years. Historically associated with the Republican party and conservative positions on many issues (Berelson, Lazarsfeld, and McPhee 1954; Lazarsfeld, Berelson, and Gaudet 1948; Lenski 1963), the mainline Protestants have been faced with growing liberal sentiment from clergy and denominational leaders (Hadden 1969; Quinley 1974). Conversely, the evangelicals have been encouraged to move in a conservative direction by some of their most vocal pastors. It cannot be assumed that ordinary members of these camps shifted in accordance with their leaders. Many mainline Protestants have strongly resisted the liberalizing tendencies emanating from the pulpit and church officials. And recent reports of evangelical leaders urging their flocks to embrace conservative political causes have diverted public attention from other evangelical voices calling for social justice and world peace through cooperative disarmament (Fowler 1982). The opinion data will reveal how mainline and evangelical white Protestants have responded to these conflicting messages.

Like Jews and African American Protestants, Catholics coalesced around the Democratic party in the 1930s; the Catholic commitment to the party was reinforced in 1960 when the Democrats conferred their presidential nomination on a Catholic candidate (Converse 1966; Scoble and Epstein 1964; Greer 1961; Fenton 1960; Baggaley 1962). Some observers have doubted the depth of this commitment, arguing that attachment to the more liberal political party was a transient stage, reflecting the immigrant and working-class background of Catholics. Under conditions of economic parity with Protestants, it has been suggested, Catholics will embrace the political conservatism that appears to be a more natural outgrowth of church doctrine (Phillips 1969, 140–175; Lipset 1964; Crosby 1978; Whyte 1981). Although many Catholics have moved into the economic mainstream and the Republicans have courted them aggressively (using the abortion controversy and other issues), it remains open to debate whether the Catholic masses have moved to the right side of the political spectrum (Hanna 1979; Fee 1976; Greeley 1977). Except on the issue of abortion, members of the Catholic religious elite—priests, bishops, and lay leaders—appear to have moved in just the opposite direction (Hanna 1984).

Expectations about religious-group patterns do not always distinguish among different political issues. It is quite possible for a group to stand out as relatively conservative on one policy but to adopt a much more liberal position on another. To take account of this possibility, I look at three broad types of political disposition. The first set relates to political identity: preference for a political party, choice of presidential candidates, and liberal versus conservative self-image. The second probes preferences on a range of public issues that have long been central to American political debate. The third taps attitudes toward sev-

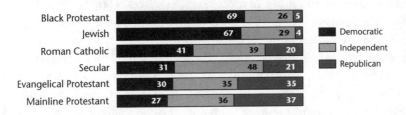

Figure 6.2 Political Partisanship by Religious Group, in percentages
(Source: Calculated by the author from the 1992 American National Election Study,
Center for Political Studies)

eral political issues of more recent vintage—including the "moral" or
"social" issues involving behavior that challenges traditional religious
teaching. Once the groups have been assessed on these three broad
dimensions, it will be possible to determine whether religious groups
adopt a consistent political standard or vary from one domain to the
next.

Political Identity

The most basic component of political identity is preference for a
political party. Despite a decline of formal party membership, a rise in
the proportion of citizens declaring themselves independent of the parties, and a greater willingness to cross party lines in voting, most
Americans still classify themselves, in greater or lesser degree, as supporters of one or the other major political party. The selection of a particular partisan label (including "independent") remains a useful predictor of basic political attitudes, electoral choice, and a wide array of
related attitudes and forms of behavior. Though finer distinctions are
possible, I have divided the ANES participants simply into Democrats
(36 percent), Republicans (26 percent), and independents (38 percent).[4] The partisan breakdown within each of the religious groups is
shown in figure 6.2.

Pronounced differences among religious groups in patterns of partisan allegiance were apparent. The two most strongly Democratic
groups—the only groups giving that party a clear majority—were
African American Protestants and Jews. At the other extreme, the
mainline and evangelical Protestants were the only groups with a plu-

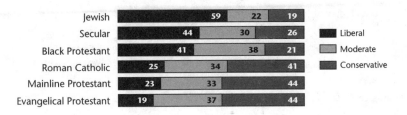

Figure 6.3 Ideology by Religious Group, in percentages (Source: Calculated by the author from the 1992 American National Election Study, Center for Political Studies)

rality of Republican identifiers. Of the remaining two groups, Catholics were twice as likely to be Democrats or independents as Republicans, and the seculars turned out to be predominantly independent in politics as well.

Another important element of political identity, ideological self-image, can be measured by asking individuals to characterize their political views on a scale from "liberal" to "conservative," with "moderate" as the neutral midpoint. Ideology is related to partisan loyalty but the fit is loose (see fig. 6.3). We find that Jewish respondents, who were overwhelmingly Democratic, were also the most willing of the six groups to embrace the liberal label. In fact, Jews were the only group with a majority in the liberal column. Evangelical and mainline Protestants, true to their strong Republican orientation, similarly were much more prone to be conservatives than liberals. For the other three groups, there was considerable slippage between partisanship and ideology. Despite their clear preference for the Democrats over the Republicans, only about 40 percent of African American Protestants and just 25 percent of Roman Catholics selected the "liberal" label. The seculars, who were only slightly more Democratic than both groups of white Protestants, were dramatically more likely than those groups to define themselves as liberal. These patterns should warn against inferring policy preferences solely from partisan loyalties. Many Catholics who embrace the Democratic label consider themselves conservative and the seculars, despite their political independence, incline heavily to a liberal self-image.

Presidential elections give citizens an opportunity to act on their more abstract political leanings. When asked whom they favored for

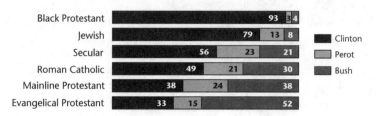

Figure 6.4 Presidential Preference in 1992 by Religious Group, in percentages (Source: Calculated by the author from the 1992 American National Election Study, Center for Political Studies)

the presidency in the 1992 ANES, 48 percent of respondents indicated a preference for Bill Clinton, 34 percent for George Bush, and 19 percent for Ross Perot.[5] Jews and African American Protestants gave virtually all their support to the Democratic nominee, far exceeding the overall level of Clinton support, while evangelical Protestants gave similarly lopsided support to the GOP candidate (see fig. 6.4). Roman Catholics mirrored the national vote distribution with a clear preference for Clinton over Bush, and about one-fifth endorsing Perot's independent candidacy. True to their independent streak, almost one-fourth of the seculars supported Perot. Among seculars who chose between the two major party candidates, Clinton did much better than Bush. Mainline Protestants were very closely split between Clinton and Bush, with a sizable fraction opting for Perot. There is no doubt that the circumstances of 1992—dissatisfaction with George Bush and the availability of Ross Perot as an independent—substantially altered the normal Democratic-Republican balance among some groups. Although Jews and African American Protestants were disproportionately Democratic and evangelical Protestants overwhelmingly Republican in both 1988 and 1992, the other three groups were less consistent from one election to the next. In 1988 mainline Protestants had been just as heavily Republican as their evangelical counterparts, and both Catholics and seculars preferred Bush over his opponent by much narrower margins than white Protestants. The 1992 results suggest that the Perot candidacy was a magnet for normally Republican Catholics, mainline Protestants, and seculars.

Looking over the three measures of basic political identity, then, African American Protestants and Jews were the most consistent supporters of what has been described as the left side of the political spec-trum—a Democratic partisan identification, self-definition as liberals, and preference for Democratic presidential nominees. The two groups of white Protestants had some striking similarities that distinguish them jointly from Jews and African American Protestants. Evangelical and mainline Protestants were much more prone to define themselves as Republicans and conservatives. In 1992, however, the two groups parted company; mainline Protestants barely preferred the Democratic nominee while the majority of evangelicals supported the Republican candidate. Apart from this deviation, the two groups of white Protestants appear to be firmly identified with the right wing. That leaves two groups with profiles intermediate between the left- and right-wing camps. Seculars were similar to Jews in their ideological identification but much more likely to support Republican presidential candidates and to define themselves as political independents. Roman Catholics had a strong affinity for the Democrats in terms of both par-tisan identification and presidential preference in 1992 but were much less liberal than the Jews and African American Protestants with whom they shared a Democratic orientation.

Political Issues

The traits of partisanship, ideology, and vote choice are broad dispo-sitions that may or may not guide positions on more specific political issues. To get a better sense of the politics of the six major religious groups, this section explores a range of policy areas. Using both the ANES and other studies, we can determine whether the group differ-ences observed on party and ideology also extend to questions about the role of government, public spending, civil rights, and so forth.

Since the 1930s the domestic policy debate in America has been dominated by disagreement about the role of government. Until 1994, when Americans elected a Republican Congress pledged to reduce the scope of government, the advocates of an active government had usu-ally managed to guide public policy. Thus the question of government's scope and effort is the logical starting place to study religious group attitudes on public issues. The American National Election Study inquires directly about this principle in two ways. First, the respon-dents were asked to choose between maintaining or expanding gov-

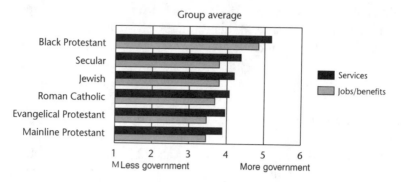

Figure 6.5 Support for Government Activity by Religious Group (Source: Calculated by the author from the 1992 American National Election Study, Center for Political Studies)

ernment services "even if it means an increase in spending" and cutting the level of government spending by providing fewer services "even in areas such as health and education." Because the choice was so stark, respondents were not forced to these extremes but could place themselves on a scale from 1 to 7 where a higher score represented a commitment to maintain or enhance governmental services. Using the same type of scale, participants were also asked a somewhat more tangible question about whether the government should see to it "that every person has a job and a good standard of living" (a score of 7) or leave that matter up to individuals (scored a 1). These two items provide a good read on general attitudes to the dominant public issue of American political life.

The top bar in figure 6.5 represents the average commitment of each religious group to maintain or increase the level of government services. With such an abstract question, we should not be surprised to find that the groups most and least supportive of active government—African American and mainline Protestants respectively—differed by a little more than 1 point on a scale with a 6-point range. Still, the pattern is reminiscent of what we found for general political identification—black Protestants, seculars, and Jews to the left; white Protestants to the right; and Catholics in between. That same pattern recurs on attitudes about the government responsibility to ensure jobs and a high standard of living, the question represented by the second bar for each religious tradition (see fig. 6.5). As on the first question,

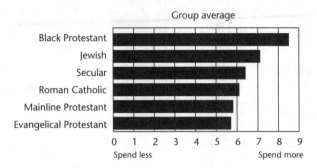

Figure 6.6 Welfare-Spending Attitudes by Religious Group (Source: Calculated by the author from the 1992 American National Election Study, Center for Political Studies)

the similarities among the groups do not disguise that African American Protestants, Jews, and seculars are most supportive of a strong economic role for government, Catholics next most positive, and white Protestants of both evangelical and mainline traditions least supportive.

Does this same pattern hold when it comes to tangible questions about *how* to spend government money? For all their philosophical commitment to small government, Americans have strongly embraced spending public funds on a wide array of specific programs and services. Rather than test support on policies that enjoy widespread approval, ANES asked about the single most controversial area of domestic spending—welfare (see fig. 6.6). The six religious groups are arrayed based on their support for welfare spending. The higher the score, the more willing the group is to increase funding for programs related to the broad goal of assisting the poor.[6] The pattern seen in figure 6.6 is familiar: The three left-wing groups (black Protestants, Jews, and seculars) scored above the scale midpoint, the two categories of white Protestants averaged somewhat lower, and Roman Catholics, as usual, occupied the middle of the distribution.

Since the 1960s Americans have debated various policy questions associated with the civil rights of racial minorities. Though virtually all Americans now accept the premises of the civil rights movement and the desire for equal treatment of African Americans, public opinion remains seriously divided about the specific means to achieve equality (see table 6.1). It appears that there is a very complicated relationship

Table 6.1 Support for U.S. Government Efforts to Assist African
Americans, by Religious Group, in percentages

	Take responsibility for integrating schools	Help ensure fair treatment in jobs	Help improve social position	Preferentially hire and promote
Black Protestants	71	90	43	54
Jews	44	73	22	7
Seculars	48	59	25	18
Roman Catholics	49	55	23	19
Mainline Protestants	37	42	19	12
Evangelical Protestants	39	49	15	13

Source: Calculated by the author from the 1992 American National Election Study,
Center for Political Studies.

between religion and public opinion on civil rights issues. On three of
the items—government's responsibility to promote integrated schools,
improve the socioeconomic position of African Americans, and accord
preference to blacks in hiring and promotion—the gap between blacks
and whites dwarfs any differences among the five predominantly
white religious traditions. Black Protestants proved to be much more
committed than any white religious group to government responsibility for school integration and socioeconomic equality and three times
as supportive of preferential hiring based on race. Only on one of these
questions, the desirability of the government helping to ensure that
African Americans have an equal shot at getting jobs, do we find large
differences among the white groups, with the familiar pattern of Jews
and seculars more to the left, white Protestants to the right, and
Catholics in the middle.

This discussion is not meant to imply that religious group differences
extend to all specific issues and controversies on the American political
agenda. Because many political issues cannot be defined exactly on the
liberal-to-conservative spectrum and because many Americans react to
specific problems without regard to any broad ideological orientation,
group opinions on these policies will not necessarily correspond to the
distribution of durable political orientations. That is why, for example,

previous research has disclosed very little difference among the religious groups in beliefs that courts have been too lenient with criminals and that the government has failed to pay enough attention to average people. On yet other issues, the dividing line between religious groups reflected racial differences. African American Protestants stood out from all other denominations by a greater sympathy for governmental action to reduce economic differences (see table 6.1). Compared with other religious groups, including those white Protestants with whom they share an evangelical heritage, they are also less prone to approve the death penalty (Young 1992). What best accounts for this type of pattern, I would venture, is not that African American religious sensibilities sound a unique theme, but rather that African Americans are represented disproportionately among those who receive both government assistance and the death penalty.

Thus, religion is not relevant to all public controversies despite the striking differences in political orientation between different religious traditions. In one policy domain, foreign policy, religious differences have proved particularly elusive. To a large degree, foreign policy opinions are typically less stable and informed than attitudes on domestic policy questions, and group differences of any kind are thus less common. In the 1950s and 1960s, when the major issue of foreign policy was clearly the cold war, strong religious group differences were apparent. As a rule, evangelical Protestants and Roman Catholics tended to call for a more aggressive military posture against communism than Jews, seculars, and African American and mainline Protestants (Wald 1994). With the end of the cold war and the collapse of the Soviet bloc, the debate over international policy entered a new era in which opinion seems to crystalize differently based on each particular case or controversy. During the Gulf War, an unlikely alliance of evangelical Protestants and Jews was most inclined to accept the case for American military intervention while the mainline churches and Roman Catholicism were far more dovish (Jelen 1994a). In the new era, when Americans debate the wisdom of military involvement in places like Haiti and Bosnia or economic alliances with Mexico and Canada, new lines of cleavage may yet form. Because each of these issues presents different concerns and problems, it may continue to prove difficult to identify strong ties between religious traditions and foreign policy priorities.

The "Social Issue"

In the late 1960s a new type of political issue appeared on the national political agenda. What was labeled the "social issue" was actually a packet of controversies revolving around drug usage, new patterns of sexual behavior, equal rights for women, and similar matters. At base, these issues all raised questions about the place of traditional social and moral values in public policy. Even though they do not touch on the institutional role of the churches in American society, the social issues have frequently been debated with reference to religious values. For many observers, the phrase "religion and politics" has come to encompass matters such as abortion, pornography, drug use, and nontraditional sexual practices. Any comprehensive discussion of religious-group differences in American politics must consider this conflict, in addition to the long-standing debates examined above.

As already noted, abortion has been a subject of intense debate in the United States for more than twenty years. For many observers, abortion is *the* social issue, and the six religious groups differ on several policy questions related to government regulation of abortion (see table 6.2). Recognizing that attitudes toward abortion depend heavily on the circumstances of the case (Granberg 1978; McIntosh, Alston, and Alston 1979), the question in the first column identifies respondents who either reject abortion on principle or accept it only under the extreme conditions of rape, incest, or danger to the mother's life. The three subsequent questions trace support for some of the limitations on abortion that the Supreme Court has permitted states to impose—parental consent for juveniles, spousal notification, and discretionary state funding. By and large, the groups are located consistently across the four questions. At first glance, noting that Jews are most liberal and evangelical Protestants most conservative, it is tempting to conclude that abortion resembles the opinion pattern observed for most policy issues. In fact, the pattern usually found is scrambled by abortion attitudes. Black Protestants, who are normally allied with Jews and seculars in a liberal mode, are closer to the restrictive views of evangelical Protestants on most abortion questions. The attitudes of mainline Protestants look much more like the proabortion opinions of secular respondents than evangelical Protestants. Even the finding that Catholics take their customary middle position is surprising in view of

Table 6.2 Support for Restrictive Abortion Law, by Religious Group, in percentages

	Oppose abortion under most circumstances	Strongly support parental consent laws	Strongly oppose state funding of abortions	Strongly support spousal notification laws
Evangelical Protestants	60	75	54	63
Black Protestants	47	71	30	57
Roman Catholics	41	64	40	57
Mainline Protestants	23	57	25	43
Seculars	18	43	21	33
Jews	3	21	22	18

Source: Calculated by the author from the 1992 American National Election Study, Center for Political Studies.

popular stereotypes of Catholics as the most militant opponents of abortion. On most items, Catholics are more permissive about abortion than either African American or evangelical Protestants.

Many debates about traditional values, such as the conflict over abortion, turn on the role of women in society. The ANES asked respondents to place themselves on a scale in which a value of "1" indicated belief that "women should have an equal role with men in running business, industry, and government" and the value of "7" represented the view "that women's place is in the home." Considering the extreme choices offered to interview participants, it may not be surprising that the overall average of 2.25 was much closer to the equality than traditionalism end of the scale and that all six religious groups were similarly clustered toward that pole (see table 6.3). Nonetheless, the six religious groups were arrayed at different places on this measuring device in a manner similar to but not identical with the pattern for abortion attitudes. Jews and seculars were much more inclined to favor an equal role for men and women (see col. 1, table 6.3), while African American and evangelical Protestants were notably less enthusiastic to (although clearly in favor of) gender equality. On this item, mainline Protestants and Roman Catholics occupied the intermediate role, less committed to women's rights than Jews and seculars but more dedicated to equality than either African American or evangeli-

Table 6.3 Position on Women's Rights Scale, by Religious Group and Church Attendance

	All members of religious tradition	Never attend church or synagogue	Regularly attend church or synagogue
Evangelical Protestants	2.74	2.17	3.17
Black Protestants	2.40	1.98	2.93
Mainline Protestants	2.11	2.10	2.19
Roman Catholics	2.06	1.73	2.23
Secular	1.89	NA	NA
Jews	1.60	1.46	1.99

Source: Calculated by the author from the 1992 American National Election Study, Center for Political Studies.

Note: Average score on women's rights scale where 1 = full equality and 7 = women belong at home; NA = not applicable.

cal Protestants. The only difference between this issue and the abortion item is that Roman Catholics were closer to the cluster of liberal groups that most strongly supported women's rights. The differences between religious groups on this issue are actually wider than the group averages suggest once we take account of religious involvement, a factor usually associated with support for traditional gender roles. The second and third columns of table 6.3 show the scale averages for members of each tradition who never attend worship services and for those who report attending weekly or more. In each case, greater involvement in the religious group promoted a more traditional understanding of women's role. Indeed, the differences between the involved and uninvolved members of the same faith tradition often exceeded the gap between the various religious groups.

The 1992 campaign brought new attention to another item on the social issues agenda, the question of legal antidiscrimination protection for homosexuals. When he proposed to end the ban on gays and lesbians serving in the U.S. military, Bill Clinton put the issue of "gay rights" on the national agenda. If one supposes that views on abortion reflect underlying moral traditionalism, it would be reasonable to

Table 6.4 Support for Policies to Prohibit Discrimination Against Homosexuals, by Religious Group, in percentages

	Should be protected from employment discrimination	Should be permitted to serve in the United States armed forces	Should be allowed to adopt children
Jews	65	54	25
Seculars	39	40	17
Roman Catholics	37	37	15
Black Protestants	46	35	12
Mainline Protestants	28	29	10
Evangelical Protestants	21	22	5

Source: Calculated by the author from the 1992 American National Election Study, Center for Political Studies.

expect the same ordering of religious groups on both abortion and gay rights. We can test this expectation by ranking groups on three questions from the 1992 ANES survey, inquiries about whether homosexuals should enjoy protection from job discrimination, the right to serve in the military, and the right to adopt children (see table 6.4). As on the abortion issue, Jews were once again the pillars of the permissive camp, giving much higher levels of support to gay rights than any other religious group. By the same token, evangelical Protestants were at the other extreme, with only about one-fifth endorsing antidiscrimination legislation and a bare 5 percent approving gay adoption. Apart from these cases, the other four groups were not found to occupy the same order as on the abortion question. When it came to job discrimination legislation, African American Protestants were the next most supportive of the aspirations of gay Americans. Mainline Protestants, who had been strong advocates of liberalized abortion, were much closer to evangelical white Protestants on this question, and seculars resembled Roman Catholics in their middle-of-the-road views.

These patterns are consistent with previous research on attitudes toward Acquired Immune Deficiency Syndrome (AIDS), the disease often associated in the public mind with homosexuality (Seltzer 1993). In a 1986 ballot referendum, California voters considered a proposition that would have declared AIDS a contagious disease and subjected infected persons to the state's quarantine and isolation laws (Le Poire et al. 1990). Although AIDS is a disease, it is often treated as a "lifestyle" issue. This was evident in exit polls on the referendum. About one-third of those surveyed voiced support for what was known as Proposition 64. In a finding consistent with the patterns discussed in this chapter, researchers found that Jews and those with no religious preference were substantially less likely to support the proposition, while "born-again" Christians, a classification roughly equivalent to white evangelical Protestants, were the strongest proponents of the quarantine. Blacks, other Protestants, and Catholics were neither more nor less likely to support the proposition than the typical voter.

Does religion affect public opinion on social issues? Yes, but not simply or consistently. While some groups are quite predictable—Jews in their resistance to the state as an instrument of moral conservatism, evangelical Protestants as staunch advocates of traditional values—other groups differ from one issue to the next. When the issue is abortion or equal roles for women, mainline Protestants part company with the conservative camp, scoring above the national average. Black Protestants, normally synonymous with liberal political outlooks, are markedly more restrictive than most religious groups on abortion and women's equality but more likely than all but Jews to support antidiscrimination laws based on sexual orientation. Roman Catholics are usually in the middle of the spectrum, regardless of the issue. They are not distinctive for their opposition to abortion, as one might suspect from following the news. These patterns demonstrate just how thoroughly social issues crosscut the patterns of group behavior on political identity or contemporary political issues.

The "Culture War" Thesis

After this review of religious group differences in contemporary politics, we can begin to address the claims of some commentators that the United States is caught up in a "culture war" (Hunter 1991). By this term, they refer to political debates that pit advocates of "traditional values" against people who adopt more liberal positions on a range of policy issues. The term itself, dating from conflicts between church and state in late nineteenth century Germany, suggests the religious basis of much cultural conflict. According to sociologist James Davison

Hunter, the two extreme poles of the modern cultural spectrum are indeed marked by very distinct world views. The advocates of traditionalism draw on religious orthodoxy for their understanding of the world and consciously reject many "modern" ideas about human standards. Their opposite number, "progressives," often reject the legitimacy of traditional religious doctrine in favor of moral authority drawn from human reason and experience. In the less abstract words of William Bennett, "America is divided between people who believe there's moral decline and people who say, 'What do you mean by moral decline?'" (quoted in Barnes 1995). These differences are manifested in political debates over federal arts funding, abortion, the causes and control of crime, feminism, educational values, welfare, and a wide range of issues. The Republican party attempted to define the 1992 presidential election precisely in such terms, suggesting that it represented traditional values against a Democratic party that had forgotten God, family, and decency. Such cultural tensions become relevant to political life when they form the basis of community controversies or serve as reference points for voters in political campaigns (Wuthnow 1988; Green and Guth 1991).

Does the pattern of religious group differences examined above confirm the "culture war" interpretation? Because the concept of "culture war" has been defined so imprecisely, the question is not easy to answer. Nonetheless, my reading of the statistical material in this chapter and related scholarly research raises substantial doubts about the value of the "culture war" hypothesis in terms of mass attitudes. As we saw in looking across a wide array of issues and dispositions, religious groups do not line up predictably across each and every political issue. While some groups were relatively consistent—Jews and seculars usually on the liberal end and evangelical Protestants at the conservative pole—most groups differed from one issue to the next. Black Protestants were liberal on partisanship, questions involving African American interests and support for antidiscrimination laws but much less prone to liberalism on ideological self-definition, abortion, or gay rights. Mainline Protestants were staunchly Republican and conservative in ideology but appreciably less right-wing on abortion and women's rights. In 1992 they deserted the Republican party in droves after the GOP embraced the prolife movement at the Republican National Convention, where it allowed conservative activists to jeer at one prochoice Republican, Ann Stone, until she left the podium. Despite spirited attempts to recruit them to the cause of "family values," Roman Catholics seem wedded to a more moderate political ethic. As these three groups demonstrate, the United States has yet to achieve the tight linkage between religious groups and political loyalties that characterizes many other societies.

Even if we grant that there has been some strengthening of religious-political ties in recent elections, that should not be taken as undeniable evidence of the severe political polarization implied by the "culture war" hypothesis. Religious groups may have developed certain political tendencies without automatically rejecting those who hold different views. Looking at the views of both seminary professors and parishioners, sociologists Daniel Olson and Jackson Carroll (1992) reported that religious liberals gave the greatest priority to what have been called "social justice" questions like poverty and peace, while religious conservatives were more concerned with sexual morality questions that fit under the "social issues" umbrella. Although this finding appears to support a "culture war" model, the authors emphasize that the two perspectives were usually not in direct conflict. That is, religious liberals did not reject the conservative agenda but simply gave it lower priority, while religious conservatives took the same stance regarding many liberal values. That finding resonates with the observation of a scholar invited to speak to an audience of religious liberals in an affluent suburb. Amitai Etzioni noted that while they were "quite keen to discuss the plight of the homeless, the American poor, the starving in Africa," the audience rejected his efforts to discuss crime, family problems, and drug use because those were "right-wing issues" (1988, 2). Rather than a war, this situation seems to resemble a political division of labor as religious groups assume primary responsibility for certain issues and consign other questions to another realm.

The limited political polarization evident in these findings has its roots in the presence of mixed tendencies in most religious groups. It helps to remember that the labels used in religious classification, terms like "evangelical" and "mainline" or "liberal" and "conservative" are simplifications, not rigid distinctions between sworn enemies. Beyond the Protestant heritage that unites white evangelicals, black evangelicals, and mainline Protestants, the three groups share a common

Christian fellowship with Catholics, and are also part of a larger Judeo-Christian tradition. Because of these common origins, we should not be surprised to find progressive and traditional factors operating in each religious tradition, preventing the sharp division into warring camps that would signal the presence of a culture war (Ammerman 1994). We need to understand the roots of political differences while remembering that they are differences of degree.

Religious Differences and Social Standing

To understand why religion may influence mass political opinions and behavior, it is necessary to consider several factors that could account for the group patterns delineated in previous sections. This task has become easier because of recent scholarship that tests various theories about the role of religion in the political outlooks of individuals and religious communities (Leege and Kellstedt 1993). Despite this promising research, we are still in the early stages of studying the linkage between religious and political loyalties.

One common reaction to revelations of some of the more dramatic political differences among religious groups, such as the pronounced disagreement over public spending or the equally significant variations in partisan identification, is denial that these patterns "really" have anything to do with religion per se. Skeptics tend to view the ties between religious and political views as spurious; members of a religious group, they argue, think alike about politics not because of their religion but because they share other characteristics that directly influence political attitudes.

The most commonly cited sources of unity linked to religion have been historical experience and economic or social standing. Jews tend toward liberalism, it is argued, because of their experience as an oppressed people whose emancipation was part of the liberal agenda and frequently resisted by conservative movements. Jews are said to have inherited from this tradition a sympathy for liberal values and a suspicion of conservatism. Similarly, proponents of an economic explanation would attribute the conservatism of mainline Protestants to their high social status and economic privileges, not to religious convictions. In this view, differences in political orientations between religious groups generally can be reduced to social characteristics that

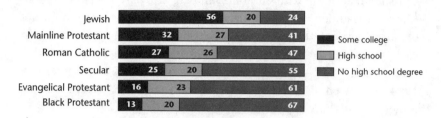

Figure 6.7 Educational Attainment by Religious Group, in percentages
(Source: Calculated by the author from the 1992 American National Election Study,
Center for Political Studies)

happen to be associated with membership in the various denominational families (Allinsmith and Allinsmith 1948).

Attempts to trace denominational political distinctiveness back to
social standing are based on the discovery of major variations in the
profiles of American religious groups. The denominational groups have
been shown to exhibit striking differences in ethnic and racial composition, geographical distribution and concentration, and, most important, social and economic achievement (Roof and McKinney 1987).
The six religious groups can be ranked according to educational
achievement, a major influence on social status and political outlooks
in the United States (see fig. 6.7). Jewish respondents possessed the
highest levels of formal education in the population, followed at some
distance by mainline Protestants, Roman Catholics, and the participants who reported no religious affiliation—findings that are consistent
with many other studies. Then, clustered at the lowest level of educational achievement, come white evangelicals and black Protestants.[7]
Analyses of religious group differences on related indicators of social
standing such as income and occupational attainment have disclosed
very similar patterns.

The claim that political differences among religious groups reflect
only the social composition of denominations can be tested by a comparison of religious group attitudes with social standing held constant.
Using party identification as an example of a political difference, one
would try to discover if, for example, Jews of high education reported
the same level of attachment to the Democratic party as did persons with
similar educational levels but different religious preferences. If religious

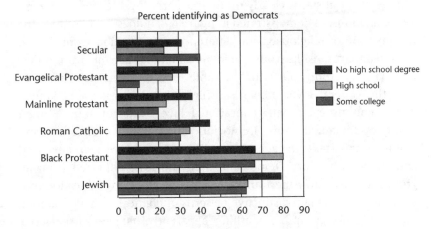

Figure 6.8 Democratic Partisanship by Religious Group and Education (Source: Calculated by the author from the 1992 American National Election Study, Center for Political Studies)

group differences were shown to narrow at each level of education, then education apparently could contribute to political variations. But if the political differences were shown to persist—if, sticking with the same example, college-educated Jews were to be still more strongly attached to the Democratic party than were college-educated Catholics, evangelical Protestants, or other groups—then religious differences in politics could not be attributed wholly to a factor such as education.

The test results for the six religious groups appear in figure 6.8. Members in each group were subdivided by education into three categories: no high school degree, a high school degree only, and a high school degree with some additional schooling. For each group, we calculated the percentage of participants who identified with the Democratic party. The figure shows social status (in the form of education) to be an important but not altogether complete explanation for denominational differences in partisanship. For three groups—Catholics, evangelical Protestants, mainline Protestants—gains in education were clearly associated with movement toward the Republican party. Put another way, the level of Democratic identification declined steadily as members of these groups moved from the least to the most educated categories. However, the three other four groups failed to exhibit this tendency.

Even if social status clearly influences party loyalties for the largest denominations, as demonstrated in figure 6.8, it does not eliminate the full measure of religious-group differences. If education were all that mattered, partisanship would be identical among persons from different religious groups but with the same level of formal education. In fact, the general level of partisanship differed considerably among denominations even with educational level held constant. Roman Catholics remained more Democratic than white evangelical and mainline Protestants in each educational category. Jews with advanced education were more Democratic than the least educated from all groups save African American Protestants. Even taking education into account, there remain distinctive patterns of political affiliation among these religious groups. Something apparently happens in religious groups to foster distinctive political identities among persons who otherwise differ on many politically relevant characteristics.

Of course, the analysis in figure 6.8 represents only a partial test of the influence of social characteristics. When more rigorous controls have been applied for additional social traits that might distinguish religious groups from one another, differences in political identity have remained significant (Wald 1989; Leege and Kellstedt 1993). Many scholars, studying a variety of political orientations and outlooks, have reported that controls for social conditions may narrow intergroup differences in various political orientations but do not eliminate them altogether (Beatty and Walter 1984; S. Cohen and Kapsis 1977; Glantz 1959; Grupp and Newman 1973; Laumann and Segal 1971; Maddox 1979; A. Miller 1974). That conclusion has stood whether the social status indicator has been education, income, urbanization, ethnicity, or occupational status. Thus the religious-group variations in attitudes to AIDS reported earlier are net differences after controlling for the impact of socioeconomic factors, gender, and age.

Even if denominational political differences are affected to some degree by social forces—the strongest conclusion warranted by current research—that still does not mean that religion is irrelevant to political attitudes and orientations. If religion confers an economic disadvantage or advantage on members of a group, it contributes in a major way to the shaping of political outlooks. From both the world and the American experience, it is not hard to identify religious groups that have suffered from economic discrimination because their creed differed from that of the majority of the community. The informal restrictions that once confined most Catholics to the working class probably go a long way toward explaining why Catholics were so receptive to Democratic party efforts to build social programs such as unemployment insurance, workers' compensation, federal aid to education, and the like (Buenker 1973). Membership in a high-status church may provide individuals with social ties, business connections, and opportunities to gain a privileged position in society. With such a strong stake in the existing order, members of prestigious denominations may develop a conservative outlook on social change.

To make the argument more strongly: religious values may be the critical element in determining the social status of the denomination and, thus, a powerful if indirect influence on political orientations. In *The Protestant Ethic and the Spirit of Capitalism,* one of the classic (and most controversial) works of modern sociology (first published in 1920), the German scholar Max Weber (1958) advanced a theory linking certain religious values to success in the economic realm. Trying to explain why Protestants had surpassed Catholics in economic achievement since the advent of capitalism in Europe, Weber suggested that the cause lay partly in the different social values inspired by the two traditions. The Protestant emphasis on discipline and self-control, born of the Puritan desire to illustrate God's blessing, was nicely suited to the demands of work life in a capitalist economy. By comparison, Weber argued, Catholic values encouraged behavior that was not conducive to economic achievement. In particular, the tendency to regard life on Earth as mere preparation for the next world and to equate material poverty with spiritual grace handicapped Catholics in competitive economic struggle. In more recent social theory that is no less controversial than Weber's "Protestant ethic" thesis, scholars have identified cultural values about family, marriage, and childbearing as critical to economic differences among religious groups (Harrison 1992; Keysar and Kosmin 1995). If this approach is correct—and there is enormous controversy about it—then the economic standing of religious groups is even more strongly connected with denominational values. Thus, although it is possible to apportion some of the credit for denominational differences in politics to economic factors, the pattern of economic status itself may ultimately have much to do with religion.

In addition to relatively "hard" differences shown on objective measurement scales of education, income, and so forth, religious groups may also differ from each other in subjective social standing. High income does not necessarily confer social acceptability, and advanced education does not invariably correlate with prestige. Too, such subjective assessments may influence the perspectives of group members and thus help to account for unique political traditions. Subjective social standing is frequently invoked to explain the persistence of Jewish liberalism. Why should Jews, by objective standards one of the highest-status groups in the United States, maintain such a firm commitment to liberal political values—a commitment that seems, contrary to all common sense, to *increase* with economic achievement (Maller 1977; L. Fuchs 1955)? As measured by social attitudes, Jewish standing in society has not matched the level of Jewish economic and educational attainment. Because of their history as a diaspora people and a strong collective memory of persecution, it has been claimed, Jews tend to think of themselves not as part of the established elite, but rather as a group on the margin of society, defensive and vulnerable to attack by the majority. The social insecurity of American Jews has been said to make them especially wary of any political movements that appear to encourage intolerance and bigotry (Cohn 1957; C. Liebman 1973; Petrusak and Steinart 1976; Rothman and Lichter 1982). Hence, Jews make common cause with other subordinate groups in clear defiance of their immediate economic interests.

The concept of subjective status can be extended to explain the political activism of the African American Protestant churches. Denied the most elementary forms of family life, access to education, and any opportunity to develop an independent community life, black slaves were allowed only the church as a focus of collective loyalty. Not surprisingly under such conditions, the church developed into the social, cultural, and intellectual center of African American life. To a degree unmatched in white society, the African American church provided its members some protection from a hostile outside world, a durable source of collective identity, training in organizational skills, and the opportunity to nurture native leadership. When blacks began to challenge the system of segregation that remained in place a century after the passing of slavery, the church became the crucible of action, and it continues today as the principal agent in African American political action. Perhaps that is why contemporary racists have expressed their hostility toward African Americans by igniting a string of fires at black churches across the South. These arsonists seem to understand instinctively that church burnings strike at the heart of the African American culture.

This same line of argument has been advanced to account for the political mobilization of evangelical Protestants in the late 1970s and 1980s. Although this subject will be examined more thoroughly in chapter 7, there is some evidence that evangelical Protestants have been driven to undertake political action in response to perceived attacks on their way of life and social standing. In a study of Protestant churchgoers in one southern community, support for the political goals of the so-called New Christian Right was strongly related to a sense that society did not accord enough respect to groups that represented "traditional" values (Wald, Owen, and Hill 1989a). For a variety of religious groups, subjective social standing may be as important in the forging of political views as factors that can be measured in dollars or years of schooling.

Religion and Political Values

Some observers have not been reluctant to attribute religious-group differences in politics to the values, teachings, and ideas of the various traditions. The application of religious creeds to politics is most visible when the leaders of a faith assert that their religion demands a particular political stance. In the United States, where official political announcements by churches have traditionally been comparatively rare, the overt linking of religious ideas with political positions has recently become much more common among almost all denominations.

The Catholic hierarchy, for example, has insisted that church teachings about the nature of life impose on Catholics the obligation to reject both artificial methods of birth control and abortion. Because the latter is governed by public policy, Catholic doctrine has drawn some members of the faith into political action. Catholic public officials who disagree with official teaching on abortion have been denied various religious rites and threatened with eternal damnation. The Catholic hierarchy has not been alone in translating faith into political principles. Members of the clergy who participated in the drive for civil rights insisted that segregation was incompatible with Judeo-Christian values. In the 1960s and 1970s, some leaders of mainline white Protestantism urged on biblical grounds that members of the churches oppose the Vietnam War and work for a broad-ranging program of social reform and welfare services. During the 1980s some leaders of the evangelical wing of Protestantism asserted biblical support for programs on the conservative agenda. Each basic plank in the program put forward by the Moral Majority, an organization supporting conservative social policy on moral grounds, was accompanied by a reference to a specific passage in Scripture. In excommunicating a supporter of the Equal Rights Amendment for disobedience, the elders of the Church of Jesus Christ of Latter-day Saints (the Mormons) surpassed other groups in enforcing compliance with political doctrine as a condition for church membership. Nonetheless, it would be hard to think of a religious group whose leaders have not defended some political position on theological grounds.

The connection between doctrine and politics may also draw on theological tradition in more subtle ways. Rather than speak directly to political issues, it has been suggested, certain common ways of thinking about religion spill over into politics (Laitin 1978). According to most observers, the differences in style and approach between a "conservative" and a "liberal" orientation in religion may well correspond to the political orientations of the same name.[8] Michael Parenti has suggested four key dimensions on which conservative and liberal religions differ:

(a) The extent to which divine teaching is considered fixed, final, and unchallengeable, as opposed to being susceptible to rational investigation and modification; and consequently, the extent to which intellectualism and many of the values associated with it are opposed or welcomed.

(b) The extent to which the drama of redemption and atonement is defined as a personal battle waged for one's soul for the sake of eternal salvation, rather than as a moral commitment to a worldly social betterment of mankind.

(c) The extent to which sin and evil are defined as inherent in human nature (e.g., original sin) and inevitable in human behavior (e.g., concupiscence), rather than as social effects of widespread environmental causes.

(d) The extent to which human well-being and natural pleasures are manifestations of a "lower," corrupting realm of nature, something to be repressed as the contamination of the spiritual, rather than responsibly cultivated as the fulfillment of God's beneficence. (1967, 268)

Recent research has suggested another major difference between conservative and liberal religions—their images of God. According to Andrew Greeley (1982), the concept of God evokes for some people a "warm" or "feminine" image of friendship, nurturance, caring, and love, but for others a "cold" and "masculine" image of discipline, order, and punishment. Additional research on the same theme has revealed that religions may convey different messages about God's presence in the world and responsibility for the flow of human events (Piazza and Glock 1979; O'Grady 1982).

How might these dimensions of religious belief take on political significance? Because of their emphasis on faith in fixed authority over the free play of intellect, persons of a conservative orientation are more likely than religious liberals to stress the need for obedience than to encourage skepticism or dissent (Rokeach 1969; J. Carroll 1995). If redemption is interpreted to mean bringing the Kingdom of God to realization on earth, as liberal religions seem to argue, movements for political change are infused with a transcendent purpose. But if, as in conservative religion, life is seen as a mere preparation for the next world or the imminent return of God to earth, then little can be done except to live as righteously as possible and to guard the integrity of one's soul from temptation and corruption (Kleppner 1970). An emphasis on sinfulness as the essential condition of humankind seems quite compatible with a skeptical orientation toward the prospect of improving conditions through political action (Rosenberg 1956). Similarly, if human pleasures are judged inferior to spiritual rewards, there is little urgency about improving material conditions. The liberal belief in "social" sin and the dignity of earthly existence, which contrasts sharply with conservative religious assumptions, spurs efforts to eradicate structural barriers to justice and to improve the material conditions of life. Belief in a warm, caring God who is part of the world tends to enhance commitment to social welfare, whereas the image of a cold and authoritative deity lends support to government's role in securing order and property.

These contrasting modes of thought are illustrated by the way in which Jews and Lutherans apply their differing religious styles to the political realm. A classic example of a liberal faith, Judaism venerates learning and charity as major virtues and is relatively silent about the origin of sin and the prospect of life after death. That combination of values encourages optimism about the human condition and a sense of urgency about the application of reason to human problems. As described by some experts, the Jewish outlook seems almost to demand social and political involvement on behalf of liberal causes:

Implicit in this style is the view that man and his environment are malleable, that he is much more the creator of history than its creature. Implicit, too, is the notion that man's environment and his polity are made for him. Implicit is a dynamic view of law, that it is changing and made for man. . . . And especially implicit in such a style is the belief that what happens in this life on this earth is very important, what happens here and now matters very much. (L. Fuchs 1984, 70)

Subject to the influence of this body of assumptions, Jewish voters have been strongly attracted to political leaders and movements that promote social change—drawn so strongly, in fact, that they have occasionally preferred activist liberals from Christian denominations to more conservative Jewish candidates (Leventman and Leventman 1976). For a people normally given to such high levels of solidarity, crossing denominational lines is strong evidence for the political impact of a liberal religious style.

The Jewish stress on human capacity to remake the world through political action finds barely an echo in Lutheran doctrine. Martin Luther taught that salvation would come only to the person who submitted thoroughly and wholeheartedly to the will of an omniscient God. In sharply contrasting the evil of mortals to the perfection of God, Lutheran thought treats humans as creatures of passion and sin who should not interfere with the divine plan for the world. Based on an extensive survey of Lutheran laypersons in the Detroit metropolitan area, Lawrence K. Kersten found that Luther's spiritual descendants accepted his counsel to take the world as it is: "Lutheran social philosophy suggests that true happiness for man and total release from the bondage of sin are not possible until after death. If earthly conditions are undesirable, man should patiently endure them, for they may actually be a test of his faith. Man must trust that God will change the social structure or social conditions when He sees fit" (1970, 31). Such religious beliefs may help to account for the Lutherans' pronounced economic, social, racial, and political conservatism (M. C. Weber 1983).

At this point, it should be emphasized that links between attitudes and religious orientations have been more often asserted than proved. Attempts to assess the connection between religious belief and political outlook have yielded mixed results. The most consistent relationships between theological beliefs and political outlooks have been found with samples of the clergy, a group that should have the firmest grasp of the political implications of religious thought. In almost every study of the clergy I have located, commitment to a conservative religious style correlated with conservative outlooks on politics and social issues (Beatty and Walter 1989; Balswick 1970; Guth, Green, Smidt, and Poloma 1991; Hadden 1969; Driedger 1974; Jeffries and Tygart 1974; B. Johnson 1966, 1967; D. Olson and Carroll 1992; Schindeler and Hoffman 1968). As for surveys of more typical people, some empirical studies have reported a relationship between commitment to the tenets of conservative religion and (1) conservative beliefs about race and ethnic relations, (2) membership in the Republican party, (3) resistance to liberal initiatives on environmental and social welfare policy, (4) support for traditional beliefs about sexual roles and behavior, and (5) a low level of toleration for "deviant" political ideas (B. Johnson 1962, 1964; Rokeach 1969; Orum 1970; Glock and Stark 1966; Stellway 1973; Hand and Van Liere 1984; Steiber 1980). Similarly, the "image of God" studies have for the most part linked the image of a stern and vengeful deity with various manifestations of political conservatism (Greeley 1988, 1993; Welch and Leege 1988; Woodrum and Davison 1992a—but see MacIver 1990).

Nevertheless, this type of relationship between theological and political outlooks has not always been borne out by empirical research. On the basis of an exhaustive review of previous research, Robert Wuthnow (1973) pointed out that well-designed studies were just as likely to report no relationship between religious beliefs and political attitudes as they were to find a positive association. Even in studies of the clergy, as Beatty and Walter (1989) discovered, the relationship was far from complete. Baptist ministers with liberal theological outlooks were still more conservative in politics than Episcopalians, Methodists, and Congregationalists of comparable religious views. Focusing exclusively on studies about racial beliefs, Gorsuch and Aleshire (1974) discovered that persons committed to religion for its intrinsic value were the least likely to hold prejudiced views of African

Americans. Responding to the emergence of organized political activity by leaders of the evangelical Protestant churches, several studies have found that, in general, church members tie religious and political attitudes together only in the domain of sexual and social roles (Wald and Lupfer 1983). The idea that Jewish political values derive from the content of the religion has been challenged by the discovery that the most religiously observant Jews, who should have the greatest exposure to the implicit liberal messages of Judaism, in fact constitute the most politically conservative element of the community (S. Cohen 1983, 143–153; C. Liebman 1973, 139–144). An inverse relationship between attachment to traditional religion and racial militance has been reported in studies of African American Protestants (Marx 1967, chap. 4; Madron, Nelsen, and Yokeley 1974; Nelsen, Madron, and Yokeley 1975). Even when survey findings have appeared to support connections between denominational belief and political outlook, the conclusions have been challenged on grounds that they really represented social background influences of the kind examined in the previous section (D. Anderson 1966; Henriot 1966; Rojek 1973; Roof 1974; Summers et al. 1970).

Those who would insist on drawing too strong a connection between religious orientations and particular forms of political belief should remember the many exceptions to the rule. Left-wing movements for social reform have frequently been inspired by Christian doctrine (Murchland 1982; Littell 1970). William Jennings Bryan, the defender of religious conservatism par excellence, had no difficulty combining a deep commitment to fundamentalist theology with passionate conviction in international arbitration, the rights of urban workers, women's suffrage, public ownership of utilities, and, in general, support for an extensive government effort to secure social and economic justice. The same Bryan who condemned evolution, in large part for its pernicious social implications, saw his commitments to social reform as the logical outgrowth of Christian morality (Levine 1975). Like Bryan, many African American Protestants, white evangelicals, and Roman Catholics find no contradiction between theological conservatism and political liberalism. Even the Pentecostal movement, normally regarded as the politically most regressive wing of Protestantism, has found biblical sanction for racial integration (Elinson 1965, 414–415). The confluence of liberal theology with conservative politics can also be found in American political life. Despite a traditional commitment to liberalism, some Jews have enlisted on behalf of conservative programs and policies. Milton Friedman, the dean of laissez-faire economists, is Jewish; so is William Kristol (himself the son of noted neoconservative Irving Kristol and historian Gertrude Himmelfarb), a conservative editor of the *Weekly Standard* and key strategist for the Republican party. Much to the dismay of many liberals in the Jewish community (see Shorris 1982), the principal leadership of the American neoconservative movement comprises Jewish intellectuals disillusioned by the liberalism they championed in the 1960s and 1970s.

These exceptions suggest that there are limits to simple theological explanations of political attitudes. On the one hand, the lack of an authoritative source of interpretation for most American religions leaves believers free to develop their own understanding of sacred texts and teachings. And even where the religious tradition seems clearly to point to a logically related political position, church members may keep the religious values segregated in their minds, limiting the application to politics. Perhaps that is why Lupfer and Wald (1985) found in their Memphis study that evangelicals did not judge humanity in the harsh manner that most laypersons assume would follow from the doctrine of original sin. On the other hand, most religious traditions are elastic enough to support very different political applications. Drawing on a common sacred text, for example, Baptists Pat Robertson and Jesse Jackson have ended up in remarkably different places. Elasticity also shows up when denominations or individuals change political behavior despite an unchanging religious outlook (Balswick, Ward, and Armstrong 1975). Where influential leaders of evangelical Protestantism once read the Bible as a blueprint for the Social Gospel, in the 1920s the predominant interpretation shifted to emphasize biblical passages that promoted political withdrawal. Before then, evangelicals provided many of the leaders of progressive causes such as the antislavery movement and populism and supported other policies, such as Prohibition, that can now be understood as sincere attempts to improve social conditions (Clark 1976; T. L. Smith 1965; J. Hammond 1974).

The environmental issue provides further evidence of the political diversity associated with religious creeds. In an influential essay published in 1967, Lynn White (1967, 1207) argued that the ecological crisis of the West was rooted in "the Christian axiom that nature has no reason for existence save to serve man." If White was correct to assert a link between this Christian belief in human "dominion" and environmental exploitation, we should find Christians as a group to be indifferent to environmental protection and those most involved in Christian churches the least environmentally conscious of all. It seems, however, that White erred in assuming that all Christians heard the same message from the Bible. Although early research on mass environmental attitudes found a greater disposition to assert human dominion among people with a Judeo-Christian background (cf. Shaiko 1987) and an apparent link between religious involvement and support for environmental exploitation (Eckberg and Blocker 1989; Kanagy and Willits 1993), subsequent research has qualified that conclusion. These studies contend that hostility to environmental protection is concentrated among those Christians who hold specific views about the relationship between humanity and nature (Woodrum and Hoban 1994; Wolkomir et al. 1995) or who perceive the end of the world as imminent (Guth et al. 1993, 1995). Other Christians have developed a "stewardship" mentality that is quite conducive to a strongly proenvironmental position.

If we still suspect a link between political and religious values, even after recognizing the potential obstacles to a relationship, what is to be done? The first step is recognizing that the deeper content of religious values is only imperfectly captured by denominational affiliation, rates of church attendance, and other simple measures of religiosity frequently employed in studies of political behavior. Demonstrating how to go beyond those traditional measures, Benson and Williams (1982) explored the "mental maps" of religion held by members of Congress. Recognizing religious belief as a complex and multifaceted phenomenon, they questioned each representative about four different aspects of his or her personal religious philosophy. These aspects or dimensions represented different ways of understanding religious truth. The "agentic-communal" dimension indicated whether religion focused more on personal or social problems. The second dimension concerned religious messages—were they restrictive, setting limits and regulating conduct, or did they offer release through forgiveness? In the third dimension, religion might be perceived as vertical, with the lines of communication flowing down from God, or horizontal, from person to person. In the final dimension, the primary task of religion was either to offer comfort to individuals or, alternatively, to challenge them to rebuild society. When used to compare voting records, the authors found that advocates of communal, horizontal, challenging, and release-oriented religions were much more likely to support liberal political causes than their religious opposites. These findings are important given the prevailing tendency to dismiss religious influences on the behavior of elected officials.

This approach has since been extended to ordinary citizens. The directors of the Notre Dame Study of Catholic Parish Life attempted to approximate the agentic-communal dimension in interviews with more than two thousand Catholic respondents (Leege 1989). The agentic, or individualist, mode was illustrated by those who selected fear of the unknown as the primary problem addressed by religion, accepting God's will as the path to salvation, and eternal life as the consequence of salvation. By contrast, the communal label was assigned to individuals who identified the human problem as lack of community and fellowship, regarded working for social justice as the route to salvation, and expected their efforts to produce peace and harmony on earth. Trying to assess the vertical-horizontal dimension, the researchers also measured individuals' feeling—was the presence of God felt most intensely in situations that linked them to other people or was God experienced primarily in formal rituals that stressed authority?

As expected, the individualist-communal dimension proved to be a strong predictor of political ideology and a significant influence on attitudes toward social regulatory policies; in both cases, the communal approach to religion was associated with more liberal outlooks (Leege and Welch 1989). Even more powerfully, those who felt close to God when working for justice and peace were disposed to political liberalism in general and to liberal preferences on issues like abortion, defense spending, and school busing (Welch and Leege 1988). These innovative measures of religion did not, however, influence a number of other important political orientations and frequently had less impact than other religious beliefs (ibid.).

A study of activists in eight religiously oriented interest groups also discovered variations in religious worldviews from one group to the next (J. Green et al. 1994). Communitarians were defined by belief in the social justice mission of the church, the need to change institutions, the societal origins of poverty, and the inadequacy of personal conversion as a means of solving social problems. This orientation was strong in three religious groups on the left side of the political spectrum. Those who instead thought in more individualist terms—seeing the church as concerned principally with individual morality and confident in the power of conversion to solve social problems—were attracted to conservative organizations. This study, together with related research, suggests that more sensitive measures of religion have a great potential to uncover the full impact of religious belief on political outlooks.

The larger point is to treat with caution the apparent compatibility of religious with political thought. Even when religious orientations are found to be consistently in league with corresponding political outlooks, the links should be treated as dispositions that allow some room for exceptions. If one should not claim too little for religion, in the manner of those who always see social standing as the "real" cause for denominational political differences, neither should one claim too much. Tocqueville and Weber were correct in using the term *affinity* instead of *cause* to examine how different denominations related the Kingdom of God and humanity.

Religion and Group Interests

Institutional interest provides another line of explanation for denominational differences in political attitudes and behavior. At first glance, churches may not appear to fit in with other organized institutions that make claims on government. The principal concern of churches, after all, is to minister to the spiritual needs of the membership. Yet because their wide scope of activity inevitably brings them into contact with government, churches, like secular groups, develop interests that may require defense in the political realm. Of concern in this regard is how the assertion of institutional interests may affect the basic attitudes and loyalties of the church and its supporters.

In the United States, as in other countries, the issue of education has frequently drawn churches into the political realm. Partly in an effort to maintain themselves (although for other reasons as well), American churches have supported extensive systems of elementary, secondary, and postsecondary education. These schools provide both instruction in basic skills and training in religious traditions and practices.

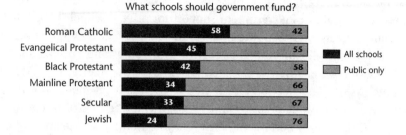

Figure 6.9 School-Funding Preferences by Religious Group, in percentages
(Source: Calculated by the author from the 1992 American National Election Study, Center for Political Studies)

According to the most recent statistics, approximately 11 percent of school-aged children attended church-related elementary and secondary institutions (U.S. Bureau of the Census 1994, 172). The Catholic parochial schools provide the best-known example of religious education, accounting for more than half the students in private education, but many denominations have built their own facilities in locations where their members are concentrated. By one recent estimate, about 700,000 students now attend Christian schools with a fundamentalist perspective and another 100,000 children are "home schooled" by their fundamentalist parents (M. Marty and Appleby 1992, 74).

As noted in chapter 4, the enormous cost of maintaining these institutions and paying for tuition gives churches and families a strong interest in securing government assistance. Under these circumstances, it is hardly surprising that studies of voting on urban bond issues dedicated to financing public education have revealed a high level of opposition from Catholics—who have a financial interest in minimizing the cost of a school system many do not utilize (Cataldo and Holm 1983). Other polls have shown very strong support for various forms of state aid among denominations that maintain schools and much more resistance in churches in which the bulk of children attend public institutions (Menendez 1977, chap. 11; Rothenberg and Newport 1984, 58–61). In the 1992 ANES, respondents were asked if government funds should be reserved for public schools or be distributed to both public and private institutions. As figure 6.9 shows, the highest levels of support for aid to private schools were found among Roman

Catholics and evangelical Protestants. At the other extreme, Jews opposed the policy of government support for private schools by a 3-1 margin. Seculars and mainline Protestants were opposed by narrower 2-1 margins, while the other two groups of Protestants, blacks and evangelicals, were closer to a 50-50 division over the question.

Interests do not have to be restricted to the financial sphere nor to single issues. In the late 1920s and 1930s, a convergence of interests brought first- and second-generation Catholics and Jews, previously inactive or pro-Republican, into the New Deal Democratic coalition fashioned by Franklin D. Roosevelt. Part of Roosevelt's appeal to these groups lay in his commitment to economic policies that addressed their economic needs; at the same time, however, Roosevelt was also seen as a defender of the religious minorities from attack by the Protestant culture. As immigrants became more numerous in cities from the late nineteenth century onward, Protestants began to look askance at the challenge to their norms and beliefs posed by the influx of Catholics and Jews. The period from approximately 1880 to the 1920s was marked by Protestant efforts to preserve their image of the Christian America by invoking the force of law to support "pious behavior" in matters of personal conduct (Handy 1984). For their part, the immigrants grew increasingly to resent Protestant crusades for immigration restriction, the prohibition of liquor, and the imposition of blue laws. The implementation of these policies represented a victory for Protestant ideas of morality, which were far more restrictive on such issues than was Jewish or Catholic thought.

As the minority party in the United States, the Democrats had a strong incentive to court the as-yet unattached potential voters. The party's urban organizations proved highly receptive to the interests and concerns of the immigrant workers, and this receptivity was finally matched at the national level in the 1928 presidential nominating convention. There, the party formally repudiated the Ku Klux Klan, then principally an extremist Protestant group attacking Catholics and Jews, and conferred the presidential nomination on New York governor Alfred E. Smith, a Catholic who embodied "the revolt of the underdog, urban immigrant against the top dog of 'old American' stock" (Lubell 1965, 53). Although he lost badly to Herbert Hoover in the 1928 presidential election, Smith brought over to the Democratic side the votes of Catholics in urban America (Lichtman 1979; Burner 1967). Four years later, Roosevelt would capitalize on that cultural conflict and on the nation's economic disarray to claim the presidency for the Democrats.

Roosevelt's policies in 1932 and thereafter cemented the alliance of Jews and Catholics with the Democratic party (Flynn 1968). Catholics were favorably disposed toward a presidential candidate who had denounced religious bigotry in the heated 1928 campaign and who quoted a papal encyclical in support of his plans for economic recovery. Roosevelt further recognized the church by appointing two Catholics to cabinet positions (half the number who had held such posts in all previous U.S. administrations combined), naming Catholics to other important positions in government, and, in an important symbolic gesture, opening up direct contacts between the church and the White House (Billington and Clark 1993). Roosevelt cultivated Jewish support with similar actions but earned the highest degree of loyalty for his leadership of the war against Hitler. Jews thereupon embraced the Democratic party with a tenacity matched by few groups—a commitment that was redoubled when Roosevelt's successor made the United States one of the first countries to recognize and endorse the formation of a Jewish state in Israel.

By means of such actions, political leaders attempt to convey to members of religious groups their understanding of the group's situation and sympathy for its goals. Eventually, if the conditions are ripe and the romance is conducted with sufficient skill, political elites can forge strong ties between a party and the members of denominations. Unlike some political parties in other countries, the major American parties have never appealed for support solely as the representatives of a specific religious interest. But they have signaled their willingness to make room for members of religious groups in the party coalition. Through the process known as "political socialization," group members may even come to regard affiliation with a particular party as one element of their religious identity (Irvine 1974). Support for the party becomes, in essence, a natural reflex for members of the religious group. Studies of group-based political loyalties have underscored the durability of the associations between religious commitment and political loyalties. Despite the obsolescence of many of the issues that prompted Jewish and Catholic support for the Democratic party under Franklin Roosevelt, the connection has persisted. Political commitments by denominations based initially on common interests thus may broaden into durable loyalties that outlive their original causes (Leege, Lieske, and Wald 1991).

The Role of Social Integration

Whether it arises ultimately from creedal forces, institutional interest, or as the by-product of a religious group's social situation, the tie between religion and politics must be activated in the mind of individuals. Very little has been said thus far about how members of groups acquire the outlooks characteristic of their religion. In order to answer the question, it is important to think of "religion" as an activity pursued (usually) in groups. The same principles that govern the organization and maintenance of other groups apply equally well to groups defined by a religious purpose:

Members of religious groups have a common identity, interact with one another regularly, and expect each other to think and act in certain ways. These expectations, which are commonly called group norms, are enforced by sanctions, i.e., rewards and punishments which group members administer to each other. The norms of a religious group constitute its special culture, a culture that is usually distinct in some ways from the culture of other groups in its environment. (B. Johnson and White 1967, 31)

In that description, Johnson and White call attention to the means by which religious groups create a common consciousness that may extend to political ideas.

By participating in a religious group, the individual learns what is expected of him or her and what behavior patterns are required for maintaining membership. When attending church, the affiliate enters a world with a communication network that reinforces the sense of group awareness. Both inside and outside the church, the member may come to have more and more social contact with like-minded persons from the religious community. In the case of the young, the church creates special educational institutions for the express purpose of transmitting group norms. These formal networks are supplemented by informal messages from various agents, especially parents, about what constitutes appropriate behavior for members of the denomination. The minister is an additional source of cues about norms. In most churches the clergy is recognized as the source of spiritual leadership and is expected, as an integral part of worship, to provide guidance about church doctrines. When these elements are put together, they provide the church with impressive potential to influence the outlooks of the membership (Cornwall 1987).

Through each of these routes—restricted communication, social interaction, formal training, informal education, ministerial guidance—the church impresses on the individual member a commitment to its norms. In American churches, these norms may include informal commitment to a party or political outlook, or at least agreement on some of the elements that can influence political perspectives: theological assumptions, a sense of social status, and a belief that group members share certain interests. Through these avenues of influence, churches may provide cues that reinforce political differences among denominations (Converse and Campbell 1969; Kaplan 1969). Most Americans, while frowning on explicit political direction from the clergy, are less resistant to the relatively subtle means of political education the church provides.

The manner in which churches promote political learning is not yet fully understood or appreciated but appears powerful nonetheless. In intensive interviews with eight women activists from a conservative Christian organization, Kristi Andersen (1988) discovered that many had experienced a gradual political conversion in which they came to see a religious basis for linking political issues as diverse as abortion, feminism, gay rights, sex education, and crime. Liberal policies on these issues were interpreted as threatening a form of social organization—the traditional family—that had its justification in the word of God. Ministers, friends from church, and other religiously inspired activists all helped these individuals learn to see a new link between religion and politics on issues that might otherwise have seemed unrelated to one another or to religious values. The same process can lead to different conclusions. Many Catholic activists in the Sanctuary movement began to pay attention to conditions in the region after learning about the murder of Catholic clergy by regimes supported by the U.S. government. Subsequent reports of church fact-finding missions and first-person accounts from Catholic missionaries in the region had a powerful impact on stimulating opposition to American policy among rank-and-file church members (Cunningham 1995).

Similarly, a key activist in the antinuclear movement in one American city reported something like an adult conversion experience when a parish priest helped him see "that an exemplary life was not so much dependent on dutifully following rules, but on examining what your faith meant for the conduct of your entire life" (cited in Holsworth 1989, 54). With this new frame of reference, he began to submit his prior political commitments to the test of faith and, eventually, to develop a very different political outlook.

Whatever the issues, this process was necessary simply because the political implications of religious belief are often difficult to discern. Consider the highly politicized question of abortion. The Bible in its Hebrew and Christian forms does not mention "abortion" or provide explicit guidance about whether the practice is permitted or prohibited. Religious arguments about abortion must thus search the text for clues about its principles regarding life, motherhood, and the dignity of persons. Precisely because the Bible speaks in abstractions or parables, those who search there for political guidance do not often agree with each other on its message. The Roman Catholic church spent centuries developing a doctrine equating abortion with infanticide. In many evangelical Protestant denominations, the understanding of abortion as a sin also came late. Regardless of the issue or faith, the religious community may be the place where individuals are guided to see how their tradition speaks to a particular political dispute.

Churches are not equally successful in prompting members to perceive connections between religious and political ideas. Richard L. Wood (1994) has reported on three Christian congregations in a California city that have actively stressed political action as a legitimate religious duty. Surprisingly, the two churches with the most homogeneous middle-class membership were much less successful at stimulating political action and sustaining it than a much poorer and diverse church. In part, the members of the more politically active church seem to have developed a strong sense of collective identity that gives them a common way of reacting to the world, a "spiritual bonding" that makes cooperative action seem both natural and rewarding. In addition, the religious understanding in the politically active church fused religious and political messages very tightly. According to one activist, her gratitude to God for giving her such a rich world virtually compelled her to repay the debt by making the world an even better place. Such a view made "faith" and "action" two inseparable components of a single religious commitment. Armed with such understanding, members of the activist church found political action a virtual religious sacrament.

These insights suggest that ties between religion and politics depend on processes that operate at the level of the individual congregation or parish. In a study of Protestant congregations in one community, my colleagues and I discovered that the acceptance of conservative or liberal politics depended less on an individual's religious outlook than on the religious values held by a majority of fellow congregants (Wald, Owen, and Hill 1988). We interpreted this finding as evidence that subtle messages from the clergy and fellow congregants provide guidance about the appropriate political conclusions that should be drawn from religious principles. Using a similar congregational design, Ted Jelen (1992) found that the impact of the religious environment was strongest precisely when the linkage between religious values and political objects was most difficult for congregants to infer on their own. The relative power of congregational influence as opposed to residential forces or other personal traits has been the focus of important research by Huckfeldt, Plutzer, and Sprague (1993) and Gilbert (1993). Recall from earlier in the chapter that mainline Protestants tend toward both Republican partisanship and liberal views on abortion. Using a unique set of interviews that assessed the views of individuals, their fellow parishioners, and neighbors, these studies found that the opinions of fellow congregants enhanced the underlying attitudes of the denomination. That is, both the level of Republicanism and prochoice sentiment among individual Protestants increased when other church members were predominantly Republican and liberal on abortion. These findings held even allowing for education, income level, and residential context. Further analysis of attitudes toward abortion in Protestant congregations suggests "that members learn more from one another than they do from abstract church pronouncements." Whatever the mechanism of influence, churches—by which I mean individual congregations—are an important crucible where the connections between religion and politics are forged.

Because individuals are not equally involved in churches, they are not equally receptive to the political messages flowing from them. Strength of commitment to the religious group has been measured in different ways—frequency of attendance at worship, involvement in the organizational life of the church, level of social interaction with church members, psychological ties to a religious label or tradition, length and intensity of exposure to church doctrine, and even the individual's subjective assessment of the importance of religious identity relative to other group loyalties. The extremes of involvement run from the person with no religious background or connection to any denomination to the cult member whose immersion in the religious community cuts off all outside sources of political information. Not surprisingly, the nonaffiliated is likely to develop political ideas independent of traditional church doctrine, whereas the cult member is likely to follow the church's political guidance with complete loyalty. Between these poles lay a wide range of religious commitments and, presumably, of responsiveness to the political cues given out directly or indirectly by the religious group. Commitment to the denomination therefore appears to strengthen conformity to the political norm of the religious group and accentuates attitude differences between persons from other groups (Guth and Green 1993; Wald, Kellstedt, and Leege 1993). Hence the discovery, to cite only one of many available from the literature, that religious group differences in party identification and presidential voting are greatest among persons with the strongest involvement in their respective religious families (C. Anderson 1973; Knoke 1974; Wald 1989). What is true for individuals also holds for congregations. The more a church dominates and circumscribes the life of its members, the greater the political cohesion among congregants (Wald, Owen, and Hill 1990).

Levels of religious participation may also minimize the impact of nonreligious factors on the political loyalties of church members. The church is an arena that frequently brings together people from different social backgrounds. Although the point should not be overstated, a strong sense of collective religious identity, with its associated political messages, may override the other sources of political cues available to the church members. Instead of picking up political orientations from the newspaper, neighbors, coworkers, or other secondary organizations, the individual may imbibe loyalties from the church members and leaders who are the principal partners in social interaction. The muted level of class differences in politics found between members of the same religious denomination appears to confirm the operation of this process (Bochel and Denver 1970). To the extent that they actually forge a common political approach among persons of diverse social standing, churches may account for the persistence of political differences independent of social forces such as income, occupation, and education.

Religion is relevant to some types of political conflict but not to all others. When they do appear, political differences among denominations cannot be reduced to a single source, be it theology, social standing, or institutional interest. All these factors may play a role in forging the patterns of belief observed at the beginning of the chapter. Whatever the source of political identity, the transmission of group-based political ideas appears to depend on the individual's level of involvement in the religious community. For individuals whose lives are the most deeply merged with the church, politically distinctive behavior appears to be the rule.

This chapter has demonstrated political differences among American religious groups on many issues that do not seem directly tied to religion per se. On both basic questions of political identity and many specific issues that have dominated political debate, the six major groups are usually arrayed across the spectrum of opinion. When the focus of attention shifts to social issues—or as they have become most recently known, "family" issues—the six groups assume positions that differ from their ordering on other kinds of public issues. To better understand the political profiles of America's major religious groups, the next two chapters review the social forces and influences that have molded distinctive political outlooks for each tradition. The first of these two chapters examines white evangelical Protestants who have recently emerged from political obscurity to the front ranks of contemporary politics. That is followed by a chapter examining the remaining groups that have exhibited more stability but are still subject to pressures for political change.

NOTES

The chapter epigraph is taken from Alexis de Tocqueville, *Democracy in America* (New York: Vintage, 1945).

1. These data are available from the Inter-University Consortium for Political and Social Research (ICPSR) as study no. 6067, "American National Election Study, 1992: Pre- and Post-Election Survey." The analysis reported in this chapter used the 1992 data on the compact disk released as ICPSR CD0010.

2. Wilcox, Jelen, and Leege (1993) have summarized the literature on what labels like "evangelical" and "fundamentalist" mean to individuals.

3. For an extended discussion of problems of religious measurement, see the excellent essays by Wade Clark Roof (1979) and John Wilson (1978, app.). In practice, apportioning individuals into categories based on religious denomination yields quite different results from classifications based on religious beliefs or orientations (Wald and Smidt 1993). For that reason, it is quite hazardous to compare the results of studies using the two different types of classification strategies.

4. The "independent" category is so large because it includes individuals who initially describe themselves as independent when asked to select a partisan label but who answer a subsequent question by indicating that they generally are closer to one of the two major parties. If these "independent partisans" were assigned a partisan identity based on the second question rather than the first, the total size of the "independent" pool would shrink and there would be more Democrats than independents.

5. The respondents who did not actually cast a ballot in 1992 were classified based on the candidate they preferred. That item, plus the normal tendency of people to "overreport" preference for the winner, accounts for the greater level of Clinton support in the sample than the actual election returns.

6. This scale was constructed by giving respondents points if they wanted to cut (0), maintain (1), or increase (2) spending on food stamps, welfare programs, programs that assist African Americans, government assistance to the unemployed, poor people, and aid to cities.

7. It should be emphasized that we are reporting group averages and that many individuals cheerfully acquire more or less education than is typical of their religious group as a whole. Moreover, there are striking differences among the denominations that compose our broad religious traditions.

8. Even though the differences are frequently used to characterize entire religious traditions as conservative or liberal, they constitute tendencies that may divide people of a common heritage.

7. The Political Mobilization of Evangelical Protestants

Get 'em saved; get 'em baptized; get 'em registered.
—Slogan at an evangelical workshop on political action

The history of recent evangelical political activity is usually written in two parts—rise and decline. The rise began in 1976, *Time* magazine's "Year of the Evangelical," when a Southern Baptist won the presidency and the self-indulgence of the "Me Decade" gave way to "born-again" religious fervor. In the political realm, so the story goes, evangelical Protestants were driven into Republican ranks by concern over abortion and other social problems, contributing in a major way to conservative dominance of the White House, the Senate, and, most significantly, the national agenda. In the last half of the 1980s, the tone of reporting shifted to the language of decline and fall. With sexual and financial scandals plaguing some media-based ministries, the Democratic recapture of the Senate, the failure of Pat Robertson's 1988 presidential campaign, and the decision to disband conservative organizations like Moral Majority, it was time to write an epitaph for the evangelical political movement (D'Antonio 1989). The perception of evangelical political weakness was further fortified by the collapse of Republican support in the 1992 presidential election and the victory of a baby-boomer Democratic candidate who was prochoice on abortion, sympathetic to the aspirations of gays and lesbians, and, in personal history and life-style, seemed very much a child of the 1960s.

The Republican resurgence in 1994, bolstered heavily by the support of conservative Protestants, showed the danger of writing off the

217

evangelical Protestant bloc. Beyond the ebb and flow of daily events, theologically conservative Christians play a key role in American public life. This chapter explores the increasing political engagement of this important religious community. What do evangelical Protestants think about contemporary political issues? What caused their apparent increase in political action? Has the attempt to mobilize them altered the pattern of American political life? Will the activism persist and in what form? These questions will guide the analysis of a new political force that some observers denounced as dangerous to the political system and others heralded as a movement to revitalize American politics.

The Political Background

Of all the shifts and surprises in contemporary political life, perhaps none was so wholly unexpected as the political resurgence of evangelical Protestantism in the late 1970s. Under the spell of modernization theory, many observers had treated traditional religion as a spent force in American life and politics (see chap. 1).[1] Like other predictions rooted in secularization theory, this assessment was rudely challenged by evidence that evangelical Christianity had achieved new strength and was ready to assert that power in political activity. The nomination of Jimmy Carter in 1976, the rise to national notice of organizations such as Moral Majority, the restoration of spirited public debate about certain "moral" issues—all these signs of evangelical political awakening marked the return to national prominence of a force that knowledgeable observers had long ago written off.

Until the 1920s evangelical Protestantism was an animating force in American political life. It had contributed greatly to the growth of antislavery sentiment in the Northern states during the period leading up to the Civil War and, paradoxically, reinforced the commitment of Southerners to the maintenance of the slave economy (Carwardine 1993). In the decades following that great conflict, evangelicals generally sided with a variety of movements designed to purify American politics of various corrupting influences. In the twenty years before World War I, when it was embodied in the national arena by William Jennings Bryan, the evangelical impulse was a driving force behind such disparate movements as currency reform, women's suffrage, regulation of corporate abuses, arbitration of international conflicts, and adoption of "direct democracy" through the initiative, referendum, and recall election (Levine 1975). These reforms of the Progressive era were advanced as means to defend the economic interests and social values of traditional Protestantism. Their widespread adoption before World War I attested to the central place of evangelicalism in American culture.

In the period following World War I, evangelical Protestantism was displaced from its perch as a major cultural force by a series of major social developments that culminated in a virtual social revolution. It is important to recognize the shattering impact of these trends.

The disintegration of traditional American values—so sharply recorded by novelists and artists—was reflected in a change in manners and morals that shook American society to its depths. The growing secularization of the country greatly weakened religious sanctions. People lost their fear of Hell and at the same time had less interest in Heaven; they made more demands for material fulfillment on Earth. . . . Most important, the authority of the family, gradually eroded over several centuries, had been sharply lessened by the rise of the city. "Never in recent generations," wrote Freda Kirchwey, "have human beings so floundered about outside the ropes of social and religious sanctions." (Leuchtenburg 1958, 158)

Under the impact of rapid urbanization, the spread of science and technology, and skyrocketing birth rates in the predominantly non-Protestant immigrant communities, the conditions that had once favored traditional Protestant religion began to lose hold. The weakening of the social values associated with evangelicalism was apparent in such disparate trends as the growth in women's employment, the loosening of restraints on sexuality, the rising prestige of science, and a general tendency to exalt hedonism and materialist values. Even many Protestants, later recognized as founders of the "mainline" approach, began to doubt the literal authority of the Bible and its superiority relative to science.

Whether these developments were ever as widespread as imagined is really beside the point. Accurately or not, evangelicals thought they were confronted with threats to orthodox Christianity, and they reacted with furious defensive activity. Attempting to resist the encroachments of secularism in the political realm, they concentrated in the 1920s on a pair of causes—the campaigns to restrict the sale of intoxicating liquor and to prohibit the teaching of evolution in the public schools. Both movements attained temporary success, but in the end, neither could withstand the shift of power to the burgeoning cities, where evangelicalism was weak and a new set of issues commanded public interest.

The fate of evangelicalism was tied to "a receding and beleaguered small-town culture" (Burner 1967, 4). As many predominantly northern denominations embraced modernity and expressed a willingness to apply scientific insight to religious belief, the center of gravity in evangelicalism shifted to the rural South. There were significant political implications in the increasing southern orientation of traditional Protestantism. Unlike northern evangelicals, who had argued that salvation depended on both faith and works, the southern variety of Protestant Christianity stopped short of demanding social transformation as a condition for salvation. To most southern theological conservatives,

salvation was an act, a transaction between God and the individual that was separable from the life that followed. Those who had been born again were expected to practice Christian morality, to behave rightly in their own lives, and to work and pray for the conversion of others. Yet these expectations were never connected with any imperative to transform their culture in the name of Christ. They did not deprecate the world about them; they simply saw religious life as something to be carried on in a separate compartment. (Kleppner 1979, 187)

From its new southern base, evangelicalism thus chose to remain outside the political arena—a withdrawal broken only by participation in sporadic rearguard actions through fringe movements and extremist crusades. Whether scholars studied the Ku Klux Klan, segregationists, book censors, or virulent anti-Communists, they found evangelical Protestants overrepresented (Clabaugh 1974; Craig 1987; Grupp and Newman 1973; Ribuffo 1983). These links between evangelicalism and regressive political movements fixed traditional religion with a public image as narrow-minded, bigoted, and backward looking—an image that obscured earlier associations between the same religious community and progressive political causes (R. Warner 1979).

Observers relied on social and theological factors to explain the political style of traditional Protestantism after World War I. The social and economic deprivation that typified evangelicals denied them the time, energy, or skill to carry on sustained political participation and isolated them from experiences that would have promoted tolerance, compromise, and other democratic values. Lesser educational opportu-

nities were said to afflict evangelicals with cognitive rigidity, an inflex-
ibility of mind that kept them at a disadvantage in genuinely democratic political competition (Lipset 1960, 100). Furthermore, the otherworldly orientation of southern religion, the divorce of religion from
social conditions, discouraged participation in the earthly process of
political action.

To the extent that evangelicals participated in national political life
after Bryan's eclipse, their sympathies remained with the Democratic
party.[2] The alliance between theological conservatives and the more
liberal of the national parties can be explained largely in regional and
class terms. The force of tradition kept white Southern Baptists, the
largest evangelical denomination, firmly attached to the party that had
reestablished white political dominance in the late nineteenth century
and usually selected its vice-presidential nominee from the region. The
linkage was further cemented in the 1930s by the popularity of the
New Deal social welfare programs that attacked poverty and agricultural distress in the region (Billington and Clark 1991). The first academic studies of public opinion and party allegiance, published in the
1940s and 1950s, confirmed what southern election returns had suggested—that white Southern Baptists were disproportionately attached
to the Democratic party and much more prone than other groups to
support government programs of economic security (Allinsmith and
Allinsmith 1948). Though the "states' rights" revolt at the 1948
Democratic National Convention had demonstrated the capacity of the
civil rights issue to draw southern whites away from a Democratic allegiance, the partisan impact of the controversy was checked by the similarity of the Democratic and Republican positions until the 1960s.

The first stirrings of change in the pattern of evangelical politics
were visible in presidential elections of the 1960s. When the
Democratic party nominated a Catholic for president in 1960, large
numbers of white, churchgoing southern Protestants defected to the
Republican candidate (Converse 1966; Dawidowicz and Goldstein
1974, 41–48). Four years later the same parts of the country that had
given William Jennings Bryan his greatest margins of support responded favorably to the candidacy of Sen. Barry Goldwater (R-Ariz.), who
had cultivated their favor by emphasizing conservative social values
(Burnham 1968). Goldwater's candidacy appeared to galvanize many
evangelicals who had previously stayed outside the political arena. In

1968 George Wallace's independent presidential candidacy showed extraordinary strength among southern whites belonging to theologically conservative denominations (Orum 1970). By the end of the decade, the level of psychological attachment to the Democratic party and voting support for its presidential candidates had eroded considerably among white southerners (Knoke 1976, 23).

These trends did not wholly prepare observers for the subsequent attempts to turn evangelical Protestants to the political right. The changing voting patterns in the South were not interpreted principally in terms of a revolt by theological conservatives but rather in racial and economic terms.[3] The Republican surge in 1960 was attributed directly to anti-Catholic sentiment, but most observers perceived it in the context of a steady postwar erosion of Democratic support in the region, occasioned by the increasing liberalism of the national Democratic party on race and social welfare issues and the corresponding move to the right by the Republican leadership. Most influential commentators on southern politics did not dwell on the role of religious values in stimulating these voter transitions.

The rise of Jimmy Carter to national power in 1976 focused public attention on the growing political significance of evangelical Protestantism and further undermined the stereotype of rabid extremism. A well-educated and scientifically trained man, comfortable with contemporary culture and familiar with modern theology, Carter advocated moderate to liberal policies without the excited appeals to emotion that had been the hallmark of evangelical politics. In the face of publicly expressed doubts by Catholic, Jewish, and black leaders who associated southern evangelicals with religious and racial bigotry, Carter's moderation seemed to promise a welcome break with that unpleasant historical tradition. In the election of 1976 he carried Catholic and Jewish voters by the same or greater margins as had most other postwar Democratic presidential candidates and, like Lyndon Johnson and Hubert Humphrey, received virtually unanimous support from African Americans (W. Miller, Miller, and Schneider 1980, 332). That Carter could appeal so strongly to liberal social groups and carry most of the southern states suggested the end of evangelical political distinctiveness. That impression might not have been so widely accepted had more people realized that a majority of white southerners voted for Carter's Republican opponent (*Public Opinion* 1985).

Roots of the "New Christian Right"

The return of evangelicals to organized political action, manifested in what has been labeled the New Christian Right (NCR), or the New Religious Right, was facilitated by a number of local movements that developed during the social ferment and upheaval of the 1970s. Alan Crawford (1980), a conservative journalist who looks with disfavor on the evangelical influence in politics, argued that three grassroots campaigns paved the way for subsequent national organizations: a textbook controversy in West Virginia, a gay-rights referendum in Dade County (Miami), Florida, and a spirited campaign in the early 1980s to defeat the proposed Equal Rights Amendment to the Constitution. In each case, evangelicals rallied strongly to the defense of traditional cultural and social values.

In the mid-1970s protesters in a mining valley of West Virginia challenged some of the English textbooks that the Kanawha County Board of Education had approved for use in public schools. Led by the wife of a fundamentalist minister, who denounced most of the books as "disrespectful of authority and religion, destructive of social and cultural values, obscene, pornographic, unpatriotic, or in violation of individual and familial rights of privacy" (Jenkinson 1979, 18), the campaign ignited a massive boycott of the schools by the parents of most students, sympathetic wildcat strikes by coal miners, mass picketing all across the county, a teachers' strike, temporary closure of the schools, and several violent assaults on people and property. Although all the books were eventually approved for classroom use, the controversy led to the resignation of the school superintendent and a new textbook adoption procedure that made it easier for parents to screen out "offensive" books. The apparent success of the parent groups in the Kanawha County "Battle of the Books" inspired similar challenges around the country (Richburg 1986) that continue today.

The seeds of the New Christian Right were also planted by the 1977 Dade County, Florida, referendum on a gay-rights ordinance. As part of a nationwide campaign to gain legal protection, homosexuals had persuaded the Dade County Commission to pass an ordinance prohibiting discrimination on the basis of sexual preference in housing, employment, and public accommodations. The ordinance prompted formation of a new organization, called Save Our Children, which claimed that the law would require private and religious schools to employ homosexuals as teachers. After a petition drive led by the singer Anita Bryant and many religious leaders, the ordinance was submitted to a popular referendum and voted down by more than a 2–1 margin. Similar ordinances were subsequently repealed elsewhere around the country.

The potential clout of religious conservatism was also on display in the remarkable campaign that defeated the proposed Equal Rights Amendment to the Constitution (Boles 1979). Approved by Congress early in 1972, the amendment prohibiting sexual discrimination by the states and the federal government quickly sailed through ratification votes in twenty-two state legislatures, leaving it only sixteen states short of formal adoption. The seemingly inevitable path to constitutional status was interrupted by the formation of "Stop-ERA" under the leadership of Phyllis Schlafly, a longtime activist in conservative political causes. In the face of determined lobbying by Schlafly's organization and allied groups, the rate of ratification dropped sharply and the amendment ultimately died three states short of the thirty-eight needed. To underline the religious dimension to the conflict, most of the states that failed to ratify had substantial concentrations of Mormons (Utah, Nevada, Arizona) or evangelical Protestants (all the southern states except Texas and Tennessee), and conservative churches supplied the recruitment base for most of the antiratification leaders and activists (Arrington and Kyle 1978; Brady and Tedin 1976; Conover and Gray 1983; Mueller and Dimieri 1982; Jones 1983; Tedin 1978; Tedin et al. 1977; Wohlenberg 1980; D. G. Matthews and De Hart 1990). Among ordinary citizens, both membership in fundamentalist churches and high rates of church attendance were associated with opposition to the amendment (Burris 1983).

Although motivated by different issues, these three campaigns were tied together by common dissatisfaction with what the participants saw as a godless society that had replaced firm moral standards with a system of relativism (Phillips 1982, chap. 14). The campaigns against "obscene" schoolbooks, gay-rights ordinances, and the ERA attracted a variety of supporters but appealed most strongly to evangelical Protestants, who saw each movement as a crusade in defense of traditional Christian values and institutions. The particular value presumed under attack ranged from respect for social conventions in West Virginia to heterosexual marriage in Miami to the maintenance of traditional social roles for women in the struggle over the ERA. Underlying the challenges to orthodox Christian values, it was argued by some leaders of the movement, was a doctrine called "secular humanism." Although definitions of that concept varied from one critic to another, social conservatives generally agreed that at its core lay a belief in the supremacy of humanity rather than of God. According to the advocates of traditional social values, the doctrine of secular humanism had become entrenched in the government, schools, media, and other institutions that molded public perceptions. Through state and local campaigns against particular outcroppings of what they saw as a pernicious idea, conservative religious activists began to forge organizational links and a common view about the source of major social problems.

These movements represented a sea change in the thinking of evangelical Protestants, a "coming out" almost as dramatic as the political awakenings of feminists and homosexuals that had triggered it. Once ridiculed as being "so heavenly minded they were of no earthly good," evangelicals had been theologically unequipped for regular participation in society. Their ministers had long warned them to steer clear of "secular" politics and focus their energies on their salvation. But now, in response to the menacing social trends unleashed in the 1960s, they were counseled to "reject the division of human affairs into the 'secular' and 'sacred' and insist, instead, that there is no arena of human activity, including law and politics, which is outside of God's lordship. The task is not to avoid this world, but to declare God's Kingdom in it" (Buzzard 1989). Animated by this ideal, evangelicals began to apply to politics the same missionary zeal they had traditionally shown in converting individuals.

Building a National Movement

The political successes of grassroots evangelicalism did not go unnoticed by "secular" conservative activists. Casting about for a strategy to restore a Republican party dispirited by consecutive electoral defeats in 1974 and 1976, they attempted to capitalize on the political energy displayed by evangelicals and to transfer it from the local to the national arena. The effort to build bridges between secular and religious conservatives was spearheaded by four activists with no background in the evangelical community: Howard Phillips of the Conservative Caucus; John "Terry" Dolan of the National Conservative Political Action Committee (NCPAC); Paul Weyrich of the National Committee for the Survival of a Free Congress; and Richard Viguerie, a major fundraiser for conservative causes.

Spurred on by the availability of a large pool of potential allies, Phillips and his colleagues offered assistance to the emerging leaders of the Christian conservative movement and urged the most vocal leaders of the evangelical community to make common cause with other single-issue groups. The basis for coalition would be a frontal attack on "big government" as a threat to traditional religious and economic values. With that theme, they hoped to harness evangelicals to a comprehensive conservative program, including opposition to liberal policies on gun control, the treaty relinquishing American control over the Panama Canal, nonrestrictive abortion laws, compulsory unionization, and defense cutbacks. Using their contacts and ample political resources—especially Viguerie's demonstrated ability to raise money through direct-mail appeals to conservative sympathizers—the secular conservatives helped to build up several national organizations designed to appeal to evangelical Protestants and other theological conservatives.

The most prominent of the new organizations, Moral Majority, was founded in 1979 by television evangelist Jerry Falwell, the minister of the nation's largest independent Baptist church, in Lynchburg, Virginia. Concentrated mostly in the southeastern states, Moral Majority drew most of its membership and leadership from other independent Baptist churches. The organization's state chapters encouraged church members to register as voters and to support staunch conservatives. To reach into the Southern Baptist Convention, the single largest evangelical denomination, Ed McAteer started the Religious Roundtable. The Roundtable (which dropped the "Religious" from its name) was intended primarily to provide a common meeting ground where theologically conservative pastors could learn the fine art of political mobilization through briefings and workshops on conservative causes. Christian Voice, the oldest of these Christian Right groups, grew out of an unsuccessful attempt by California evangelicals to pass a state law limiting the public employment of homosexuals or homosexual advocates. Concentrated in the western and southwestern states and composed primarily of members of the Assemblies of God, Christian

Voice concentrated its efforts on electioneering—compiling information on candidates, offering lists of favored and opposed candidates, and raising funds to support independent campaigns for favored candidates. It also had an active lobbying presence in Washington, D.C. Initially formed to defend the interests of the burgeoning Christian schools movement in 1977, the National Christian Action Coalition (NCAC) was a multipurpose organization (Moen 1989, 71–73). To secure its goal of defending Christian schools from governmental intrusion, it lobbied on Capitol Hill, raised funds for candidates, and compiled the first "family issues" scorecard for congressional representatives. The founder, Bob Billings, was named by President Reagan to a post in the U.S. Department of Education.

There were other smaller groups that focused on a narrower range of issues yet drew in one way or another on the same concerns that motivated the larger organizations. Although the existence of so many different organizations reflected some of the diversity in the evangelical community and a degree of rivalry among the prominent television ministers, the different groups shared members, staff, support services, funding sources, and office space (Hill and Owen 1982, 56). The principal leaders formed something of an interlocking directorate, holding seats on the boards of one another's organizations and leadership positions in the secular conservative groups with whom they were allied. All the organizations established at the end of the 1970s also drew on the experience and expertise of earlier movements designed to spur evangelicals into political action, including some with ties to Ronald Reagan's unsuccessful bid for the 1976 Republican presidential nomination (Blumenthal 1984).

These organizations also shared a common agenda (Shriver 1981). Described by the Christian Right as the "profamily" program, the same specific proposals showed up in the literature of all four organizations. The Reverend Falwell's "Christian Bill of Rights" stressed opposition to abortion, support for voluntary prayer and Bible reading in public schools, the responsibility of government to encourage the "traditional family unit," maintenance of tax exemption for churches, and noninterference by the authorities with Christian schools. In an effort to explain the need for mobilizing evangelicals, Christian Voice expanded the list of social evils to include the teaching of evolution, pornography, the celebration of "immoral" behavior on television, and liquor and drug abuse. True to its roots in the Christian school movement, NCAC pressed relentlessly for income tax credits to offset private school tuition.

Although assigning preeminence to family issues, the leaders of these movements did not ignore the issues that concerned "secular" conservatives, including increased defense spending, support of anti-Communist movements around the globe, anti-inflationary policies, efforts against street crime, and calls for a balanced budget. In each case, conservative positions on these issues were advocated with a religious rationale. Thus, increased defense spending was justified as a way of keeping the nation free for the continued preaching of the Gospel, and support for the governments of Taiwan and South Africa was defended as necessary to protect Christian allies from the "Godless forces of anti-Christ Communism." Similarly, Falwell asserted a scriptural basis for low inflation, flat-rate taxation, and a balanced federal budget. In practice, however, conservative social values drove the formation and activity of the New Christian Right.[4]

Evangelical Political Action in the 1980s

The New Christian Right, as it was styled by media and academic observers, first gained widespread national attention during the presidential campaign of 1980, when its leaders coalesced around the candidacy of Ronald Reagan. Divorced, an intermittent churchgoer from a mainline denomination, the father of children who have pursued unconventional lives, and a veteran of show business, Reagan seemed a most unlikely object of support for the devout—doubly so in a race with two other evangelical Protestants, Jimmy Carter and John Anderson. But as Reagan alone embraced the political efforts of the conservative evangelical leaders and pledged to work for enactment of their agenda, he increasingly drew the New Christian Right into his camp. All the groups encouraged pastors to sign up evangelicals on the voter rolls and to impress upon churchgoers the necessity of expressing their religious convictions in the polling booth. These efforts led to a substantial evangelical presence in political party activities during the 1980 campaign (see chaps. 5–7 in T. Baker, Steed, and Moreland 1983).

Despite criticism of the administration's failure to push hard enough on the social agenda, the leaders of the New Christian Right lined up even more enthusiastically behind the Reagan reelection effort in 1984. The Republican convention opened with a prayer by the Rev. James Robison, a Texas evangelist who had been vice president of the Roundtable, and closed with a benediction from Moral Majority president Jerry Falwell, who referred to the Republican nominees as "God's instruments in rebuilding America." [5] The platform committee called for a constitutional amendment to restrict abortion, legalization of prayer and religious meetings in public schools, a ban on abortion, and withheld support from the Equal Rights Amendment. In language that spoke directly to the concerns that had prompted formation of the evangelical political movement, the platform accused the Democrats of "assaulting our basic values," stating: "They attacked the integrity of the family and parental rights. They ignored traditional morality. And they still do." To hammer home the point about the differing stands taken by the two major parties, speakers referred constantly to their opponents as "the San Francisco Democrats," linking the freewheeling city where the Democrats had met for their convention with the policies pursued by the party. And on the morning of his renomination, President Reagan brought religion even more firmly into the campaign by giving a speech at a prayer breakfast that had been organized by the convention host committee (Reagan 1984). The groups followed up on these convention efforts by devoting yet more funds to mount voter-registration drives in evangelical churches.

Without the unifying presence of Ronald Reagan at the head of the ticket, evangelical leaders split during the 1988 Republican primary campaign. Jerry Falwell endorsed George Bush, while Jack Kemp and Robert Dole drew support from other New Christian Right activists. With the decline of the four major groups active in 1980, the significance of these endorsements was dubious. Moreover, the major focus of evangelical activism in 1988 was the campaign for the Republican nomination by Pat Robertson, an ordained Southern Baptist minister who had built the Christian Broadcasting Network into the nation's largest religious broadcasting empire. But Robertson's hopes of riding to the nomination on the basis of a strong showing in the "Super Tuesday" southern primaries in March were dashed by his poor showing throughout the region. He eventually withdrew, a victim of the strong competition, his own verbal gaffes and limited experience, and strong divisions within the evangelical camp (Wald 1991).

Though he was a member of the impeccably mainline Episcopalian church and a former congressional advocate of the prochoice position, George Bush sought Christian Right support in both his presidential campaigns. The scandals engulfing several television ministries made Bush wary of too public an embrace by the movement in 1988. Nonetheless, the Republican campaign stressed conservative cultural themes (J. White 1990), and the Religious Right reciprocated by mobilizing for the GOP ticket. Facing a strong Democratic challenge in 1992 and under criticism from several Christian Right groups for having refused to exclude homosexuals from his administration, Bush's 1992 reelection campaign pushed the "profamily" agenda much more aggressively. In several well-publicized talks, Vice President Dan Quayle attacked moral relativism, unmarried mothers, and the low moral standards of the mass media. At the Republican convention in Houston, delegates heard prime time addresses on the same subjects from Pat Buchanan, Pat Robertson, and Marilyn Quayle. Bush himself criticized the Democrats for omitting God from their platform. When Bush's defeat was attributed in part to the concerns of moderate voters about the Christian Right's "capture" of the party, several moderate Republicans announced plans to challenge Christian Right influence. The movement that seemed so promising in the early 1980s was now perceived by some as an albatross around the necks of the GOP.

The Next Generation

After the 1988 presidential campaign there was a period of soul searching among evangelical activists. Deeply dissatisfied by how little public policy had changed after their years of intense activity, evangelicals began to question both the strategy and the tactics of the movement. The strategic decision to focus on the national government exposed the New Christian Right to the immobilism built into the American political system. With its fragmented structure and multiple centers of power, the U.S. political system has long resisted radical attempts to reshape public policy. The movement might have done better had it chosen to remain active primarily at the state and local levels, where it was incubated and generally faced fewer obstacles. Beyond this strategic mistake, the movement also committed a number of tactical blunders. Deceived by poll reports into thinking that their agenda commanded overwhelming public support, evangelical activists frequently disdained "basic rules of politics, such as respect for opposing views, an emphasis on coalition-building and compromise, and careful rhetoric" (Atwood 1990, 45). Although such defects are common to religious groups that enter political life (Donnelly 1987), the mistakes may have been reinforced by the NCR's fundamentalist religious heritage. Confident of their ability to the will of God, conservative evangelicals were quick to claim divine approval for their efforts and to treat any opposition as rebellion against God's will. An insistence on purity of purpose and absolute standards, derived from evangelical doctrine, disposed NCR activists to reject small but attainable victories in favor of grandiose and implausible goals. Thomas Atwood, a member of the Robertson campaign, also accused some evangelicals of "triumphalism," the belief they should rule by virtue of moral superiority, and of ascribing to the state the capacity to redeem humankind (1990). These traits may have been useful in rallying the evangelical faithful, but they hindered efforts to appeal to voters outside the evangelical community.

The kind of behavior that occasioned this criticism was illustrated by the North Carolina congressman who charged that his Democratic opponent denied "the principles outlined in the Word of God" (H. Johnson 1986). Another favorite of the Christian Right, Rep. Mark Sijlander (R-Mich.), appealed to fundamentalist voters to help him "break the back of Satan" (cited in Diamond 1989, 71). Because she was "tired of having the devil's people run things," an Indiana woman told a reporter, she had volunteered for a campaign "to get some of God's people" in office.[6] The same tone pervaded the "report cards" issued by several of the NCR organizations. Using roll-call votes on "moral issues," the evangelical lobbies assigned scores to public officials and pledged to defeat candidates who seldom took positions endorsed by the group. Although the use of such voting scores is common, the New Christian Right approach seemed unusual by suggesting that there was only one "moral" position on such complicated issues as abortion and school prayer.[7] (The flavor of the conflict is reflected in a Christian Voice flyer distributed in 1984; see box on following page.) Furthermore, by attaching the "moral" label to its preferred vote and treating the index as a measure of adherence to the "godly principles" of the nation's Founders, sponsoring organizations seemed to accuse opponents of per-

Christian Voice's "Report Card" on Key 1984 Presidential Candidates

REPORT CARD:
Reagan vs. Mondale vs. Hart

Take the issues test. The following are the Presidential candidates' positions on issues important to Christian Voters. Match your position with the candidates'.

Issue	Ronald Reagan		Walter Mondale		Gary Hart		Your position	
	yes	no	yes	no	yes	no	yes	no
Prayer in School	✔		✔		✔			
Taxpayer-Funded Abortion		✔	✔		✔			
Gay Rights Amendment		✔	✔		✔			
Equal Rights Amendment		✔	✔		✔			
Unverifiable U.S.-Soviet Arms Agreement		✔	✔		✔			
Excessive Government Spending		✔	✔		✔			

Source: Christian Voice Moral Government Fund, Washington, D.C., 1984

sonal immorality and "unchristian" voting (Congressional Quarterly 1980, 2624; Simon 1984, 89–90).[8]

To overcome these barriers, the movement underwent a stunning transformation. Originally a collection of "direct-mail lobbies, led by prominent fundamentalists who championed a moralistic agenda on Capitol Hill," the Christian Right has become "a variety of well-established membership organizations, whose leaders use mainstream language and organize followers in the grassroots" (Moen 1995, 131). As part of this transformation, which critics simply cannot resist describing as a "resurrection" or "second coming," the movement has tried to shed sectarianism and stridency. Most of the pioneering organizations, Moral Majority, American Coalition for Traditional Values (ACTV), and

NCAC, folded. The impetus shifted to the broad-based organizations (listed in table 7.1) that tried to avoid theological language and religious leadership. When candidates of "traditional values" ran for public office, they were advised to run "stealth" campaigns that did not mention religious motivations or some of the policies they wanted to implement. Pat Robertson himself organized a new organization, Christian Coalition, which followed the principle that "the real battles of concern to Christians are in neighborhoods, school boards, city councils and state legislatures." By 1995 the organization claimed 1.6 million members in more than 1,600 local chapters, access to a network of 60,000 churches, and $25 million in funds. During the 1994 election it distributed 35 million voter guides, 17 million congressional scorecards, and made telephone calls to 3 million voters.

Christian Coalition soon emerged as a persistent lobbying force on behalf of the "Contract with America," the platform of the new Republican majority in Congress. In doing so, the movement emphasized such "secular" policies as the Balanced Budget Amendment, tax relief for families, welfare reform, and term limits (Christian Coalition 1995). Scrupulously avoiding religious language, the organization described Republican policies as "profamily" rather than ordained by God. That same reticence marked the coalition's own "Contract with the American Family," introduced with great fanfare on the steps of the U.S. Capitol in mid-1995 (ibid.). The document called for

1. restoring religious equality
2. local control of education
3. promoting school choice
4. protecting parental rights
5. family-friendly tax relief
6. restoring respect for human life
7. encouraging support of private charities
8. restricting pornography
9. privatizing the arts
10. punishing criminals, not victims.

These priorities represent a mix of themes from the early days of the Christian Right as well as more recent concerns. The moral traditionalism evident at the origins of the movement persists in the calls to restrict abortion, pornography, and funding for obscene art (nos. 6, 8, 9). The desire to shield Christian schools and "home schoolers" from state reg-

Table 7.1 Christian Right Organizations and Their Opponents

Organization	Members	Purpose and Methods
	Christian Right Groups	
American Family Association Tupelo, Miss. (gocin.com/afa) Rev. Donald Wildmon	600,000	Formerly the National Federation for Decency, it concentrates primarily on fighting obscenity in the mass media and favors consumer boycotts against television programs (and their sponsors) that have sex, violence, and profanity
Christian Coalition Chesapeake, Va. (cc.org) Ralph Reed	1.6 million	Formed out of Pat Robertson's 1988 presidential campaign, the organization emphasizes legislative lobbying and mobilizing conservative Christians
Citizens for Excellence in Education Anaheim, Calif. Rev. Robert Simonds	NA	An offshoot of a Christian educators association, this group has been active in trying to elect fundamentalists to local school boards
Concerned Women of America San Diego, Calif. (kma.com/cwa.html) Beverly LaHaye	600,000	Concentrates primarily on opposing gay rights legislation
Eagle Forum Alton, Ill. (basenet.net/~eagle) Phyllis Schlafly	80,000	This group now concentrates primarily on educational issues—opposition to Outcomes Based Education, national standards, sex education, or use of the schools to promote self-esteem
Family Research Council Washington, D.C. (townhall.com/townhall/ FRC) Gary Bauer	250,000	Principally a research and lobbying organization, this group deals with a wide range of issues relevant to "traditional" families. Opposes gays in the military, parental notification of abortions, government sex research, etc.

Table 7.1 *Continued*

Organization	Members	Purpose and Methods
Focus on the Family Colorado Springs, Colo. (cs.albany.edu/~ault/fof) Rev. James Dobson	2,000,000 mailing list	Provides a Christian perspective on questions of child-raising and family matters. Less engaged in politics, it has become active in the anti-gay rights movement and strongly opposes contemporary feminism
Traditional Values Coalition Orange County, Calif. Rev. Lou Sheldon	50,000	This group has led the anti-gay movement on the West Coast
Groups Opposed to the Christian Right		
Americans United for Separation of Church and State Silver Spring, Md. (netplexgroup.com/ americansunited) Rev. Barry Lynn	50,000	Once an organization known for its opposition to Catholic power, AU has broadened into an ecumenical organization that undertakes litigation on behalf of church-state separation
American Civil Liberties Union New York, N.Y. (gopher://aclus.org:6601) Ira Glasser	280,000	This organization has a broad agenda but works to defend a separationist policy in the name of religious freedom. It has also taken the cases of several fundamentalist students who charge their religious rights were abridged by local schools. Major work is litigation
Institute for First Amendment Studies Great Barrington, Mass. (berkshire.net/~ifas/) Skipp Porteous	NA	A clearinghouse for information and research on right-wing Christian movements
Interfaith Alliance Washington, D.C. (intr.net/tialliance) Rev. Herbert Valentine	20,000	An educational and lobbying group that publicizes actions of the Christian Right through reports, press releases, and public statements

Continued on next page

Table 7.1 *Continued*

Organization	Members	Purpose and Methods
People for the American Way Washington, D.C. (gopher.com/11/ Artswire/pfaw)	300,000	Begun in response to Moral Majority, conducts extensive research on conservative Christian movements and lobbies against their proposals

Note: The organizations' electronic addresses are listed in parentheses. In order to make contact, the address must be preceded by: http://. To contact Christian Coalition, for example, the Internet location (URL) is: http://cc.org.

ulations is also apparent in priorities 2 and 4, and the first item on the list is part of a strategy to undermine Supreme Court separationism. Other items are aimed much more broadly at secular conservatives who want to preserve the legality of corporal punishment for children (no. 4), lower taxes (no. 5), dismantle welfare programs (no. 7), and increase the stringency of criminal law (no. 10).

Even when today's Christian Coalition embraces the same policies as yesterday's Moral Majority, the differences in language reveal a striking tactical shift. Whereas Jerry Falwell cited Scripture as the basis for each plank of his ten political commandments, Christian Coalition spokesmen like Ralph Reed speak in the liberal language of "rights, equality, and opportunity" (Moen 1995, 130). In this framework, school prayer is defended as the right of religious students to free speech, state subsidies for religious schools become a policy of "choice," and abortion is criticized for denying opportunity to the fetus. In using such language, Christian Coalition has demonstrated an understanding that the American public offers little support to sectarians who bombard them with nonnegotiable demands but is much more open to reasonable appeals that expand the scope of freedom.

The new organizations also worked diligently to appeal to groups outside evangelical Protestantism. The heritage of fundamentalist involvement in the Ku Klux Klan and radical anticommunism included racism, anti-Semitism, and anti-Catholicism. Although the Moral Majority reached out directly to Catholics, Jews, and blacks, offering a common cause on behalf of what they termed Judeo-Christian values, these efforts were easily undercut by the occasional unguarded anti-

Semitic statements of movement activists. The Christian Coalition's Ralph Reed declared such bigotry unacceptable, the product of the movement's infancy, and assured Jewish audiences that his organization stood for

a nation that is not officially Christian, Jewish, or Muslim. A nation where the separation of church and state is complete and inviolable. Where any person may run for elective office without where they attend church or synagogue ever becoming an issue. A nation where no child of any faith is forced by government to recite a prayer with which they disagree. (Reed 1995)

When critics pointed out that the coalition's founder and director, the Rev. Pat Robertson, had used language that was much less tolerant and inclusive, or denounced specific proposals as efforts to give legal support to fundamentalist values under the cover of neutral principles, the critics were themselves condemned as religious bigots.[9] By turning the language of religious pluralism into a shield, the New Christian Right of the 1990s tried to overcome another of the singular weaknesses it displayed in the 1980s.

Even without the national publicity that has focused on Christian Coalition, many conservative Christians have already redirected their efforts to the states and localities, working diligently for goals as disparate as banning "obscene" lyrics in popular music, challenging sex education programs, fighting against gay rights legislation, and providing options to abortion. By concentrating on the lower levels of American political life and doing so without emphasizing their religious orientations, these activists represent an important new stage in evangelical political mobilization.

Theories of Evangelical Mobilization

Describing the origins and development of the New Christian Right is much easier than explaining it. The emergence of the movement contradicted social science research about the secularization of political conflict and the social and doctrinal bases for evangelical political apathy. Initially caught off guard by the upsurge in evangelical political action, scholars soon began to analyze the new coalition according to theories and concepts that have been applied to similar social movements of the past. Because no single factor is sufficient to explain such an unexpected social development, the responsibility for the New Religious Right must be apportioned among the three facets of religion previously shown to have political relevance: social group, institution, and values.

Social Influences

Although evangelical Protestants rate below average on factors like education, income, and occupational status, the group has achieved dramatic socioeconomic gains in the last half-century (Roof and McKinney 1987). From the late 1940s and through the mid-1950s, white Southern Baptists averaged just under eight years of formal education, and roughly two-thirds did not complete high school. By the 1970s the average years of school completed by the same group had risen to almost eleven, and the proportion with less than a high school degree declined to substantially less than half. These gains in education signaled the growing presence of evangelicals in urban areas, higher income brackets, and white-collar occupations. Though evangelicals continued to lag behind the rest of the white population on most measures of socioeconomic achievement, the younger members of the community came to resemble mainstream American groups. The development of an evangelical middle class was symbolized by the replacement of modest, ramshackle churches with lavish and well-appointed centers of worship.

This objective gain in economic standing contributed in several ways to undercutting evangelical traditions of political apathy and Democratic partisanship. As evangelicals moved into the middle class, they gained resources that encouraged political participation, such valuable assets as increased free time and energy, organizational skills, access to social and communication networks, contacts with government officials, and greater exposure to information. As it often does for other groups, social change also produced an evangelical leadership class of clergy and secular activists. With their increasing economic standing, evangelicals also tended to acquire more of an interest in the policies of low taxation and limited government unceasingly advocated by the Republican party. By moving to cities and suburban communities, evangelicals came face to face with direct assaults on the social values dominant in their rural and small-town strongholds. Such "transitional" environments where conservative Christians faced challenges to traditional values were far more likely to generate Christian Right activity than the sheltered rural areas dominated by evangelicals (Green, Guth, and Hill 1993).

As a result of social transformation, evangelicals emerged in the 1970s with both greater capacity and disposition for political action. But to explain why evangelicals were mobilized principally on the basis of traditional moral and social values, rather than economic appeals, reference to changes in objective economic achievement is not suffi-cient. For many observers, the critical factor in preparing the ground for the New Christian Right was change in subjective social status. According to the "status politics" model that has been used to explain different types of right-wing political action, moral crusades such as those mounted by the Religious Right represent a symbolic response by groups to declines in their social prestige (Lipset and Raab 1981). Joseph Gusfield described "status politics" in the following terms:

As his own claim to social respect and honor [is] diminished, the . . . citizen seeks for public acts through which he may reaffirm the dominance and pres-tige of his style of life. Converting the sinner to virtue is one way; law is anoth-er. Even if the law is not enforced or enforceable, the symbolic import of its passage is important to the reformer. It settles the controversies between those who represent clashing cultures. The public support of one conception of morality at the expense of another enhances the prestige and self-esteem of the victors and degrades the culture of the losers. (1963, 4–5)

The evangelicals, it has been argued, watched with dismay as society turned away from the values represented by traditional morality and opinion leaders appeared to give priority to the interests and aspira-tions of groups, such as African Americans, who had long ranked below them in social esteem. Under this interpretation, resentment about declining social respect paid to devout members of the evangel-ical community prompted their support for movements pledged "to reestablish, through formal political processes, the social support that the group's values once commanded" (Crawford 1980, 149).

Challenging the assumption that evangelicals were necessarily los-ing social prestige, some observers have broadened the status-politics framework into a "politics of life-style concern." In this view, move-ments such as the New Christian Right, rather than trying to recapture lost prestige or social honor, have attempted to defend the values, cus-toms, and habits that form the basis of their life-style (Conover 1983;

Lorentzen 1980; Moen 1984; A. Page and Clelland 1978). Through early training and later participation in group life, evangelicals are exposed to a culture that emphasizes "adherence to traditional norms, respect for family and religious authority, asceticism and control of impulse" (M. Wood and Hughes 1984, 89). When social policies appeared to challenge this frame of reference by endorsing attacks on religion or encouraging self-indulgence and alternatives to the traditional family, it has been argued, evangelicals fought back by supporting policies more in tune with their cultural values.

The concerns of the evangelicals were not entirely symbolic. They criticized the federal government for taking over a number of tasks once reserved for the family (Moen 1989). Medicare was condemned for encouraging people to shirk family obligations, welfare benefits were alleged to encourage promiscuity, and high rates of taxation were blamed for forcing women from the household into the workplace. Of course, the long string of Supreme Court decisions restricting government action in support of religion did hamper the expression of evangelical faith in public schools. Although claims of a conspiracy of "secular humanists" were an effective rhetorical device rather than an empirical reality, there is undeniable evidence of a broadly secular orientation among strategically placed members of the American elite (McCloskey and Zaller 1984, 26). Evangelicals had something to worry about.

Whether couched in its narrow or broad form, status-politics theory asserts that the roots of evangelical political mobilization can be found in perceived social-group interests. That hypothesis has been examined carefully and remains the object of debate.[10] Several studies of moral conservatism have failed to find evidence of status discontent among advocates and the rank and file. Noting that these studies had not measured the degree to which moral conservatives actually felt deprived of social respect, Wald, Owen, and Hill (1989a) assessed the relationship between perceived social respect and support for NCR goals and organizations among a sample of Protestant churchgoers. They found strong support for status politics in the acute sense of status deprivation felt by the most enthusiastic supporters of evangelical political action. To the extent that study is supported by additional research, it suggests that both objective and subjective social forces interacted to foster the New Christian Right.

Institutional Influences

The role of religious institutions was important in this regard. The social transformation of evangelicals produced a major emphasis on what was called "church planting." The so-called super churches, like Jerry Falwell's Thomas Road Baptist Church, took on a wide range of functions and developed into religious equivalents of major corporations (Fitzgerald 1981). Less ambitious local churches also began to provide a wide array of services for their members. As the ministry became more professional, the seminaries produced clerical leaders who managed church entry into such fields as education, day-care, and counseling. The evolution of the churches from places of worship to social service centers brought them under the authority of government regulations affecting zoning, educational practices (curriculum content, teacher certification, desegregation mandates, tax-exempt status), day-care facilities, minimum-wage laws, and working conditions. The result was a series of classic confrontations between the state's interest in regulating the private provision of social services and the church's claims of immunity under the free-exercise clause. With such substantial investments, the churches could no longer afford a policy of political disengagement.

Whatever their motivation, evangelical clergy gradually took up more active political involvement than recorded previously. In studies conducted during the 1960s, scholars found that clergy from conservative Protestantism were much less likely than their liberal counterparts to take public stands on political concerns and were themselves less likely to participate in politics (Quinley 1974). The emphasis on converting sinners took precedence over changing laws. More recent research finds much lower participation differences among clergy from different denominations (Beatty and Walter 1989; Guth et al. 1991). The parishioners appear to be listening. Those from doctrinally conservative Protestant denominations do not report receiving less political direction than mainline Protestants or Catholics (Welch et al. 1993). As we would expect, the priorities of the communication differ, with conservative clergy stressing the profamily agenda while liberal ministers emphasize "peace and justice" issues like hunger and poverty. But the conservative clergy appear to have caught up with their mainline counterparts in the degree to which they preach about politics.

The rapid expansion of the "electronic church" was another manifestation of evangelical growth that stimulated political involvement

(Hadden and Swann 1981). Although estimates vary considerably from one source to another, there are more than one hundred religious television stations, over a thousand religious radio stations, and more than twenty cable networks devoted to religious programming (Bandow 1995). Of the latter, three now broadcast around the clock, several others offer similar programming for parts of the day, and there are fifteen nationally syndicated Christian radio programs; together these networks reach an audience estimated at 25 million people (J. Kennedy 1994). Still more such activity can be expected with the growth of cable television coverage and the proliferation of low-power television stations. Because the airwaves are regulated by the Federal Communications Commission (FCC), religious broadcasters have a natural interest in government decision making.

These institutional interests appeared to function as "trigger issues," particular concerns that may have stimulated evangelical elites to enter the political arena. In the mid-1970s the FCC considered regulations that would have effectively limited the access of religious groups to the public airways. The Carter administration, responding to a Supreme Court decision, took steps to eliminate the tax exemption for segregated religious schools. Both these actions seemed to strike at the heart of the institutions built by evangelical entrepreneurs. Although these issues were enough to give religious leaders an incentive to enter the political arena, it was doubtful that mass movements could be founded on matters that concerned a relatively small portion of the evangelical population. Hence the emphasis on the broader "profamily" agenda, of which religious broadcasting and tax exemption were but two elements.

The growth of evangelical institutions affected not only the interests but also the political capacity of the Religious Right. According to resource mobilization theory, social movements cannot convert grievances into political action unless they have access to potential supporters and other organizational resources that can be pressed into service. Potentially powerful political forces in their own environment, local evangelical churches are also aligned with central organizations that can coordinate nationwide political action. Part of Moral Majority's strength was its direct access to local preachers through the network of churches affiliated with the Baptist Bible Fellowship (R. Liebman 1983). Television evangelists have direct access to viewers and the capacity to tap into mailing lists with millions of names. Not surprisingly in view of these resources, the major political movements targeting evangelicals were initiated by pastors with access to vast broadcasting empires. Falwell had his "Old Time Gospel Hour," the Christian Voice was connected to Robertson's Christian Broadcasting Network, and the Roundtable's leading spokesman, James Robison, had a nationally syndicated program. The extent and effectiveness of their televised political appeals remain a subject of debate (Jelen and Wilcox 1993).

Of course, reliance on broadcasting and national church alliances cannot guarantee success in political life. As some of the liberal clergy discovered in the 1960s, an evangelist who preaches politics instead of the Gospel may lose those in the audience who want religion to address their spiritual concerns. Moreover, constant demands for funds may produce decreasing returns from a weary audience. Competition among media ministers may undermine the unity required for effective political action. The local churches that serve as the base of operations for the New Religious Right, finally, may also fiercely resist attempts at central coordination, fragmenting the energy of the group and giving unwanted publicity to loose cannons such as the Moral Majority chapter head from California who publicly advocated the execution of homosexuals.

Values

The third aspect of religion, comprising theology and values, has also played a part in stimulating the New Christian Right. The new willingness of evangelicals to apply their religious values to public policy has been especially puzzling to the social theorists who used to explain evangelical abstention from politics by citing religious values. How could a theology that once emphasized otherworldliness and personal salvation now become a basis for political activism? Of course, not all evangelicals approved of the new political activism; enough embraced it, however, to require an explanation.

Robert Wuthnow (1983) has suggested that in engaging in politics, the evangelicals were responding to changes in society that encouraged the application of religious values to public policy. At the national level, several trends blurred the traditional view of "morality" as a matter largely for individual behavior and thus raised new public concern about the ethical standards of public institutions. As evidence of the growing trend to approach public policy from an ethical viewpoint, Wuthnow cited "criticism of the Vietnam war as an act of public immorality, the various legislative actions taken in the aftermath of Watergate to institutionalize morality as a matter of official concern, and major Supreme Court decisions symbolically linking government with morality" (ibid., 176). Ironically, Jimmy Carter helped to point the way for evangelicals when he hinged his 1976 campaign on the need to restore trust, honesty, and morality to American public life. All these developments reflected growing recognition that government should not be totally independent of moral considerations and paved the way for morally based criticism of national policy (Lienesch 1993).

Few groups were as receptive to this approach as the evangelicals. Contrary to their historical image, evangelicals have a long tradition of fighting back against perceived assaults by public authority on their favored social values. In the past, this tendency had surfaced mostly in local and state conflicts over issues such as liquor licensing, sex education, and pornography. In the 1970s, however, the challenge appeared to emanate from a national government that seemingly had loosened restraints in hundreds of ways. Faced with a Supreme Court that reduced limits on public expressions of sexuality to an administration that allowed homosexuals to meet with a presidential assistant, evangelicals felt their values under siege in the national arena.

The actions of secular authority not only offended traditional moral values—reason enough to act—but also seemed to threaten the ability of evangelicals to protect themselves and their families from corrupting influences. Encouraged by the politicizing of morality exhibited in the reaction to the civil rights struggle, Vietnam, and Watergate, theological conservatives sought to draw from the same reservoir of moral outrage to influence social policy. And to prosecute the crusade, they could call on an increasingly affluent constituency through several organizational channels.

The New Christian Right as a Mass Movement

Do the organizations of the New Christian Right actually speak for a large majority of the American public, as they have claimed, or do they primarily represent the views of theologically conservative Christians

Table 7.2 Public Agreement on Issues of Government and Morality, in percentages

Our government would be better if policies were more directed by moral values	84
The president should be a moral and spiritual leader	78
God is a heavenly father who can be reached by prayers	76
Individual freedom is critical to democracy in this country	91
Each individual must determine what is right or wrong	70
God is the moral guiding force of American democracy	55

Source: U.S. News poll, 5–7 March 1994, cited in Jeffery L. Sheler, "Spiritual America," *U.S. News and World Report,* 4 April 1994, 48–59.

who are principally concerned with social issues? Thanks to the development of tools such as public opinion polls, some of these claims can be assessed.

Popular support for moral traditionalism is ambiguous (see table 7.2). The first three questions in the survey shown in the table portray a population seemingly hungry for moral leadership and a government inspired by godly values—a population ripe, in other words, for the moral appeals of the New Christian Right. Yet responses to the questions in the bottom of the table show a population equally committed to letting individuals chart their own moral paths. Uncertain that God directs the nation, this resilient individualism creates barriers to using the state to enforce traditional morality. The contradiction embodied in these questions, a yearning for authoritative values coupled with a reluctance to impose them by law, creates an opening for moral reform movements like the Christian Right but also limits their mass appeal.

The limitations are apparent from the poor public reputation of the organizations and standard-bearers. When asked recently about "conservative Christian groups that are active in politics, sometimes called the religious right," only 11 percent of a national sample admitted to knowing much about the movement and just 9 percent of respondents claimed to think of themselves as members (Berke 1994b).[11] Pat Robertson, the movement's standard-bearer in 1988, ranked at the bottom of the list of candidates for the GOP nomination, evoked far more negative than positive assessments and did not win a single primary.[12] The personification of the movement in its early phase, the Rev. Jerry Falwell, was one of the least popular figures on the national political scene and an electoral liability for candidates he endorsed (cited in Sigelman, Wilcox, and Buell 1987, 879). Falwell's organization, Moral Majority, enrolled many fewer people than it claimed and suffered a very negative public image among the relatively small share of the population familiar with it (Buell and Sigelman 1985; Hadden and Swann 1981, 164–165). Using a composite measure, Sigelman, Wilcox, and Buell (1987) found only about 10 percent of the population supportive of NCR organizations, whereas two-thirds to three-fourths were critical.

During the civil rights movement, the cause of racial equality proved more popular than the organizations campaigning for it. In a similar manner, do the NCR's issue preferences, if not the organizations themselves, engage the support of the public? One scholar (Simpson 1983) used poll data to estimate that as much as 70 percent of the adult population was receptive to the "sociomoral" platform advocated by the Christian Right. As we saw in chapter 6, some NCR positions command the blessing of a majority, while others alienate far more people than they attract. Because of variations in question wording and other survey features, the level of public support for the Christian Right platform is extremely difficult to assess. Although the public might give overwhelming support to the principles mentioned in the Christian Coalition priority list, this evaporates when those abstract principles are translated into specific pieces of legislation. Although demurring that their estimate was merely a rough indicator of public sentiment, Sigelman and Presser (1988, 334) revealed that only about 5 percent of the public supported all the Moral Majority policy positions on abortion, sex education, the Equal Rights Amendment, and school prayer. Support for the core items making up the entire "profamily" agenda, limited to a minority of the population, has declined over the course of the 1970s and 1980s as the public has apparently become *more* liberal on issues like abortion, tolerance for homosexuality, and women's rights (Mueller 1983; T. W. Smith 1982).

These numbers reflect the limitations of a movement rooted in a minority constituency. The profamily agenda and the organizations that propagate it have struck the most responsive chord precisely where they might be expected to make a strong appeal—to persons deeply attached to evangelical Protestant denominations and values (Barrett and Harris 1982; Buell and Sigelman 1985; Baker, Epstein, and Furth 1981; Brudney and Copeland 1984; Hertel and Hughes 1987; Kellstedt 1989b; Nemeth and Luidens 1989; Patel, Pilant, and Rose 1982; Shupe and Stacey 1983; Sigelman, Wilcox, and Buell 1987; Smidt 1989c; Tamney and Johnson 1983; Wilcox 1986, 1989a; Wald and Lupfer 1983). As secularization theory suggests, the traditional values of orthodox Christianity appeal disproportionately to groups with the most limited exposure to modernizing institutions—respondents who are older, less educated, less affluent, women not employed outside the house, and residents of the South.[13] Robertson's 1988 presidential campaign drew both electoral and financial support from the same well of Protestant theological conservatism (Green and Guth 1988; Wilcox 1992b). As many studies have suggested, involvement in theologically conservative churches seems to breed a strong attachment to traditional moral values and a tacit willingness for clergy and church members to try to enshrine these values in public policy (Himmelstein 1986).

The constituency for these appeals is smaller than often assumed by journalists (see Yankelovich 1981, 5) and even by Pat Robertson, who confidently claimed "the seventy million evangelical Christians in this country" as his political base (cited in Reid 1987). The sheer size of the target constituency for NCR mobilization varies with the measurement system. The method used in chapter 6, identifying "denominational" evangelicals by counting the number of persons affiliated with specific Protestant traditions, encompasses about one-fourth of the adult population. A common alternative, using survey questions to identify evangelicals by doctrinal convictions (e.g., having a "born again" experience, encouraging others to believe in Jesus, interpreting the Bible literally), can generate larger or smaller estimates depending on the specific question. The "born again" measure, which has occasionally been used alone to identify evangelicals, is subject to dramatic shifts in agreement depending on how the question is worded (Smidt 1989b; Dixon, Levy, and Lowery 1988; Jelen, Smidt, and Wilcox 1993).

Similarly, the percentage of people who take a literal view of the Bible changes with each survey's measure of literalism (Smidt 1989b; Kellstedt and Smidt 1993). Reserving the evangelical label for individuals who meet a number of these doctrinal conditions (a more reliable way to identify adherents), encompasses a somewhat smaller proportion of the population—perhaps 15–20 percent (Gallup 1981). The share of the population in the evangelical camp can be reduced further, to only about one in ten, if membership is determined by asking individuals if they accept the evangelical label (Green et al. 1993).

By saying that the Christian Right is anchored in evangelical Protestantism, I am *not* claiming that it enjoys the unanimous support of that community. The evangelical community as a whole has been surprisingly resistant to the appeals of many organizations campaigning in its name (Smidt 1993, 102). In a 1983 survey of registered voters with evangelical theological convictions, more than a quarter did not recognize Falwell and his organization; opinions were equally divided pro and con among those who did recognize the names (Rothenberg and Newport 1984, 100, 140). Remarkably, among a population heavily targeted by Moral Majority, that organization was less well regarded than two liberal rivals long condemned as purveyors of secular humanism— the National Organization for Women and the National Education Association. Even when the sample was purged of blacks, Catholics, and those with minimal church involvement—groups less disposed to accept the NCR platform—the evangelical community hardly embraced the sociomoral platform associated with Moral Majority (Kellstedt 1989b). Though majorities of the sample approved the Christian Right agenda on school prayer, American support for Israel, and tuition tax credits, substantial majorities also took positions diametrically opposed to the leadership of the conservative Christian organizations on other issues. In supporting the distribution of birth control information in the schools, favoring passage of the Equal Rights Amendment, and rejecting the notion that Acquired Immune Deficiency Syndrome (AIDS) is a form of divine retribution for homosexuality, the evangelicals broke ranks with some of their spokesmen. On other issues on which the New Christian Right has conveyed clear preferences—supporting increases in defense spending, opposing a nuclear freeze, calling for restrictive abortion policy—evangelical opinion was split, with no single opinion clearly preferred over the alternatives. Using data from the same period, Wilcox

(1989a, 408–410) likewise found a large majority of white evangelical Protestants to be either ignorant of Moral Majority, opposed to it on ideological grounds, or sympathetic to its views but committed to the Democratic party. Given this pattern, Robertson's 1988 candidacy had no hope of gaining majority support among evangelical groups (S. Johnson, Tamney, and Burton 1989; Langenbach 1989; Guth et al. 1991, 85).

The lack of evangelical political unity is partly the result of the NCR's narrow agenda."Profamily" issues are not the only questions on the national agenda. When the focus shifts to economic policy, foreign relations, or the environment, evangelicals are not nearly so cohesive, nor do they diverge so much from the attitude patterns of other religious groups (Iannaccone 1993; S. Hart 1992, chap. 7). Like other groups of voters from a common religious tradition, evangelicals tend to divide along lines of class, region, gender, and the like when the issue does not relate to profamily issues, and sometimes even when it does (Pyle 1993). Political diversity explains some part of the movement's failure to monopolize its natural constituency of evangelicals. Contrary to the notion of a "natural" constituency, however, the evangelical bloc is also marked by religious diversity that impedes common political action.

A Fractious Family

Outsiders seldom appreciate the degree of *religious* diversity among the large and heterogeneous population suggested by the "evangelical" label. Nor do they always recognize that these religious differences carry over into politics.

The Christian Right has yet to make much headway among African Americans or the substantial number of white Catholics who subscribe to the doctrines of evangelicalism. Despite their social conservatism, African Americans remain committed to the Democratic party and most of the liberal political agenda (R. Smith and Seltzer 1992, 125–132). Catholic evangelicals and "prolife" advocates are also markedly more liberal than Protestant evangelicals, particularly on questions where church leaders have transmitted a "peace and justice" orientation (Welch and Leege 1991; Wilcox and Gomez 1990a).

Even among white Protestants in evangelical denominations—a group of about 40 million adults that constitutes one of the three largest electoral blocs (J. Green et al. 1993)—there is more "family resemblance" than homogeneity (Dayton and Johnston 1991). Consider the three subcategories composed of fundamentalists, charismatics, and evangelicals. Beyond respect for the authority of the Bible, a sense that salvation is bound up with Jesus, and a commitment to spread the Gospel, these groups follow different paths. Since the traditionalist/modernist debate of the late nineteenth century, fundamentalists have rejected much of modern culture, insisted on the importance of maintaining purity by separation from other faiths, and tended more than other evangelicals to a literal understanding of the Bible. Charismatics, once found only in Pentecostal churches but now present in many evangelical denominations, emphasize the "baptism of the Holy Spirit," based on events recorded in Acts 2, whereby they are infused with divine power by the Holy Ghost. The "indwelling of the Spirit" enables them to speak in tongues, heal by faith, and utter prophecies based on the Bible. These views are often regarded as heretical and perhaps even satanic by fundamentalists who assign exclusive religious authority to Scripture. Both fundamentalists and charismatics may seem strange or extreme to those evangelicals who maintain the essential theological principles mentioned earlier but find a way to accommodate modern culture, recognize that religious truth is embodied in other faiths, and see the Bible as authoritative but not determinative in all matters.

The three categories exhibit some political differences (Wilcox, Jelen, and Leege 1993). Fundamentalists have been found to be considerably more conservative than nonfundamentalist evangelicals and have enlisted much more wholeheartedly in New Christian Right organizations (Green and Guth 1988; Jelen 1987; Smidt 1988; Wilcox 1986; Kellstedt and Smidt 1991; Green et al. 1994). Among ministers, for whom social issues are likely to be paramount, self-identified fundamentalists are three to four times as likely as nonfundamentalists to adopt conservative positions on a broad range of public issues (Beatty and Walter 1988). Fundamentalist clergy in the Southern Baptist Convention were about twice as likely as nonfundamentalists to prefer Pat Robertson over George Bush in 1988 (Guth 1989a). Among the fundamentalist laity, political attitudes were less distinctive except on social issues (Hood and Morris 1985).

The evangelical Protestants who accept the charismatic label are more conservative than their brethren on social morality issues (Smidt 1989c).[14] Pat Robertson, an evangelical who enlisted in the charismatic revival while a seminary student, drew his strongest support from ministers in charismatic denominations such as the Assemblies of God (Langenbach 1989). Charismatic self-identification was the single largest factor distinguishing donors to Robertson's political action committee, his delegates to state conventions, and primary voters (J. Green and Guth 1988, 156; Smidt and Penning 1988, 1991; Penning 1991; Wilcox 1992b; Jelen and Wilcox 1992; J. Green 1993). In the absence of Robertson during the 1992 campaign, charismatics were much less committed than other Protestant evangelicals to the Republican party, ideological conservatism, or the Bush candidacy (J. Green et al. 1993).

These groups are not simply different but may in some cases be antagonistic toward one another. Some leaders of the fundamentalist wing, believing the only task of the churches is to win souls for Christ, preach against any political involvement and denounce with real venom attempts to yoke fundamentalists into unholy alliances with the unsaved. Pat Robertson's involvement in the charismatic renewal movement made him the object of considerable scorn among fundamentalists, while Falwell, rooted in fundamentalism, had limited appeal among charismatics (Jelen 1993). From the other wing of evangelicalism, Social Gospel advocates such as the Sojourners have protested against an unholy alliance between the "prolife" forces on abortion and such "antilife" causes as militarism, capital punishment, apartheid, and social inequality.

Within the mainstream of evangelicalism, those who accepted neither fundamentalism nor the charismatic approach, the New Christian Right received a guarded reception. As Robert Booth Fowler (1982) documented, the leaders of this wing of evangelical Protestantism had been moving toward a more moderate political position throughout the 1960s. The most widely recognized spokesman for this perspective, the Rev. Billy Graham, is a case in point (Pierard 1983; Stockton 1989). At the beginning of his career, Graham exhibited some of the political and social tendencies that were typical of fundamentalist Protestants. But over the course of the years, Graham moved toward the center of the political system by integrating his crusades, speaking out in favor of civil rights legislation, and advocating limits on the nuclear arms race. Graham repeatedly warned that any attempt to identify a particular political agenda with Christianity is likely to bring discredit on religion and to interfere with evangelization.

The Electoral Dimension of the NCR

As an electoral movement, the New Christian Right has three major goals—to get evangelical Protestants to participate in politics, to bring them into the Republican coalition, and to elect social conservatives to public office. Because so many evangelicals lived in the Democratic South and had a reputation for political passivity, achieving these objectives required changing ingrained patterns of behavior. After more than a decade of Christian Right involvement in national elections, we should be able to assess the progress of this effort. Unfortunately, our ability to reach a verdict is hampered by both the inherent difficulty of identifying evangelicals in polls and changes in polling questions over time. Nonetheless, evangelicals do seem to have experienced significant political change on some measures, and the direction of change is in the path advocated by the organized movement. Whether the Christian Right is the cause or consequence of these changes is harder to determine.

In trying to overcome the evangelical tradition of low political involvement, the New Right groups have devoted considerable energy to persuading conservative Protestants that political action is compatible with the Scriptures. This effort *appears* to have paid off in some elections more than others, but the findings of different studies are not wholly consistent. Among white evangelicals defined by membership in denominations, the level of voter turnout rose from 61 to 66 percent between 1972 and 1976, remained at about that level in both 1980 and 1984, and then dropped back to 61 percent in 1988. Despite their turnout surge, the denominational evangelicals voted at a rate consistently below other whites in all these elections (Wilcox 1992a, 220). The doctrinal measures available only since 1980 suggest higher levels of evangelical participation—the low to mid-70 percent range—and less consistent differences between evangelicals and nonevangelicals. According to this system of classification, evangelicals were slightly more likely than nonevangelicals to participate in 1980, significantly less likely to vote in 1984, and equally likely to travel to the polls in 1988 (ibid.). These patterns disguise some significant differences based on region. Except in 1980, evangelicals who resided in the South were much less likely to vote than their northern counterparts (Smidt 1993, 95). Because southerners account for such a large proportion of the doctrinal evangelicals, their lower turnout rates tend to exaggerate the evangelical/nonevangelical participation gap.

Tempting as it is to credit these changes to the Christian Right, the evidence simply does not warrant that conclusion. The sharp increase in turnout among denominational evangelicals in 1976 predated the emergence of the Christian Right on the national scene and seems primarily a function of the modernization of the South or the appeal of Jimmy Carter. There is a stronger case for attributing the 1980 turnout advantage of doctrinal evangelicals to the mobilizing efforts of the various groups that coalesced around the Reagan candidacy. Yet, as noted, evangelical turnout subsequently declined relative to nonevangelicals despite the extensive mobilization efforts in subsequent elections. The most we can say from this evidence is that evangelicals may vote more heavily in national elections but only under extraordinary conditions.

Even if they did not succeed in increasing the evangelical presence in the electorate, perhaps the Christian Right promoted a more Republican self-image among that community. The evidence of change is much clearer on this matter. In the 1970s denominational evangelicals were less prone to Republicanism than other whites. During the 1980s that distinction disappeared and by 1992, as we saw in chapter 6, the evangelicals were almost as pro-Republican as mainline Protestants. Doctrinal measures emphasize even sharper divisions. Already by 1980 evangelicals defined on the basis of beliefs were somewhat more Republican than other whites. In subsequent elections, the gap between the groups has widened. Considering that evangelicals were once the most reliable component of the Democratic voting coalition, the movement toward Republican parity or advantage in this group is stunning. Even this conclusion understates the magnitude of change because the group experiencing the largest shift from the Democrats to Republicans, younger evangelicals in the South, will become an increasingly large bloc in years to come (Kellstedt 1989a).

The evangelicals' growing psychological identification with Republicanism was accompanied by their shift to Republican presidential candidates. In both 1976 and 1980, when the Democratic candidate was a Southern Baptist from Georgia, denominational evangelicals were slightly less likely than other whites to favor the Republican nominee. About the only hint of evangelical distinctiveness in 1980 was the overwhelming support for Reagan—86 percent—among the small share of voters who felt close to evangelical groups like Moral Majority (Brudney and Copeland 1984, 1075). In 1984 and 1988 denominational evangelicals favored the Republican candidate by at least 10 percent more than whites who were not members of the evangelical family. In 1992 the Republican gap between evangelicals and members of other denominations swelled to more than 20 percent, and evangelicals, by virtue of their loyalty to George Bush, surpassed even mainline Protestants as the single largest component of the Republican constituency (Kellstedt et al. 1994). The doctrinal measure tells the same story, although it reports even larger voting differences between evangelicals and nonevangelicals (Smidt and Kellstedt 1992). These changes have given the Republicans a considerable advantage in the South and West (Olson and Beck 1990; Nesmith 1994, chap. 6).

What is particularly telling as a testament to the influence of the Christian Right is not merely the movement of evangelicals toward Republican presidential candidates—most of the electorate is shifting in the same direction—but a change in the basis of the voting decision. In 1980 evangelicals treated the election largely as a referendum on Carter's performance as president, not as a choice between divergent moral platforms (Himmelstein and McRae 1984). Since then, the Christian Right has apparently taught many evangelicals to weigh moral issues heavily in choosing between presidential candidates (Kellstedt 1989a; Hammond, Shibley, and Solow 1994; S. Johnson 1994; Layman and Carmines 1994). In the 1992 election, commentators told us, the outcome was essentially determined by dissatisfaction with the state of the national economy. Asked to explain their presidential choice, voters in most religious groups were three times more likely to cite economic conditions than social issues. But among evangelicals asked the same question, social issues and family values were deemed equal in importance or more substantial a concern than the economy (Kellstedt et al. 1994). Because of their economic standing, evangelicals were probably more exposed than other religious groups to the harsh recession. Their continuing commitment to the Republicans in the face of such powerful pressure—and the presence of two Southern Baptists on the Democratic ticket—testifies to the depth of their newfound partisanship.

The scope of these changes can be traced with particular clarity in the evolution of the largest evangelical denomination, the Southern Baptist Convention (SBC) (Morgan 1995). Once believers in a strong wall of separation between church and state, church delegates had endorsed abortion as a right just two years before the Supreme Court decision of *Roe v. Wade* and had repeatedly endorsed Supreme Court rulings prohibiting organized prayer in public schools (S. Green 1991). Through its membership in the Baptist Joint Committee, the church had lobbied for the types of welfare policies consistent with a Social Gospel approach to Christianity. By contrast, the annual convention has now shifted into a much more activist mode, attacking nearly every policy the SBC once supported, and has withdrawn from the Baptist Joint Committee. A continuing survey of Southern Baptist pastors begun in 1980 shows dramatic change among the clergy in support for state action to reinforce traditional values and in commitment to the Republican party (Guth 1989b; Guth et al. 1991). To borrow a phrase once used to describe the Conservative Party in Great Britain, today's SBC resembles the Republican party at prayer.

How much of this transformation should be credited to the New Christian Right organizations? Using a longer time frame helps us understand that the social movement was responsible for some of this change but also capitalized on changes occurring independently. Evangelicals had shown a willingness to vote Republican *before* the New Christian Right was formed. Kellstedt and Noll's (1990, 360) analysis of denominational evangelicals shows that they had been more Republican than the rest of the nation as far back as 1956. The evangelicals who entered the electorate for the first time in 1980 were actually *more* likely to support the Democratic presidential candidate than were nonevangelicals or evangelicals who had voted before (Smidt 1983, table 8). The apparent increase in Republican voting among evangelicals in 1984 was less impressive than it seems, occurring against a backdrop of abnormally high Democratic support for the candidacy of a fellow evangelical in both 1976 and 1980. Although they have played a role, the leaders of the New Christian Right can claim only partial responsibility for the partisan transformation of the evangelical constituency.

Prior to 1994 NCR-sponsored candidates for lower offices do not appear to have enjoyed similar success (S. Johnson, Tamney, and Burton 1989—but see A. Miller and Wattenberg 1984, 313). Anecdotal evidence supports the claim that evangelicals newly registered by Moral Majority were crucial in the primary defeat of a moderate Republican congressman from Alabama in 1980 (Congressional Quarterly 1980), but other congressional candidates recruited directly from local Christian Right affiliates did poorly (J. Green, Guth, and Hill 1993). Conservative religious themes and organizations have contributed to the successful Senate campaigns of North Carolina's Jesse Helms. For his vociferous and unwavering support of the NCR platform in the Senate and on the campaign trail, Helms was designated "a national treasure" by Jerry Falwell. In a battle against a strong opponent in 1984, Helms benefited from a massive effort to register white voters in conservative churches. Countering Democratic efforts to place more blacks on the voter roles, the Helms campaign relied on an organization headed by the Moral Majority state chairman, a minister, to eke out a narrow victory (H. Johnson and Edsall 1984; Luebke 1985–1986). During the 1990 campaign Helms renewed his "politics of values" by framing the campaign as a choice between "decent, God-fearing people" against an unholy coalition of "gays, radical feminists, and arts people," the latter referring to supporters of federal funding for allegedly blasphemous and pornographic works of art.[15] Helms's cultural conservatism helped him win the vote of more than two-thirds of white Protestants, well above his statewide percentage of the total vote.[16]

The 1994 congressional campaigns may have marked a turning point. The sweeping Republican gains in the U.S. Senate and House of Representatives were credited in large measure to the mobilization of two key constituencies, gun owners and Christian conservatives (Schneider 1995). By blaming liberal programs like welfare spending for a breakdown of family structure, fueling a rise in crime and undermining the social order, the Republican campaign themes echoed the language of the Christian Right (Edsall 1994a). Christian Right activists played a key role in a number of states, often tilting the Republican primary to their favored candidates (Rozell and Wilcox 1995b) and electing an unprecedented number of evangelical Protestants to Congress (Hertzke 1995). As in 1992, evangelicals contributed more votes to the Republican cause than any other religious group (J. Green et al. 1995). Some caution is in order before concluding that the 1994 results mean that evangelicals have come to dominate national politics. In many races, candidates who were portrayed as card-carrying members of the Christian Right lost elections precisely because of that association (Rozell and Wilcox 1995b). Moreover, the conditions of 1994—a midterm election with participation from only about one-fourth of the electorate—were much more favorable to a highly motivated minority bloc of voters than the vastly different circumstances of a presidential election year. The results of 1994 do confirm the Republican loyalty of evangelicals but do not ordain their electoral dominance.

A Republican Dilemma?

Whatever its strengths and weaknesses as a mass movement, the New Christian Right has channeled many of its activists into Republican party organizations. Conservative Christians have flocked to local and state party caucuses, taking control of the Republican apparatus in at least eighteen states—not only evangelical strongholds in the South but also such apparently unlikely places as California, Minnesota, Iowa, and Oregon (Persinos 1994). Perhaps as many as one-fourth of the delegates to the 1992 Republican national convention were part of this bloc, giving them substantial platform influence. That Christian Right activists have gained a virtual veto on the choice of the 1996 Republican presidential nomination was suggested by the early exit from the race of the only prochoice candidates—California governor Pete Wilson, Pennsylvania senator Arlen Specter, and Gen. Colin Powell.

Despite the prospect of attracting new partners to their coalition, longtime Republicans have not always welcomed the converts (Hertzke 1993, 158–171). Describing the Robertson forces as something like "the bar scene out of *Star Wars*" (cited in Hertzke 1989, 6), the Republican state chairman of Michigan articulated the repugnance that many in the GOP establishment felt toward the newcomers. His counterpart in Georgia declared that the Christian Rightists who took over that state's party had the attitudes "that brought you the burning of Joan of Arc, the Salem Witch trials, and the Ayatollah Khomeini" (Gurwitt 1989, 54). The tendency of the evangelicals to portray this conflict as a battle of "Christians vs. Republicans" did not smooth over the situation. Republican elites in several states were particularly aggrieved at the seizure of party power by neophytes who had only recently left the Democratic party. Stung by charges that the association with the Christian Right hurt the party in 1992, moderates formed organizations to counter the influence of Christian activists and soften platform language about abortion.

To some extent, the resentment directed by party regulars against the evangelical newcomers is an inevitable by-product of a struggle for power. But it also reflects a cultural conflict—what one participant called "the God Squad versus the Regulars" (ibid., 7). The conservative Christian activists who have moved into Republican party circles bring different values, priorities, and styles. Compared to party regulars, they are decidedly more religious, and they are religious in a different, more intense manner. Although sharing the economic conservatism of the regulars, they attach much greater priority to social issues and take an extremely nationalistic line in foreign policy. They disdain political compromise, believe parties must stand clearly for issues, and see little virtue in harboring diverse viewpoints (J. Green and Guth 1988; Smidt and Penning 1988). This "purist," or amateur, political style puts them at odds with party regulars who have learned to bargain and negotiate if it advances the fortunes of the party. The evangelical activists tend to see the Republican party as a vehicle for implementing their social vision; the regulars view the party as a worthy end in itself.

The entry of the evangelical activists threatens both the internal harmony and larger electoral prospects of the Republican party. According to Rebecca E. Klatch (1988), social and economic conservatives disagree fundamentally over the individual and society, the role of the state, and the position of women. Unlike economic conservatives, who believe society will thrive when individuals are free to pursue self-interest, social conservatives entertain a model wherein "society brings the individual under the moral authority of God, the church, and the family, thereby restraining man's instincts and curbing individual self-interest" (ibid., 31). It follows that economic conservatives want to limit and dismantle the state while social conservatives want to use the state to achieve a different set of goals from those it has recently pursued under the influence of "secular humanism." Thus proposals to regulate the entertainment media, set federal standards on sex education, or control the flow of information across computer networks, just some of the legislation implied by the various conservative "contracts," appeal to social conservatives but conflict with economic conservatives' desire for smaller and less intrusive government. Finally, according to Klatch, social conservatives assign priority to defending a traditional role for women as housewives and caregivers; they oppose day-care, liberalized abortion, and gay rights as threats to traditional sex roles. "Laissez-faire women, on the other hand," writes Klatch, "are prochoice and support day care, as long as it remains in private hands; they firmly reject any government role in legislating sexuality or moral matters as an intrusion on individual liberty" (ibid., 34). It may prove difficult for the Republicans to contain two such contradictory worldviews within the same party.

The Republicans also face a strategic dilemma in their drive to secure a national majority. To get more evangelical voters into the Republican camp will require a consistent emphasis on social conservatism. That is the goal of the evangelical elites who have penetrated the inner circles of Republicanism. Yet to become the majority party at all levels of government, Republicans also have to appeal to a large bloc of nonevangelical voters. Reagan thrived primarily because his conservative economic policies appealed to many young voters and affluent members of the post–World War II baby boomers. Such voters respond to economic conservatism but take a libertarian line on social issues (Ladd 1982, chap. 3; W. E. Miller and Levitin 1976; Maddox and Lilie 1984). Moreover, members of this target constituency want day-care facilities, environmental protection, spending on public education—issues that leave conservative evangelicals either indifferent or alienated (Berke 1995). An emphasis on New Right concerns is thus likely to drive nonevangelicals away from the GOP.

The warning that Republican support for severe limits on abortion access and other Christian Right priorities "could drive a stake through the heart of the Reagan coalition" (Schneider 1989, 2) seems to have been vindicated by subsequent election results. In 1989, shortly after the *Webster* decision gave states more discretion to regulate abortion, prochoice gubernatorial candidates actually gained votes by virtue of their position on abortion (Cook, Jelen, and Wilcox 1994). Several studies suggest that George Bush lost net electoral support because of his commitment to the prolife cause and public perceptions of his association with the Christian Right (Abramowitz 1995; Alvarez and Nagler 1995; A. Miller 1993, 205–209; Strand and Sherrill 1993). Christian Right activists succeeded in packing the Virginia Republican convention and obtaining the senatorial nomination for Oliver North but saw North lose his campaign to Chuck Robb, the single most vulnerable Democratic incumbent of 1994 (Rozell and Wilcox 1995a).

Despite the costs of such inner-party conflict, the battle was once again fought out in public during the 1996 presidential campaign.

During the competition for the Republican nomination, Pat Buchanan carried the banner for the prolife forces and constructed a movement of voters "disproportionately attracted to him because of his moral and social views and . . . disproportionately concerned about moral problems." [17] Once the nomination was decided in favor of Bob Dole, the Christian conservatives focused their energy on keeping uncompromising antiabortion language in the party platform and forcing Dole to choose a vice-presidential nominee who supported that position without reservation. Where they controlled Republican state parties, the conservatives threatened to keep prochoice supporters or even less ardent prolifers off the state delegations to the national convention. [18]

The full extent of the public backlash against Christian conservatives has been seen most clearly at the local level. As part of the return to the grassroots, Christian activists have tried to elect conservative Christians to local school boards to cleanse public schools of the "alien philosophy" and "secular humanism" pervading them (Nazario 1992; Simonds 1985). In many cases, such candidates ran so-called stealth campaigns in which they disguised their commitment to Christian Right priorities by using broad slogans about maintaining discipline and values. Once in office, they pressed for replacing sex education curricula with abstinence-only policies, mandated the teaching of creationism in biology, encouraged school prayer, and generally tried to implement the social conservatism that resides at the heart of the movement. In Lake County, Florida, a school board majority associated with the Christian Right advised teachers to instruct their students in the superiority of American culture. Even in conservative areas like Lake County, these policies generated enormous controversy, and many of the high-profile representatives of the Christian Right were summarily voted out of office at the first available opportunity.

The internal problems of the Republicans do not automatically spell recovery for the Democrats. After all, the growth in Republicanism among evangelicals comes at the expense of Democrats. Moreover, the growing concern about moral issues in politics also increases the tensions within the Democratic coalition. The Republican evangelical activists have something of a mirror image in the "secular left" of the Democratic party. This group, predominantly unattached to churches and distinguished by an almost militant commitment to free choice in personal behavior, has assumed a growing importance within the

Democratic elite (Guth and Green 1986, 1990). The priorities of this important group do not square with the fundamental social conservatism of many core Democratic groups. In a delicate balancing act designed to steer a way between these two divergent groups, the Clinton reelection campaign of 1996 endorsed such conservative themes as school uniforms, teen curfews, and heterosexual marriage while remaining staunchly prochoice on the abortion debate.

The Consequences for Public Policy

Because much of this electoral activity has been aimed at changing public policy at the national level, it is appropriate to examine the success of Christian political action at that level. Until the Republican seizure of Congress in 1994, the record was one of failure. To quote David Frum (1994), a conservative journalist, most politicians refused to regard the New Christian Right as "anything more than a nuisance to be managed." Despite the prodding of the evangelical groups, lobbying by church members, the vocal support of Presidents Reagan and Bush, the presence of important allies in the House and Senate, and fear of electoral retribution, the major programs advocated by Christian Right groups were not enacted during the Reagan-Bush era. The Senate voted down a constitutional amendment permitting organized school prayer and did not enact the tuition tax credit requested by supporters of religious schools. Another primary objective of the movement, prohibiting abortion, remains elusive. In the *Webster* decision of 1989 (profiled in chap. 8), the Supreme Court accepted certain state restrictions on abortion but did not invalidate the *Roe v. Wade* precedent by returning complete control over abortion to the states. Even if the Court were to take that step, both pre-*Roe* practice and the responses to the *Webster* decision suggest that legal abortion would remain the rule in many communities. Moreover, it is not at all clear that the Christian Right can claim much credit for any restrictions imposed on abortion.

The symbolic nature of most of the New Christian Right's victories is exemplified by a 1985 Education Department regulation prohibiting local school districts from using certain federal funds to support courses in "secular humanism." As noted above, that term has come to symbolize the philosophy that many evangelical spokesmen regard as the root of American problems—that is, a belief in humanity as the supreme force in the universe. Because secular humanism has been identified as the foundation of such topics as biological evolution, prohibitions on prayer in public schools, and any number of other practices (Eidsmoe 1984, chap. 15), the ruling might seem to have been an important victory. However, the regulation left the concept undefined, and any attempt to specify it would almost certainly fail to pass judicial scrutiny. From "victories" such as this, the members of the Religious Right may have learned, as have other change-oriented persons before them, that the American political system has a genius for resisting external pressure.

With the Republican seizure of Congress in 1994, as noted above, the playing field tilted appreciably in the Christian Right's favor. Although Christian Coalition offered strong support for the "Contract with America," many activists were disappointed by the absence of their core priorities from the list. Several contract items that were popular among evangelicals, including a constitutional amendment to ban flag desecration, passed the House of Representatives but fell short of the votes needed to pass the Senate. Though the Christian Coalition postponed its own family contract until mid-1995, the 1996 presidential election campaign doomed most of the controversial legislation.

The willingness of Christian Coalition to subordinate its specific priorities to Republican goals with broader appeal highlights the central dilemma facing interest groups like the NCR (Judis 1994). On the one hand, most groups that want a piece of the pie learn that they must ask nicely. That means compromising, avoiding extreme tactics, forming useful alliances, and deferring goals. On the other, such a strategy risks alienating the activists who enter politics because they want change. Their continuing mobilization cannot be taken for granted. Disappointed by the glacial pace of political change to date and difficult to mobilize on the basis of rather incremental policy changes, evangelicals may simply retreat from the political world into their thriving Christian subculture with its own bookstores, mass media, celebrities, and institutions (Bandow 1995). Alternatively, the evangelical constituency may itself become more tolerant and sophisticated as a consequence of its increasing exposure to reasonable groups that nevertheless hold differing views on fundamental cultural and social issues. As evangelicals partake more fully of American culture, they will be exposed to the same tensions, challenges, and opportunities that have changed the political orientations of other Americans. This may blunt the hard edges of evangelical activism.

Still, evangelical groups have affected national policies in ways short of changing public policy. As Matthew C. Moen has argued, the New Christian Right succeeded in obtaining passage of national legislation offering partial redress of its grievances (1989). In place of organized school prayer, it received "equal access" for religious group meetings in class and later saw the Religious Freedom Restoration Act passed into law.[19] Many states have sheltered evangelical Christian schools from educational regulation and permitted parents to teach their own children in "home schools." Abortion has not been prohibited, but federal funds no longer support it and abortion access has been severely limited in many parts of the country. The Equal Rights Amendment was defeated and attempts to add sexual orientation to national antidiscrimination policy seem similarly doomed. Outraged by federal subsidies to artists who purveyed offensive art, critics managed to instruct the National Endowment for the Arts to consider "decency" as a criterion in making grants. At the state and local levels, where they are often the best-organized groups, local chapters of NCR organizations have carried other proposals into law (Pierard and Wright 1984).

Moen also noted that the efforts to challenge national policy on social issues have kept those controversies from falling off the national agenda. The emphasis in New Christian Right rhetoric on traditional values has encouraged politicians of all stripes to discuss those values in the public realm (Stanfield 1994; Edsall 1994b). As illustrated by New York governor Mario Cuomo's keynote address to the 1984 Democratic National Convention and President Clinton's repeated emphasis on values, both parties have come to believe in the importance of appeals to moral concerns. Or perhaps more cynically, the presence of the New Christian Right may have "made politicians think about the moral quotient before casting their votes" (cited in Moen 1989, 145).

We have considered the New Christian right from a number of angles. In concluding the chapter, it would be useful to remember that the movement is not quite as innovative as it may appear. Indeed, the NCR movement may be new, but it draws on well-established traditions of

American life. Some observers have even interpreted the new Christian conservatism as an attempt to revitalize the civil religion discussed in chapter 3. The idea of the United States as a redeemer nation and its people as "chosen" to lead humankind took a severe beating in the 1960s and 1970s. These developments may have accelerated an ongoing shift in cultural values that undermined the moral consensus in American society. Hence, in a 1975 book describing the status of civil religion, Robert Bellah referred to the "broken covenant." By insisting on official support of traditional moral values and of the view of the United States as a nation under divine judgment, the leaders of the New Christian Right have sounded themes with a strong civil religious orientation. As I argued when the concept of civil religion first came up in chapter 3, that tradition has both noble and seamy aspects.

As new players in the game of national politics, the evangelical Protestants have attracted most of the attention of trend spotters. But the evangelicals have not been the only religious group to reassess traditional political loyalties. As the next chapter will make clear, Catholics have also undergone a profound political transition at the same time that mainline Protestant churches have appeared to lose enthusiasm for constant political engagement. Only black Protestants and Jews seem to have resisted pressures for political change.

NOTES

The chapter epigraph is taken from Mark Silk, *Spiritual Politics: Religion and America Since World War II* (New York: Simon and Schuster, 1988).

1. To the extent religion remained a force in politics, advocates of modernization theory expected the action to come primarily from "peace and justice" supporters on the Christian Left.

2. It is very difficult to find information about the political behavior of northern evangelicals after the 1920s. John Hammond's (1974) study of the revivalist ethos in Ohio and New York suggests that northern evangelicals strongly supported both restrictive social policies and the Republican party.

3. A slew of unpublished studies, documenting the political conservatism of southern evangelicals, did not influence mainstream electoral analysis (e.g., Freeman 1962; Reinhardt 1975).

4. In the hands of some scholars, "social issues" are said to encompass not just questions of moral regulation like abortion, homosexuality, and school

prayer but virtually every controversy on the public agenda including school busing, affirmative action, free speech, and crime (Glazer 1986; Wattenberg 1995). Although these issues undoubtedly have a moral dimension, including them so broadens the concept of social issues as to make it useless for analysis. There is no empirical evidence that these other issues correlate substantially with the core items on the Christian Right agenda.

5. "Religion Is Powerful GOP Theme," *Washington Post,* 24 August 1984, 8A.

6. "Evangelist Gets Scant Support from GOP in House Campaign," *Wall Street Journal,* 23 October 1986, 68.

7. The responsibility for raising the temperature of the political atmosphere with strident appeals did not rest exclusively with the evangelical action groups. The opponents of the New Christian Right were not reluctant to indulge in some of the same tactics they condemned in the conservative movement. Although thoughtful and reasoned critiques of the NCR were presented, careful examination of the literature of groups such as People for the American Way or well-established organizations like the American Civil Liberties Union reveals examples of self-righteousness, distortion, oversimplification, and attempts to "monopolize the symbols of legitimacy" by staking exclusive claim to the flag, national traditions, and common American values (Hunter 1983a, 162). As Hunter has pointed out, members of the evangelical movements are expressing their dissatisfaction with momentous changes in American society. If the methods and language of their advocacy have not always been moderate, it is also true that their claims have not always been treated with the respect and civility they deserve.

8. Ironically, the "moral voting" test was failed by several of the most widely respected representatives in Congress, as well as most of the ordained clergy in the legislative branch. The highest-scoring group of congressmen included a representative who was caught on videotape accepting a bribe, another who was convicted of tax evasion, and two who confessed to sexual misconduct.

9. Robertson has dabbled in a number of conspiracy theories that put a cabal of "European bankers" at the center of a plot for world domination. In anti-Semitic circles, such phrases have commonly served as code words to describe Jews. Robertson strongly denies any such motivation.

10. Critics like Moen (1988) argue that the "status politics" model does not fit groups with a broad agenda and concerns, such as tuition tax credits, which are tangible rather than symbolic. In my own judgment, the status-politics approach does not limit moral reform to symbolic acts, and the issue of tuition tax credits can be interpreted as defending an institution (in this case, Christian schools) perceived as central to a threatened way of life. Some skeptics (Conover 1983) have converted status-politics theory to an economic model, an approach that does not do justice to its assumptions.

11. Gallup polls have found from 14 percent to 22 percent of adults claiming membership in "the religious right movement" but the question wording and order likely inflate the level of support (Gallup and Bezilla 1995). In a mid-

1994 poll, only 11 percent of respondents said they had a very positive view of the Religious Right (defined as "conservative Christian groups active in politics"), and many were unfamiliar with the movement (cited in Jost 1994, 892).

12. Robertson's campaign was also discredited by his penchant for uttering "funny facts": claims, for example, that George Bush had engineered a sex scandal involving a fellow televangelist or that Nancy Reagan had urged her husband to "go soft" on communism.

13. Describing the supporters of the movement as "poor, uneducated, and easy to command," a *Washington Post* reporter showed how easy it is to overgeneralize about the social composition of the Christian Right base. It is worth emphasizing that these differences are relative: Compared with persons of other faiths, evangelicals have lower *average* levels of education and income, higher proportions of women, greater concentration in the South, etc. The group differences are not huge and allow considerable latitude for individual differences.

14. The charismatic movement has attracted large numbers of Catholics and black Protestants who are strikingly less traditionalist and politically engaged than white Protestant charismatics (Smidt 1989c).

15. "Unseating Helms: Rival Charts His Uphill Climb," *New York Times*, 16 July 1990, 1A, 12A; "In North Carolina's Senate Race, a Divisive TV Fight Over 'Values'," *New York Times*, 23 September 1990, 1, 32; "Helms Kindled Anger in Campaign and May Have Set Tone for Others," *New York Times*, 8 November 1990, 3B.

16. "The 1990 Elections," *New York Times*, 6 November 1990, 8B.

17. David Moore, "Buchanan Polls," communication to the "Public Opinion Research" electronic discussion list (por@ripken.oit.unc.edu), 27 February 1996.

18. Richard L. Berke, "Abortion Continues to Divide G.O.P. at State Level," *New York Times*, electronic edition (http://www.nytimes.com), 20 June 1996; Thomas B. Edsall, "GOP Convention Delegates Face Abortion Test," *Washington Post*, 12 June 1996, A1.

19. Many in the Christian Right viewed equal access as a "sellout" of school prayer and were dragged along rather reluctantly (Moen 1989, 114).

8. Continuity and Change Outside the Evangelical Camp

> The really big story is that amid the clamor of invisible armies and righteous empires, there is a noticeable silence in the way most Americans bring their values and beliefs to bear upon the democratic process.
>
> —Wade Clark Roof

The past few years have been marked by great ferment in the relationship between religion and American political life. As previous chapters have demonstrated, religious issues and controversies have assumed much greater importance in political debate than they had commanded previously. With public attention so concentrated on attempts to forge the evangelical Protestants into a cohesive voting bloc, it has been easy to lose sight of the constant pressures for political change also faced by the majority of Americans affiliated with nonevangelical churches. Like the evangelicals, the other major religious groups in America have been encouraged to modify their traditional political patterns and to increase their involvement in public affairs. The response of the various nonevangelical groups to a changing political environment is the subject of this chapter.

After a period of dramatic internal change, the Catholic church has shed its predictable conservatism, especially on foreign and military policy, to adopt a new role as gadfly and activist on a wide range of issues. Although Catholic thought has generally moved to the left, the church fathers have maintained a staunchly conservative outlook on the issue of abortion. In the process, members of the Catholic clergy have largely replaced the ministers from mainline Protestantism as the leading political activists among the clergy. The mainline denominations in American Protestantism, once the driving force for many social reform campaigns, seem to have pulled back somewhat from active engagement in the political realm. The patterns of African American politics have shifted the least, with Protestant clergy continuing to play a leading role as spokespersons for the minority community. And Jews, though still a mainstay of the liberal coalition, have had occasion to reassess their traditional alliances.

In examining the new political tendencies of American religious groups, I will emphasize the role of religious leaders. In many religious communities, the clergy take the lead in defining institutional interests and applying theology to public issues. If social change alters the perspective of church members, the impact will usually register first with the ministry. Hence my discussion of trends in the political behavior of religious groups would be incomplete without close attention to those exhibited by members of the clergy. At the same time, it is important to recognize that religious leaders do not control the political perspectives of church members. Rather, in their attempt to shape the political outlook of coreligionists, ministers compete for influence with secular politicians, the media, and many other organized groups. The political attitudes of congregants are also shaped by personal experiences and the perspectives derived from living in a variety of social contexts that cannot be manipulated by the church. In each religious group under study here, even the most centralized and hierarchical, some discrepancy between the attitudes of the religious elite and the views from the pews is inevitable.

Catholicism: The Conservative Political Heritage

For persons whose impression of Catholic politics was formed during the 1980s, it must be hard to imagine just how radically the situation has changed in a short time. During that decade, the church came to public attention because of its opposition to many of the policies pursued by the Reagan and Bush administrations. The bishops issued critical pastoral letters on nuclear strategy and the economy, priests and nuns participated enthusiastically in mass movements against nuclear weapons, and members of the church spearheaded opposition to U.S. policy in Central America. By contrast, for most of the twentieth century the Catholic church in the United States was closely associated with conservative political causes. Although that political tradition has not been extinguished—as testified to by the national prominence of Catholic conservatives like Patrick Buchanan, Phyllis Schlafly, William Bennett, and Henry Hyde—it must compete for Catholic allegiance with a liberal tradition represented by Mario Cuomo and Edward Kennedy. As we saw in chapter 6, Catholic attitudes on most issues now cluster around the middle of the U.S. political spectrum (Penning 1986). This leftward shift among Catholics has been every bit as substantial as the more publicized right-wing movement of the Protestant evangelicals.

The traditional pattern of Catholic politics in the United States was epitomized by the career of Francis Cardinal Spellman, from 1939 to 1967 the archbishop of New York. As head of the major Catholic center in the United States and a person of considerable persuasive ability, he imposed a distinctly conservative tilt to the church's effort to influence the public realm (Cooney 1984). Intensely anti-Communist, suspicious of the civil rights and labor movements, and a strong advocate of government efforts to prohibit public displays of "immorality," Spellman forged strong links between the church and leaders of secular conservative movements. Under his influence, the Catholic hierarchy enthusiastically endorsed the active involvement of the United States in military conflicts wherever communism was thought to be a threat. From Spain in the 1930s through Vietnam in the 1960s, Spellman consistently favored a policy that has been satirized by the phrase "Pass the Lord and praise the ammunition."

Spellman's views on world affairs seem to have resonated with rank-and-file members of the church (Lipset 1964). Two major ultranationalistic mass movements of the twentieth century, the Coughlinite and McCarthy crusades, were led by Catholics and drew somewhat more support from Roman Catholics than from other religious groups.[1] The John Birch Society, a right-wing organization that gained notoriety in the 1960s, also drew greater backing from Catholics than from the population at large. Because all these movements enjoyed substantial support from Protestants and were opposed by some Catholics, their special appeal to Catholics should not be exaggerated (Crosby 1978). Nonetheless, when compared with the rest of the population, Catholics exhibited greater readiness to support U.S. military involvement around the globe.

The militaristic tendency was apparent among young Catholics who participated in a number of studies about attitudes toward the use of force in international politics (Klineberg 1950, 175; Eckert and Mills 1935). In a 1952 survey of almost three thousand students on eleven university campuses, Peter Blau (1953) found that devout Catholics scored higher than other religious groups on a scale measuring emphasis on power (rather than cooperation) in world affairs. When a similar study was conducted in 1967 by Connors, Leonard, and Burnham (1968), the same pattern was noted. Among approximately one thousand students from four eastern colleges, Catholics exhibited the most warlike attitudes. In both studies, which controlled for social characteristics associated with religion, the disposition to support the use of force was greatest among Catholics who were most deeply attached to the church and exposed to Catholic institutions (but see Starr 1975 for conflicting evidence).

The strong conservatism evinced by American Catholics during the time of Spellman's reign as the "American pope" has been explained by the familiar forces of group interests, social standing, and creed. Because the Catholic church was a dominant force in many of the countries where communism sought to gain power, communism represented a fundamental threat to the established power of Catholic institutions. The outspoken antireligiousness of Communist leaders and the active persecution of the church wherever communism had come to power further inflamed Catholic opinion. This concern helped to build early Catholic support for the U.S. military effort in Vietnam. The dispatches from the National Catholic News Service made it seem "as though the big story in Vietnam is how the war affects Catholic missionaries, Catholic institutions, Catholic programs, Catholic political personalities, Catholic villages, Catholic soldiers, Catholic anything" (Deedy 1968, 126). In domestic politics, too, the church leaders fought innovative national government programs when they threatened their local institutions and authority (Byrnes 1991).

Social factors, principally the insecure social status of Catholic immigrants, also contributed to the tendency of Catholic spokesmen "to identify their Americanism with their Catholicism" (Dohen 1967, 175). Militant native-stock Protestants had long impugned the "Americanism" of Catholics, citing Pope Leo XIII's hostility to church-state separation as proof that "Romanism" threatened American religious liberty. One way to challenge this claim was to "overidentify" with American nationalism (Hofstadter 1965). Hence, Catholic immigrants and their descendants flocked to patriotic societies and veterans' groups, eager to display extreme vigilance through acts of superpatriotism. From the viewpoint of status politics theory, the fervent anticommunism of Catholics represented an opportunity to assert their oneness with American values.

The conservatism of American Catholics has also been attributed to creedal factors. From the eighteenth-century Enlightenment through the middle of the twentieth century, "Catholicism and liberalism stood in a vigorously adversarial relation to each other" (Hollenbach 1990, 103). Catholic teaching looked askance at liberalism's distrust of tradition and authority, stress on religious freedom and skepticism, and philosophical individualism. Domestic or international movements associated with such values—such as communism or even milder schemes of social reform—drew opposition from the church. Moreover, the church often considered political issues through the haze of "nostalgia for agrarian, local, organic forms of social life" (ibid.), values rooted in the peasant cultures that Catholic immigrants brought to America from the Italian and Irish countryside. The Catholic emphasis on authority and hierarchy may have further disposed American Catholics to support national leaders who undertook military intervention in the name of national security.

On the basis of such explanations, Catholics acquired a reputation for extreme political conservatism that has been hard to shake—even in the face of polls showing that Catholics now occupy the middle of the American political spectrum (see chap. 6). That reputation was never entirely warranted, even in the heyday of anticommunism during the 1950s. Catholic politicians like Alfred E. Smith and Robert F. Wagner, who served as New York's governor and senator, respectively, helped to lay the foundations for the welfare system in the United States (O'Brien 1968). During the period that Cardinal Spellman tried to steer Catholics in the New York diocese to conservative causes, a Catholic woman named Dorothy Day founded the Catholic Worker movement in an attempt to identify the church with progressive views on issues like poverty, labor, social justice, civil liberties, and international disarmament (Piehl 1982). Catholic theologians, too, were steadily moving away from traditional beliefs about the rigid separation between heaven and earth, forging a new concern with social ethics (Curran 1982).

Even if they dismissed the signs of liberalization as unrepresentative of mainstream Catholic thought, political analysts could not overlook hard evidence of Catholic support for the Democratic party. Yet rather than acknowledge that this partisan tradition indicated the potential for Catholic liberalism, most scholars attempted to explain away the Democratic affiliation with the same economic self-interest argument used to account for the Democratic affiliation of southern evangelicals. By addressing the economic problems of the working class, they argued, Franklin D. Roosevelt had safeguarded the immediate interests of most American Catholics. Out of gratitude for his policies and for his appointments of Catholics to public jobs, Roosevelt and his immediate successors enjoyed continuing electoral support from the Catholic voter. But as the memory of the New Deal eroded and issues of foreign policy and civil rights replaced economic security on the Catholic political agenda, the "natural" conservatism of American Catholics once again came into play. During the late 1960s, when conservative political activists hoped to replace the New Deal coalition with a right-wing majority more to their liking, Catholics were perceived as the most likely converts and became the target of special appeals. Despite these efforts, the subsequent political movement of Catholics has not been toward a wholehearted embrace of conservatism but, at least among the clergy, toward a more liberal posture on most major national issues.

The Transformation of Catholic Attitudes

If the conservatism of traditional Catholic politics had been due to communal isolation and immigrant culture, the social transformation of Catholic life was bound to produce new departures in political action. Indeed, during the decades after World War II, Catholics in America experienced dramatic upward mobility. Even when allowance is given for the enormous variation among individual Catholics, the community as a whole enjoyed substantial increases in economic status, social acceptance, and the acquisition of politically relevant skills and resources.[2] Having "left the ghetto" (Hanna 1979, 22) economically and psychologically, Catholics were primed to assume a larger role in national political life. The direction of that new energy was principally determined by events in Rome.

What changed the Catholic church in America—or what gave official approval to trends that might have been developing independently—was a meeting of the world's bishops called in 1962 by Pope John XXIII. Known as Vatican II, or the Ecumenical Council, this historic meeting of church fathers revolutionized church liturgy and ritual. Most important from a political standpoint was that the leaders of the Catholic church called on the members to apply their Christian values to the problems of the world. In documents condemning the sinfulness of poverty, war, injustice, and other social ills, the church put its authority squarely behind the worldwide movement for social change. This profound shift of mood, coinciding with the assumption of the presidency by an energetic and vigorous Catholic, prompted an enthusiastic response from the American Catholic community (ibid., chap. 2). In developments that did not always meet with the approval of the older and more conservative bishops or of many Catholic laypersons, many young priests and nuns enrolled in the civil rights and antipoverty movements.

The enthusiasm for political change among Catholic leaders might not have survived into the 1980s without a corresponding transformation in the organization of the American church (E. Kennedy 1985). Under the impact of Vatican II, the American bishops established the United States Catholic Conference to speak with one voice about public issues. Absorbing several older institutions, the newly established organization developed departments specializing in domestic antipoverty efforts, campaigns for Third World economic development, and the promotion of world peace and social justice. This action-oriented church bureaucracy was increasingly staffed by professionals with substantial secular training and a commitment to broad-ranging social reforms. As Mary Hanna (1985, 15) notes, the reform impulse has persisted to the present day because it was embodied in new institutions that "push the Church as a whole and the bishops toward action on social and political questions." A new breed of bishops, large in number because a mandatory retirement age produced more openings than normal in the hierarchy, has proved highly receptive to the Vatican II outlook. Although the differences between the current and pre–Vatican II bishops can easily be overstated (see the data in E. Kennedy 1985, chap. 2), contemporary leaders of the Catholic church, like the parishioners, experienced a much more cosmopolitan upbringing than their predecessors. Young enough to have absorbed the liberalism of the 1960s and more familiar with secular environments, they have imparted a much more liberal cast to Catholic social and political thought.

Another influence that propelled the American Catholic elite in new directions during the 1970s was the movement known as "liberation theology." In response to the papal call for a renewed emphasis on social justice, some Latin American bishops and many clergy abandoned the traditional alliance between the church and the ruling classes of the region. Instead of defending the status quo, liberation theologians argued, the church should join the poor in resisting large landowners and their allies in military governments. Many priests and lay Catholics acted on this belief by forming a "church of the people" that engaged oppressive regimes in direct political, economic, and military challenges. Liberation theology imparted a willingness to challenge the power of the state in pursuit of the prophetic mission of the church. This example stimulated many American Catholics (and Protestants) similarly to reconsider the role of their church in struggles between rich and poor.

The liberalization of American Catholic attitudes did not occur overnight, nor was it always clear that the church was moving in that direction. The most dramatic evidence of the new mood came in Catholic reactions to the war in Vietnam. As it did for so many other Americans, the Vietnam War eventually prompted many Catholics to rethink their traditional support for U.S. military involvement around the globe. At the extreme wing of the antiwar movement, a Catholic was the first young man to be imprisoned for publicly destroying his draft card, and a pair of Jesuit priests, Daniel and Phillip Berrigan, became leaders of a campaign of civil disobedience launched to protest U.S. military action in Vietnam (Meconis 1979). Among the young men who fled to Canada rather than serve as conscientious objectors, Catholics were apparently represented to a disproportionate degree (Surrey 1982). Despite these passionate expressions of antiwar feeling, most Catholics did not abandon their strong support for military action during the early years of the war. In Gallup polls taken between 1965 and 1967, Catholics were more supportive than Protestants of U.S. military participation by about 10 percent (calculated from data in Mueller 1973, 143). Whereas many Protestant and Jewish spokesmen condemned U.S. participation in the war, the Catholic bishops issued a statement that concluded "it is reasonable to argue that our presence in Vietnam is justified" (reprinted in Drinan 1970, 192). Cardinal Spellman was perhaps the most enthusiastic supporter of military action in American religious circles.

But as the war dragged on into the late 1960s, Catholic support gradually eroded. In 1968 the bishops issued a new pastoral letter that was notably less enthusiastic than its 1966 predecessor (ibid., 195). While raising more questions than answers, the new statement called on Catholics to judge the legitimacy of U.S. participation in Vietnam by the "just war" principle—a doctrine that deems military action appropriate only if all other methods have failed to achieve an equitable settlement and if the use of force is proportional to the goal of the war. Recognizing that Catholics differed among themselves over whether the Vietnam conflict passed the test of a just war, the bishops pointedly refrained from reaching a judgment. One Catholic clergyman who decided that Vietnam violated the standard set by the just war doctrine, Father Robert Drinan of Boston, ran for a seat in the U.S. Congress on an antiwar platform and became the first priest elected to the House in many years. By 1971 the bishops moved explicitly into the antiwar camp, passing a resolution calling for an immediate halt to U.S. military participation in Southeast Asia. Consistent with this new "dovish" emphasis, they also took a strong position in favor of amnesty for draft evaders and war resisters and expressed opposition to the use of conscription outside the context of a genuine national emergency. As the hierarchy moved toward positions taken up earlier by the religious leadership of mainline Protestantism and Judaism, the Catholic lay population also developed attitudes toward the Vietnam War that were indistinguishable from the rest of the American public (J. Mueller 1973, 143).

Since those watershed years, the American bishops have consistently called for conciliation and negotiation in preference to military action in world affairs. In Latin America, for example, the Catholic church has spearheaded opposition to U.S. financial and military assistance to governments threatened by leftist insurgents. As noted earlier, Catholics have played a key role in providing illegal sanctuary for refugees from the strife in Central America. Through acts of civil disobedience ranging from nonpayment of income taxes to assaults on military property, individual Catholics, including members of the clergy, have protested efforts by the U.S. government to take the side of conservative forces in that region. In addition, missionaries from the Maryknoll order have worked throughout Latin America to promote social change through programs of land reform, social welfare benefits, and the like.

In 1983, when the bishops issued a well-publicized letter on nuclear weapons, the American hierarchy bid a final farewell to the Spellman era. Entitled "The Challenge of Peace: God's Promise and Our Response," the lengthy letter was intended to educate Catholics about church doctrine on war and violence in world affairs. It expanded on many of the themes that first appeared in the Vietnam-era statements, emphasizing the relevance of the just war standard and the need for individual Catholics to reach their own, independent judgments rather than accept governmental decisions as inherently worthy of support. Catholics were also told that although military service was a worthy endeavor when motivated by a generous love of country, the church fathers supported persons whose conscience prompted them to refuse to bear arms or to otherwise defend themselves with tools of violence. On the issue of nuclear weapons, the major focus of the statement, the bishops declared that the idea of deterring war by matching the weaponry of an opponent—a cornerstone of U.S. nuclear strategy—was an inadequate basis for long-term peace on earth. Indeed, because deterrence was credible only if it rested on a willingness actually to use nuclear weapons, some bishops found the entire concept immoral. Noting that nuclear weapons could almost never be used in a manner that satisfied Catholic standards for a just war, they called on governments to accelerate efforts to achieve disarmament.

As abstract expressions, these statements could be endorsed in principle by nearly all public officials, even those identified as conservative on the issue of nuclear policy. But the letter provoked controversy because it challenged the Reagan administration policy on several counts. Specifically, the bishops called on the U.S. government to undertake some exploratory, independent initiatives of weapons reduction; to set up a regular schedule of summit meetings with the leaders of adversary governments; to tighten controls on the export of nuclear materials with potential military uses; and, in an effort to promote research and teaching on the peaceful resolution of conflicts, to establish a national peace academy. Each of these actions had previously been rejected by administration policy makers. Moreover, the bishops condemned as "morally reprehensible in its hypocrisy" Reagan's policy of supporting repressive governments when he thought that the likely alternative would be even less desirable. By noting that the United States shared responsibility for the conditions that generated world tension and had not always behaved honorably in global affairs, the bishops further took on the president who had publicly attributed global disorder to the "evil empire" of the Soviet Union. For the first time in American history, the Catholic hierarchy had lined up against a president on questions of fundamental military policy.

Did the hierarchy carry the parishioners? The question may seem inappropriate because the letter was not portrayed as a mandate for Catholics to support specific policies. Rather, the bishops claimed, their goal was to suggest a moral framework that Catholics could use in thinking about this difficult question. Nonetheless, practical politicians wondered about Catholic reaction to specific proposals. Although some conservative Catholics denounced the letter as naive or inappropriate, it apparently stimulated the Catholic rank-and-file to reconsider their positions on questions of peace and war. As Andrew Greeley (1985) first pointed out, Catholic opinion on military spending underwent a dramatic shift after the issuance of the pastoral letter in 1983. Protestant and Catholic attitudes on U.S. military spending were very similar in 1983 (see fig. 8.1). Although Catholics were, even then, more likely than Protestants to believe that the United States was overspending for military purposes, the group differences were small enough to be attributable to chance.

But in 1984 Catholics shifted dramatically into the "too much" category and opened up substantial differences between themselves and Protestants. By comparison with both their 1983 attitudes and the 1984 Protestant preferences, Catholics in 1984 had moved significantly toward the view that the United States was devoting too many resources to military purposes. Coupled with evidence that Catholic attitudes on other issues had not changed much or moved further away from Protestant opinion, this finding made a strong case for attributing the transformation to the bishops' pastoral letter on nuclear weapons. To bolster that interpretation, a study in one midwestern city

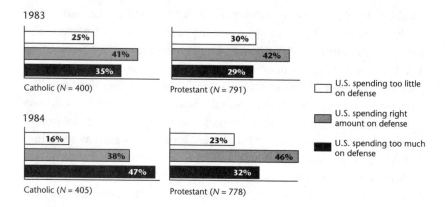

Figure 8.1 Catholic Versus Protestant Attitudes on Defense Spending, 1983 and 1984 (Source: General Social Surveys, 1983, 1984). Respondents were asked if they thought the United States was spending "too much money, too little money, or about the right amount" in a series of program areas. In 1983, the subject of military spending was introduced with the phrase "the military, armaments, and defense." In 1984, about one-third of the respondents were asked about "national defense" and another third about "strengthening national defense"; the remaining third were asked the question as it had been posed in 1983. Because the distribution of responses was similar using all three question forms, they were combined as one for analysis.

found that Catholics were substantially more likely than Protestants to know of their church's position on nuclear weapons and that knowledge of the hierarchy's position produced greater approval for a "freeze" on the further construction and deployment of nuclear warheads (Tamney and Johnson 1985). Gallup surveys also found sharp growth in Catholic support for the nuclear freeze after "The Challenge of Peace" was issued (Gallup and Castelli 1987, 83).

Subsequent research has qualified Greeley's interpretation by pointing out the apparently short-lived nature of the change induced by "The Challenge of Peace." In 1985 Catholic opposition to military spending dropped while polls recorded a rise in the proportion of Protestants who thought the United States was spending too much on defense. As a result, the opinions of the two groups converged and have remained together in subsequent polls. Even more damaging to the reputation of the pastoral was the report from a 1987 poll that only 29 percent of Catholics claimed they were familiar with the bishops' message on nuclear weapons (Davidson 1989). When that subgroup was asked to evaluate the document, only 57 percent said they approved its contents. If just 17 percent of the entire Catholic community knew *and* supported the pastoral a mere four years after it was issued in a blaze of publicity, then its long-term impact is dubious.

Nonetheless, considering the many barriers between the bishops and the Catholic population, the magnitude of the change the pastoral produced is more impressive than its rapid demise (Wald 1992). In the first place, the message of the pastoral seems to have penetrated Catholic opinion despite a formidable range of obstacles that include inattention, selective perception, distortion, and other devices by which people screen out new information that challenges old beliefs. Second, even if Catholic attitudes ceased to be distinct from Protestant opinion after 1984, this may merely reflect the delayed impact of the pastoral on Protestant opinion (cf. D. Curry 1984). In any case, both communities remained significantly less enthusiastic about defense spending after 1984 than they had been in 1983. Finally, the bishops weighed in at a critical moment in the public debate on nuclear policy (T. Byrnes 1991, 130). At a time when the Reagan administration derided arms control to concentrate instead on a major buildup of U.S. military strength, the public deliberations leading up to the pastoral letter gave moral support to the emerging "nuclear freeze" movement. The conservative reputation of the bishops enhanced the impact of their message, adding to the other forces that eventually persuaded the Reagan administration to move to the negotiating table. In these terms, "The Challenge of Peace" stands out as a remarkably effective political intervention by a modern religious group.

The leftward shift on international politics was accompanied by a growing concern among Catholic clergy about questions of economic policy. Rather than speak of this concern as a break with tradition, it is more accurate to describe it as renewed emphasis on a traditional theme in Catholic social thought. In its modern statements on economic questions, the papacy had never wholeheartedly endorsed the doctrine of capitalism and had criticized the system for its undue emphasis on competition and individualism. Reflecting that skepticism about the merits of unrestricted market economies, the American bishops had in 1919 issued a "Program of Social Reconstruction" that called for major changes in economic arrangements, and Catholic clergy watched with approval as most of the proposals were enacted by Franklin Roosevelt's New Deal (Billington and Clark 1993).

Questions of economic justice regained primacy as part of the heightened social consciousness that accompanied Vietnam War protests. In the 1966 statement on Vietnam, the bishops had hinted that the ultimate source of world tension was to be found in social conditions like hunger, poverty, and unemployment. With each successive statement on national or international conflict, this theme grew stronger. The church became more active in the economic arena, concentrating resources to combat poverty and giving strong support to Cesar Chavez, a Catholic activist, first to organize farm workers and then to boycott corporations that undermined contracts between agricultural producers and the union (Ortiz 1984). From this experience and their own firsthand experience with the poverty in inner-city parishes, the bishops developed a strong interest in economic policy and began preliminary work in 1980 on a pastoral letter.

Issued late in 1986 under the title "Economic Justice for All," the letter emphasized the prevalence of economic inequality, denounced such suffering in biblical terms, and attributed economic problems to the U.S. economic and political system. Putting the church on the side of the poor and underprivileged, the bishops endorsed proposals for a substantial increase in the minimum wage, statutory limits on personal income and wealth, federally mandated welfare standards, federal support for new job programs, and pay scales that reflected the intrinsic worth of a job as well as market considerations. A chapter on agricultural policy called for massive emergency aid to farms and rural banks damaged by defaulted loans. Apart from these reformist proposals, the bishops showed considerable sympathy for such capitalist and market-based practices as tax incentives, small business, multinational corporations, and policies designed to promote entrepreneurial activity. Nonetheless, many of the specific proposals embedded in the report had already been rejected by the Reagan administration and its recommendations collided with the administration's announced commitment to reduce governmental involvement in the domestic economy.

The bishops faced considerable difficulty in swinging Catholic opinion to their side on this issue. A group of conservative Catholics, including business leaders, public officials, and scholars, published a letter of their own before the bishops' pastoral got into print.[3]

Described as "a strong celebration of the capitalist system and the individual entrepreneur, not the government, as the true benefactors of the poor and jobless," the letter from the Lay Commission on Catholic Social Teaching and the U.S. Economy, as the group called itself, argued that the political freedom accompanying free enterprise economies promotes the living standards of all citizens.[4] The issuance of such a missive indicated that influential Catholics were not unanimously in favor of the bishops' economic proposals, and other reports have suggested that the official statement was greeted unenthusiastically by the rank-and-file (Davidson 1989; Tamney, Burton, and Johnson 1988).

The greater impact of the pastoral letter on nuclear war compared to the economic message underscores the importance of process, timing, and content in church political action. The credibility of the nuclear letter was enhanced by the careful and public deliberations that preceded it. The letter on war and peace was framed and issued at a time of grave public concern over the possibility of nuclear war; the economic letter, by contrast, emerged when the economy seemed buoyant and the extent of problems like homelessness and unemployment were not fully recognized. Furthermore, war and peace is the kind of issue that more readily lends itself to sudden shifts of opinion. Calls for reducing military spending can be simple and powerful, appealing both to altruism and self-interest. By contrast, calls for higher rates of taxation and redistribution of resources may strike at the very economic system that provided advantages to many Catholics. As such, they will inspire greater resistance.

Abortion: The Catholic Response

During the same period that the Catholic religious elite was rethinking traditional positions on a wide range of political issues, the church also gained public attention as the major force resisting the liberalization of abortion laws in the United States.[5] That stance was derived from Catholic doctrine defining the fetus as a form of human life that should enjoy a nearly absolute right to existence. From that perspective, abortion, along with any other deliberate interference with the gestation of a fertilized human egg, constitutes the moral equivalent of murder (Callahan 1970, chap. 12). This position, reiterated in the 1968 papal encyclical *Humanae Vitae,* had undergirded the church's opposition to making birth control devices freely available to the public and motivated subsequent activism against liberalized abortion. Before 1973, when the U.S. Supreme Court struck down most existing state abortion laws, the church was active in fighting state efforts to loosen restrictions on abortion through so-called Right to Life organizations. These activities increased dramatically after the *Roe* decision.[6]

In *Roe v. Wade,* the Supreme Court argued that a constitutional right to privacy prohibited states from limiting abortion during the first three months of pregnancy. Concerns for maternal health could justify medical regulations in the second trimester, and the government's interest in encouraging "normal childbirth" permitted restrictive policies in the last three months. The decision wiped out state laws that forbade abortion without regard to circumstance or timing. Armed with a record of public opposition to what the advocates of liberalization called abortion reform and the network to organize parishioners, the Catholic church was well placed to provide leadership when the *Roe v. Wade* decision brought the issue to national prominence.

The attack on liberalized abortion laws was waged on several fronts. Shortly after *Roe* was announced, the bishops created the National Committee for a Human Life Amendment, whose goal was to reverse the Supreme Court decision by passage of a constitutional amendment extending legal protection to the fetus. When the Senate Judiciary Committee held hearings on proposed antiabortion amendments in 1974, four Catholic bishops appeared among the many clergy who testified on the issue. When the Senate Judiciary Committee deadlocked over the issue, failing to send any of the nearly sixty proposed amendments to a vote on the Senate floor, abortion opponents decided to press the attack through a variety of interim measures. While keeping as their ultimate objective a constitutional amendment prohibiting abortion, antiabortion forces focused on the more immediate goal of limiting the availability of abortion by restricting government funding and by adopting administrative regulations to deter women from using abortion facilities.

Like other groups that seek to wield influence in the legislative process, the opponents of abortion have attempted to accumulate power through the development of grassroots electoral organization. Although they have intervened in presidential politics, even to the extent of sponsoring a symbolic campaign for the Democratic presidential nomination, their major focus has been on electing antiabortion candidates to state and congressional office. The full extent of church involvement in these actions was spelled out in the highly detailed "Pastoral Plan for Pro-Life Activities" issued in 1975 by the bishops. The bishops' plan called for the development in each congressional district of an identifiable, tightly knit, and well-organized "prolife" unit (Jaffe, Lindheim, and Lee 1981, 75) that would provide financial assistance, campaign workers, and publicity to antiabortion candidates. The plan envisioned close ties between the secular Right to Life organizations and the Catholic parish. In practice, the church has supplied the movement with physical, financial, and human resources, leading some critics to the conclusion that the right-to-life movement is largely an expression of the Catholic hierarchy (Merton 1981; Jaffe, Lindheim, and Lee 1981, 76–83; Paige 1983). Although academic researchers have expressed skepticism about the electoral impact of the abortion issue in national elections (Traugott and Vinovskis 1980; Granberg and Burlison 1983; Granberg 1987; Vinovskis 1979; Bolce 1988), the antiabortion movement has gained a reputation for political clout that has prompted many lawmakers to pay it careful heed (Margolis and Neary 1980).

As the prospect of amending the Constitution faded, the opponents of abortion confronted the Supreme Court with a variety of laws testing the limits of the *Roe* decision. In several states and localities, legislative bodies tried to qualify the Court's ruling by imposing preconditions on women seeking abortions—permission of the spouse or parents, mandatory waiting periods—or by setting medical requirements intended to make the operation impractical. Some localities adopted zoning regulations to prevent the operation of abortion facilities and required that physicians warn prospective patients to expect serious physical and psychological aftereffects. The Supreme Court struck down most of these restrictive features as religiously motivated laws with no overriding secular purpose (L. Friedman 1983).

Other laws and regulations received Court approval, however. Most important, the Court upheld the legality of a ban on the use of Medicaid funds for abortion under most circumstances and permitted publicly funded hospitals to refuse to perform elective abortions. Given the green light in the Medicaid decision, Congress put similar antiabortion restrictions on military benefits, District of Columbia appropriations, federal employee health insurance, and the foreign assistance program. In addition, many states prohibited their health-care contributions from being used to support elective abortion. Consistent with President Reagan's vocal condemnation of elective abortion, his administration championed most of these efforts and extended them to the international sphere. On the domestic front, the administration joined the efforts of antiabortion groups to eliminate federal support for birth control activities that had proceeded under Title X of the Public Health Act. George Bush endorsed these efforts during the 1988 presidential campaign and supported an executive order, known as the "gag" rule, prohibiting federally funded family planning agencies from mentioning abortion as an option.

With the replacement of three justices from the majority faction in *Roe* by conservative appointees, many observers expected that decision to be overturned during the 1988–1989 session of the Supreme Court. When it finally issued its ruling in the case known as *Webster v. Reproductive Health Services*, the Court severely qualified the guarantees extended in 1973 but did not invalidate the earlier decision. Specifically, the five justices in the *Webster* majority gave Missouri the right to forbid public employees and facilities from conducting discretionary abortions or counseling in favor of it and to insist the physicians must determine whether the fetus is "viable" outside the womb before performing abortions on women who are twenty or more weeks pregnant. More generally, the decision signaled the Court's willingness to consider new state restrictions on the availability of abortion and it subsequently upheld parental notification laws for abortion seekers under the age of eighteen, mandatory waiting periods, and other such limits. But despite furious activity by prolife advocates in state legislatures, the *Roe* principle of liberal access to abortion held steady (Byrnes and Segers 1992).

Beyond its legal consequences, *Webster* seemed to energize the prochoice movement. In several 1989 gubernatorial races where candidates differed on abortion, the abortion-rights advocates received additional electoral support because of their position on the issue (Cook, Jelen, and Wilcox 1994). The prochoice Democratic president elected in 1992 reversed most of the Reagan-Bush restrictions. Among his earliest official acts, Bill Clinton repealed the "gag" order, authorized the resumption of medical research using fetal tissue, restored the authority of overseas military hospitals to perform abortions, permitted impor- tation of a "morning after" abortion pill (RU-246), and reinstated for- eign aid to groups that advocated abortion. He urged states to fund abortions for poor women who were pregnant as the result of rape or incest. In response to a mounting tide of violence aimed at family plan- ning clinics and abortion providers, Clinton also supported a 1994 law that made it a federal crime to intimidate women seeking abortion or to impede their access to clinics. In a decision that drew a sharp rebuke from the nation's Roman Catholic cardinals, Clinton also vetoed a bill that prohibited a rare form of abortion used late in pregnancy.[7] The tide swung back somewhat in favor of the prolife side as a result of the Republican congressional victories in 1994, most notably in the Senate's rejection of a surgeon general nominee who had performed abortions. Nonetheless, abortion remains established as a legal right.

Abortion: A Catholic Issue?

Can abortion be considered a Catholic issue? To some extent, the answer depends on whether the church—both the hierarchy and the laity—is wholeheartedly united around an antiabortion stance. At the level of religious elites, there is no question that the Catholic bishops have invested enormous energy and passion in the abortion issue, assigning it priority over many other concerns (Byrnes 1991). Even though the church's position on the issue has not produced the same level of dissent as its policy against artificial contraceptives, visible signs of disagreement within the Catholic community have cropped up. A small group of scholars and members of various religious orders, orga- nized in "Catholics for Free Choice," has publicly argued that church teaching is in fact compatible with the public availability of abortion under some circumstances (Segers 1992). Roughly one-third of the parish priests interviewed in a *New York Times*/CBS News poll support- ed that view, against the remaining two-thirds who endorsed official church teaching against abortion under any circumstances.[8] The two- to-one margin in favor of the bishops' position constitutes a strong consensus but falls short of unanimity.

But do the parishioners accept the guidance of the church on abor- tion? On many public questions that impinge on personal behavior, including the use of artificial birth control methods, the Catholic laity clearly does not welcome the counsel of its clergy (Leege 1988; McNamara 1992). Similarly, as the bishops' decision to engage actively in public relations confirms, the hierarchy does not enjoy unanimous support from the Catholic community when it speaks in its name about abortion (see chap. 5). In the most active form of disagreement, many Catholic women have utilized the freedom brought by *Roe v. Wade* to obtain legal elective abortions.[9] Less dramatically, Catholics have split over the question of abortion policy, with many favoring a liberalized policy in cases of rape, probable birth defects, or serious threat to maternal health. Indeed, it appears that most lay Catholics now favor access to abortion under those conditions, believe that "good Catholics" can reject church teaching on abortion, and strongly disapprove of church efforts to change national abortion policy directly or by pressuring Catholic officials (D. Moore 1993; Cook, Jelen, and Wilcox 1992). The "blatantly prochoice tone" of the 1992 Democratic campaign did not prevent Catholics from handily favoring Bill Clinton over George Bush nor have Catholics generally shown much willingness to vote against candidates who favor abortion access (Toner 1993). If defining abortion as a Catholic issue implies unanimity of opinion, then the label does not fit.

Abortion still might be considered a Catholic issue if it is uniquely salient to members of that faith. More so than other groups, the *Roe* decision stimulated Catholics to adopt antiabortion positions, and the church unquestionably took the lead in mobilizing opposition and resistance (Franklin and Kosaki 1989; Hofman 1986). Yet even in this sphere, Catholics cannot be depicted accurately as the sole source of opposition to liberalized access, and in fact are not the most intransigent opponents of abortion; that status fell to evangelical Protestants, white and black alike (see table 6.2).[10] Religious behavior and doctrine, not denominational affiliation, most strongly relate to abortion attitudes (Harris and Mills 1985; Cook, Jelen, and Wilcox 1992). The most radical forms of attack on abortion—sit-ins, acts of civil disobedience, clinic bombings, and murders of clinic workers—have primarily been the province of fundamentalist Protestants.

If opposition to abortion is not a Catholic monopoly nor a position accepted by all members of the church, neither is support for *Roe v. Wade* a wholly secular phenomenon. While public leadership of the prochoice movement has been associated with feminist organizations like the National Organization for Women and the family-planning advocate, Planned Parenthood, several Protestant and Jewish groups have worked to resist restrictive abortion policy. The Religious Coalition for Reproductive Choice, a Washington-based umbrella group with more than thirty institutional members, has gained a reputation for effective lobbying in Congress (Mills 1991). It has recently branched out to monitor abortion-related activity in the administrative agencies and has tried to raise public support for the principle of free choice in reproductive decisions. The group does not take a theological position on the abortion issue but rather emphasizes the diversity among American faiths over the status of the fetus as a human being. With such divergent views, the organization argues, extending legal protection to the fetus amounts to enshrining one theological view—the Catholic doctrine—as law. The alleged Catholic basis for antiabortion legislation is then cited as a violation of the antiestablishment clause of the First Amendment, and *Roe v. Wade* is portrayed as a contribution to religious freedom in America (Wenz 1992).

Although abortion cannot be reduced to an exclusive Catholic issue, the most active opponents of liberalization have indeed been recruited from the Catholic community. Several studies of the antiabortion movement have identified the typical activist (outside the South) as a Catholic housewife of limited education, much of it obtained in church-affiliated schools. Deeply devout and a regular churchgoer, she was likely to come from a large family and to be the mother of several children (Granberg 1981b, 1982a, 1982b). According to a study of California right-to-lifers conducted by sociologist Kristin Luker (1984), these women overcame a background of political inactivity out of anger at a Supreme Court decision that seemed to strike directly at their fundamental values about motherhood, the role of women, and the purpose of sex. Assuming that men and women differ in nature, the former best suited for the role of public work and the latter for raising children, the women chose to forgo opportunities for attaining professional skills in favor of stressing their role as caregivers to children and husband. Luker points out that liberalized abortion laws undermine that set of values in three respects:

First, it is intrinsically wrong because it takes a human life and what makes women special is their ability to nourish life. Second, it is wrong because *by giving women control over their fertility*, it breaks up an intricate set of social relationships between men and women that has traditionally surrounded (and in the ideal case protected) women and children. Third and finally, abortion is wrong because it fosters and supports a world view that de-emphasizes (and therefore *downgrades*) the traditional role of men and women. Because these roles have been satisfying ones for pro-life people and because they believe this emotional and social division of labor is both "appropriate and natural," the act of abortion is wrong because it plays havoc with this arrangement of the world. (1984, 161–162)

The supporters of liberalized abortion have proved to be almost the complete opposite of these traditionalist Catholics in social condition and outlook. On the evidence available from this type of intensive interview and from sample surveys, the apparent Catholic versus non-Catholic dimension to the abortion debate is part of a broader conflict over the place of traditional values and sexual norms in society (Jelen 1984; Wagenaar and Bartos 1977; Legge 1985; Tamney, Johnson, and Burton 1992; Woodrum and Davison 1992b). Liberalized abortion is particularly abhorrent to persons enmeshed in traditional social settings and imbued with conservative norms—many, but not all, of whom are Catholic—and acceptable to persons who have been part of modernizing institutions. The conflict is less a denominational fight or a battle between religion and irreligion than a dispute between differing styles of religious belief.

Because abortion touches on such fundamental differences in how some people view the world and their own place in it, it should not be surprising that the debate has unleashed so much passionate energy. The tension has been particularly acute for Catholics in public office. Traditionalist Catholics, whose views were formed in the pre–Vatican II era, have tended to justify opposition to abortion in terms of a universal doctrine of the sanctity of life that need not be restricted to Catholics. But other Catholic officials, including those sympathetic to liberalized abortion on social grounds or representatives of constituencies with mixed attitudes, have not found it easy to stake out an acceptable position. If they were to honor their Catholic background by opposing the free availability of abortion, they could be criticized for representing Catholic interests—a charge that historically has handicapped Catholics seeking public office in the United States. Yet coming down on the side of liberalized abortion would endanger their ability to draw Catholic electoral support.

The Catholic officials who have supported liberalization have justified their position by claiming that their primary responsibility as public officials is to uphold decisions legitimately promulgated by the Supreme Court. Just how fiercely church officials have reacted to this claim was illustrated in 1984, when Rep. Geraldine Ferraro (D-N.Y.), a devout Catholic, received the Democratic nomination for vice president. Though personally opposed to abortion, she had voted against curbs on the use of federal funds to prohibit elective abortion and indicated that her votes on abortion policy would not be influenced by her private faith. This position drew a rebuke from the head of the U.S. Catholic Conference, Bishop James Malone of Youngstown, Ohio, who criticized attempts by candidates to distinguish between private and public morality. More pointedly, the archbishop of New York, John Cardinal O'Connor, wondered aloud during a television interview how Catholics could vote in good conscience for a candidate who did not pledge to support restrictive abortion policies. The steady drumbeat of criticism directed at Representative Ferraro and the appearance of several bishops at Reagan campaign rallies amounted to a virtual endorsement of the Republican ticket. Recognizing an opportunity to make inroads on the traditional allegiance of Catholics to the Democratic party, Republican spokesmen called attention to the bishops' criticism of prochoice Catholics and emphasized that the GOP platform more closely mirrored the church's teachings on abortion.

By seeming to endorse a candidate in a partisan election, the church hierarchy came in for its own share of criticism from political leaders. While endorsing the church's right to speak out on issues with a moral dimension, leading Catholic Democrats asserted that the clergy had overstepped the proper "wall of separation" between church and state. Sen. Edward Kennedy publicly asserted the impropriety of church attempts to impose a restrictive abortion policy on the nation:

Where decisions are inherently individual ones or in cases where we are deeply divided about whether they are, people of faith should not invoke the power of the state to decide what everyone can believe or think or read or do. In such cases—cases like abortion or prayer or prohibition or sexual identity— the proper role of religion is to appeal to the free conscience of each person, not the coercive rule of secular law.[11]

In his defense of Ferraro and other Catholic politicians who opposed restrictive abortion policies, New York governor Mario Cuomo revived the notion of "civil peace" first enunciated in the 1950s by the Catholic theologian John Courtney Murray. In a religiously diverse society like the United States, Murray had argued, attempts by one religious group to prohibit what it regards as evil practices might endanger the harmony of the social order. Hence, he reasoned, it is better to tolerate such evil rather than undermine a society that has permitted such a wide degree of freedom to Catholics and other religious minorities (Wolf 1968, chap. 1). By insisting on the need for an abortion policy that did not enjoy national consensus, Cuomo argued, the Catholic church might well encourage other religious groups to press for policies that endangered religious liberty.

The Catholic public official lives the political truth most Catholics through most of American history have accepted and insisted on: the truth that to assure our freedom we must allow others the same freedom, even if occasionally it produces conduct by them which we would hold to be sinful. We know that the price of seeking to force our beliefs on others is that they might someday force theirs on us.[12]

Thus, according to Cuomo, Catholics should not threaten the peace of society and the freedom accorded to religion by using the state to impose policies deeply offensive to many people. He conceded that the church had every right to condemn abortion and to work for conditions that would eliminate its necessity but, echoing Senator Kennedy, he believed it should attempt to implement its views by appealing to the consciences of individuals.

As the campaign progressed, the church leadership appeared to draw back from the implied attack on Ferraro and other Catholic politicians who had supported *Roe v. Wade*. In a statement issued on behalf of his fellow members of the U.S. Catholic Conference, Bishop James Malone emphasized that the church had no intention of supporting candidates for office and insisted that abortion was one issue among many that Catholics should use to judge potential officeholders. In the end, nearly 60 percent of Catholic voters supported the Republican ticket in 1984, and the defections from the Democratic party appeared to have been highest among those Catholics most deeply involved in parish life. That the Democratic ticket fared so poorly among Catholics, even with a Catholic on the ballot, indicated the potential of abortion to disrupt traditional alliances.

Despite Bishop Malone's attempt to defuse tension, the 1984 debate revealed a church leadership deeply divided over tactics. For some bishops, abortion is still the paramount moral issue of the day and a candidate's position on that single issue remains a litmus test of acceptability. The other camp, represented by Joseph Cardinal Bernardin of Chicago, has taken the position that abortion should be part of a "seamless garment" of issues—including nuclear war, human rights, capital punishment, doctor-assisted suicide, and poverty—all involving threats to human life. The call for "a consistent ethic of life" produced an ecumenical political action committee, "JustLife," that funded congressional candidates in favor of liberal social welfare programs, disarmament, and the prolife position on abortion.[13]

Despite the apparent support of the pope, those who subscribe to the "seamless garment" approach face an uphill battle to restructure Catholic opinion along new lines. Research reveals that abortion opponents are not noted for their opposition to capital punishment, military spending, and the use of force in world affairs—all positions that the bishops have treated as expressions of the prolife ethic. Neither, despite the prolife implications, are antiabortionists more favorable than supporters of liberalization to increased spending on health, gun control laws, or the mandatory use of seatbelts (Granberg 1981a; Granberg and Granberg 1981; Sawyer 1982; Cleghorn 1986; Johnson and Tamney 1988). JustLife could identify only about eighty congressional supporters of the consistent life ethic. What distinguishes the prolife activists— aside from resistance to abortion, euthanasia, and suicide—is conservative preferences on social issues relating to traditional sex roles. To date, most prolife Catholics compartmentalize this sentiment rather than extend the principle to other areas of public policy.

Standing apart from the traditional lines of political debate, the abortion dispute constitutes an exception to the recent trend of liberalized thinking among the clergy. But because its leaders have been so vocal about the issue, the antiabortion movement has sometimes obscured the trend in Catholic politics—even from Catholic parishioners themselves. During the next few years, the church hierarchy will have to decide on the priority to be given abortion relative to the other issues on the national agenda. To date, concern over abortion has dominated the church's political action whenever it entered the equation. As noted earlier, the church's concern that it might be required to provide abortion services in Catholic hospitals delayed passage of the Civil Rights Restoration Act in 1989. When President Clinton proposed a national system of health insurance, the church withheld support because abortion services were part of the package. Continuing concern over the implications of feminism on abortion rights has been one of the factors preventing the bishops from passing a pastoral letter on the status of women in the church. The church also opposed conservative proposals for welfare reform in 1995, fearing that reductions in aid to single mothers would stimulate pregnant poor women to seek abortion. These acts contribute to the widespread impression that abortion is the only priority that the Roman Catholic church is prepared to enforce.

The church's dilemma is made more acute by the increasing polarization of American political life. By taking the prolife position, the Roman Catholic bishops have appeared to side with a conservative movement that does not share its priorities on economic justice questions. The Catholic Alliance, a Conservative Coalition auxiliary that attempts to attract Catholic support, uses a "family-friendly" voting scorecard that celebrates certain policies explicitly condemned by the bishops—cuts in welfare benefits, support for capital punishment, restrictive immigration policy, and so forth. Such policies may be attractive to a middle class constituency that is several generations removed from immigrant status and imbued with the notion that individual Catholics are free to pick and choose from church teachings. Catholics who identify with the evangelical movement do seem to acquire much of its political conservatism, at least on issues that have not been the subject of pastoral letters (Welch and Leege 1991). But such policies alienate the "other" Catholic church—the "urban, ethnically diverse and economically precarious" church of recent immigrants (Hampson 1995). To maintain connections with an increasingly Hispanic constituency, church officials have often embraced liberal social welfare programs and active support for generous treatment of immigrants (Rogers 1990). Negotiating a coherent path between these competing agendas will remain a vivid challenge for the bishops.

The challenge is even greater owing to growing tension between the American Catholic hierarchy and the increasingly conservative disposition of the Vatican. Under Pope John Paul II, considerable efforts have been made to bring rebellious national churches closer in line to Vatican policy. The sympathy of many American bishops for movements such as feminism and, more broadly, to the moral authority of the laity has collided with the pope's insistence on church discipline and moral absolutism. To the extent they side with their more liberal laity, the American church leaders incur the wrath of Rome. But if they opt unreservedly for the social positions advocated by Pope John Paul II, the bishops could find themselves generals without an army.

The Political Traditions of Mainline Protestants

Unlike evangelical Protestants or Roman Catholics, mainline Protestants had established a strong and active presence in American political life well before the 1970s and still control a disproportionate share of public offices (Davidson 1994, 431; Duke and Johnson 1992). Most presidents have been members of a mainline Protestant church; especially strongly represented have been Episcopalians and Presbyterians. For most of the twentieth century, Catholics and Protestants from an evangelical background were rarely considered serious candidates for the nation's highest elective position. The political predominance of mainline Protestants, largely due to their high socioeconomic status, was usually enlisted to resist governmental programs of social welfare and economic regulation. As noted in chapter 6, this tradition survives in the high levels of Republican identification and economic conservatism among rank-and-file members of mainline denominations.

The conservative orientation of the membership has frequently collided with a more liberal outlook among church leaders. Clergy from the mainline Protestant denominations have periodically given birth to movements that cast a skeptical eye on prevailing social and economic arrangements. In this "Social Gospel" tradition, the distinctive feature of reform sentiment has been a belief that God's spirit pervades the world. Rather than seeing God as aloof to human social patterns, the liberal theological tradition has insisted that God is immanent, or present, in human life. Consequently, love of one's neighbor, not personal holiness, should be the principal ethical concern of Christianity (Gilkey 1968). According to this perspective, the will of God is associated with social reform, so it falls to the Christian, as a religious duty, to strive to bring about change in human social conditions. The clergy have usually been the most active carriers of this particular vision (Garrett 1973). As noted in chapter 5, the Washington offices of the mainline Protestant churches have also represented this view in their lobbying efforts.

At the beginning of the twentieth century, when the Social Gospel movement was particularly strong, it contributed to the split in American Christianity between the mainline denominations and their evangelical and fundamentalist adversaries. Although the conflict was rooted in a number of sources, the traditionalists who appropriated the evangelical label objected to the tendency among modernist theologians to equate Christianity with support for social reform. Though the evangelicals were not indifferent to social problems, they emphasized the priority of spiritual communion between God and individuals. Hence, they interpreted social problems as the outgrowth of individual moral failings and supported solutions such as conversion or spiritual rebirth. As pointed out in the previous chapter, the evangelical wing eventually found itself cast in the role of defending traditional social values against the onslaught of modern forces and largely retreated from the national political arena after repeated defeats during the 1920s.

Even though members of what became known as the mainline wing were divided internally over the proper definition of Christianity, much of the clergy moved into the Social Gospel camp. Their enthusiasm for social reform waxed and waned with national political circumstances (P. Carter 1954; Meyer 1961). Enthusiasm was high in the period before World War I, low in the decade after, and high again during the presidency of Franklin D. Roosevelt. Interest in social problems dropped to the bottom of the church agenda during the prosperous years of the post–World War II era, when many churches concentrated their energies on building new facilities for their suburban congregants. By the late 1950s the Protestant churches from the mainline denominations were the target of strong attacks for their supposed indifference to social problems.

Few of the critics could have imagined just how sharply the situation would change in a short time. During the 1960s, social reform moved back to the top of the Protestant agenda. In the churches, a "new breed" of social action-oriented clergy jumped enthusiastically into a variety of progressive causes (Cox 1968). Members of the new breed led rent strikes, organized pickets around city hall, served in community action organizations, financed low-cost housing projects, and helped welfare recipients form unions to better press their claims on reluctant government bureaucracies. At the same time that such action flourished in isolated communities, national attention was drawn to the Protestant clergy's participation in civil rights demonstrations and their leadership role in organizations that opposed U.S. involvement in the Vietnam War (Hall 1990).

In a 1968 survey of parish ministers in California, taken when political activism was at its height, political scientist Harold Quinley (1974) reported on the extent of clergy involvement in three social movements—a campaign to defend California's "fair housing" ordinance from a repeal effort, to support efforts to unionize migrant farm workers, and to oppose the Vietnam War. Among the 1,580 clergy who responded to Quinley's survey, the rate of activism was pronounced—though uneven—across the three issue areas. On the fair housing campaign, a civil rights issue that attracted the highest level of activism, a clear majority of the Protestant ministers took public action in the form of sermons, petitions, or other public statements conveying support for maintenance of the ordinance. For Methodist, Congregationalist, Episcopalian, and Presbyterian clergy, who most enthusiastically endorsed the social reform ministry, antirepeal activity also included prayers about the issue, organization of study or advocacy groups in the church, service on public committees, and the writing of letters to public officials. Roughly one-fourth of the ministers took similar high-profile stances on the Vietnam War, including a substantial number who attended protest meetings, belonged to antiwar organizations, or participated in public marches. The plight of farm workers drew somewhat lower rates of involvement but still gained attention and support from a sizable share of the sample.

The impression of a united bloc of liberal clergy was further reinforced by their high visibility in some of the most dramatic protests of the era. In a number of southern communities where conflict over desegregation of public schools raised social tension to a fever pitch, clergymen played a key role on the front lines, frequently exposing themselves to intimidation and violent assaults from segregationists (Campbell and Pettigrew 1959, 3–4). Shortly before the 1965 Selma-to-Montgomery march to secure voting rights, the civil rights movement gained another martyr in the Rev. James Reeb of Boston. A Unitarian minister who had answered the call of Martin Luther King Jr. for ministerial involvement, Reeb died from a savage beating inflicted by opponents of the planned march. Other ministers similarly risked their lives in boarding buses bound for the South during the "Freedom Summer" campaigns. In expressing their opposition to racial segregation and, later, to U.S. policy in Vietnam, some clergy departed from conventional political activity to perform acts of civil disobedience or even violence. The nation grew accustomed to pictures of clergymen being led off to jail for participation in illegal sit-ins or other such activities.

It is important to keep in mind, however, that a great many ministers did not conform to this description of social action. In their study of the Little Rock (Arkansas) school desegregation crisis of 1957–1958, Campbell and Pettigrew (1959) stressed that most ministers from the mainline churches, while not supporting school segregation, kept their distance from the controversy engulfing their community. Similarly, if Quinley's study of California ministers held true nationwide, many clergy apparently kept their Sunday sermons free of any sustained commentary on the divisive political and social issues of the 1960s (Stark et al. 1971, chap. 5). Neither would it be accurate to conclude that the politically active mainline clergy uniformly supported the liberal side on these issues; some members of Quinley's sample reported undertaking activities in favor of repealing the housing ordinance, defending U.S. military involvement in Southeast Asia, or resisting the unionization campaign on the farms. Similarly, several community surveys revealed that substantial numbers of mainline ministers continued to preach the traditional Protestant perspective, emphasizing personal piety as the best response to social problems (Koller and Retzer 1980; Nelsen 1975). Such conservative activism was much less common than liberal mobilization (Tygart 1977).

In attempting to account for the different levels of political activism among mainline clergy, scholars have stressed both individual and structural factors. As individuals, the activist clergy were more likely than their inactive counterparts to have received advanced education from secular institutions and to have been raised in urban areas (Ammerman 1981). These traits reflect exposure to agents of modernization that probably undermined a traditional conception of religion and encouraged clergy to view their task in much broader terms. Indeed, according to the research of sociologist Hart Nelsen (1975; Nelsen, Madron, and Yokeley 1975), activists and nonactivists exhibited very different understandings about the role of religion in society and adjusted their ministerial priorities accordingly. Nelsen discovered

that clergymen who regarded themselves principally as spiritual leaders, personal counselors, church administrators, or educators tended to
embrace conservative political ideas and to preach the traditional
moral concerns about individual rectitude. The activists were recruited
from the ranks of clergy who defined their principal responsibility as
community problem solving. Believing they were meant to address a
wide range of problems that could not necessarily be solved by personal piety, these clergy were more likely to sermonize on social problems and to favor direct political involvement as a solution.

These differences in role orientation were reinforced by participation
in supportive social networks. Protestant parish ministers were more
likely to engage in civil rights activity—even in the face of congregational resistance—when they belonged to national denominations that
issued clear directives in support of the civil rights movement (J. Wood
1981). It was equally important for activists to find a local haven to sustain their liberal activities. In her study of civil rights involvement
among Protestant ministers in Tuscaloosa, Alabama, Nancy Ammerman
(1981) found that geographical proximity to a university campus and a
perception of pro–civil rights attitudes in the local community were
important factors drawing clergymen into public activism.

Mainline Activism: Sources and Reactions

To understand why the "new breed" clergy emerged when it did, it
is important to consider the social, creedal, and institutional aspects of
mainline Protestantism. I noted earlier that changes in the national
political climate drew both evangelicals and Catholics more fully into
the political arena. The same factors had some influence on the mainline Protestants. The political issues that engaged clergy during the
activist era—civil rights, Vietnam, social justice—touched on profound
moral values at the core of Christian thought. As Quinley (1974, 3) put
it, "The churches could hardly preach Christian brotherhood and love
for one's fellow man and at the same time remain silent on such issues
as civil rights and the war in Vietnam." But the explanatory power of
this theological explanation is limited by awareness that Protestant
clergy had historically kept silent in the face of social conflicts no less
harmful to the spirit of brotherhood and love for one's fellow man and
that many ministers did refrain from speaking out publicly even in the

turbulent 1960s. Another explanation of the clergy's decision to speak out points to a perceived need to preserve the institutional strength of the church and the social influence of the ministry. According to this theory, the liberal Protestant churches saw an emphasis on social action as a bridge to the well-educated and modernized members of their parishes. The demand for relevance was particularly urgent at a time of radical challenge to Christian orthodoxy, when a scientific worldview had undermined some traditional elements of belief and Americans seemed disposed to experiment with Eastern religions. Unless the churches could seem "relevant" to contemporary social problems, in other words, they would lose their appeal to young people and progressive thinkers. For the clergy, who had been criticized earlier for silence on pressing moral matters, participation in social movements may have presented an opportunity to maintain a leadership role in society, through aggressive championing of liberal causes. This interpretation of the clergy's motivation amounts to yet another application of the "status politics" framework.[14]

If the causes of activism among the clergy were debatable, the immediate effect was clear-cut. In church after church, the activist clergy ran headlong into the status quo sentiments of more conservative congregants (Quinley 1974; Hadden 1969). In what another author described as a "gathering storm," the clergy encountered substantial resistance to their attempts to speak for the church on controversial public issues. By majorities ranging from 55 percent on the farm worker issue to 83 percent on the fair housing referendum, the clergy in the California sample reported encountering opposition from at least some members of their congregation. On the race relations campaign, about one-third indicated conflict with the church board, and one in ten said their position had produced efforts to remove them from the pulpit. The Vietnam issue and the farm worker dispute incited conflicts of similar intensity, although with lower rates of opposition.

Faced with this resistance from congregations who apparently preferred a priority on worship and spirituality, many clergy sought safe havens in appointments outside the local parish. Accordingly, the liberal ministers took refuge in campus ministries, denominational "social action" bureaucracies, the seminaries, and other environments that were more supportive of political activity by church leaders. Freed from accountability to a conservative constituency, ministers in these positions supplied a disproportionate share of the activist clergy (Hadden and Rymph 1971). To this day, nonparish environments continue to harbor many politically liberal clergy who would probably find it difficult to coexist with typical members of their denomination (IEA and Roper Center 1982). Other reform-minded members of the clergy and seminary students, weary of the constant battles within the church, simply opted to leave the ministry for opportunities in secular agencies.

Those who remain in the pulpit have continued to press for a liberal and activist social agenda. In a 1988 poll of Protestant ministers, clergy from mainline denominations gave greater emphasis than their evangelical counterparts to the social reform mission of the church and assigned less importance than evangelicals to missionary activities (Guth 1989a). Compared with Baptists, ministers from the Presbyterian church and the Disciples of Christ reported giving more attention to social problems in sermons and sponsoring more church study groups. Many mainline churches were also active in the nuclear freeze movement and in programs to combat homelessness. As in the 1960s, they preach to congregations with many members who do not welcome the "intrusion" of politics in religion (see Welch et al. 1993, table 3).

The problems faced by the progressive clergy stem in large measure from the social perspectives of church members. As Wade Clark Roof (1978) has demonstrated in his study of North Carolina Episcopalians, the social basis of contemporary Christianity has shifted because of the declining plausibility of religious doctrine to persons most deeply affected by modernization. Traditional religious teachings have the greatest appeal for persons with limited exposure to education, urbanization, and impersonal bureaucracies. Such persons who are deeply anchored in their local communities tend to exhibit a narrow perspective on the world and to defend vigorously those traditional social values that have lost favor among the progressive clergy. As a consequence, even liberal denominations with many new-breed clergy drew their church members and activists disproportionately from theological and political conservatives. It is *not* the case, as Roof stressed, that theological conservatism brings about traditional attitudes on social and political issues. Rather, he contended, traditional religious values are the most plausible to persons whose limited exposure to the outside world had safeguarded them from the challenge of modern social thought.

Retrenchment

In a religious marketplace in which churches compete for membership, the individual Protestant faces a wide choice of potential churches with which to affiliate. From the late 1960s through the current period, membership trends have run against the mainline denominations and in favor of the evangelical confessions. Some observers have interpreted the erosion of mainline membership in terms of parishioner resistance to the social activism characteristic of liberal Protestantism. What people want from their churches, declared Dean Kelley (1977) of the National Council of Churches, is comfort rather than challenge. When the liberal ministers nonetheless insisted on social reform as the first priority, Kelley and others maintained, the members voted with their feet, deserting in favor of evangelical churches that spoke to the personal needs and fears of Christians. The mainline clergy seem to have ended up with the worst of both worlds: too action-oriented to suit the preferences of many congregants, and too conventional to maintain the faith of their young, affluent, well-educated constituents (Hoge, Johnson, and Luidens 1995).

Faced with fewer resources and some pressure from parishioners, mainline churches have given renewed attention to problems of church vitality and less energy to political action (Woodward 1993). To make more effective use of limited resources, smaller denominations have joined together in merged confessions or considered such unions. Because endorsement of controversial social and political policies might threaten the harmony of these new unions, the denominations have been reluctant to tread too deeply into the realm of public action. The eroding membership base and membership dissatisfaction have also diminished the "peace and justice" ministries of national church offices and ecumenical organizations. Much conservative criticism had come to focus on the National Council of Churches (NCC), an ecumenical organization of mainline denominations that spearheaded church social action during the 1960s (Pratt 1972). The NCC has not abandoned such commitments—condemning U.S. military action in the Gulf War and challenging Republican cutbacks in federal social programs—but has since given more attention to traditional religious issues such as the extent of sex and violence in popular media. In contrast to their previous willingness to enter the political arena, the mainline churches have been conspicuously silent during the last few presidential elections.

In all facets of the mainline church, then, the recent period has been marked by political retrenchment. The new breed, who never represented more than a minority force within a largely conservative tradition, succeeded for a time in altering the image of liberal Protestantism but eventually succumbed to pressures for a lower profile. Though individuals continue to press for liberal political causes, the family of mainline Protestants has let the leading role go by default to the newly energized evangelicals and Roman Catholics.

African American Protestants: The Perpetuation of Liberalism

The above discussion of political trends among evangelical Protestants, Roman Catholics, and mainline Protestants has emphasized change—from inaction to mobilization for the first two groups, and a shift in the opposite direction for the mainline Protestants. But for the two remaining religious groups, Jews and African American Protestants, the operative word has been "stability." Although neither group was unmoved by the events of the 1970s, they have remained the most reliable pillars of national support for liberal candidates and causes.

That African Americans have stayed on the political left is hardly surprising. As an identifiable minority group, the object of continuing discrimination, subject to the highest rates of unemployment and the lowest levels of economic security, the African American community has remained overwhelmingly in favor of an activist government. In the 1980s, Republican attacks on many programs and policies that African Americans ardently supported cemented their ties to the Democratic party. In the last three national elections, African Americans surpassed all other groups in their level of commitment to the Democratic party and their electoral support for Democratic nominees at all levels of office. The commitment of African Americans to public spending on social welfare programs remains strong (see fig. 6.6).

At first glance, it seems that African Americans manage to combine two loyalties often characterized as opposites—traditional religion and political liberalism. The extent of black political liberalism has already been documented; African Americans are also distinguished by strong adherence to evangelical doctrine, intense religiosity, and high levels of church commitment (Jacobson, Heaton, and Dennis 1990). Do these qualities, normally associated with a conservative stance on many so-called life-style issues, fail to influence African Americans in the same manner? Not entirely. Recall from chapter 6 the strong social conservatism exhibited by blacks on a number of social issues. Compared with many white religious groups, black Protestants were much less enthusiastic about abortion and were much more reluctant to permit gays to serve in the military. Such differences have been confirmed in other studies and shown to extend to related issues such as school prayer (R. Smith and Seltzer 1992; Combs and Welch 1982; Secret, Johnson, and Welch 1986). Religious beliefs largely account for African American opposition to abortion (Wilcox 1992b).

But on other issues that have been linked to the profamily agenda, African American religiosity either fails to instill moral conservatism or actually promotes liberal views. Susan Marshall (1990) found for example that church attendance, correlated strongly with opposition to the Equal Rights Amendment among white women, had no impact on the attitudes of black women to the amendment. In a similar analysis of women's views on discretionary abortion, membership in a Protestant denomination was associated with opposition to abortion among whites but had no such effect on black women (Dugger 1991). Religious identification and private devotionalism appear to encourage whites to accept the "priestly" version of civil religion that sanctifies the nation; they have precisely the opposite effect on African Americans (Woodrum and Bell 1989). Among whites, as we learned in the previous chapter, charismatic identification, personal religiosity, and high levels of church attendance were associated with greater levels of support for the conservative presidential candidacy of Pat Robertson. Among African Americans sampled in Washington, D.C., these qualities were related to support for Jesse Jackson, a candidate whose platform was the polar opposite of Robertson's (Wilcox 1990). The data in chapter 6 suggest that African Americans draw a sharp distinction between rejecting a certain type of behavior and enacting public policy to forbid it. Though clearly hostile to homosexuality, African Americans were more likely than all but one white group to oppose employment discrimination against gays (see table 6.4) and to support state funding of abortions for poor women even though blacks were opposed to abortion in general (see table 6.2).

The solution to this apparent puzzle may be the rich, multifaceted evangelicalism conveyed in black churches that has the potential to encourage either liberal or conservative political tendencies. One component of black evangelical theology emphasizes the innate sinfulness of humankind and the consequent importance of family values in restraining immorality. Social traditionalism may encourage blacks, as it does whites, to favor restrictions on abortion and to oppose limitations on school prayer. Yet African American Protestantism also contains a strong prophetic component, a response to centuries of oppression. Portraying Jesus primarily as a force for liberation, this aspect of black theology makes religion a spur to social justice. The prophetic element guides religious African Americans to a critical stance regarding the United States and attracts them to the candidacy of a Jesse Jackson.

The political response of blacks seems to depend on which aspect of theology is evoked by a particular public issue. Because white women saw the ERA primarily as a challenge to traditional sex roles, evangelical religious commitment inspires opposition to the proposal. For African Americans, however, the amendment represented the salient value of equality and legal protection against discrimination. As such, African Americans who are imbued with a strong religious commitment are more sympathetic to the proposal. On the issues of paramount concern for most black Americans—economic security and civil rights—religious commitment is likely to reinforce the liberal thrust of that community.

The Infrastructure of African American Politics

More surprising than the persistence of liberalism has been the continued presence of members of the African American clergy in political leadership roles. Through the Southern Christian Leadership Conference (SCLC) and local ministerial alliances, the Rev. Martin Luther King Jr. and like-minded black clergymen provided vital organizational resources and strategy for the civil rights movement in the late 1950s and early 1960s. In a fascinating reconstruction of the early days of the civil rights campaign, Aldon Morris (1981, 1984) has demonstrated the critical role of black ministers and churches in training and recruiting volunteers, communicating with supporters, and providing havens for the early sit-ins, boycotts, and mass marches. Even those southern African Americans who were outside the centers of organized resistance to segregation recognized ministers as the natural leaders of political activism (Matthews and Prothro 1966, 180–185). The same pattern held in the early 1970s, according to a national survey of African American adults conducted by political scientist Hanes Walton (1985, 47–49). When asked to identify the major influences on their thinking, respondents identified the "black church" and "black minister" more frequently than any other institution or organization.

But with time and changes in the political and social situation of African Americans, the political leadership of ministers came to be challenged by new elites. The first signs of competition for leadership emerged when the civil rights movement entered what was described as its "black power" phase. Disappointed with the limited consequences of the civil rights legislation passed into law in 1964 and 1965, younger activists from outside the churches called on blacks to pursue more aggressive action to achieve social, economic, and political progress. As part of their appeal to black nationalist sentiment, the more militant leaders frequently denounced the clergy of the major black denominations for a supposed unwillingness to challenge the white power structure. To the extent that the black power movement was church-related, its center of gravity was located in nontraditional religious faith rather than in the mainstream African American churches. The religious group most critical of Christianity, the Black Muslims, called for a complete separation of African Americans from the white community and developed a theology that identified the white man as the incarnation of the devil. Although these non-Christians have never come close to displacing the traditional denominations, the assassination of Martin Luther King Jr. robbed the civil rights movement of the most prominent leader with a distinctly Christian orientation to political action.

The black power revolt represented dissatisfaction with the limited progress of the civil rights movement under the leadership of the mainline clergy. Ironically, however, the very successes of the movement also produced a rival set of claimants for community leadership. With some relaxation of segregation and expanded educational opportunities, limited numbers of African Americans were able to move into formerly white-dominated voluntary associations specializing in policy areas such as health, employment, education, and social welfare. With professional training, administrative skills, and political sophistication, such experts assumed some of the political and social responsibilities previously monopolized by the ministers (J. Q. Wilson 1965, 297–300). The growing corps of African Americans in government positions— another consequence of the civil rights movement—further accentuated the transition away from clergy domination. Today, the typical black candidate for public office, be the position elective, appointive, or administrative, is most likely to emerge not from the clergy but from the sector of African American professionals trained in law, business, public administration, or another field outside the church (Cole 1976, 43; R. Smith 1981, 210). Unlike the leadership of the black power revolt, however, the African American professionals and public officials have remained closely tied to the mainstream churches (Salamon 1973, 628–629; Fenno 1978, 113–124).

Despite the emergence of a secular leadership class, the clergy have continued to provide major political leaders of the black community. Until his recent retirement, the Rev. Walter Fauntroy of Washington, D.C., was one of the leading spokesmen for the concerns of the African American community. A New York preacher, the Rev. Floyd Flake, has emerged as a congressional expert on urban redevelopment, while John Lewis, a representative from Georgia trained as a Baptist minister, was an influential deputy whip among House Democrats. In social action, too, black ministers have continued to play leading roles in such organizations as the National Association for the Advancement of Colored People (NAACP), the Chicago-based "People United to Save Humanity" (PUSH), and the Opportunities Industrialization Commission (OIC) in Philadelphia. The founder of OIC, the Rev. Leon Sullivan, was also instrumental in forging U.S. opposition to the white minority regime in South Africa.

Black ministers have been able to play such a strategic role because they command the resources of the strongest institution in African American life (C. Lincoln and Mamiya 1990, esp. chap. 5). The roots of the church run deep enough to make it the natural focus of organized activity in the black community and to enable it to withstand competition from secular organizations. As a typical example, the minister of the Shiloh Baptist Church in the nation's capital presides over a community outreach program that provides more than ninety separate services to neighborhood residents and over five thousand parishioners.[15] In other urban centers, there have been church-based organizations such as the East Brooklyn Churches (EBC), described by an observer as "a powerful, politically independent, dues-paying organization that can turn out 7,000 people for a rally, register 10,000 new voters in a year, and persuade politicians to put up new street signs [and] inspect local grocery stores" (Hornblower 1985). The EBC was instrumental in the building of low-cost housing that has restored to viability parts of Brooklyn that were once written off as terminally blighted. On a smaller scale, such activities are performed by many churches in the African American community. Black congregations are significantly more likely than predominantly white churches to engage in social action involving provision of meals, housing and shelter, community development, and civil rights activity (Chaves and Higgins 1992).

From the perspective of organizational theory, leaders of the church enjoy (1) regular opportunities to communicate their views on issues to members of the community, (2) immense prestige and credibility, and (3) control over a network of social agencies that meet human needs. Such resources can easily be turned to political advantage. When black politics was restricted by law and custom, the African American church could still provide a basis for some limited bargaining with the white political elite. In Chicago during the turn of the century, a bishop of the local African Methodist Episcopal church used his pulpit, personal influence, and administrative control over an extensive system of welfare activities to mold African Americans into a cohesive voting bloc. In exchange for supporting a victorious white mayoral candidate, the clergyman was able to obtain new public facilities in the African American community and some patronage positions in municipal government for congregants (Katznelson 1976, 92–93).

To judge by the role of black churches in more recent Chicago elections, the stakes may have changed but the methods have not. With the prospect of electing an African American to the mayor's office, the churches played a crucial role in a dramatic voter registration drive late in 1982 (Kleppner 1985, 145–150). One prominent black minister bluntly told his parishioners that nonregistrants were not welcome in the congregation. A voter registration card was the price of access to the free food distributed by one of the major Baptist churches in the African American community. Under the slogan "Praise the Lord and

Register," the black churches committed themselves wholeheartedly to serving as registration centers. Because of the massive increase in black voter enrollment and high turnout among the newly registered, the black candidate, Harold Washington, won the Chicago mayoral election in 1983. The churches provided similar support for successful African American mayoral candidates in many American cities.

When public office–holding came to be a realistic possibility, the political options of black clergymen expanded well beyond the limits of the segregation era. In fact, securing public office has frequently come to be viewed as an extension of the pastoral role. As one black minister with congressional experience told another who was considering running for office, "Congress will not be difficult. It is essentially pastoring, ministering to the folks in your district" (C. Hall 1985, 13). Combined with a gospel of social action, these institutional and social forces have provided a powerful impetus to organized political action.

The presidential campaigns of Jesse Jackson reinforced the trend by providing the clergy-activist with a national platform. An associate of Martin Luther King Jr., Jackson had concentrated on black economic development during the 1970s. In Chicago, he founded PUSH, an organization that encouraged blacks to cultivate conservative social values (self-help, strong discipline, drug avoidance) in the pursuit of what most conservative whites must surely regard as radical social, economic, and political objectives. True to his background in the civil rights movement, Jackson has not shied away from the use of boycotts, demonstrations, and sit-ins to protest alleged discrimination. Although failing to win either the 1984 or 1988 Democratic presidential nominations, he succeeded in mobilizing impressive political support and produced a surge in electoral participation by African Americans (Henry 1990, 88–91).

Jackson's campaign was deeply rooted in the black churches (Hertzke 1993; Wald 1991). They provided the forum in which his candidacies were first explored and the base for voter registration drives essential to its success. Churches also served as the key organizational units of the campaign and generated most of the activists and money to fuel the cause. The religious dimension of Jackson's campaign was most apparent to whites in the candidate's religious language and appeals. Jackson's entire platform rested on a belief in the kinship of humankind through its common link to God; in this view, poverty, racism, and sexism are not merely social problems but sins against the divine spark in all people. He portrayed political action in messianic terms, constantly invoking biblical metaphors and turning an attack on drug use into something resembling a religious crusade. The Jackson platform bore strong traces of both the Social Gospel and liberation theology.

There is every reason to believe that the church will continue as the vanguard of political action for black Protestants. This does not mean that all African American clergy should be expected to play a leadership role in political life. Like its white Protestant counterpart, the black religious community contains ministers who firmly believe that political mobilization ought to be a secondary concern lest it detract the church from the paramount task of saving souls. Even in the heyday of the civil rights movement, the SCLC was regarded with suspicion by some leaders of major black confessions, and many preachers refrained from taking aggressive or challenging political stances (C. Hamilton 1972, chap. 5; Paris 1978).The most politically active ministers of black churches closely resembled their white counterparts in the new-breed clergy of the mainline Protestants (Berenson, Elifson, and Tollerson 1976). But because the laity of the largest and most active African American churches recognizes a need for an activist government to promote social change, black clergymen face much less resistance to social and political activism (C. Lincoln and Mamiya 1990, 223–227).

Scholars continue to debate the impact of strong religious feeling on the development of African American politics. The root of the debate is the historical tendency of the black church to act at times as a force for resisting African American subordination while in other circumstances as an advocate of accommodation to white domination. Advocates of the so-called opiate interpretation insist that religion has primarily been a conservative force, its otherworldly nature encouraging blacks to wait for justice in heaven rather than to pursue it here on earth. At the other extreme, the contrasting "inspiration" view contends that "it was precisely through the Biblical story, the Negro Spiritual, and the event of Christian worship that black people knew the existence of being bound together in the persecuted family of a righteous God who destined them someday to break the bonds of oppression" (Gayraud Wilmore, cited in S. Johnson 1986, 311). The coexistence of conservative and radical themes in black theology, noted earlier in this chapter, may provide support for each interpretation under appropriate circumstances. Indeed, research on the role of religion during the civil rights movement disagreed as to whether ministerial leadership and religious consciousness helped or hindered the development of African American political consciousness (Marx 1967, chap. 4; Hunt and Hunt 1977; Nelsen, Madron, and Yokeley 1975).

Speaking of "the black church" as though it were a singular entity obscures the astonishing array of diverse religious impulses among African Americans (Baer and Singer 1992). Among the seven major Protestant denominations that incorporate the vast majority of African American churchgoers, the evidence suggests that religion contributes to political assertiveness. Blacks who are active in such churches are more likely to vote even when taking into account their socioeconomic status and other related factors (F. Harris 1994). Black churches apparently teach their congregants to identify with the African American community, and this sense of group solidarity, in turn, encourages blacks to pursue collective political remedies for their problems (Allen, Dawson, and Brown 1989; Brown and Wolford 1993; Wilcox and Gomez 1990b; Dawson, Brown, and Allen 1990; Bledsoe et al. 1995; Ellison 1991).

This recent research emphasizes the role of religious environments in providing two major stimulants to African American political action, the acquisition of organizational skills and exposure to political information. Although these traits may be acquired in the workplace or other voluntary organizations, the centrality of religious congregations in African American life makes them critical environments for generating African-American participation. According to the results of national surveys, blacks are appreciably more likely than whites or Hispanics to practice in church such politically relevant skills as letter writing, participation in group decision making, running meetings, or making formal presentations (Verba et al. 1993). Some of this difference relates to the greater concentration of blacks in Protestant congregations that encourage individual participation and congregational decision making. Comparatively speaking, African Americans are also much more likely than other population groups to attend church meetings about politics and to hear discussion of political issues from the pulpit (ibid.). If white evangelical churches can be described with considerable hyperbole as the "Republican party at prayer," the common practice of beginning NAACP meetings at the conclusion of worship services led the black church to be depicted as "the NAACP on its knees" (Gayraud Wilmore, cited in C. Lincoln and Mamiya 1990, 209). Together, the transmission of organizational skills and platforms for political learning make the black church an important resource that enables African Americans to overcome the other resource shortages that would hinder their political involvement.

As with all generalizations, this conclusion has limits and does not apply to many of the religious traditions outside the mainline black denominations (Baer and Singer 1992). Participation in pentecostal and Holiness sects that stress turning inward and personal piety often inhibits political commitment among African Americans. So does involvement in spiritualist movements that seek to overcome oppression by invoking magic. Messianic movements that emphasize black nationalism do not look for deliverance in the hereafter or the realm of the senses but may nonetheless discourage involvement in such mundane political actions as voting and campaigns. Whether the impact is toward political engagement or withdrawal, there can be little doubt that the African American religious tradition continues to shape the form of modern black political action.

Jews and U.S. Political Trends

Given their relatively small numbers, Jews might not seem to warrant special attention in a general volume about religion in U.S. politics. But several aspects of Jewish political behavior have prompted scholars to pay close attention to this particular community. To begin with, Jews are extremely active in American political life. They are represented well beyond their numerical share of the population as candidates and officials, campaign activists, political contributors, members of interest groups, and—not least—as regular voters in primary and general elections. Their high rate of voting, coupled with geographic concentration in large and competitive states, makes them especially important in presidential elections. The nature, as well as the amount, of Jewish activism also stands out. Collectively an affluent religious group, Jews nonetheless hold liberal political views that seem contrary to their economic self-interest. In fact, unlike non-Jews who typically become much more Republican as their income increases, Jewish voters do not "vote their pocketbooks" to the same degree (Sigelman 1991; A. Fisher 1989, 43). Although most religious groups define themselves in terms of theological beliefs or prescribed codes of behavior, many Jews actually regard liberalism as the very essence of Judaism itself (Sklare and Greenblum 1967, chap. 10; C. Liebman and Cohen 1990, 97).

In chapter 6 we noted several explanations for the strength of Jewish liberalism. The popular theory that liberalism was somehow implicit in Jewish theology has been undercut by repeated findings that the most religiously observant Jews are also the most politically conservative (S. Cohen 1983, 143–153; Lazerwitz, Winter, and Dashefsky 1988).[16] If their liberalism is not mandated by creed and seems counter to group interest, then social standing probably seems the best explanation. Scholars generally attribute Jewish political preferences to the community's sense of itself as a potential target of hostility from the non-Jewish majority. Despite attaining objective levels of prominence undreamed of by earlier generations, American Jews still feel vulnerable to persecution and anti-Semitism (C. Liebman and Cohen 1990, 42–50). Why should a sense of social marginality attract American Jews to the left side of the political spectrum? From history, Jews learned that the left historically favored the cause of minorities, and liberalism is still seen as more sympathetic to minority groups than the political alternatives. Even if they do not benefit directly from the social programs sponsored by liberals, Jews regard such programs as a safeguard against the social tensions that breed religious bigotry (Fein 1988).

Since the 1960s some observers have predicted that urban unrest, affirmative action, and concern for the fate of Israel would eventually drive Jews out of the Democratic coalition and into alliance with conservative forces. One powerful impetus to political change was the upsurge in conflict between Jews and African Americans. Before the "black power" movement, when the civil rights campaign concentrated principally on attacking formal barriers to equality, Jews were the single most ardent supporters of the movement in the white community. Aside from membership and leadership roles in interracial civil rights organizations, Jews made up a massively disproportionate share of the young white students who went South as volunteers for desegregation (M. Friedman 1995, chaps. 6–8). White politicians who developed a reputation as civil rights activists enjoyed nearly unanimous electoral support from Jewish voters; those who became symbols of white resistance, such as George Wallace of Alabama, looked elsewhere.

Once the civil rights movement moved to northern cities and came to focus on de facto expressions of racism, however, the two communities began to divide. Tensions arose over demands by the advocates of black power for "community control" of ghetto life. As the immigrant group that had preceded African Americans to the city, Jews still occupied an important place in private businesses and public institutions in the central city. Hence, though directed at whites in general, demands for black ownership of businesses, black-only leadership in civil rights groups, and increased African American representation in public employment challenged Jews in particular. The bitter expressions of hostility from some protagonists on both sides conveyed the impression of a fundamental estrangement rooted in a rising tide of black anti-Semitism and Jewish racism.

In New York, the city with the largest concentration of Jews, these clashes became particularly intense. Attacks on Jewish-owned businesses during ghetto riots and conflicts between African Americans and Jews in the public schools brought national publicity. Relationships eventually deteriorated to the point that a Brooklyn-born rabbi, Meier Kahane, formed the Jewish Defense League (JDL) to patrol inner-city neighborhoods with sizable concentrations of Jews. By offering armed protection to Jews who felt threatened by crime and anti-Semitic attacks, the JDL bore a strong resemblance to the most militant black organizations in the ghetto. Condemned by many Jewish leaders as a thinly disguised appeal to racist sentiment, the JDL nonetheless played on fears of racial violence widespread in the Jewish community.

On a more general level, tensions arose over the development of affirmative action programs in public employment, graduate and professional school admission, and other important sectors. The principle of affirmative action is that past discrimination against African Americans or any other group can most effectively and justly be overcome by giving temporary preference to African American applicants in competition for channels to upward mobility. The legitimacy of the principle and its application to concrete situations have generated considerable conflict within the liberal community. The doctrine goes well beyond the traditional understanding of "equality" into realms that have been described by unfriendly observers as "reverse discrimination" or "affirmative discrimination." Some of the most trenchant criticisms of the new policy came from Jews who regarded the programs as tantamount to setting up governmentally approved "quotas" for access to social advancement. Because such quotas had once been used to exclude Jews from careers in prestigious and remunerative occupations, their proposed introduction for purposes of spurring African American advancement called forth strong opposition from much of the Jewish community. When the Supreme Court considered cases about the constitutionality of specific affirmative action programs, the major Jewish organizations that had once joined African American plaintiffs in discrimination cases usually weighed in on the side challenging the new schemes.

Once the closest of allies, the two groups began to trade charges of racism and anti-Semitism. Blacks attributed the deteriorating relationship to Jewish unwillingness to admit their legitimate claims for jobs, housing, and political power, whereas Jews tended to blame racial agitation and envy. In retrospect, the clash seems to have been a predictable outcome of the process of ethnic succession in American cities, the process by which each newly arrived ethnic group stakes its claim to power at the expense of its predecessors. Even at the height of the conflict in New York, a specially commissioned public opinion poll revealed an underlying harmony between African Americans and Jews (L. Harris and Swanson 1970, chap. 2). According to the poll, Jews were more likely than white Catholics and no less likely than white Protestants to acknowledge that blacks suffered discrimination, and only African Americans shared the Jewish perception that the latter were still victims of discrimination in the city.

The Jewish commitment to liberalism was thought to have been further undermined by the issue of Israel. As noted earlier, the Jewish community was galvanized by the outbreak of the Six-Day War in 1967 between Israel and its Arab neighbors, which immeasurably strengthened the commitment of American Jews to the Zionist cause. As American Jews increased their support for the Jewish homeland in the Middle East, many self-identified liberals moved the other way by showing greater sympathy for the claims of Palestinian nationalists. Jews who had once championed the United Nations and given verbal support to some national liberation movements watched with dismay as the 1975 General Assembly declared Zionism to be a form of racism and equated Israelis with white South Africans as colonial oppressors.

During the administration of President Jimmy Carter, the Israeli issue fused with concern over African American attitudes toward the

Jewish community (Feuerlicht 1983, chap. 6; for an earlier tie, see Carson 1984). At the United Nations, Amb. Andrew Young had forged strong ties with some of the Third World representatives who had been the most vociferous critics of U.S. support for Israel. In August 1979 it was revealed that Ambassador Young had held a meeting with a representative of the Palestine Liberation Organization (PLO), the umbrella group of Palestinian nationalism. Since the United States had an official policy to boycott the PLO until it granted recognition to Israel, Young's meeting was condemned by Israel and by leaders of American Jewish organizations. Under pressure from the State Department, Young eventually resigned. Blacks were angry about the apparent Jewish attack on their most influential advocate in the administration and felt that Young had been singled out for retribution. The Jews were outraged at the sympathy that African Americans had shown to an organization that advocated violence in order to achieve Palestinian aims.[17] In 1980 Jewish voters appeared to repay the Carter administration for its alleged pro-Arab tilt by giving President Carter less than a clear majority of their vote in his reelection bid. Although Israel was not the only reason for the decline in Jewish support for the Democratic ticket, it surely contributed in a major way.

These various tensions prompted a small group of Jewish intellectuals to argue that it was time for a permanent change in alliance. In journals like *Commentary* and *Public Interest*, neoconservatives like Irving Kristol urged Jews to reconsider their traditional attachment to liberalism. Jewish interests, it was argued, were most likely to be served by the conservative policies of the Republican administration that took office in 1981. In national defense, for example, Jews were told that Israel would benefit from the massive rearmament undertaken by the Defense Department. The administration's hostility to affirmative action programs fell well within the Jewish opposition to the use of quotas to increase African American representation in the public sector and other places. Similarly, some of the neoconservatives encouraged Jews to vote their pocketbooks by supporting the anti-inflation and tax-cutting programs launched by the Reagan White House.

The attempt to move Jews out of the Democratic camp received an unexpected push from the presidential campaigns of the Rev. Jesse Jackson. During a public appearance in 1984, Jackson was overheard to refer to Jews as "Hymies" and New York City as "Hymietown."

Although Jackson apologized for his offensive language, bad feelings were revived as the public learned more about his ties with Minister Louis Farrakhan, the head of a Black Muslim sect known as the Nation of Islam. By meeting with Libyan leader Col. Muammar Qaddafi in 1995 and referring to Judaism as either a "gutter" or "dirty" religion, Farrakhan revived all the Jewish fears about the growth of black anti-Semitism. Jackson's insistence on condemning Farrakhan's remarks but not the man himself did not placate Jewish anger.[18] Neither were Jews endeared to a candidate so clearly sympathetic toward Palestinian nationalism. Though Jackson endorsed the existence of Israel and called for secure borders, Jews were more persuaded by the photograph of him in the physical embrace of PLO leader Yasir Arafat and the candidate's (unsuccessful) efforts to pass a platform plank endorsing an independent Palestinian state. Usually much more supportive of black candidates than other white voters, Jews rejected Jackson because they regarded him as antagonistic. The Republicans spared no effort to tie the Democratic presidential nominees to Jackson's position on the Middle East and to publicize his alleged anti-Semitism (Madison 1984).

Despite Jackson's lower profile after 1988, black-Jewish tensions remained high (Berman 1994). The increasing prominence of the Nation of Islam, symbolized by Louis Farrakhan's prominence in the "Million Man March" of 1995, raised concern about the power of anti-Semitic appeals in the African American community. The problem took on concrete form in the Crown Heights section of Brooklyn in 1991. The accidental death of a black child at the hands of a Jewish driver set off several days of anti-Jewish rioting in which a rabbinical student was targeted and killed. The eventual acquittal of his accused murderers angered many in the Jewish community.

Despite predictions that Jewish liberalism would decay under the combined onslaught of all these factors, both the data presented in chapter 6 and the findings of other studies show Jews still much more likely than others to favor liberal policies on a wide range of public issues (Lerner, Nagai, and Rothman 1989; A. Fisher 1985; S. Cohen 1989). This liberalism has continued to translate into very high levels of Jewish support for Democratic congressional and gubernatorial candidates. In 1986 Jews typically preferred Democrats to Republicans by margins of three or four to one (Singer 1987). Despite fond hopes that 1980 signaled a permanent conversion to Republicanism in presidential elections, Jews soon returned to their traditional preferences. Depending on which poll is consulted, the Democratic nominees in 1984 and 1988 carried somewhere between two-thirds and three-fourths of the Jewish vote. The gap in Democratic support between Jews and non-Jews, which had dropped to only 14 percent in 1980, returned to the same mid–20 percent range it had reached during the 1950s (A. Fisher 1989, 43).

The failure of Jews to respond to Republican overtures evidently meant that Jewish voters were more worried about the new political prominence of the evangelical Protestants than about the conflicts with African American leaders. In support of this interpretation, a 1984 *Los Angeles Times* poll revealed that Jewish voters were actually more hostile to the Rev. Jerry Falwell, who had actually courted them on behalf of the Reagan campaign, than to Jesse Jackson (Schneider 1985, 58). And while 58 percent of Falwell's Jewish critics supported Walter Mondale, a whopping 78 percent of the anti-Jackson Jews stayed with the Democratic ticket on election day. Why do Jews react so much more negatively to a white Protestant preacher who supported Israel unreservedly than to a black Protestant preacher who flirted with the Arab cause? According to political scientist Seymour Martin Lipset (1985, 23), "The answer would seem to lie in the millennia-old history of European Jewry as a minority, persecuted and discriminated against by conservative religious and secular establishments." The evangelical Protestants are associated in the Jewish mind both with the policies of "Christian government" and with skepticism about the value of government support for welfare. Neither association endeared Jews to the Republican ticket in 1984 or 1988.

The growing strength of the Christian Right in the Republican party has not been lost on many Jews. Fear that the Republican party saw itself as the "Party of God" was one of the factors accounting for the 80–85 percent support that Jewish voters gave to Bill Clinton in 1992 and their continuing loyalty to the Democrats in 1994 (J. Goldberg 1992). In response to the second coming of the Christian Right in the 1990s, the Anti-Defamation League (ADL), a Jewish human rights agency, issued a stinging critique of the movement for its alleged anti-democratic and antipluralistic orientation (Cantor 1994). Although the Christian Coalition's executive director later addressed the ADL in an attempt to mend fences, the strongly antiseparationist posture of the

Christian Right is likely to reinforce Jewish doubts and concerns about the movement's respect for religious pluralism.

Jews today are cohesive but certainly not unanimous in their preferences for liberal issues and candidates. There are signs of willingness by some members of the community to reconsider their traditional ties. Younger Jews, though still much more Democratic than their non-Jewish counterparts, are more sympathetic to Republican candidates than their grandparents (A. Fisher 1989). Pro-Israel political action committees donate roughly one-third of their funds to Republican candidates (Malbin 1986). But still, in all, Jews remain politically where they have been for more than half a century—well to the left on the American political spectrum.

Strong ties bound religion and politics in the 1980s. Yet it has also been demonstrated in this and the previous chapter that religious groups have reacted quite differently to national political trends. They have not all responded to the same issues nor responded similarly to common developments. Although some of the uniqueness reflects group tradition and the pull of old loyalties, equal weight must be given to factors rooted in creedal, social, and institutional traits. The larger consequences of the relationship for the health of the body politic—the important question of whether religious involvement is good or bad for the political system—will be taken up in the concluding chapter.

NOTES

The epigraph for this chapter is taken from the *Wall Street Journal*, 24 February 1988.

1. Charles E. Coughlin was a Detroit priest who had become a national celebrity with his radio broadcasts in the 1920s. During the 1930s, his broadcasts combined economic radicalism with attacks on Jews, communists, and the "New Deal" of Franklin D. Roosevelt. A U.S. senator from Wisconsin, Joseph McCarthy drew fame for his accusations of Communist penetration of the U.S. government in the late 1940s and early 1950s.

2. This upward mobility was true mostly for Catholic natives who were at least the third generation of their family in America. For more recent immigrants, especially Hispanic Catholics from Mexico and Puerto Rico, economic conditions and social integration were much less advanced.

3. "Catholic Group Extols Capitalism as Bishops Ready Economic Study," *New York Times*, 7 November 1984, 1, 21.

4. "In Celebration of Creative Capitalism in Society," *New York Times*, 7 November 1984, 21.

5. Terms such as "liberal" and "conservative" do not fit well on issues such as abortion. In describing support for legalized abortion as "liberal" and opposition as "conservative," I do not mean to suggest that there is anything intrinsically liberal about supporting abortion as a right or anything inherently conservative about a restrictive policy. My use of these terms refers to liberal or conservative access to abortion.

6. For excellent summaries of the Catholic role in the abortion controversy, see Jung and Shannon (1988) and Rubin (1994).

7. The procedure, known as intact dilation and evacuation, was labeled "partial birth abortion" by its opponents. See Gustav Niebuhr, "Catholic Cardinals Condemn Clinton Abortion Bill Veto," *New York Times*, 17 April 1996 (electronic edition available at http://www.nytimes.com).

8. "Poll Shows Most Priests Want the Right to Marry," *New York Times*, 11 September 1987, 1.

9. Catholics comprise about 30 percent of the women receiving abortions, roughly the same proportion as their population share, but the rate varies appreciably by ethnic and racial groups within the church (Henshaw and Silverman 1988).

10. In their comprehensive study of abortion attitudes, Cook, Jelen, and Wilcox (1992, 122–124) found that Roman Catholicism had a stronger impact on opposition than membership in an evangelical denomination after taking account of a wide range of demographic, attitudinal, and religious factors.

11. "Excerpts from Speech by Kennedy," *New York Times*, 11 September 1984, 10.

12. "Excerpts from Cuomo Talk on Religion and Public Morality," *New York Times*, 14 September 1984, 13.

13. JustLife eventually folded.

14. Interestingly, the historian Richard Hofstadter (1955, 148–152) offered a similar explanation to account for the initial surge of mainline activism during the Progressive era.

15. "D.C.'s Shiloh Baptist Is a Symbol of Black Political Activism," *Gainesville Sun*, 1 September 1984, 1C.

16. Jerome Legge (1995) has recently argued that Jewish religious involvement—not orthodoxy per se but religious attachment—does correlate strongly with liberal political outlooks.

17. Whatever the views of African American leaders toward Israel, black Americans remained favorably disposed to that country and preferred it to its Arab enemies (Gilboa 1987, 275–277). The Congressional Black Caucus has also been a consistent supporter of aid to Israel.

18. For black reaction to the Farrakhan movement, see the special polls of a national black sample in Simon Wiesenthal Center (1986).

9. Religion and American Political Life

The challenge of practical politics is to combine the passion of religion with the civil tolerance of democratic pluralism.
—Clarke E. Cochran

Viewed against the backdrop of history, the recent rise in political activism among some religious groups is not a departure from national tradition but only the renewal of a long-standing pattern in American political life. As previous chapters have documented, religion—in the guise of sacred values, institutions, and social groups—has operated at several levels of politics. Religion was present at the creation of the U.S. political system and was one of several elements contributing to the design of governmental institutions and to the core of beliefs that grew into the national political culture. The place of religion in a pluralistic society has generated a seemingly endless supply of legal disputes about the proper relationship between church and state. Religious affiliation has long been a potent influence on mass partisan loyalties and has been a factor inspiring the positions taken by political elites on a wide range of pressing national issues. If the past few years are any indication, religion has retained a potency that will keep it among the social forces likely to fuel political conflict.

What may not be clear are the political and social consequences that result from the interaction between the spheres of religion and politics. By referring to "consequences," I do *not* mean either the impact of political activism on religion or the effect of religious intervention on the disposition of particular policies. Both are legitimate issues that have been examined elsewhere in the book. Rather, this chapter's theme is the effect of religious activism on the general tenor of political life in the United States. Specifically, I will assess the benefits and costs to democracy and the functioning of the political system of the religious presence in public life. My conclusion, that religion in politics is neither an unvarying source of good nor a consistent evil influence, is unlikely to please either the most ardent advocates of a "Christian America" or secularists who want to keep religion safely outside the public arena. It is consistent, however, with the historical record, which has shown that religion has the capacity both to ennoble and to corrupt political life.

The Case Against Religious Influence in Politics

Even if they were to lower their profile, religious groups would still be important actors in American political life. Does this reality bode good or ill for the future of politics in the United States? The question is not merely academic, for although certain forms of religious influence cannot be controlled, the government has some limited power to encourage or discourage organized political involvement by the churches (Kelley 1982, 64–83, 111–128, 151–164). To cite one important example, the regulations governing the tax-free status of churches are generally interpreted to give churches substantial leeway for public involvement but could be tightened to make it more difficult for clergy to engage in political action. Beyond governmental power, individuals also have the authority to decide how much they combine or segregate their roles as congregants and citizens. That makes it even more important to assess the pros and cons of active political involvement by churches and religiously inspired activists.

The rise of religious activism in politics has been a source of concern and apprehension for many observers, including those who are sympathetic to religion as an institution (see, for example, Maguire 1982). At the heart of that concern lies the fear that religious controversy in politics will lead to extremism and polarization, infecting the body politic with unhealthy doses of fanaticism and ill will. Carried to extremes, critics have contended, the entry of religious issues into the public agenda may produce violence, undermining the very foundations of democratic politics.

Why should religion have such dire consequences for the stability of government? Many commentators have insisted that democratic government depends on a willingness to negotiate, to bargain, to approach politics in the spirit of compromise. Some issues naturally lend themselves to this type of treatment. Conflicts over money—demands for pay raises, proposals to increase taxes, competition for federal funding—are inherently subject to bargaining, because financial benefits are divisible in terms of dollars. Economic conflicts can usually be managed within the framework of a stable political system. But when conflicts take on an either/or dimension, the impediments to compromise can prompt antagonists to subvert the political system. "Charged with symbolic freight," Peter McDonough (1994, 124) says of these conflicts, "some issues have the capacity to threaten identities, jeopardize world views, and galvanize intense minorities." Issues that involve fundamental social and moral values "are intrinsically harder to be reasonable about than others" (ibid.).

Because they do not lend themselves so readily to compromise solutions, religious issues may challenge the normal system of governance. If you regard abortion as murder, and I see it as a neutral medical procedure, it will be hard to find a middle ground that either one of us will accept as a legitimate public policy. Perhaps that attitude explains why bombing attacks against abortion clinics are concentrated in states where opponents of abortion have failed to restrict the practice (Nice 1988). The same kind of problem may arise in the context of debates over prayer in public schools, the rights of homosexuals, traditional sex roles, and other policy areas in which religious groups have been active. Without realistic hope for a compromise solution that is minimally acceptable to all sides, such issues are likely to fester and breed support for extremist action.

A related problem raised by critics of church activism involves the potential impact of religious values on the *style* of political activists. As religious issues do not easily permit compromise solutions, so, too, religious values may produce rigidity, dogmatism, and contempt for alternative points of view. Such destructive traits, far from being accidental, may actually be the consequence of religious commitment (C. Liebman 1988, chap. 3). One aspect of religious faith that encourages extremism, its claim to possess the truth, inspires believers with unshakable confidence in the rightness and inevitability of their efforts. Religion also provides standards of truth and justice; believers may push relentlessly to bring all of society under these ideals. Finally, because "religious adherence becomes a criteria by which other people can be evaluated" (ibid., 40), people of strong faith may not respect the motives and values of their political opponents. A person who believes that he or she is acting under God's direct command may be prone to regard compromise as a betrayal of divine intention and perceive opponents as not merely misguided or confused but as evil and malevolent. As the philosopher Martin Buber (1937) taught us, the first step toward barbarism is to treat an opponent as an "it" rather than a "thou."

The dangers posed by religious involvement in politics can be arranged in a hierarchy. At the lowest level, religious passions may inspire displays of individual intolerance and uncivil behavior. Though troubling, such incidents probably do not threaten the social order. The danger escalates greatly when religious commitment is expressed in violent acts such as property crimes, assaults, terrorist attacks, and killings. As repugnant as they are, such crimes still stop short of the next level of danger—organized, systematic violence against people or nations stimulated by conflicting religious identities. At that level, religious passion can truly overwhelm the political system and promote a collapse of social order.

We do not have to look hard for examples of all three levels of religiously inspired hostility. As we saw in chapter 6, the emergence of the Christian Right troubled observers who saw in the movement many expressions of religious bigotry and arrogant narrow-mindedness. For symptoms of the tendency to fuse religious and political truth, consider the demonstrator at the 1988 Republican convention whose placard boasted that "BUSH WILL WIN BECAUSE GOD IS A REPUBLICAN" or the 1992 flier warning Christians that "TO VOTE FOR BILL CLINTON IS TO SIN AGAINST GOD," or the "prayer alert" network that urged members to call down divine curses on Democratic candidates in the 1994 elections.[1] Such arrogance is not restricted to one side of the political spectrum. A former American hostage in the Middle East reported that the "smug self-righteousness" of nuclear freeze advocates in the United States reminded him of his Iranian captors (M. Kennedy 1985). This style of political combat also entails demonizing political opponents. A New York homemaker told pollsters she was attracted to the Religious Right because it "still stands for morals, and the liberal people, the Democrats, don't have any morals" (quoted in Berke

1994b). Another poll participant, a self-described Republican, did not want her party to admit people who were tolerant of homosexuality or abortion "because they don't have moral values." Escalating the rhetoric a notch, the leader of a militant antiabortion movement assigned to feminists a "very antimale, lesbian-oriented, Marxist-oriented, put-your-kids-in-day-care-and-go-out-and-pursue-a-career, proabortion mentality" that was nothing less than "Satan's agenda" (quoted in Lacayo 1991).

The clearest manifestation of religiously based intolerance, the "Christian Reconstructionist" movement, has exerted some influence on leaders of the New Christian Right. Leaders of this fringe movement propose a radical reconstruction of American society on the basis of their reading of Old Testament law (Barron 1992). The blueprint includes severe punishment for assorted "deviants"—"homosexuals, incorrigible children, adulterers, blasphemers, astrologers" as well as Sabbath breakers and practitioners of witchcraft—the reimposition of slavery, and the abolition of democracy. Under this regime, religious pluralism would be redefined as heresy, a crime punishable by death. The assurances by activists that these changes will be introduced by popular consensus hardly makes reconstructionism a democratic movement.

What of the next level of threat, the use of violence to further religious ends? Though we associate religious terrorism with Third World societies, places where children offer themselves up as virtual human sacrifices in "holy wars," the United States has not escaped religiously inspired political violence. In the first half of the 1990s, two doctors, one driver, and three clinic employees were murdered by antiabortion activists, and thousands of violent attacks have been launched against medical facilities offering reproductive health care. Many of these actions were the result of individual extremists or amateurish conspiracies (Blanchard and Prewitt 1993). With much less fanfare but a much more systematic campaign, so-called Christian patriots have since the late 1970s been engaged in a murderous war against what they call the "Zionist Occupation Government" (Aho 1990; Barkun 1994). Participants in this extremist movement perceive the government as the tool of a satanic conspiracy that is devoted to subverting the word of God by promoting racial equality, multiculturalism, and gun control. As "true" Christians, they see themselves obligated to resist with whatever means are necessary the authority of this illegitimate occupying power. More than fifty people have died in violent collisions with this movement and at least one sympathizer, Louisiana's David Duke, attained a state legislative seat and ran a strong gubernatorial campaign. There are some signs that this movement, implicated in the Oklahoma City bombing of 1995, has joined forces with the radical wing of the antiabortion movement (Rich 1995).

Fortunately, the United States has been spared the most intense type of religious-political conflict, the organization of political conflict on strictly religious lines as evident in places like Northern Ireland, Lebanon, Rwanda, Somalia, India, and Bosnia. All these countries have experienced the dangerous fusion of national identity with religious, racial, and ethnic loyalty. Linking religion and land in a sacred bond, the essence of religious nationalism, invariably produces territorial conflicts, wars of conquest, and battles over immigration (Akenson 1992). By making citizenship a badge of exclusivity, it promotes an "us versus them" mentality that may be fatal to the political system. A systematic study of seventeen Western nations with strong electoral traditions confirmed the dangers of a strong religious presence in national party politics (Rose and Urwin 1969). In approximately half the countries, the principal line of electoral conflict was defined by religious affiliation or practice; the remaining nine nations lacked a strong religious dimension to party competition. According to Rose and Urwin, the countries with the strongest religious divisions had experienced much more strain, violence, and political instability than those whose politics were largely free of religious controversy. In some cases, religious conflict in the former group had even contributed to the collapse of governmental systems and the emergence of antidemocratic politics. The correlation between the strength of "ethnocultural" cleavages and political instability appears to have persisted to the present day (Powell 1982, 44–47).

Does the entry of religious groups in the political arena threaten the stability of the American political system, perhaps leading to the levels of systematic breakdown evident in other nations? Do the instances of individual intolerance and the sporadic cases of violence mentioned above point to a larger and more pervasive climate of hostility? These are not easy questions to answer and we shall start by looking for evidence relevant to the core assumption that strong religious convictions (of whatever kind) promote an antidemocratic outlook. Many social scientists have interpreted the weight of evidence to support a link between the intensity of religious belief and various indicators of an antidemocratic orientation. That conclusion has been based on comparisons of the expressed political and social attitudes of people with different reported levels of exposure to religious influence.

The link between religious attachment and political intolerance was supported by one of the first major academic surveys of American attitudes toward civil liberties (Stouffer 1966). Using a format that would be widely imitated in subsequent research, the investigator gauged tolerance in 1954 by asking members of a national sample if they would support various forms of freedom for unpopular groups—Socialists, Communists, and atheists. The results indicated that general attachment to religion was associated with low levels of support for basic civil liberties. Specifically, a high level of tolerance characterized 28 percent of respondents who had attended church in the month before the survey but a substantially higher 36 percent of the people who were not churchgoers (ibid., 142). The difference held up with controls for social factors related to religion that might independently reduce political tolerance. Stouffer also discovered that some kinds of religion were less conducive to tolerance than others (ibid., 143–144). At one extreme, only 21 percent of southern Protestants fell into the "most tolerant" category whereas 73 percent of Jewish respondents were so classified. Northern Catholics and Protestants, who scored about the same on the tolerance scale, held a position midway between the extremes.

In the three decades since Stouffer's findings were first published, they have been repeatedly confirmed by other researchers. In periodic national surveys about willingness to extend civil liberties to unpopular groups, major religious groups differ roughly the same way they did in 1954. The nonaffiliated are substantially more likely than persons attached to religion to score high on a scale of support for civil liberties. Among religious groups, the same ordering reported by Stouffer has been in evidence: low tolerance among evangelical Protestants (black and white alike), intermediate support for civil liberties by Catholics and mainline Protestants, the highest commitment to democratic norms among Jews. These findings have also been extended to other antidemocratic orientations. Thus, researchers have found that hostility to blacks, Jews, and other minority groups has most often been expressed by adherents of theologically conservative churches and has been least common in persons outside the churches (Byrnes and Kiger 1992; Gibson and Tedin 1988).

The initial explanations for the intolerance of fundamentalism concentrated on the social or organizational components of traditional religion. Stouffer attributed the connection to the religiously threatening nature of nonconformity, that is, the direct challenge that atheism and communism posed to religious belief. Advocates of the social explanation linked intolerance to the limited education, social isolation, and parochial life-styles of fundamentalist churchgoers. Both explanations suggest that intolerance is not inherent in religion but largely a product of circumstances. If religious traditionalists did not feel directly threatened by political dissenters or broadened their perspectives through modernization, they would show more tolerance for views and groups outside the mainstream.

Less comforting is another possibility we have already entertained—that intolerance might be built into religious commitment. Amid mounting empirical evidence connecting particular types of religious attachment with antidemocratic orientations, researchers began to look for explanations of the relationship in the creedal aspects of religion—either what people believed or the manner in which they believed it. Milton Rokeach (1971) called attention to the mixed nature of religious messages—their dual emphasis on the oneness of humankind and the rigid separation between true believers and heathen. He argued that the latter tendency frequently overwhelmed the benevolent impulse at the root of religious traditions. Other investigators, influenced by Rokeach's work on styles of thinking, hypothesized that conventional religion attracted people who could not accept doubt, ambiguity, or challenges to their belief systems, and who were prone to reject people who did not share their attitudes or outlooks (Budner 1962, 38–40; Raschke 1973). Finding that the intolerance of fundamentalists and pentecostals could not be explained wholly by low socioeconomic standing, hostility to specific groups, or the strength of religious commitment, Wilcox and Jelen (1990) attributed narrow-mindedness primarily to doctrine.[2] Persuaded they already have the truth, true believers see nothing valuable about hearing dissenting views (see Kirkpatrick 1993). This tendency to ascribe intolerance to the very nature of religious commitment can be captured in the conclusion of an influential study by Nunn and his colleagues (1978, 140): "Traditional Christians, who participate actively in their churches and who find themselves with limited resources to comprehend and affect the larger world, closely link God and political authority and are also likely to see political nonconformity as the work of the Devil."

Assessing the Evidence

These results paint a disturbing portrait of the capacity for democratic thinking and action among deeply religious people and lead to concern about the implications of their increasing involvement in political life. Dogmatism, close-mindedness, and intolerance are not traits that promote civility or the free exchange of ideas. If such traits are pronounced among religious activists and their opponents, there is a solid basis for concern about the increasing politicization of religious issues. In my view, however, the evidence supporting a link between religiosity and the propensity to intolerance is not strong enough to warrant alarm.

In the first place, studies on the relationship between religious commitment and various forms of antidemocratic orientations have not uniformly pointed to a strong connection. In his careful review of relevant research published during the 1960s, Wuthnow (1973, 122) found that religious commitment was positively related to social conservatism in only about one-half of the reported analyses; more commonly, the variables were unrelated or negatively associated.[3] Wuthnow further demonstrated substantial methodological deficiencies in many of the studies that contributed to the conventional wisdom. Typical weaknesses included a lack of appropriate controls for external influences, the use of unrepresentative samples, and reliance on overly simple measures of complex political and religious orientations.[4] An additional flaw has recently been noted in studies that have purported to measure the impact of religious affiliation on political tolerance. Even though they have claimed to measure general orientations toward civil liberties, most studies have commonly asked respondents about their willingness to extend constitutional rights to left-wing groups or other organizations perceived as especially threatening to Christian values. When the target groups have included those that threaten the values of liberal religious groups, the interdenominational differences in tolerance narrow appreciably (Sullivan, Piereson, and Marcus 1982, 137–139; Beatty and Walter 1984, 322–327) or may disappear altogether (Raymond and Norrander 1990). Even with such elaborations, however, persons outside the churches seem substantially more tolerant of opposing viewpoints than church members (Smidt and Penning 1982).

A second problem has been the reliance of all such studies on attitudes rather than on behavior. People do not always act consistently with their expressed beliefs. The crisis that enveloped the American Civil Liberties Union (ACLU) over the *Skokie* case in 1977 showed that the attitude-behavior gap can be especially large in the realm of civil liberties. In Skokie, a Chicago suburb with a high concentration of Jewish refugees from the Nazi Holocaust, local authorities tried to block a planned march by members of a Nazi organization. When the ACLU provided support for the Nazis' legal challenge to the Skokie ordinance—an action for which there was ample precedent in its history—the organization lost thousands of members and a vital proportion of financial resources. Even for supporters of an organization whose sole purpose was the defense of civil liberties, it was easier to express tolerance in the abstract than in practice (Gibson and Anderson 1985). The higher levels of tolerance expressed by the nonreligious might erode under similar pressure—as, indeed, religious activists have charged.

Moreover, those who have viewed religious commitment as a source of antidemocratic sentiment have not always distinguished among different types of commitment. Most studies have simply examined the attitude differences between church members and nonaffiliates, or between different denominations, or, in a few cases, between churchgoers of varying frequency. These are poor approximations of what might well turn out to be the real source of variation in the linkage between religious commitment and tolerance—differences in the manner in which people absorb religious values. In a pioneering survey of democratic attitudes in the United States, researchers from the University of California stressed that people hold their religious values in different ways (Adorno et al. 1950, chap. 18). For example, some attend church only out of a sense of duty to parental expectations or because it conforms to social practice in their community. They find in religion support for their way of life and sanctification of the social order—but nothing of a prophetic vision that might challenge them to change their behavior or act more sensitively to others. What is missing from such conventional or nominal religiosity is deeply rooted acceptance of the nobler values associated with major religious traditions—love, charity, compassion, and forgiveness. Some adherents do not hear these messages either because they do not attend often enough or, more likely, because "while hearing they do not hear, nor do they understand" (Matt. 13:13). But other persons who take religion seriously—meaning that they embrace the ethical messages transmitted by a religious tradition—internalize that tradition and assign the highest priority to acting righteously. Before condemning individuals for falling short of biblical standards, they are likely to recall the admonition to hate the sin but love the sinner. Hence, the authors predicted:

The more "human" and concrete a person's relation to religion, the more human his approach to those who "do not belong": their sufferings remind the religious subjectivist of the idea of martyrdom inseparably bound up with his thinking about Christ. (Adorno et al. 1950, 731)

In a moving illustration of precisely that style of deep commitment, the psychiatrist Robert Coles (1985) reported about six-year-old Ruby. The first black child to integrate a New Orleans school in 1960, she had to march every day past a howling and vicious mob threatening her life: "As she walked by the mob, sometimes a hundred or so strong, protected by federal marshals on her way to a sadly deserted classroom, she said, 'Please, dear God, forgive those folks, because they don't know what they're doing.' She'd heard in Sunday school that Jesus had once reached out similarly and she was trying to follow suit." That type of religious commitment—which is precisely what is meant by "taking religion seriously"—could very likely militate against the arrogance that threatens democratic interchange.

This argument about a link between "genuine" religious commitment and thoughtful, reasoned behavior has attracted some research support. Gordon Allport (1958, 421–422) reported an intriguing study in which standard prejudice scales were administered to Catholic and Baptist laymen. The process of selecting respondents was designed to produce persons who exhibited diverse styles of religiosity—commitment to the essence of the faith versus commitment for social or professional reasons. These different styles of commitment were labeled, respectively, as "intrinsic" and "extrinsic" orientations to religion. The Catholic participants were selected by a knowledgeable parishioner who was asked to recommend some church members who were deeply influenced by faith and others who participated for secular advantages. In an attempt to match this distinction between "devout" and "institutional" church members, the Protestant participants were recruited from regular and irregular attenders at Bible class. In both cases, "the most devout, more personally absorbed in the religion, were far less prejudiced than the others."

The negative association between "intrinsic" religious commitment and prejudice has been found to hold in larger and more systematic studies (Gorsuch and Aleshire 1974; Wilson and Bagley 1973). The findings point to a curvilinear pattern: broad-mindedness is endorsed by people on the extremes of religious commitment—those outside the churches and those most deeply involved in religious groups—and the association between religion and various forms of prejudice is highest among people who are only moderately involved with churches. H. Wesley Perkins (1983, 1985, 1992) has further rehabilitated strong religious commitment by linking it empirically to social compassion and concern for inequality, as well as to lower levels of racial prejudice. When intrinsic religious commitment is coupled with an open and tolerant religious environment, the probability of prejudice is reduced. But if the religious environment sends a narrow and particularistic message, the intrinsically committed may also absorb that perspective (Griffin, Gorsuch, and Davis 1987; Fisher, Derison, and Polley 1994).

In an important qualification, C. Daniel Batson has refined Allport's "intrinsic" category by introducing a third form of religious commitment, the "quest" dimension. In this "mature" form of religiosity, faith encourages believers to accept complexity, criticize and doubt their own motivations, and keep an open mind as they search for truth. This third style of attachment is designed to distinguish between intrinsics whose commitment to orthodoxy makes them intolerant and highly committed persons who do not demand from their faith "black and white" answers to all of life's dilemmas. Persons with high scores on the "quest" scale generally turn out to be less prejudiced (Batson et al. 1986; Fisher, Derison, and Polley 1994; Leak and Randall 1995) and to employ more sophisticated standards of moral judgment (Sapp and Jones 1986).

Hence, it seems reasonable to maintain that religion versus irreligion is not the crucial dimension underlying political attitudes but that religious people differ politically based on the nature and motivation of their religiosity and the political norms transmitted in their religious communities. Specifically, some forms of religious commitment, far from threatening democracy, may reinforce constructive tendencies in public life. Unfortunately, I have not yet found any studies that examine directly the relationship between political tolerance and styles of religious commitment. In the closest such research project, support for unquestioning loyalty to the president was positively related to religious orthodoxy, high levels of ritual involvement, and strong belief in God but was negatively associated with the incidence of private prayer (Schoenfeld 1985). The author interpreted his findings in a manner consistent with the hypothesis suggested here, finding the more "priestly" aspects of religion conducive to support for political authority, but the spontaneous, unstructured, and unmediated act of prayer imparting a healthy sense of skepticism about public officials. Until more direct studies become available, it will remain arguable that intense religious commitment—measured in qualitative rather than quantitative terms—actually promotes healthy democratic orientations.

Finally, I am comforted by the belief that political participation may actually teach religious activists to moderate their style and tame their expectations. There is fairly consistent evidence that political activists are more tolerant than nonparticipants. Although it has not yet been shown that political participation actually *causes* more tolerant outlooks, a logical case can be made for such a relationship. From the perspective of social learning theory, political participation should bring the individual into contact with others who value the opportunity to influence policy through democratic means. This experience might enhance the individual's respect for a system that facilitates such opportunities (Sullivan et al. 1993). The only evidence relevant to the argument has been provided by Guth and Green's (1984) mail survey of financial contributors to various party and ideological political action committees (PACs). Contributors to religiously oriented PACs and antiabortion electoral efforts were not less tolerant than the sample as a whole or than some mainstream groups. In fact, the (admittedly) small number of "religiously" conservative activists were more supportive of political liberties than were many "secular" conservative givers—contributors to antitax, gun ownership, libertarian, and Republican causes. Though far from proving the assertion about the moderating influence of political involvement, such fragmentary findings give hope that religious extremists will learn the rules of the game as a consequence of participation in conventional political action.

For all these reasons, some observers have retreated from earlier predictions about the baleful effect of religious activism on the political system. Of course, people tend to find what they are looking for, so I want to point with caution at some signs that the American political system can indeed accommodate religiously inspired campaigns for candidates or issues. The essence of the argument is that while such issues may strain the system by making compromise difficult and attracting the attention of persons with passionate commitments, the system can cope with this situation. To some extent, such activity may even enhance the vitality of political life.

The abortion issue provides perhaps the best illustration of how the political system adapts to the pressure applied by deeply committed activists. When advocates throw phrases like "baby killer" and "Nazi" at one another, the rhetoric does not elevate the tone of political discourse. In Congress and other governmental arenas, the issue has from time to time undermined a civil decision-making process. The fear about abortion's disruptive potential has certainly been intensified by the alarming outbreaks of murderous violence on the fringes of the antiabortion movement. Taken together, those trends have persuaded some observers that the abortion debate might actually threaten the American form of government.

Despite such fears, careful study suggests that most of the abortion-related activity has stayed well within the bounds of democratic norms (Steiner 1983). Despite the excesses alluded to, most leaders have seemed committed to defusing the issue, channeling it in ways that do not threaten the political process. Without abandoning their beliefs, some staunch supporters of abortion restriction have nevertheless forgone the use of certain weapons out of a concern for the larger health of the political system. As chair of the Senate Appropriations Committee, Sen. Mark Hatfield (R-Ore.) resisted attempts to attach antiabortion bills to appropriations legislation, and Sen. Jake Garn (R-Utah), a leader of the antiabortion movement in Congress, resigned from the advisory board of a prolife political action committee because of its decision to target several incumbents for defeat solely because they voted against restrictive policies on abortion. In both cases, techniques that might have advanced the cause were rejected because their use seemed to undermine procedural norms that contributed to effective governance. The prochoice coalition has also demonstrated concern for the maintenance of accepted procedure by approving several prolife nominees for federal jobs.

It is noteworthy that despite its bitterly divisive nature, the abortion issue has engendered a willingness to compromise. The advocates of restriction by constitutional amendment have seemingly withdrawn from a position of favoring only an absolute prohibition on abortion to one that would permit abortion under certain conditions. Supporters of liberalized policies might not appreciate the magnitude of these compromises nor their divisive impact on prolife activists, but they do in fact constitute a significant revision of earlier positions, indicating the willingness of antiabortion forces to adapt to political realities.

The search for compromise is also apparent in the courts and the legislative branch. Ever since *Roe v. Wade,* the Supreme Court has steered a middle course by rejecting the extreme options of allowing abortion on demand or returning to the pre-1973 situation. Instead, the Court has granted its approval to some limitations on access to abortion while continuing to uphold the principle of abortion as a constitutionally protected right of privacy. Similarly, Congress has moved the issue to the familiar terrain of the budgetary process, debating whether federal funds should be used to pay for abortion. This conflict follows a well-established precedent of using control over appropriations as a means for settling policy debates. In both the legislative and judicial arenas, the debate has focused on bargainable questions of implementation of the law.

To go one step further, it can be argued that the abortion debate has actually invigorated public life in the United States. This argument challenges the standards of democracy used by critics of religiously inspired political activism. Those who have criticized the place of such passionate issues on the public agenda have sometimes argued from a conception of democracy that treats mass involvement in policy making as suspect or potentially dangerous to governmental stability. These critics contend that high-energy issues like abortion may promote an excess of public excitement and involvement, inhibiting the possibility of rational policy making or intelligent compromise. Rather than treating active citizen participation as a requirement of the democratic process, these "revisionist" democrats have tended to approach it as a threat to the stability of democratic governance and look benignly on apathy as a useful way of managing intense political conflict.

But this particular view of democracy is not the only model available. Another view defines the continuous and active involvement of the people in public decision making as the key characteristic of a democratic system (Pateman 1970; Tesh 1984). In this view, issues like abortion enhance democracy by forcing ordinary men and women to take a stand on issues of public significance and by encouraging them to act on their beliefs in the public realm. The rise of the abortion issue challenges not democracy per se, but rather a particular conception of democracy that keeps important issues off the agenda, or limits their focus, or leaves decision making to political elites (Casanova 1994, 102ff). When religious convictions propel groups to enter the political process, they add a new voice to the public debate on issues like abortion. These new activists "try to politicize that which had been private, to broaden that which had been narrow, and to bring ordinary citizens into that which had been the province of professionals" (Tesh 1984, 44). That may not be orderly—but perhaps orderliness is not an appropriate standard for democratic politics.

The Case for Religion in Politics

In the previous section, I evaluated the case against religious activism in politics and found it wanting. Though the rise of religiously based political issues may present challenges to the capacity of a democratic political system, the American political process seems adequate to the task. Now it is time to consider the positive claims for religion in politics.

Earlier in this book, I reported the belief of some scholars that religion contributed to the development of democratic values and the acceptance of democratic practices in the United States. Some observers have gone well beyond that statement, debatable as it is, to make an even larger claim for religion. They argue that religion is an *essential* support for a democratic political orientation and warn that the decay of religious values or their exclusion from policy debate will weaken the health of the American political system. While acknowledging that problems accompany political debate over moral values, they have asserted that the departure of faith from the political realm is far more dangerous to democracy than is an excess of passion.

Whatever its role in the past, how might religion today be expected to sustain democratic political institutions? According to some advocates, the dominant religions in the United States uphold beliefs that are essential to the maintenance of democratic values. Consider the notion of "human rights," a fundamental element of American political culture. On what basis can we assert that human beings, simply because they are human beings, are entitled to the various liberties spelled out in the U.S. Constitution? Although the idea of human rights is so deeply embedded in American thought that it almost seems natural, it has usually been justified in religious terms. The religious traditions that have dominated American life commonly assert the equality of human beings before God. By virtue of humankind's common link to God, it is declared, all people deserve to be treated with a minimum of decency and respect. The Bill of Rights, supported by public opinion, embodies a religiously grounded teaching (Garrett 1987).

Other elements in the American creed have been said to originate in some conception of a divine presence. The political scientist Ernest Griffith and his coauthors, John Plamenatz and J. Roland Pennock, once attempted to list the beliefs essential to the survival of democracy and to show how each one depended on the Judeo-Christian heritage:

1. Love for and belief in freedom: best based upon belief in the sacredness of the individual as a child of God.
2. Active and constructive participation in community life: best based upon the obligation of the Christian, the Jew, and other believers to accept responsibilities, cooperating with and working for their brother men.
3. Integrity in discussion: best based upon the inner light of truth being primary in a world God meant to be righteous.
4. The freely assumed obligation of economic groups to serve society: best based upon the Christian insight into the nature of society as set forth, for example, by the parable of the body and its members.
5. Leadership and office holding regarded as public trusts: best based upon or inspired by the example and teachings of religious prophets, such as Jesus, who accepted such a service "to the death."

6. Attitudes assuring that passion will be channeled into constructive ends: best based upon religious faiths that unite an obligation to love and serve with a recognition of the primacy of individual personality.

7. Friendliness and cooperation among nations: best based upon the vision of world brotherhood derived from a faith that we are all children of a common Heavenly Father. (1956, 113)

In this view, religion provides the standards for judgment that are necessary to give meaning to concepts such as fairness, justice, goodness, and dignity.

The bald claim that religion is essential to maintain democratic values immediately inspires two critical questions. First: is religion the only basis for supporting the democratic outlook, or are other secular systems of belief capable of performing the same task? If alternatives are available, then religion can hardly be treated as essential to the survival of democratic government. But even if religious values do undergird freedom, that does not necessarily suggest that religious groups should enter the political arena. Hence the second question: should religion fulfill its public function only by speaking to the consciences of individuals or by entering the political arena more directly?

To maintain that religion is the only basis for morality, a position that President Reagan appeared to endorse during the 1984 campaign, is to ignore the existence of secular philosophies that also support respect for human rights and liberties. In fact, the research of many political scientists has suggested that the health of democracy depends less on public opinion of any sort than on favorable social and economic conditions (Lipset 1960, chap. 2). Nonetheless, advocates of religion have argued that it supplies a more powerful rationale for democracy than does any competing system of thought. In particular, they have claimed, religion—and religion alone—has the capacity to impart a sacred character to democratic values, to make them objects of faith that can resist all threats. By grounding a respect for human dignity in a force beyond human comprehension, like a transcendent God, the values rise above debate and are protected from the whims of public opinion or the challenges of competing philosophies. Only religion can provide a standard of judgment that transcends human authority (Bird 1990). In the United States, the major religious groups thus contribute to the preservation of a democratic order by making support for political liberty an article of faith.

But does this necessarily mean that religious groups should enter the political order? Can't they contribute to the defense of democratic values without becoming embroiled in political activity and partisan debate? The advocates of a strong religious presence have answered these questions by pointing to the danger of a rigid separation between private conscience and public activity. When religious groups refrain from taking stands on controversial public issues, they may give the impression that religion speaks only to the concerns of private life. If religion is rigidly confined to the sphere of private morality, it has been argued, society runs the risk of enacting public policy without regard for moral consequences. It is important that religious claims enjoy a legitimate status in political debate, if only to guard against the danger of amoral government actions. This argument recalls the emphasis on the prophetic role of the churches, a familiar theme in the American civil religion discussed in chapter 3.

Religious groups thus perform the important task of reminding us that public decisions inescapably involve and reflect values. Without such reminders, political conservatives have warned us, society might be willing to sacrifice the aged and the ill in the name of "efficiency" or some other standard.[5] Liberals have relied just as much on transcendent values when they demanded protection for the poor and oppressed, even at the cost of economic growth. The values operating in these examples—respect for life and compassion—will carry greater force in public consciousness when they are defended with the same resources as are competing secular values. The political activity of religious groups can thus be seen as necessary for the defense of moral judgment in public policy making. Even in a society where religious commitment is widespread, the churches have a duty to insist on its application to the problems of the day. Contentious though that might be, the alternative is even less satisfactory for the health of society.

In the modern world, Richard J. Neuhaus has argued, religion supplies a counterweight to the greatest threat faced by democracy—a slide into totalitarianism. In a passage worth quoting at length, Neuhaus summarized the importance of religion in keeping government under popular control:

Once religion is reduced to nothing more than privatized conscience, the public square has only two actors in it—the state and the individual. Religion as a mediating structure—a community that generates and transmits moral values—is no longer available. Whether in Hitler's Third Reich or in today's sundry states professing Marxist-Leninism, the chief attack is not upon individual religious belief. Individual religious belief can be dismissed scornfully as superstition, for it finally poses little threat to the power of the state. No, the chief attack is upon the *institutions* that bear and promulgate belief in a transcendent reality by which the state can be called to judgment. Such institutions threaten the totalitarian proposition that everything is to be within the state, nothing is to be outside the state. (1984, 82)

If that analysis is correct, the church alone stands between the individual and the government, preventing the latter from swallowing up the former.

In truth, world history has supplied notable examples of religious values inspiring stubborn resistance to governments that demand complete obedience. Although the German churches as a group did not cover themselves with glory during the rise of Nazism, some of the most courageous resisters to Hitler were motivated by belief in divinely inspired values transcending the norms of national loyalty. In the 1980s the Catholic church preached on behalf of the autonomy of individuals against both leftist governments—as in Poland and Nicaragua—and right-wing regimes in countries like El Salvador and the Philippines. The contemporary movements mentioned previously in this book—Sanctuary, the nuclear freeze, antidraft activity, refusal to pay taxes for military programs—seem to draw disproportionately from Catholics attuned to the message that emanated from the Second Vatican Council. In all such cases, religion can provide a sense of perspective that may prompt the individual to challenge the authority of the state. By forcefully reminding individuals that their behavior must conform to higher standards, a religious tradition can promote disobedience to the excessive demands of government or other authority figures.

Religious values may guard against totalitarian sympathies in yet another manner. One great source of evil behavior is certainty, the unshakable conviction that the individual possesses some higher truth. Armed with certainty about the "one true master race" or the "inevitable destiny" of communism, human beings have committed some of the greatest crimes in history. Doubt is a potential antidote to such monstrousness because it activates the conscience. A person who is not wholly certain may question the rightness of a particular behavior—including his or her own actions.

Christianity may engender doubt by its insistence on the fallenness of humankind. The doctrine of original sin teaches that humans are depraved and cannot be certain even of the righteousness of their own behavior. Sustained by this assumption, the Founders devised a governmental system that would make it difficult for would-be tyrants to accumulate enough power to overwhelm democratic institutions. One who assumes that humans are imperfect may counsel against the type of utopianism that has occasionally disfigured the world. While doubt can lead to confusion and paralysis, it may also prompt a pause that enables people to rethink the possible consequences of a particular course of action. In that way, the doctrine of original sin may serve as a hedge against extremism (W. Marty 1980; R. Niebuhr 1944).

Each facet of religion may contribute to the protection of a democratic political system. Religious *values* can supply a basis for rejecting the claims of the state by giving precedence to sacred obligations. For example, slavery and other systems of oppression have been condemned by some church leaders as incompatible with the dictates of religion and the content of the Bible. Religious *institutions* transmit the beliefs that can stand as a buffer between individuals and the state. They expose congregants to standards of right and wrong and may preach about how best to apply values to concrete situations. And when the individual is deeply attached to a religious *community*, he or she may prove more resistant to recruitment by political causes that threaten human rights. People bonded to others by social ties are probably less susceptible to the allure of totalitarian movements than are social isolates (Kornhauser 1959).

I believe the foregoing argument provides the strongest case for an active religious presence in all aspects of society, including the political arena. Like the case against religious activism in politics, it is best treated as a hypothesis. Note that I described religion's impact on democracy in terms that emphasized potential—*can, may, might,* and *could.* Those conditional verbs were used because they convey the conditional impact of religion. According to one eminent historian (Muller 1963), the record of religion with regard to human freedom is remarkably mixed. As has just been pointed out, religious values have in some instances supported the spirit and practice of democratic government. Yet the concept of democracy arose with the Greeks, well before the beginning of the Judeo-Christian era, and the church has often been a bulwark of resistance to the spread of democratic values. In a conclusion that dramatically calls attention to the coexistence of democratic and antidemocratic impulses in Western religion, Muller concluded that "Christianity did more to promote the growth of freedom than did any other of the higher religions . . . while it also opposed freedom of thought, speech, and conscience more fiercely than did any other religion except Mohammedanism" (ibid., 3).

If religion is to fulfill its promise as a bulwark against tyranny, it must encourage its followers to resist rulers who demand actions that are inconsistent with religious values. The evidence on that point does not suggest that religious commitment necessarily works to produce more reasoned behavior. The ambivalent relationship between religion and support for constituted authority was revealed in a disturbing study conducted by two psychologists from Atlanta (Bock and Warren 1972). They built on the famous experiments devised by another psychologist, Stanley Milgram (1974), who put laboratory subjects in a situation where an authority figure encouraged them to help with an experiment that involved inflicting pain on other subjects. Specifically, the participants were ordered to administer what they thought were electrical shocks to fellow subjects who had been unsuccessful in what was portrayed as a learning experiment. Milgram's finding that most persons obeyed the commands—even in the face of loud protests from the purported victim of the shocks—raised fundamental questions about what human qualities accounted for refusal to go along with destructive behavior.

The scenario devised by Milgram seemed an excellent opportunity to investigate one issue not carefully considered in his original experiments, the role of religious values in distinguishing between compliance and resistance. The Atlanta psychologists thus recruited thirty college students, measured their religious values and commitment, and then put them through what amounted to a facsimile of the original Milgram experiments. In findings that will recall the studies of prejudice described earlier in the chapter, Bock and Warren discovered a strong but nonlinear relationship between religious commitment and willingness to inflict pain on others. Those with low or high levels of attachment to religion were substantially more likely than persons of moderate attachment to resist the instructions to administer shocks. To explain this finding, the investigators suggested that the nature of religious commitment—rather than its amount—was a critical factor in the subjects' decision to comply or refuse:

> In the Judeo-Christian tradition, a high value is placed on a strong, well-defined response to "the will of God." In fact, a decisive response even if negative is to be preferred over neutrality. The Biblical position is that the man who is undecided about basic religious issues is unable to be decisive when confronted by an ethical dilemma. His tendency is to forfeit his choice to any impinging power. On the other hand, having taken a definite religious stance, one is in a position to act in accord with conscience. (1972, 190)

If the findings of this study can be assumed to hold for the general population in real-world settings—both untested assumptions—then they should diminish our confidence that religious commitment will automatically inspire resistance to tyranny. Once again, it depends on the quality of religious commitment that brings people into the public sphere. People who appear to have internalized the ethical principles of religion—along with those who have minimal contact with religious institutions—will probably prove most likely to resist orders that conflict with widely accepted ethical principles. Based on the limited experimental data, those whose religious commitment is moderate do not seem endowed with a tendency to challenge rulers who demand that citizens abdicate conscience.

According to various attitude surveys, the disposition to challenge authority appears quite weak among the white fundamentalist Protestants who have greatly increased their political involvement since the 1980s (Altemeyer 1988; Altemeyer and Hunsberger 1992). The veneration for authority said to characterize fundamentalism (Wald, Owen, and Hill 1989b) seems to pervade many of the institutions that compose the subculture. Thus, the dynamic evangelical churches that have provided leadership for the New Christian Right conform to fairly rigid and hierarchical authority patterns that give members very little experience of democratic decision making (Fitzgerald 1981). The law school founded and led by Pat Robertson has been sued by students and faculty alleging a lack of academic freedom (Myers 1994). At the Christian university he founded and continues to lead, the Rev. Jerry Falwell has provided a code of conduct that is similarly weighted toward authority (D. Baker 1985). Under the rules, students at Liberty University may not participate in unauthorized demonstrations, are obliged to attend church, and may be expelled for participation in demonstrations or petition drives not approved by university authorities. Students are thus asked to waive a number of rights guaranteed under the Constitution, including protection against warrantless searches of their rooms. These rules reflect a more generalized emphasis on obedience in the worldview of fundamentalist Protestantism (Ellison and Sherkat 1993). Again, we cannot know for certain if these practices are widespread in evangelical Protestantism or common among all types of religions; nor is it guaranteed that adherents of such churches draw lessons about governance from religious institutions or that such lessons would carry over to the behavior of church members in other settings. Nonetheless, these tendencies should dissuade observers from asserting too confidently that religious commitment in politics necessarily acts as a brake on totalitarian tendencies.

What, then, can we finally conclude about the impact of religion on democracy in the contemporary situation? There is little alternative but to conclude that religion may sometimes sustain democratic values and sometimes undermine them. The source of the paradox is simply that religious values are ambiguous with regard to politics. They contain messages that can lead persons of common faith in different directions. The multiple political uses of religious ideas have been demonstrated repeatedly throughout history. In the period leading up to the Civil War, Northerners and Southerners alike found ample justification for slavery and abolition in the same religious document. During the Prohibition era in this century, learned clergymen argued earnestly about the message of the Scriptures with regard to intoxicating beverages. The problem arises today even in the unlikely context of environmental policy, a subject of conflicting biblical images. Just as some interpret God's intention that people have dominion "over all the earth" (Gen. 1:26) as license to exploit the environment in the interests of human happiness, others cite the Twenty-fourth Psalm, "The Earth is the Lord's," to promote reverence for the natural environment and support a preservationist ethic. The problem is no less vexing at the general level of democracy. Jesus' call in Matt. 22:21 to "render therefore unto Caesar the things which are Caesar's; and unto God the things that are God's" does not define precisely what it is that humanity owes to state and to church. Depending on how responsibility is allocated between God and Caesar, that biblical injunction may be interpreted as a call to revolution or, at the other extreme, as a plea for servility.

The problem of limited guidance even extends to such fundamental questions as the best form of human government. The doctrine of original sin is interpreted by some theologians as a call to caution, an injunction against committing evil in the name of higher values. As such, it may promote a belief in the wisdom of limited government. Yet it has also been used as an argument against the human capacity for self-government. If mortals are prone to greed, jealousy, rapaciousness, envy, pride, and other expressions of sinfulness, then they are simply not worthy of basic rights or opportunities to exercise their free will in politics. Even today, people of faith continue to argue if the Bible is capitalistic or socialistic, supportive of abortion or not, militaristic or pacifistic. The most careful students of religious thought simply cannot agree on the precise relevance of Christian doctrine to specific issues or if Christianity is inherently conducive to democracy or dictatorship (Wolin 1956). I submit that the obstacle is not deficient understanding, but the mixed political messages contained in the major religious creeds.

Given the ambiguity of religious texts and teachings, the mixed historical record, and the empirical evidence cited earlier in the chapter, it would be foolhardy to assert that religious faith necessarily upholds democratic values. In some contexts and for some types of people, it may enhance freedom. Or it may encourage particular types of freedom while enforcing conformity in other realms of human endeavor. It seems to matter less if people are religious than how they hold their religious values and attempt to apply them in concrete situations. An upsurge in religiously based political activity is neither to be welcomed uncritically nor condemned out of hand.

The richness and complexity of religious thought should also moderate *how* individuals carry their religious faith into the public square. When it is difficult to discern with confidence what a religious tradition actually says about a moral issue—and the very brevity, intricacy, and abstractness of religious creeds often make it so—individuals should be reluctant to assert with confidence that they and they alone possess unique insight. But even if the individual can be confident about the relevant moral judgment, it is still a large step from philosophical principle to public policy. As Kent Greenawalt (1994, 155) reminds us, "there is a difference between telling people that an active homosexual life is sinful and telling them that they should support criminal sanctions for that behavior." And even if the individual is confident that a specific political application flows directly from a religious principle, he or she may have more success if the arguments for the policy are made in terms that transcend the particular religious tradition and speak with equal force to persons who inhabit different moral universes. That may be the price for political coexistence in a nation that is religiously and morally pluralistic.

It seems appropriate to end this work by stressing that science cannot establish whether religious claims are true or false. But science, especially social science, can attempt to discover the consequences of religious values, institutions, and communities for the political system. This book has attempted to describe how religion interacts with the political system in one country and has explained why some patterns recur. Because of the limitations of previous research and the inherent tentativeness of science, I have emphasized the provisional status of my conclusions. More and better research might clarify the patterns of religious influence in politics and might even provide a basis on which to offer confident predictions about the future of the relationship between the two domains. The impact of religion on American political life is surely important enough to warrant the effort.

NOTES

The epigraph for this chapter was taken from Clarke E. Cochran, *Religion in Public and Private Life* (New York: Routledge, 1990).

1. "Fliers Denounce Clinton," *Gainesville Sun*, 15 October 1992, p. 17A (originally published in the *Washington Post*); "Prayers Target Politicians," *Cincinnati Inquirer*, 4 November 1994, 12A.
2. Wade Clark Roof (1974) has suggested that the apparent prejudice of churchgoers is principally an outgrowth of their localistic orientation, a consequence of their limited exposure to agents of modernity.
3. Lest it be thought that conservative preferences are antidemocratic sentiments, let me emphasize that most of the scales Wuthnow examined really measured what has aptly been called "pseudo-conservatism," surface agree-

ment with right-wing goals but usually involving means that most conservatives would reject. What passes for mass conservatism often lacks the subtlety and respect for democratic means that characterizes the conservative intellectual tradition (McClosky 1958).

4. These studies may also be suspect due to a bias against certain types of religious commitment. Specifically, such scales may be constructed in a way that virtually guarantees that people of strong religious belief appear to be authoritarian and rigid. For examples of measuring devices loaded with items that tap support for traditional religious values, see the "conventionality" scale developed by Raden (1982) and Fagan and Breed's (1970) dogmatism scale. So, too, a well-known test of abstract reasoning style appears almost by definition to consign religious fundamentalists to a low level of intellectual complexity (Richards 1991).

5. Opponents of liberalized abortion make just such an argument when they contend that the prochoice position is grounded in values that lead to disrespect for human life and dignity. Supporters of liberalized abortion would respond that forcing women to bear unwanted children is a greater denial of respect for human life and dignity. Hence, the abortion debate is a conflict between different interpretations of what is right rather than a clash between advocates of morality versus amorality.

References

Abraham, Henry J. 1987. "Religion, the Constitution, the Court and Society: Some Contemporary Reflections on Mandates, Words, Human Beings, and the Art of the Possible." In *How Does the Constitution Protect Religious Freedom?*, ed. Robert A. Goldwin and Art Kaufman, 15–42. Washington, D.C.: American Enterprise Institute.

Abramowitz, Alan I. 1995. "It's Abortion, Stupid: Policy Voting in the 1992 Presidential Election." *Journal of Politics* 57:176–186.

Adams, Arlin. 1986. "Is the Supreme Court Making a Significant Shift in Church-State Jurisprudence?" In *Government Intervention in Religious Affairs, II*, ed. Dean M. Kelley, 69–78. New York: Pilgrim.

Adams, Arlin M., and Charles J. Emmerich. 1990. *A Nation Dedicated to Religious Liberty: The Constitutional Heritage of the Religion Clauses*. Philadelphia: University of Pennsylvania Press.

Adams, James L. 1970. *The Growing Church Lobby in Washington*. Grand Rapids, Mich.: Eerdman's.

Adorno, T. W., Else Frenkel-Brunswik, Daniel J. Levinson, and R. Nevitt Sanford. 1950. *The Authoritarian Personality*. New York: Harper and Brothers.

Ahlstrom, Sydney. 1965. "The Puritan Ethic and the Spirit of American Democracy." In *Calvinism and the Political Order*, ed. George L. Hunt, 88–107. Philadelphia: Westminster.

———. 1975. *A Religious History of the American People*. New York: Image.

Aho, James A. 1991. *The Politics of Righteousness: Idaho Christian Patriotism*. Seattle: University of Washington Press.

Akenson, Donald Harman. 1992. *God's People: Covenant and Land in South Africa, Israel, and Ulster*. Ithaca: Cornell University Press.

Allen, Richard L., Michael C. Dawson, and Ronald Brown. 1989. "A Schema-Based Approach to Modelling an African-American Racial Belief System." *American Political Science Review* 83:421–442.

Alley, Robert S. 1994. *School Prayer: The Court, the Congress, and the First Amendment*. Buffalo, N.Y.: Prometheus.

Allinsmith, Wesley, and Beverly Allinsmith. 1948. "Religious Affiliation and Politico-Economic Attitudes: A Study of Eight Major U.S. Religious Groups." *Public Opinion Quarterly* 12:377–389.

Allport, Gordon W. 1958. *The Nature of Prejudice*. Abridged ed. Garden City, N.Y.: Doubleday-Anchor.

Altemeyer, Bob. 1988. *Enemies of Freedom: Understanding Right-Wing Authoritarianism*. San Francisco: Jossey-Bass.

348   References

Altemeyer, B., and B. Hunsberger. 1992. "Authoritarianism, Religious Fundamentalism, Quest and Prejudice." *International Journal for the Psychology of Religion* 2:113–133.

Althauser, Robert P. 1990. "Paradox in Popular Religion: The Limits of Instrumental Faith." *Social Forces* 69:585–602.

Alvarez, R. Michael, and Jonathan Nagler. 1995. "Economics, Issues, and the Perot Candidacy: Voter Choice in the 1992 Presidential Election." *American Journal of Political Science* 39:714–745.

Ammerman, Nancy T. 1981. "The Civil Rights Movement and the Clergy in a Southern Community." *Sociological Analysis* 41:339–350.

———. 1994. "Telling Congregational Stories." *Review of Religious Research* 35:289–301.

Andersen, Kristi. 1988. "Sources of Pro-Family Belief." *Political Psychology* 9:229–243.

Anderson, Charles H. 1973. "Religious Communality and Party Preference." In *Research in Religious Behavior,* ed. Benjamin Beit-Hallahmi, 336–352. Monterey, Calif.: Brooks Cole.

Anderson, Donald. 1966. "Ascetic Protestantism and Political Preference." *Review of Religious Research* 7:167–171.

Anderson, John B., ed. 1970. *Congress and Conscience.* Philadelphia: J. B. Lippincott.

Aptheker, Herbert, ed. 1968. *Marxism and Christianity.* New York: Humanities.

Arrington, Theodore S., and Patricia A. Kyle. 1978. "Equal Rights Amendment Activists in North Carolina." *Signs* 3:666–680.

Atkins, Rt. Rev. Stanley, and Rev. Theodore McConnell, eds. 1986. *Churches on the Wrong Road.* Chicago: Regnery Gateway.

Atwood, Thomas C. 1990. "Through a Glass Darkly." *Policy Review* 5:44–53.

Baer, Hans A., and Merrill Singer. 1992. *African-American Religion in the Twentieth Century: Varieties of Protest and Accommodation.* Knoxville: University of Tennessee Press.

Baggaley, Andrew. 1962. "Religious Influence on Wisconsin Voting." *American Political Science Review* 56:66–70.

Baker, Donald. 1985. "It's Not Exactly 'Animal House'." *Washington Post Weekly Edition,* 27 May, 7–8.

Baker, James T. 1977. *A Southern Baptist in the White House.* Philadelphia: Westminster.

Baker, Ross K., Laurily K. Epstein, and Rodney D. Furth. 1981. "Matters of Life and Death: Social, Political, and Religious Correlates of Attitudes on Abortion." *American Politics Quarterly* 9:89–102.

Baker, Tod A., Robert P. Steed, and Laurence W. Moreland, eds. 1983. *Religion and Politics in the South: Mass and Elite Perspectives.* New York: Praeger.

Balswick, Jack O. 1970. "Theology and Political Attitudes Among Clergymen." *Sociological Quarterly* 11:394–404.

Balswick, Jack, Dawn M. Ward, and David E. Armstrong. 1975. "Theological and Socio-Political Belief Change Among Religiously Conservative Students." *Review of Religious Research* 17:61–67.

Bandow, Doug. 1995. "The Parallel Universe." *American Enterprise* 6:58–61.

Bard, Mitchell. 1991. *The Water's Edge and Beyond: Defining the Limits to Domestic Influence Upon United States Middle East Policy.* New Brunswick, N.J.: Transaction.

Barkun, Michael. 1994. *Religion and the Racist Right.* Chapel Hill: University of North Carolina Press.

Barnes, Fred. 1992. "The New Covenant." *New Republic,* 9 November, 32–34.

———. 1995. "The Orthodox Alliance." *American Enterprise* 6:70–71.

Barrett, Sharon W., and Richard J. Harris. 1982. "Recent Changes in Predictors of Abortion Attitudes." *Sociology and Social Research* 66:320–334.

Barringer, Felicity. 1985. "A Ban on Teaching 'Secular Humanism'." *Washington Post Weekly Edition*, 28 January, 32.

Barron, Bruce. 1992. *Heaven on Earth? The Social and Political Agendas of Dominion Theology*. Grand Rapids, Mich.: Zondervan.

Bates, Stephen. 1993. *Battleground: One Mother's Crusade, the Religious Right, and the Struggle for Control of Our Classrooms*. New York: Poseidon.

Batson, C. Daniel, et al. 1986. "Religious Orientation and Overt and Covert Racial Prejudice." *Journal of Personality and Social Psychology* 50:175–181.

Bean, Clive. 1991. "Participation and Political Protest: A Causal Model With Australian Evidence." *Political Behavior* 13:253–283.

Beatty, Kathleen Murphy, and Oliver Walter. 1984. "Religious Preference and Practice: Reevaluating Their Impact on Political Tolerance." *Public Opinion Quarterly* 48:318–329.

———. 1988. "Fundamentalists, Evangelicals, and Politics." *American Politics Quarterly* 16:43–59.

———. 1989. "A Group Theory of Religion and Politics: The Clergy As Group Leaders." *Western Political Quarterly* 42:129–146.

Beck, Paul Allen, and Suzanne Parker. 1985. "Consistency in Policy Thinking." *Political Behavior* 7:37–56.

Bell, Daniel. 1977. "Return of the Sacred? Argument on the Future of Religion." *British Journal of Sociology* 28:419–449.

Bellah, Robert N. 1975. *The Broken Covenant: American Civil Religion in a Time of Trial*. New York: Seabury.

Bellah, Robert N., and Phillip E. Hammond, eds. 1980. *Varieties of Civil Religion*. New York: Harper and Row.

Bellah, Robert N., Richard Madsen, William M. Sullivan, Ann Swidler, and Steven M. Tipton. 1985. *Habits of the Heart: Individualism and Commitment in American Life*. Berkeley and Los Angeles: University of California Press.

Benson, Peter L., and Dorothy L. Williams. 1982. *Religion on Capitol Hill: Myths and Realities*. San Francisco: Harper and Row.

Bercovitch, Sacvan. 1975. *The Puritan Origin of the American Self*. New Haven, Conn.: Yale University Press.

Berelson, Bernard, Paul Lazarsfeld, and William N. McPhee. 1954. *Voting: A Study of Opinion Formation in a Presidential Campaign*. Chicago: University of Chicago Press.

Berenson, William, Kirk W. Elifson, and Tandy Tollerson III. 1976. "Preachers in Politics: A Study of Political Activism Among the Black Ministry." *Journal of Black Studies* 6:373–392.

Berger, Peter L., and Richard John Neuhaus. 1977. *To Empower People: The Role of Mediating Structures in Public Policy*. Washington, D.C.: American Enterprise Institute.

Bergstrom, Charles, and David Saperstein. 1984. "God and Politics." *Washington Post Weekly Edition*, 10 September, 28.

Berke, Richard L. 1994a. "At Church, the Sermon Is Often How You Vote." *New York Times*, 7 November, 10A.

———. 1994b. "Christian Right Defies Categories." *New York Times*, 22 July, A1, A9.

———. 1995. "Poll Finds G.O.P. Primary Voters Are Hardly Monolithic." *New York Times*, 30 October, A10–A11.

Berman, Paul, ed. 1994. *Blacks and Jews: Alliances and Arguments.* New York: Delacorte.

Billington, Monroe, and Cal Clark. 1991. "Baptist Preachers and the New Deal." *Journal of Church and State* 33:255–270.

———. 1993. "Catholic Clergymen, Franklin D. Roosevelt, and the New Deal." *Catholic Historical Review* 79:65–82.

Bird, Frederick B. 1990. "How Do Religions Affect Moralities? A Comparative Analysis." *Social Compass* 37:291–314.

Birkby, Robert H. 1966. "The Supreme Court and the Bible Belt: Tennessee Reactions to the 'Schempp' Decision." *Midwest Journal of Political Science* 10:304–319.

Blakeley, William Addison. 1970. *American State Papers Bearing on Sunday Religion.* Rev. and enlarged ed. New York: Da Capo.

Blanchard, Dallas A., and Terry J. Prewitt. 1993. *Religious Violence and Abortion: The Gideon Project.* Gainesville: University Press of Florida.

Blau, Peter M. 1953. "Orientation of College Students Toward International Relations." *American Journal of Sociology* 59:205–214.

Bledsoe, Timothy, Susan Welch, Lee Sigelman, and Michael Combs. 1995. "Residential Context and Racial Solidarity Among African Americans." *American Journal of Political Science* 39:434–458.

Bloch, Ruth H. 1990. "Religion and Ideological Change in the American Revolution." In *Religion and American Politics,* ed. Mark A. Noll, 44–61. New York: Oxford University Press.

Blumenthal, Sidney. 1984. "The Righteous Empire." *New Republic,* 22 October, 18–24.

Bochel, J. M., and D. T. Denver. 1970. "Religion and Voting: A Critical Review and a New Analysis." *Political Studies* 18:205–219.

Bock, David C., and Neil Clark Warren. 1972. "Religious Belief As a Factor in Obedience to Destructive Commands." *Review of Religious Research* 13:185–191.

Bolce, Louis. 1988. "Abortion and Presidential Elections: The Impact of Public Perceptions of Party and Candidate Positions." *Presidential Studies Quarterly* 28:815–829.

Boles, Janet K. 1979. *The Politics of the Equal Rights Amendment.* New York: Longman.

Bond, Jon R., and Charles A. Johnson. 1982. "Implementing a Permissive Policy: Hospital Abortion Services After *Roe v. Wade.*" *American Journal of Political Science* 26:1–24.

Bonomi, Patricia U. 1994. "Religious Dissent and the Case for American Exceptionalism." In *Religion in a Revolutionary Age,* ed. Ronald Hoffman and Peter J. Albert, 31–51. Charlottesville: University Press of Virginia.

Boothby, Lee. 1986. "Government As an Instrument of Retribution for Private Resentments." In *Government Intervention in Religious Affairs, II,* ed. Dean M. Kelley, 79–106. New York: Pilgrim.

Boston, Rob. 1994. "Slow Learners." *Church and State* 47: 4–6.

———. 1995. "Politics, Pulpits, and the IRS." *Church and State* 48:129–133.

Bradley, Martin B., Norman M. Green Jr., Dale E. Jones, Mac Lynn, and Lou McNeil. 1992. *Churches and Church Membership in the United States 1990.* Atlanta: Glenmary Research Center.

Brady, David W., and Kent L. Tedin. 1976. "Ladies in Pink: Religious and Political Ideology in the Anti-ERA Movement." *Social Science Quarterly* 56:564–575.

Brett, Edward T. 1994. "The Attempts of Grassroots Religious Groups to Change U.S. Policy Toward Central America: Their Methods, Successes, and Failures." *Journal of Church and State* 36:773–794.

Brickner, Balfour. 1980. "Social Policy-Making Structures of the Jewish Community." In *The Formation of Social Policy in the Catholic and Jewish Traditions,* ed. Eugene J. Fisher and Daniel F. Polish, 5–14. Notre Dame, Ind.: University of Notre Dame Press.

Bridenbaugh, Carl. 1962. *Mitre and Sceptre: Transatlantic Faiths, Ideas, Personalities, and Politics, 1689–1775.* New York: Oxford University Press.

Brogan, D. W. 1960. *Politics in America.* Garden City, N.Y.: Doubleday-Anchor.

Brooks, Juanita. 1962. *The Mountain Meadows Massacre.* Norman: University of Oklahoma Press.

Brown, Ronald E., and Monica L. Wolford. 1993. "Religious Resources and African American Political Action." *National Political Science Review* 4:30–48.

Brudney, Jeffrey L., and Gary W. Copeland. 1984. "Evangelicals As a Political Force: Reagan and the 1980 Religious Vote." *Social Science Quarterly* 65:1072–1079.

Buber, Martin. 1937. *I and Thou.* Edinburgh, Scotland: Clark.

Buchanan, Pat. 1992. "The Election Is About Who We Are." *Vital Speeches* 58:712–715.

Budner, Stanley. 1962. "Intolerance of Ambiguity As a Personality Variable." *Journal of Personality* 30:29–50.

Buell, Emmett H., and Lee Sigelman. 1985. "An Army That Meets Every Sunday? Popular Support for the Moral Majority in 1980." *Social Science Quarterly* 66:426–434.

Buenker, John D. 1973. *Urban Liberalism and Progressive Reform.* New York: Charles Scribner's Sons.

Bullis, Ronald K. 1991. "The Spiritual Healing 'Defense' in Criminal Prosecutions for Crimes Against Children." *Child Welfare* 70:541–555.

Burkett, Randall K. 1978. *Garveyism As a Religious Movement.* Metuchen, N.J.: Scarecrow.

Burner, David. 1967. *The Politics of Provincialism: The Democratic Party in Transition, 1918–1932.* New York: W. W. Norton.

Burnham, Walter Dean. 1968. "American Voting Behavior and the 1964 Election." *Midwest Journal of Political Science* 12:1–40.

Burris, Val. 1983. "Who Opposed the ERA? An Analysis of the Social Bases of Antifeminism." *Social Science Quarterly* 64:305–317.

Butler, Jon. 1990. *Awash in a Sea of Faith: Christianizing the American People.* Cambridge: Harvard University Press.

Buzzard, Lynn. 1989. "The 'Coming Out' of Evangelicals." In *Contemporary Evangelical Political Involvement: An Analysis and Assessment,* ed. Corwin E. Smidt, 133–146. Lanham, Md.: University Press of America.

Byrnes, Deborah A., and Gary Kiger. 1992. "Social Factors and Responses to Racial Discrimination." *Journal of Psychology* 126:631–638.

Byrnes, Timothy A. 1991. *Catholic Bishops in American Politics.* Princeton, N.J.: Princeton University Press.

Byrnes, Timothy, and Mary C. Segers, eds. 1992. *The Catholic Church and the Politics of Abortion.* Boulder: Westview.

Caldeira, Gregory A., and James L. Gibson. 1992. "The Etiology of Public Support for the Supreme Court." *American Journal of Political Science* 36:635–664.

Calhoon, Robert M. 1994. "The Evangelical Persuasion." In *Religion in a Revolutionary Age,* ed. Ronald Hoffman and Peter J. Albert, 156–183. Charlottesville: University Press of Virginia.

Calhoun, Charles W. 1993. "Civil Religion and the Gilded Age Presidency: The Case of Benjamin Harrison." *Presidential Studies Quarterly* 23:651–667.

Callahan, Daniel, ed. 1970. *Abortion: Law, Choice, and Morality.* New York: Macmillan.

Campbell, Angus, Philip E. Converse, Warren E. Miller, and Donald Stokes. 1960. *The American Voter.* New York: John Wiley.

Campbell, Ernest Q., and Thomas F. Pettigrew. 1959. *Christians in Racial Crisis.* Washington, D.C.: Public Affairs Press.

Cantor, David. 1994. *The Religious Right: The Assault on Tolerance and Pluralism in America.* New York: Anti-Defamation League.

Caplow, Theodore. 1985. "Contrasting Trends in European and American Religion." *Sociological Analysis* 46:101–108.

Caplow, Theodore, Howard M. Bahr, and Bruce A. Chadwick. 1983. *All Faithful People: Change and Continuity in Middletown's Religion.* Minneapolis: University of Minnesota Press.

Capps, Walter H., ed. 1972. *Ways of Understanding Religion.* New York: Macmillan.

Carey, George W. 1982. "Religion and American Government Textbooks." *Teaching Political Science* 10:7–19.

Carmines, Edward G., and James A. Stimson. 1980. "The Two Faces of Issue Voting." *American Political Science Review* 74:78–91.

Carmody, Denise Lardner, and John Tully Carmody. 1990. *The Republic of Many Mansions: Foundations of American Religious Thought.* New York: Paragon House.

Carroll, F. M. 1978. *American Opinion and the Irish Question, 1910–1923: A Study in Opinion and Policy.* Dublin, Ireland: Gill and Macmillan.

Carroll, Jackson W. 1995. "Culture Wars? Insights from Ethnographies of Two Protestant Seminaries." *Sociology of Religion* 56:1–19.

Carson, Claybourne, Jr. 1984. "Blacks and Jews in the Civil Rights Movement." In *Jews in Black Perspective: A Dialogue,* ed. Joseph Washington, 113–131. Rutherford, N.J.: Fairleigh Dickinson University Press.

Carter, Paul A. 1954. *The Decline and Revival of the Social Gospel.* Ithaca: Cornell University Press.

Carter, Stephen L. 1993. *The Culture of Disbelief: How American Law and Politics Trivialize Religious Devotion.* New York: Basic Books.

Carwardine, Richard. 1993. *Evangelicals and Politics in Antebellum America.* New Haven, Conn.: Yale University Press.

Casanova, José. 1994. *Public Religions in the Modern World.* Chicago: University of Chicago Press.

Casey, Shaun. 1993. "The President's Religion." *Nieman Reports* 47:32–35, 54.

Cataldo, Everett F., and John D. Holm. 1983. "Voting on School Finances: A Test of Competing Theories." *Western Political Quarterly* 36:619–631.

Center for Political Studies. 1989. *American National Election Study: 1989 Pilot Study Codebook.* Ann Arbor, Mich.: Institute for Social Research.

Chaves, Mark, and Lynn M. Higgins. 1992. "Comparing the Community Involvement of Black and White Congregations." *Journal for the Scientific Study of Religion* 31:425–440.

Cheal, David. 1975. "Political Radicalism and Religion: Competitors for Commitment." *Social Compass* 22:245–249.

Cherry, Conrad, ed. 1972. *God's New Israel: Religious Interpretations of American Destiny.* Englewood Cliffs, N.J.: Prentice-Hall.

Chresanthis, George A., Kathie S. Gilbert, and Paul W. Grimes. 1991. "Ideology, Constituent Interests, and Senatorial Voting: The Case of Abortion." *Social Science Quarterly* 72:588–600.

Christenson, James, and Ronald C. Wimberly. 1978. "Who Is Civil Religious?" *Sociological Analysis* 39:77–83.

Christian Coalition. 1995. *Contract With the American Family.* Nashville, Tenn.: Moorings.

Christiano, Kevin J. 1988. "Religion and Radical Labor Unionism: American States in the 1920s." *Journal for the Scientific Study of Religion* 27:378–388.

Clabaugh, Gary K. 1974. *Thunder on the Right: The Protestant Fundamentalists.* Chicago: Nelson-Hall.

Clark, Norman H. 1976. *Deliver Us From Evil: An Interpretation of American Prohibition.* New York: W. W. Norton.

Cleghorn, J. Stephen. 1986. "Respect for Life: Research Notes on Cardinal Bernardin's 'Seamless Garment'." *Review of Religious Research* 28:129–141.

Clements, Kendricks. 1982. *William Jennings Bryan: Missionary Isolationist.* Knoxville: University of Tennessee Press.

Clinton, Bill. 1992. "Acceptance Address." *Vital Speeches* 58:642–645.

Cochran, Clarke E. 1990. *Religion in Public and Private Life.* New York: Routledge.

Cohen, Naomi. 1992. *Jews in Christian America.* New York: Oxford University Press.

Cohen, Steven M. 1983. *American Modernity and Jewish Identity.* New York: Tavistock.

———. 1989. *The Dimensions of American Jewish Liberalism.* New York: American Jewish Committee.

Cohen, Steven M., and Robert E. Kapsis. 1977. "Religion, Ethnicity, and Party Affiliation in the United States: Evidence from Pooled Election Surveys, 1968–1972." *Social Forces* 56:637–653.

Cohn, Werner. 1957. "The Politics of American Jews." In *The Jews*, ed. Marshall Sklare, 614–626. New York: Free Press.

Cole, Leonard. 1976. *Blacks in Power.* Princeton, N.J.: Princeton University Press.

Coleman, John A. 1970. "Civil Religion." *Sociological Analysis* 31:67–77.

Coles, Robert. 1985. "Out of the Mouths of Babes: When Ethics and Reality Collide." *Washington Post Weekly Edition,* 2 September, 24.

Combs, Michael, and Susan Welch. 1982. "Blacks, Whites, and Attitudes Toward Abortion." *Public Opinion Quarterly* 46:510–520.

Committee on Post Offices and Post Roads. 1830. *Report No. 271.* Twenty-first Congress, 1st sess. Washington, D.C.: U.S. House of Representatives.

Congressional Quarterly. 1980. "Lobbying for Christ." *Congressional Quarterly Weekly Report,* 6 September: 2627–2634.

Connors, John F., Richard C. Leonard, and Kenneth E. Burnham. 1968. "Religion, Church Attitudes, Religious Education, and Student Attitudes to War." *Sociological Analysis* 29:211–219.

Conover, Pamela Johnson. 1983. "The Mobilization of the New Right: A Test of Various Explanations." *Western Political Quarterly* 36:632–649.

Conover, Pamela Johnson, and Virginia Gray. 1983. *Feminism and the New Right.* New York: Praeger.

Converse, Philip E. 1966. "Religion and Politics: The 1960 Election." In *Elections and the Political Order,* ed. Angus Campbell, Philip E. Converse, Warren E. Miller, and Donald Stokes, 96–124. New York: John Wiley.

———. 1974. "Some Priority Variables in Comparative Electoral Research." In *Electoral Behavior,* ed. Richard Rose, 727–745. New York: Free Press.

Converse, Philip E., and Angus Campbell. 1969. "Political Standards in Secondary Groups." In *Readings in Reference Group Theory and Research,* ed. Herbert H. Hyman and Eleanor Singer, 473–489. New York: Free Press.

Cook, Elizabeth Adell, Ted G. Jelen, and Clyde Wilcox. 1992. *Between Two Absolutes: American Public Opinion and the Politics of Abortion.* Boulder: Westview.

———. 1994. "Issue Voting in Gubernatorial Elections: Abortion and Post-*Webster* Politics." *Journal of Politics* 56:187–199.

Cooney, John. 1984. *The American Pope.* New York: Times Books.

Cord, Robert L. 1982. *Separation of Church and State: Historical Fact and Current Fiction.* New York: Lambeth.

Cornwall, Marie. 1987. "The Social Bases of Religion: A Study of Factors Influencing Religious Belief and Commitment." *Review of Religious Research* 29:44–56.

Cousins, Norman, ed. 1958. *In God We Trust: The Religious Beliefs and Ideas of the American Founders.* New York: Harper and Brothers.

Coutin, Susan Biber. 1993. *The Culture of Protest: Religious Activism and the U.S. Sanctuary Movement.* Boulder: Westview.

Cox, Harvey. 1968. "The 'New Breed' in American Churches: Sources of Social Activism in American Religion." In *Religion in America,* ed. William G. McLaughlin and Robert N. Bellah, 368–383. Boston: Beacon.

Craig, Wyn. 1987. *The Fiery Cross: The KKK in America.* New York: Simon and Schuster.

Crawford, Alan. 1980. *Thunder on the Right.* New York: Pantheon.

Crosby, Donald F. 1978. *God, Church, and Flag: Senator Joseph R. McCarthy and the Catholic Church, 1950–1957.* Chapel Hill: University of North Carolina Press.

Cunningham, Hilary. 1995. *God and Caesar at the Rio Grande.* Minneapolis: University of Minnesota Press.

Curran, Charles E. 1982. *American Catholic Social Ethics: Twentieth-Century Approaches.* Notre Dame, Ind.: University of Notre Dame Press.

Curry, Dean C., ed. 1984. *Evangelicals and the Bishops' Pastoral Letter.* Grand Rapids, Mich.: Eerdman's.

D'Antonio, Michael. 1989. *Fall From Grace: The Failed Crusade of the Christian Right.* New York: Farrar, Straus, and Giroux.

Davidson, James D. 1989. "The Pastoral Letters on Peace and the Economy: A New Approach to Church Teachings." In *Catholic Laity in a Changing Church,* ed. Dean Hoge, 121–131. Kansas City, Mo.: Sheed and Ward.

———. 1994. "Religion Among America's Elite: Persistence and Change in the Protestant Establishment." *Sociology of Religion* 55:419–440.

Davis, Derek. 1991. "The Supreme Court, Public Policy, and the Advocacy Rights of Churches." In *The Role of Religion in the Making of Public Policy,* ed. James E. Wood Jr. and Derek Davis, 101–126. Waco, Texas: Baylor University, J. M. Dawson Institute of Church-State Studies.

———. 1995. "Assessing the Proposed Religious Equality Amendment." *Journal of Church and State* 37:493–508.

Dawidowicz, Lucy S., and Leon J. Goldstein, eds. 1974. *Politics in a Pluralist Democracy: Studies of Voting in the 1960 Election.* Westport, Conn.: Greenwood.

Dawson, Michael C., Ronald E. Brown, and Richard Allen. 1990. "Racial Belief Systems, Religious Guidance, and African-American Political Participation." *National Political Science Review* 2:22–44.

Daynes, Bryon W., and Raymond Tatalovich. 1984. "Religious Influence and Congressional Voting on Abortion." *Journal for the Scientific Study of Religion* 23:197–200.

Dayton, Donald W., and Robert K. Johnston, eds. 1991. *The Variety of American Evangelicalism.* Knoxville: University of Tennessee Press.

Deedy, John G., Jr. 1968. "The Catholic Press and Vietnam." In *American Catholics and Vietnam,* ed. Thomas E. Quigley. Grand Rapids, Mich.: Eerdman's.

Deloria, Vine, Jr. 1992. "Secularism, Civil Religion, and the Religious Freedom of American Indians." *American Indian Culture and Research Journal* 16:9–206.

Dexter, Lewis Anthony. 1938. "Administration of the Social Gospel." *Public Opinion Quarterly* 2:294–299.

Diamond, Martin. 1977. "Ethics and Politics: The American Way." In *The Moral Foundations of the American Republic,* ed. Robert Horwitz, 39–72. Charlottesville: University Press of Virginia.

Diamond, Sara. 1989. *Spiritual Warfare: The Politics of the Christian Right.* Boston: South End.

Dierenfeld, R. B. 1967. "The Impact of the Supreme Court Decisions on Religion in the Public Schools." *Religious Education* 62:445–451.

Diggins, John P. 1984. *The Lost Soul of American Politics: Virtue, Self-Interest, and the Foundations of Liberalism.* New York: Basic Books.

Dixon, Richard D., Diane E. Levy, and Roger C. Lowery. 1988. "Asking the 'Born-Again' Question." *Review of Religious Research* 30:33–39.

Dohen, Dorothy. 1967. *Nationalism and American Catholicism.* New York: Sheed and Ward.

Dolbeare, Kenneth. 1967. "The Public Views the Supreme Court." In *Law, Politics, and the Federal Courts,* ed. Herbert Jacob, 194–212. Boston: Little, Brown.

Dolbeare, Kenneth, and Phillip Hammond. 1977. *The School Prayer Decisions: From Court Policy to Local Practices.* Chicago: University of Chicago Press.

Donnelly, Brenda W. 1987. "The Social Protest of Christian and Nonreligious Groups: The Importance of Goal Choice." *Journal for the Scientific Study of Religion* 26:309–326.

Driedger, Leo. 1974. "Doctrinal Belief: A Major Factor in the Differential Perception of Social Issues." *Sociological Quarterly* 15:66–80.

Drinan, Robert F., S.J. 1970. *Vietnam and Armageddon.* New York: Sheed and Ward.

Dudley, Roger L., and Edwin I. Hernandez. 1992. "Religiosity and Public Issues Among Seventh-Day Adventists." *Review of Religious Research* 33:330–348.

Dugger, Karen. 1991. "Race Differences in the Determinants of Support for Legalized Abortion." *Social Science Quarterly* 72:570–587.

Duke, James T., and Barry L. Johnson. 1992. "Religious Affiliation and Congressional Representation." *Journal for the Scientific Study of Religion* 31:324–329.

Dunn, Charles W., ed. 1984. *American Political Theology.* New York: Praeger.

Eastland, Terry, ed. 1993. *Religious Liberty in the Supreme Court: The Cases That Define the Debate Over Church and State.* Washington, D.C.: Ethics and Public Policy Center.

Ebersole, Luke E. 1951. *Church Lobbying in the Nation's Capital.* New York: Macmillan.

Eckberg, Douglas Lee, and T. Jean Blocker. 1989. "Varieties of Religious Involvement and Environmental Concern: Testing the Lynn White Thesis." *Journal for the Scientific Study of Religion* 28:509–517.

Eckert, Ruth E., and Henry C. Mills. 1935. "International Attitudes and Related Academic and Social Factors." *Journal of Educational Sociology* 9:142–153.

Edmondson, Brad. 1995. "Unclaimed by God." *American Demographics* 17:60.

Edsall, Thomas B. 1994a. "Revolt of the Discontented." *Washington Post Weekly Edition,* 21 November, 28.

———. 1994b. "An Up-Close Look at the 'Values' Battle." *Washington Post Weekly Edition,* 17 October, 24–25.

Ehrenhalt, Alan, ed. 1983. *Politics in America 1984.* Washington, D.C.: CQ Press.

Eidsmoe, John. 1984. *God and Caesar.* Westchester, Ill.: Crossway Books.

Elazar, Daniel J. 1976. *Community and Polity: The Organizational Dynamics of American Jewry.* Philadelphia: Jewish Publication Society of America.

———. 1980. "The Political Theory of Covenant: Biblical Origins and Modern Developments." *Publius* 10:3–30.

———. 1984. *American Federalism: A View from the States.* Third ed. New York: Harper and Row.

Elifson, Kirk W., and C. Kirk Hadaway. 1985. "Prayer in Public Schools: When Church and State Collide." *Public Opinion Quarterly* 49:317–329.

Elinson, Howard. 1965. "The Implications of Pentecostal Religion for Intellectualism, Politics, and Race Relations." *American Journal of Sociology* 70:403–415.

Ellison, Christopher G. 1991. "Identification and Separatism: Religious Involvement and Racial Orientations Among Black Americans." *Sociological Quarterly* 32:477–494.

Ellison, Christopher G., and Darren E. Sherkat. 1993. "Obedience and Authority: Religion and Parental Values Reconsidered." *Journal for the Scientific Study of Religion* 32:313–329.

Epstein, Leon D. 1967. *Political Parties in Western Democracies.* New York: Praeger.

Ermann, M. David, and William H. Clements II. 1984. "The Interfaith Center on Corporate Responsibility and Its Campaign Against Marketing Infant Formula in the Third World." *Social Problems* 32:185–196.

Etzioni Amitai. 1988. "Evading the Issues: Progressives' Political Taboos." *Public Opinion* (March–April), 2–3, 53.

Fagan, John, and George Breed. 1970. "A Good, Short Measure of Religious Dogmatism." *Psychological Reports* 26:533–534.

Fairbanks, James David. 1977. "Religious Forces and 'Morality' Policies in the American States." *Western Political Quarterly* 30:411–417.

———. 1979. "Politics, Economics, and the Public Morality: Why Some States Are More 'Moral' Than Others." *Policy Studies Journal* 7:714–720.

———. 1981. "The Priestly Function of the Presidency: A Discussion of the Literature on Civil Religion and Its Implications for the Study of Presidential Leadership." *Presidential Studies Quarterly* 11:214–232.

Fee, Joan L. 1976. "Party Identification Among American Catholics, 1972, 1973." *Ethnicity* 3:53–69.

Fein, Leonard. 1988. *Where Are We? The Inner Life of America's Jews.* New York: Harper and Row.

Fenno, Richard F. 1978. *Home Style: House Members in Their Districts.* Boston: Little, Brown.

Fenton, John H. 1960. *The Catholic Vote.* New Orleans: Hauser.

Fenton, John H., and Kenneth N. Vines. 1967. "Negro Registration in Louisiana." In *Negro Politics in America,* ed. Harry A. Bailey, 166–177. Columbus, Ohio: Charles E. Merrill.

Festinger, Leon. 1947. "The Role of Group Belongingness in a Voting Situation." *Human Relations* 1:154–180.

Feuerlicht, Roberta Strauss. 1983. *The Fate of the Jews: A People Torn Between Israeli Power and Jewish Ethics*. New York: Times Books.

Findlay, James F. 1990. "Religion and Politics in the Sixties: The Churches and the Civil Rights Act of 1964." *Journal of American History* 77:66–93.

Finke, Roger, and Rodney Stark. 1992. *The Churching of America, 1776–1990: Winners and Losers in Our Religious Economy*. New Brunswick, N.J.: Rutgers University Press.

Fisher, Alan M. 1979. "Realignment of the Jewish Vote." *Political Science Quarterly* 94:97–116.

———. 1985. "The Jewish Vote in 1982: A Good Look, A Good Predictor." *Jewish Social Studies* 47:281–294.

———. 1989. "Where the Jewish Vote Is Going." *Moment* 14:41–43.

Fisher, Eugene J., and Daniel F. Polish, eds. 1980. *The Formation of Social Policy in the Catholic and Jewish Traditions*. Notre Dame, Ind.: University of Notre Dame Press.

Fisher, Randy D., Donna Derison, and Chester F. Polley III. 1994. "Religiousness, Religious Orientation, and Attitudes Toward Gays and Lesbians." *Journal of Applied Social Psychology* 24:614–630.

Fitzgerald, Frances. 1981. "A Disciplined, Charging Army." *New Yorker*, 18 May, 53–141.

Flowers, Ronald B. 1983. "President Jimmy Carter, Evangelicalism, Church-State Relations, and Civil Religion." *Journal of Church and State* 25:113–132.

———. 1994. *That Godless Court?* Louisville, Ky.: Westminster–John Knox.

Flynn, George Q. 1968. *American Catholics and the Roosevelt Presidency, 1932–1936*. Lexington: University of Kentucky Press.

Fowler, Robert Booth. 1982. *A New Engagement: Evangelical Political Thought, 1966–1976*. Grand Rapids, Mich.: Eerdman's.

———. 1989. *Unconventional Partners: Religion and Liberal Culture in the United States*. Grand Rapids, Mich.: Eerdman's.

———. 1995. *The Greening of Protestant Thought*. Chapel Hill: University of North Carolina Press.

Francis, John G. 1992. "The Evolving Regulatory Structure of European Church-State Relationships." *Journal of Church and State* 34:775–804.

Frankel, Carl. 1984. "A Legacy." *American Scholar* 52:159–166.

Franklin, Charles E., and Liane C. Kosaki. 1989. "Republican Schoolmaster: The U.S. Supreme Court, Public Opnion, and Abortion." *American Political Science Review* 83:751–777.

Freeman, Donald M. 1962. "Religion and Southern Politics: A Study of the Political Behavior of Southern White Protestants." Ph.D. diss., University of North Carolina.

Friedman, Lawrence M. 1983. "The Conflict Over Constitutional Legitimacy." In *The Abortion Dispute and the American System*, ed. Gilbert Y. Steiner, 13–29. Washington, D.C.: Brookings.

Friedman, Murray. 1995. *What Went Wrong? The Creation and Collapse of the Black-Jewish Alliance*. New York: Free Press.

Frum, David. 1994. "Dead Wrong: Christian Conservatism's Losing Record." *New Republic*, 12 September, 17–20.

Fuchs, Lawrence H. 1955. "American Jews and the Presidential Vote." *American Political Science Review* 49:385–401.

———. 1956. *The Political Behavior of American Jews*. Glencoe, Ill.: Free Press.

———. 1984. "The Political Behavior of American Jews." In *American Political Theology*, ed. Charles W. Dunn, 70–78. New York: Praeger.

Funderburk, Charles. 1986. "Religion, Political Legitimacy, and Civil Violence: A Survey of Children and Adolescents." *Sociological Focus* 19:289–298.

Gallup, George, Jr. 1981. "Divining the Devout: The Polls and Religious Belief." *Public Opinion* 4:20, 41.

Gallup, George H., Jr., and Robert Bezilla. 1995. "Who Belongs to the Religious Right?" *Christian Century*, 26 April, 451–452.

Gallup, George, Jr., and Jim Castelli. 1987. *The American Catholic People*. Garden City, N.J.: Doubleday.

———. 1989. *The People's Religion*. New York: Macmillan.

Gamoran, Adam. 1990. "Civil Religion in American Schools." *Sociological Analysis* 51:235–256.

Ganin, Zvi. 1979. *Truman, American Jewry, and Israel, 1945–1948*. New York: Holmes and Meier.

Garrett, William R. 1973. "Politicized Clergy: A Sociological Interpretation of the 'New Breed'." *Journal for the Scientific Study of Religion* 12:383–397.

———. 1987. "Religion, Law, and the Human Condition." *Sociological Analysis* 47:1–34 (supplement).

Gehrig, Gail. 1979. *American Civil Religion: An Assessment*. Storrs, Conn.: Society for the Scientific Study of Religion.

Getz, Irene R. 1984. "Moral Judgment and Religion: A Review of the Literature." *Counseling and Values* 28:94–116.

Gibson, James L., and Arthur J. Anderson. 1985. "The Political Implications of Elite and Mass Tolerance." *Political Behavior* 7:118–146.

Gibson, James L., and Kent L. Tedin. 1988. "Etiology of Intolerance of Homosexual Politics." *Social Science Quarterly* 69:587–604.

Gilbert, Christopher P. 1993. *The Impact of Churches on Political Behavior: An Empirical Study*. Westport, Conn.: Greenwood.

Gilboa, Eytan. 1987. *American Public Opinion Toward Israel and the Arab-Israeli Conflict*. Lexington, Mass.: D. C. Heath.

Giles, Michael, and Thomas G. Walker. 1975. "Judicial Policy-Making and Southern School Desegregation." *Journal of Politics* 37:917–936.

Gilkey, Langdon. 1968. "Social and Intellectual Sources of Contemporary Protestant Theology in America." In *Religion in America*, ed. William G. McLoughlin and Robert N. Bellah, 137–166. Boston: Beacon.

Glantz, Oscar. 1959. "Protestant and Catholic Voting Behavior in a Metropolitan Area." *Public Opinion Quarterly* 23:73–82.

Glazer, Nathan. 1986. "The 'Social Agenda'." In *Perspectives on the Reagan Years*, ed. John L. Palmer, 5–30. Washington, D.C.: Urban Institute.

Glick, Edward Bernard. 1982. *The Triangular Connection: America, Israel, and American Jews*. London: George Allen and Unwin.

Glock, Charles Y., and Rodney Stark. 1966. *Christian Beliefs and Anti-Semitism*. New York: Harper and Row.

Gohmann, Stephan F., and Robert L. Ohsfeldt. 1990. "U.S. Senate Voting on Abortion Legislation: A More Direct Test for Ideological Shirking." Working Paper Series #90-14. Birmingham: Department of Health Care Organization and Policy, School of Public Health, University of Alabama.

Goldberg, David Howard. 1990. *Foreign Policy and Ethnic Interest Groups: American and Canadian Jews Lobby for Israel*. New York: Greenwood.

Goldberg, J. J. 1992. "On the Winning Side, At Last." *Jerusalem Report*, 3 December, 30–32.

Goldman, Sheldon. 1966. "Voting Behavior on the U.S. Court of Appeals, 1961–64." *American Political Science Review* 60:374–383.

———. 1975. "Voting Behavior on the U.S. Court of Appeals Revisited." *American Political Science Review* 79:491–506.

———. 1993. "Bush's Judicial Legacy: The Final Imprint." *Judicature* 76:282–297.

Goldscheider, Calvin, and William D. Mosher. 1991. "Patterns of Contraceptive Use in the United States: The Importance of Religious Factors." *Studies in Family Planning* 22:102–115.

Goodenough, Erwin R. 1972. "Religion As Man's Adjustment to the Tremendum." In *Ways of Understanding Religion*, ed. Walter H. Capps, 45–48. New York: Macmillan.

Gorsuch, Richard L., and Daniel Aleshire. 1974. "Christian Faith and Ethnic Prejudice: A Review and Interpretation of Research." *Journal for the Scientific Study of Religion* 13:281–307.

Granberg, Donald. 1978. "Pro-Life or Reflection of Conservative Ideology? An Analysis of Opposition to Legalized Abortion." *Sociology and Social Research* 62:414–429.

———. 1981a. "The Abortion Activists." *Family Planning Perspectives* 13:157–163.

———. 1981b. "Comparison of Members of Pro- and Anti-Abortion Organizations in Missouri." *Social Biology* 28:239–252.

———. 1982a. "Comparison of Pro-Choice and Pro-Life Activists: Their Values, Attitudes, and Beliefs." *Population and Environment* 5:75–94.

———. 1982b. "Family Size Preferences and Sexual Permissiveness As Factors Differentiating Abortion Activists." *Social Psychology Quarterly* 45:15–23.

———. 1985a. "An Anomaly in Political Perception." *Public Opinion Quarterly* 49:504–516.

———. 1985b. "The United States Senate Votes to Uphold *Roe v. Wade*." *Population Research and Policy Review* 42:115–131.

———. 1987. "The Abortion Issue in the 1984 Elections." *Family Planning Perspectives* 19:59–62.

Granberg, Donald, and James Burlison. 1983. "The Abortion Issue in the 1980 Elections." *Family Planning Perspectives* 15:231–238.

Granberg, Donald, and Beth Wellman Granberg. 1981. "Pro-Life versus Pro-Choice: Another Look at the Abortion Controversy in the U.S." *Sociology and Social Research* 65:424–433.

Greeley, Andrew M. 1977. "How Conservative Are American Catholics?" *Political Science Quarterly* 92:199–218.

———. 1982. *Religion: A Secular Theory*. New York: Free Press.

———. 1985. *American Catholics Since the Council: An Unauthorized Report*. Chicago: Thomas More.

———. 1988. "Evidence That a Maternal Image of God Correlates With Liberal Politics." *Sociology and Social Research* 72:150–154.

———. 1989. *Religious Change in America*. Cambridge: Harvard University Press.

———. 1991. "Religion and Attitudes Toward AIDS Policy." *Sociology and Social Research* 75:126–132.

———. 1993. "Religion and Attitudes Toward the Environment." *Journal for the Scientific Study of Religion* 32:19–28.

Greeley, Andrew, and Gregory Baum, eds. 1973. *The Persistence of Religion*. Concilium—Religion in the Seventies. New York: Herder and Herder.

Green, John C. 1993. "Pat Robertson and the Latest Crusade: Religious Resources and the 1988 Presidential Campaign." *Social Science Quarterly* 74:157–168.

Green, John C., and James L. Guth. 1988. "The Christian Right in the Republican Party: The Case of Pat Robertson's Supporters." *Journal of Politics* 50:150–168.

———. 1991. "The Bible and the Ballot Box: The Shape of Things to Come." In *The Bible and the Ballot Box,* ed. James L. Guth and John C. Green, 207–225. Boulder: Westview.

———. 1991. "Religion, Representatives, and Roll Calls." *Legislative Studies Quarterly* 16:571–584.

Green, John C., James L. Guth, and Kevin Hill. 1993. "Faith and Election: The Christian Right in Congressional Campaigns, 1978–1988." *Journal of Politics* 55:80–91.

Green, John C., James L. Guth, Lyman A. Kellstedt, and Corwin E. Smidt. 1993. *National Survey of American Evangelicals: Preliminary Report.* Akron, Ohio: Ray C. Bliss Institute of Applied Politics, University of Akron.

———. 1994. "The Characteristics of Christian Political Activists: An Interest Group Analysis." In *Christian Political Activism at the Crossroads,* ed. William R. Stevenson, 133–172. Lanham, Md.: University Press of America.

———. 1995. "Evangelical Realignment: The Political Power of the Christian Right." *Christian Century,* 5 July, 676–679.

Green, Steven K. 1991. "Evangelicals and the Becker Amendment: A Lesson in Church-State Moderation." *Journal of Church and State* 33:541–568.

Greenawalt, Kent. 1994. "The Participation of Religious Groups in Political Advocacy." *Journal of Church and State* 36:143–160.

Greer, Scott. 1961. "Catholic Voters and the Democratic Party." *Public Opinion Quarterly* 25:611–625.

Griffin, G. A., R. L. Gorsuch, and A. L. Davis. 1987. "A Cross-Cultural Investigation of Religious Orientation, Social Norms, and Prejudice." *Journal for the Scientific Study of Religion* 26:358–365.

Griffith, Ernest S., John Plamenatz, and J. Roland Pennock. 1956. "Cultural Prerequisites to a Successfully Functioning Democracy." *American Political Science Review* 50:101–137.

Grupp, Frederick W., and William M. Newman. 1973. "Political Ideology and Religious Preference: The John Birch Society and the Americans for Democratic Action." *Journal for the Scientific Study of Religion* 12:401–413.

Gurwitt, Rob. 1989. "The Christian Right Has Gained Political Power. Now What Does It Do?" *Governing* (October), 52–58.

Gusfield, Joseph. 1963. *Symbolic Crusade: Status Politics and the American Temperance Movement.* Urbana: University of Illinois Press.

Guth, James L. 1989a. "Pastoral Politics in the 1988 Election." Paper delivered at the annual meeting of the American Political Science Association, Atlanta.

———. 1989b. "Southern Baptists and the New Right." In *Religion in American Politics,* ed. Charles W. Dunn, 177–190. Washington, D.C.: CQ Press.

Guth, James L., and John C. Green. 1984. "Political Activists and Civil Liberties: The Case of Party and PAC Contributors." Paper delivered at the annual meeting of the Midwest Political Science Association, Chicago.

———. 1986. "Faith and Politics: Religion and Ideology Among Political Contributors." *American Politics Quarterly* 14:186–200.

———. 1990. "Politics in a New Key: Religiosity and Participation Among Political Activists." *Western Political Quarterly* 43:153–179.

———. 1993. "Salience: The Core Concept?" In *Rediscovering the Religious Factor in American Politics,* ed. David C. Leege and Lyman A. Kellstedt, 157–176. Armonk, N.Y.: M. E. Sharpe.

Guth, James L., John C. Green, Lyman A. Kellstedt, and Corwin E. Smidt. 1995. "Faith and the Environment: Religious Beliefs and Attitudes on Environmental Policy." *American Journal of Political Science* 39:364–382.

Guth, James L., John C. Green, Corwin E. Smidt, and Margaret M. Poloma. 1991. "Pulpits and Politics: The Protestant Clergy in the 1988 Presidential Election." In *The Bible and the Ballot Box,* ed. James L. Guth and John C. Green, 73–93. Boulder: Westview.

Guth, James L., Lyman A. Kellstedt, Corwin E. Smidt, and John C. Green. 1993. "Theological Perspectives and Environmentalism Among Religious Activists." *Journal for the Scientific Study of Religion* 32:373–382.

Guysenir, Maurice G. 1958. "Jewish Vote in Chicago." *Jewish Social Studies* 20:195–214.

Hadaway, C. Kirk, Penny Long Marler, and Mark Chaves. 1993. "What the Polls Don't Show: A Closer Look at U.S. Church Attendance." *American Sociological Review* 58:741–752.

Hadden, Jeffrey K. 1969. *The Gathering Storm in the Churches.* Garden City, N.Y.: Doubleday-Anchor.

———. 1987. "Toward Desacralizing Secularization Theory." *Social Forces* 65:587–611.

Hadden, Jeffrey K., and Raymond C. Rymph. 1971. "The Marching Ministers." In *Religion in Radical Transition,* ed. Jeffrey K. Hadden, 99–110. New Brunswick, N.J.: Transaction.

Hadden, Jeffrey K., and Charles Swann. 1981. *Prime-Time Preachers.* Reading, Mass.: Addison-Wesley.

Haeberle, Steven H. 1996. "Gay Men and Lesbians at City Hall." *Social Science Quarterly* 77:190–197.

Hahn, Dan F. 1984. "The Rhetoric of Jimmy Carter, 1976–1980." *Presidential Studies Quarterly* 14:265–288.

Haider-Markel, Donald P., and Kenneth J. Meier. 1996. "The Politics of Gay and Lesbian Rights: Expanding the Scope of Conflict." *Journal of Politics,* forthcoming.

Hall, Carla. 1985. "How a Philadelphia Preacher Won Converts to His Budget Gospel." *Washington Post Weekly Edition,* 10 June, 12–13.

Hall, Mitchell K. 1990. *Because of Their Faith: CALCAV and Religious Opposition to the Vietnam War.* New York: Columbia University Press.

Hallowell, John. 1951. *Religious Perspectives on College Teaching in Political Science.* New Haven, Conn.: Edward W. Hazen Foundation.

Hallum, Anne Motley. 1989. "Presbyterians As Political Amateurs." In *Religion in American Politics,* ed. Charles W. Dunn, 63–74. Washington, D.C.: CQ Press.

Hamilton, Charles V. 1972. *The Black Preacher in America.* New York: William Morrow.

Hamilton, Howard D. 1970. "Voting in Open Housing Referenda." *Social Science Quarterly* 51:715–729.

Hammond, John L. 1979. *The Politics of Benevolence: Revival Religion and American Voting Behavior.* Norwood, N.J.: Ablex.

Hammond, John M. 1974. "Revival Religion and Anti-Slavery Politics." *American Sociological Review* 39:175–186.

Hammond, Phillip E., and Eric M. Mazur. 1995. "Church, State, and the Dilemma of Conscience." *Journal of Church and State* 37:555–572.

Hammond, Phillip E., Mark A. Shibley, and Peter M. Solow. 1994. "Religion and Family Values in Presidential Voting." *Sociology of Religion* 55:277–290.

Hampson, Rick. 1995. "Immigrants and the Church: Who's Changing Whom?" *Gainesville Sun*, 1 November, 1G, 4G.

Hand, Carl M., and Kent D. Van Liere. 1984. "Religion, Mastery-Over-Nature, and Environmental Concern." *Social Forces* 63:555–570.

Handy, Robert T. 1984. *A Christian America?* Second ed. New York: Oxford University Press.

Hanna, Mary T. 1979. *Catholics and American Politics.* Cambridge: Harvard University Press.

———. 1984. "From Civil Religion to Prophetic Church: The Bishops and the Bomb." In *American Political Theology,* ed. Charles W. Dunn, 144–153. New York: Praeger.

———. 1985. "The Catholic Bishops' Pastoral Letter on Poverty." Paper delivered at the annual meeting of the American Political Science Association, New Orleans.

Hansen, Susan B. 1980. "State Implementation of Supreme Court Decisions: Abortion Rates Since *Roe v. Wade.*" *Journal of Politics* 72:372–395.

Harley, Brian, and Glenn Firebaugh. 1993. "Americans' Belief in an Afterlife: Trends Over the Past Two Decades." *Journal for the Scientific Study of Religion* 32:269–278.

Harris, Frederick C. 1994. "Something Within: Religion As a Mobilizer of African-American Political Activism." *Journal of Politics* 56:42–68.

Harris, Louis, and Bert E. Swanson. 1970. *Black-Jewish Relations in New York City.* New York: Praeger.

Harris, Richard J., and Edward W. Mills. 1985. "Religion, Values, and Attitudes to Abortion." *Journal for the Scientific Study of Religion* 24:137–154.

Harrison, Lawrence E. 1992. *Who Prospers? How Cultural Values Shape Economic and Political Success.* New York: Basic Books.

Hart, Roderick. 1977. *The Political Pulpit.* West Lafayette, Ind.: Purdue University Press.

Hart, Stephen. 1992. *What Does the Lord Require? How American Christians Think About Economic Justice.* New York: Oxford University Press.

Hastings, Philip K., and Dean R. Hoge. 1986. "Religious and Moral Attitude Trends Among College Students, 1948–84." *Social Forces* 65:370–376.

Hatch, Nathan O. 1990. "The Democratization of Christianity and the Character of American Politics." In *Religion and American Politics,* ed. Mark A. Noll, 92–120. New York: Oxford University Press.

Haughey, John C., ed. 1979. *Personal Values in Public Policy.* New York: Paulist.

Healy, James B. 1989. *Northern Ireland Dilemma: An American Irish Imperative.* New York: Peter Lang.

Heath, Anthony, Bridget Taylor, and Gabor Toka. 1993. "Religion, Morality and Politics." In *International Social Attitudes: The Tenth BSA Report,* ed. Roger Jowell, Lindsay Brook, and Lizanne Dowds, 49–80. Aldershot, England: Dartmouth.

Henriot, Peter. 1966. "The Coincidence of Political and Religious Attitudes." *Review of Religious Research* 8:50–58.

Henry, Charles P. 1990. *Culture and African American Politics.* Bloomington: Indiana University Press.

Henshaw, Stanley K., and Jane Silverman. 1988. "The Characteristics and Previous Contraceptive Use of U.S. Abortion Patients." *Family Planning Perspectives* 20:158–168.

Hero, Alfred O., Jr. 1973. *American Religious Groups View Foreign Policy: Trends in Rank-and-File Opinion, 1937–1969.* Durham, N.C.: Duke University Press.

Hertel, Bradley R., and Michael Hughes. 1987. "Religious Affiliation, Attendance, and Support for 'Pro-Family' Issues in the United States." *Social Forces* 65:858–882.

Hertzke, Allen D. 1988. *Representing God in Washington*. Knoxville: University of Tennessee Press.

———. 1989. "Pat Robertson's Crusade and the GOP: A Strategic Analysis." Paper delivered at the annual meeting of the Midwest Political Science Association, Chicago.

———. 1991. "An Assessment of the Mainline Churches Since 1945." In *The Role of Religion in the Making of Public Policy*, ed. James E. Wood Jr. and Derek Davis, 43–80. Waco, Texas: J. M. Dawson Institute of Church-State Studies, Baylor University.

———. 1993. *Echoes of Discontent: Jesse Jackson, Pat Robertson, and the Resurgence of Populism*. Washington, D.C.: CQ Press.

———. 1995. "Religion and the Republican Congress." *Extensions* 7–10.

Hibbs, Douglas A., Jr. 1982. "President Reagan's Mandate from the 1980 Elections: A Shift to the Right?" *American Politics Quarterly* 10:387–420.

Hill, Samuel S., and Dennis E. Owen. 1982. *The New Religious Political Right in America*. Nashville, Tenn.: Abingdon.

Himmelstein, Jerome. 1986. "The Social Bases of Antifeminism: Religious Networks and Culture." *Journal for the Scientific Study of Religion* 25:1–15.

Himmelstein, Jerome L., and James A. McRae Jr. 1984. "Social Conservatism, New Republicans, and the 1980 Election." *Public Opinion Quarterly* 48:592–605.

Hirsch, H. N. 1981. *The Enigma of Felix Frankfurter*. New York: Basic Books.

Hodgkinson, Virginia A., Murray S. Weitzman, and Arthur D. Kirsch. 1988. *From Belief to Commitment: The Activities and Finances of Religious Congregations in the United States*. Washington, D.C.: Independent Sector.

Hofman, Brenda D. 1986. "Political Theology: The Role of Organized Religion in the Anti-Abortion Movement." *Journal of Church and State* 28:225–248.

Hofrenning, Daniel. 1995. *In Washington but Not of It: The Prophetic Politics of Religious Lobbyists*. Philadelphia: Temple University Press.

Hofstadter, Richard. 1955. *The Age of Reform*. New York: Vintage.

———. 1965. *The Paranoid Style in American Politics*. New York: Vintage.

Hoge, Dean R., Benton Johnson, and Donald A. Luidens. 1995. "Types of Denominational Switching Among Protestant Young Adults." *Journal for the Scientific Study of Religion* 34:253–258.

Hoge, Dean R., and Ernesto Zulueta. 1984. "Salience As a Condition for Various Social Consequences of Religious Commitment." *Journal for the Scientific Study of Religion* 24:21–38.

Hollenbach, David, S.J. 1990. "Liberalism, Communitarianism, and the Bishops' Pastoral Letter on the Economy." In *Church Polity and American Politics*, ed. Mary C. Segers, 99–118. New York: Garland.

Holsworth, Robert D. 1989. *Let Your Life Speak: A Study of Politics, Religion, and Antinuclear Weapons Activism*. Madison: University of Wisconsin Press.

Hood, Ralph W., Jr., and Ronald J. Morris. 1985. "Boundary Maintenance, Social-Political Views, and Presidential Preference Among High and Low Fundamentalists." *Review of Religious Research* 27:134–145.

Hoopes, Townshend. 1973. *The Devil and John Foster Dulles*. Boston: Atlantic–Little Brown.

Hornblower, Margot. 1985. "Now a Suburb Grows in Brooklyn—and Without Federal Help." *Washington Post Weekly Edition*, 29 July, 31–32.

Horwitz, Robert H. 1977. "John Locke and the Preservation of Liberty: A Perennial Problem of Civic Education." In *The Moral Foundations of the American Republic,* ed. Robert Horwitz, 129–156. Charlottesville: University Press of Virginia.

Hougland, J. G., and J. A. Christenson. 1983. "Religion and Politics: The Relationship of Religious Participation to Political Efficacy and Involvement." *Sociology and Social Research* 67:405–420.

Howe, Daniel Walker. 1990. "Religion and Politics in the Antebellum North." In *Religion and American Politics,* ed. Mark A. Noll, 121–145. New York: Oxford University Press.

Huckfeldt, Robert, Eric Plutzer, and John C. Sprague. 1993. "Alternative Contexts of Political Behavior: Churches, Neighborhoods, and Individuals." *Journal of Politics* 55:365–381.

Hudson, Winthrop S. 1965. "John Locke: Heir of Puritan Political Theories." In *Calvinism and the Political Order,* ed. George L. Hunt, 108–129. Philadelphia: Westminster.

Hughes, D. L., and Charles W. Peek. 1986. "Ladies Against Women: Explaining the Political Participation of Traditional and Modern-Role Females." *Political Behavior* 8:158–174.

Hughey, Michael W. 1984. "The Political Covenant: Protestant Foundations of the American State." *State, Culture, and Society* 1:113–156.

Hunt, Larry L., and Janet G. Hunt. 1977. "Black Religion As Both Opiate and Inspiration of Civil Rights Militance: Putting Marx's Data to the Test." *Social Forces* 56:1–14.

Hunter, James Davison. 1983a. *American Evangelicalism: Conservative Religion and the Quandary of Modernity.* New Brunswick, N.J.: Rutgers University Press.

———. 1983b. "The Liberal Reaction." In *The New Christian Right,* ed. Robert C. Liebman and Robert Wuthnow, 150–167. New York: Aldine.

———. 1991. *Culture Wars: The Struggle to Define America.* New York: Basic Books.

Hutcheson, John D., and George A. Taylor. 1973. "Religious Variables, Political System Characteristics, and Policy Outputs in the American States." *American Journal of Political Science* 17:414–421.

Hutchison, William R. 1993. *Errand to the World: American Protestant Thought and Foreign Missions.* Chicago: University of Chicago Press.

Iannaccone, Laurence R. 1993. "Heirs to the Protestant Ethic? The Economics of American Fundamentalism." In *Fundamentalisms and the State,* ed. Martin E. Marty and R. Scott Appleby, 342–366. Chicago: University of Chicago Press.

IEA and Roper Center. 1982. "Theology Faculty Survey." *This World* 1:27–108.

Inkeles, Alex. 1983. *Exploring Individual Modernity.* Cambridge: Harvard University Press.

International Social Survey Program. 1994. *International Social Survey Program: Religion, 1991.* Ann Arbor, Mich.: Inter-University Consortium for Political and Social Research.

Irvine, William P. 1974. "Explaining the Religious Basis of the Canadian Partisan Identity: Success on the Third Try." *Canadian Journal of Political Science* 7:560–563.

Ivers, Gregg. 1995. *To Build a Wall: American Jews and the Separation of Church and State.* Charlottesville: University Press of Virginia.

Jacobson, Cardell K., Tim B. Heaton, and Rutledge M. Dennis. 1990. "Black-White Differences in Religiosity: Item Analyses and a Formal Structural Test." *Sociological Analysis* 51:257–270.

Jaffe, Frederick S., Barbara Lindheim, and Philip R. Lee, eds. 1981. *Abortion Politics: Private Morality and Public Policy*. New York: McGraw-Hill.

Jeffries, Vincent, and Clarence Tygart. 1974. "The Influence of Theological Denomination and Values Upon the Positions of Clergy on Social Issues." *Journal for the Scientific Study of Religion* 13:309–313.

Jelen, Ted G. 1984. "Respect for Life, Sexual Morality, and Opposition to Abortion." *Review of Religious Research* 25:220–231.

———. 1987. "The Effects of Religious Separatism on White Protestants in the 1984 Presidential Election." *Sociological Analysis* 48:30–45.

———. 1992. "Political Christianity: A Contextual Analysis." *American Journal of Political Science* 36:692–714.

———. 1993. "The Political Consequences of Religious Group Attitudes." *Journal of Politics* 55:178–190.

———. 1994a. "Protestant Clergy As Political Leaders: Theological Limitations." *Review of Religious Research* 36:23–42.

———. 1994b. "Religion and Foreign Policy Attitudes: Exploring the Effects of Denomination and Doctrine." *American Politics Quarterly* 22:382–400.

Jelen, Ted G., Corwin E. Smidt, and Clyde Wilcox. 1993. "The Political Effects of the Born-Again Phenomenon." In *Rediscovering the Religious Factor in American Politics*, ed. David C. Leege and Lyman A. Kellstedt, 199–215. Armonk, N.Y.: M. E. Sharpe.

Jelen, Ted G., and Clyde Wilcox. 1992. "The Effects of Religious Self-Identification on Support for the New Christian Right: An Analysis of Political Activists." *Social Science Journal* 29:199–210.

———. 1993. "Preaching to the Converted: The Causes and Consequences of Viewing Religious Television." In *Rediscovering the Religious Factor in American Politics*, ed. David C. Leege and Lyman A. Kellstedt, 255–269. Armonk, N.Y.: M. E. Sharpe.

Jenkinson, Edward B. 1979. *Censors in the Classroom*. New York: Avon.

Jensen, Richard. 1980. "Armies, Admen, and Crusaders: Strategies to Win Elections." *Public Opinion* 3:44–53.

John, Richard R. 1990. "Taking Sabbatarianism Seriously: The Postal System, the Sabbath, and the Transformation of American Political Culture." *Journal of the Early Republic* 10:517–567.

Johnson, Benton. 1962. "Ascetic Protestantism and Political Preference." *Public Opinion Quarterly* 26:35–46.

———. 1964. "Ascetic Protestantism and Political Preference in the Deep South." *American Journal of Sociology* 69:359–366.

———. 1966. "Theology and Party Preference Among Protestant Clergymen." *American Sociological Review* 31:200–208.

———. 1967. "Theology and the Position of Pastors on Public Issues." *American Sociological Review* 32:433–442.

Johnson, Benton, and Richard H. White. 1967. "Protestantism, Political Preference, and the Nature of Religious Influence: Comment on Anderson's Paper." *Review of Religious Research* 9:28–35.

Johnson, Charles A. 1976. "Political Culture in American States: Elazar's Formulation Examined." *American Journal of Political Science* 20:491–509.

Johnson, Haynes. 1986. "The Ambassador for Christ Race." *Washington Post Weekly Edition*, 13 October, 24.

Johnson, Haynes, and Thomas B. Edsall. 1984. "North Carolina's Three Rs: Race, Religion, and Registration." *Washington Post Weekly Edition*, 15 October, 12–13.

Johnson, Richard M. 1967. *The Dynamics of Compliance: Supreme Court Decision-Making from a New Perspective*. Evanston, Ill.: Northwestern University Press.

Johnson, Stephen D. 1986. "The Role of the Black Church in Black Civil Rights Movements." In *The Political Role of Religion in the United States*, ed. Stephen D. Johnson and Joseph B. Tamney, 307–324. Boulder: Westview.

———. 1994."What Relates to Vote for Three Religious Categories?" *Sociology of Religion* 55:263–275.

Johnson, Stephen D., and Joseph B. Tamney. 1988. "Factors Related to Inconsistent Life-Views." *Review of Religious Research* 30:40–46.

Johnson, Stephen D., Joseph B. Tamney, and Ronald Burton. 1989. "Pat Robertson: Who Supported His Candidacy for President?" *Journal for the Scientific Study of Religion* 28:387–399.

Johnston, Michael. 1983. "Corruption and Political Culture in America: An Empirical Perspective." *Publius* 13:19–39.

Joliceur, Pamela M., and Louis K. Knowles. 1978. "Fraternal Organizations and Civil Religion: Scottish Rite Freemasonry." *Review of Religious Research* 20:3–22.

Jones, Ethel B. 1983. "ERA Voting: Labor Force Attachment, Marriage, and Religion." *Journal of Legal Studies* 12:157–168.

Jost, Kenneth. 1994. "Religion and Politics: What Impact Will the Religious Right Have on Politics." *CQ Researcher* 4:891–907.

Judis, John B. 1994. "Crosses to Bear: The Many Faces of the Christian Right." *New Republic*, 12 September, 21–25.

Jung, Patricia Beattie, and Thomas A. Shannon, eds. 1988. *Abortion and Catholicism: The American Debate*. New York: Crossroads.

Kamin, Leon J. 1958. "Ethnic and Party Affiliations of Candidates As Determinants of Voting." *Canadian Journal of Psychology* 12:205–212.

Kanagy, Conrad, and Fern Willits. 1993. "A 'Greening' of Religion? Some Evidence from a Pennsylvania Sample." *Social Science Quarterly* 74:674–683.

Kaplan, Norman. 1969. "Reference Groups and Interest Group Theories of Voting." In *Readings in Reference Group Theory and Research*, ed. Herbert H. Hyman and Eleanor Singer, 461–472. New York: Free Press.

Katz, Ellis. 1965. "Patterns of Compliance With the *Schempp* Decision." *Journal of Public Law* 14:396–408.

Katznelson, Ira. 1976. *Black Men, White Cities*. Chicago: University of Chicago Press.

Kelley, Dean M. 1977. *Why Conservative Churches Are Growing*. Second ed. San Francisco: Harper and Row.

———, ed. 1982. *Government Intervention in Religious Affairs*. New York: Pilgrim.

Kellstedt, Lyman A. 1989a. "Evangelicals and Political Realignment." In *Contemporary Evangelical Political Involvement: An Analysis and Assessment*, ed. Corwin E. Smidt, 99–118. Lanham, Md.: University Press of America.

———. 1989b. "The Falwell Issue Agenda: Sources of Support Among White Protestant Evangelicals." In *Research in the Social Scientific Study of Religion*, ed. Monte L. Lynn and David O. Moberg, 109–132. Greenwich, Conn.: JAI.

Kellstedt, Lyman A., and John C. Green. 1993. "Knowing God's Many People: Denominational Preferences and Political Behavior." In *Rediscovering the Religious Factor in American Politics*, ed. David C. Leege and Lyman A. Kellstedt, 53–71. Armonk, N.Y.: M. E. Sharpe.

Kellstedt, Lyman A., John C. Green, James L. Guth, and Corwin E. Smidt. 1994. "Religious Voting Blocs in the 1992 Election: The Year of the Evangelical?" *Sociology of Religion* 55:307–326.

Kellstedt, Lyman A., and Mark A. Noll. 1990. "Religion, Voting for President, and Party Identification, 1948–1984." In *Religion and American Politics*, ed. Mark A. Noll, 355–379. New York: Oxford University Press.

Kellstedt, Lyman A., and Corwin Smidt. 1991. "Measuring Fundamentalism: An Analysis of Different Operational Strategies." *Journal for the Scientific Study of Religion* 30:259–278.

———. 1993. "Doctrinal Beliefs and Political Behavior: Views of the Bible." In *Rediscovering the Religious Factor in American Politics*, ed. David C. Leege and Lyman A. Kellstedt, 177–198. Armonk, N.Y.: M. E. Sharpe.

Kennan, George F. 1951. *American Diplomacy, 1900–1950*. Chicago: University of Chicago Press.

Kennedy, Eugene. 1985. *Reimagining American Catholicism*. New York: Vintage.

Kennedy, John W. 1994. "Mixing Politics and Piety: Christian Talk Radio." *Christianity Today*, 15 August, 42–47.

Kennedy, Morehead. 1985. *The Ayatollah in the Cathedral*. New York: Hill and Wang.

Kenyon, Cecelia. 1955. "Men of Little Faith: The Anti-Federalists on the Nature of Representative Government." *William and Mary Quarterly* 12:3–43.

Kersten, Lawrence K. 1970. *The Lutheran Ethic*. Detroit: Wayne State University Press.

Kessel, John H. 1966. "Public Perceptions of the Supreme Court." *Midwest Journal of Political Science* 10:167–191.

Kessler, Sanford. 1992. "Tocqueville's Puritans: Christianity and the American Founding." *Journal of Politics* 54:776–791.

Keysar, Ariela, and Barry A. Kosmin. 1995. "The Impact of Religious Identification on Differences in Educational Attainment Among American Women in 1990." *Journal for the Scientific Study of Religion* 34:49–62.

King, Martin Luther, Jr. 1963. *Strength to Love*. New York: Harper and Row.

Kirby, James C. 1977. "*Everson* to *Meek* and *Roemer*: From Separation to Detente in Church-State Relations." *North Carolina Law Review* 55:563–575.

Kirkpatrick, Lee. 1993. "Fundamentalism, Christian Orthodoxy, and Intrinsic Religious Orientations As Predictors of Discriminatory Attitudes." *Journal for the Scientific Study of Religion* 32:256–268.

Kirwin, Harry W., ed. 1959. *The Search for Democracy*. Garden City, N.Y.: Doubleday-Christendom.

Klatch, Rebecca E. 1988. "The New Right and Its Women." *Society* 25:30–38.

Kleppner, Paul. 1970. *The Cross of Culture*. New York: Free Press.

———. 1979. *The Third Electoral System*. Chapel Hill: University of North Carolina Press.

———. 1985. *Chicago Divided: The Making of a Black Mayor*. DeKalb: Northern Illinois University Press.

Klineberg, Otto. 1950. *Tensions Affecting International Understanding: A Survey of Research*. New York: Social Science Research Council.

Klingman, David, and William W. Lammers. 1984. "The 'General Policy Liberalism' Factor in American State Politics." *American Journal of Political Science* 28:598–610.

Knoke, David. 1974. "Religious Involvement and Political Behavior: A Log-Linear Analysis of White Americans, 1952–1968." *Sociological Quarterly* 15:51–65.

———. 1976. *Change and Continuity in American Politics: The Social Bases of Political Parties*. Baltimore: The Johns Hopkins University Press.

Kobylka, Joseph F. 1995. "The Mysterious Case of Establishment Clause Litigation: How Organized Litigants Foiled Legal Change." In *Contemplating Courts*, ed. Lee Epstein, 93–128. Washington, D.C.: CQ Press.

Koller, Norman B., and Joseph D. Retzer. 1980. "The Sounds of Silence Revisited." *Sociological Analysis* 41:155–161.

Kondos, Elena M. 1992. "The Law and Christian Science Healing for Children: A Pathfinder." *Legal Reference Services Quarterly* 12:5–71.

Kornhauser, William. 1959. *The Politics of Mass Society*. Glencoe, Ill.: Free Press.

Kosmin, Barry A., and Seymour P. Lachman. 1993. *One Nation Under God? Religion in Contemporary American Society*. New York: Harmony.

Kurland, Philip B. 1995. "Of Faith and Freedom." In *All Imaginable Liberty: The Religious Liberty Clauses of the First Amendment*, ed. Francis Graham Lee, 147–166. Lanham, Md.: University Press of America.

Lacayo, Richard. 1991. "Crusading Against the Pro-Choice Movement (interview of Randall Terry)." *Time*, 21 October, 26.

Kurtz, Howard. 1985. "Opposition to Reagan's Choice for Legal Policy Is Mounting." *Washington Post Weekly Edition*, 5 August, 34.

Ladd, Everett Carll. 1982. *Where Have All the Voters Gone?* Second ed. New York: Norton.

———. 1989. "Trouble for Both Parties." *Public Opinion* 12:3–8.

Laitin, David D. 1978. "Religion, Political Culture, and the Weberian Tradition." *World Politics* 30:563–592.

Langenbach, Lisa. 1989. "Evangelical Elites and Political Action: The Pat Robertson Presidential Candidacy." *Journal of Political and Military Sociology* 17:291–304.

Laumann, Edward O., and David R. Segal. 1971. "Status Inconsistency and Ethnoreligious Group Membership As Determinants of Social Participation and Political Attitudes." *American Journal of Sociology* 77:36–61.

Laycock, Douglas. 1986. "The Right to Church Autonomy As Part of Free Exercise of Religion." In *Government Intervention in Religious Affairs, II*, ed. Dean M. Kelley, 28–39. New York: Pilgrim.

Layman, Geoffrey C., and Edward G. Carmines. 1994. "The Impact of Cultural Cleavages on American Political Behavior: A Comparison of Competing Notions of Cultural Conflict." Typescript, Department of Political Science, University of Indiana.

Lazarsfeld, Paul F., Bernard Berelson, and Hazel Gaudet. 1948. *The People's Choice: How the Voter Makes Up His Mind in a Presidential Campaign*. New York: Columbia University Press.

Lazerwitz, Bernard, J. Allen Winter, and Arnold Dashefsky. 1988. "Localism, Religiosity, Orthodoxy, and Liberalism: The Case of Jews in the United States." *Social Forces* 67:229–242.

Leak, Gary K., and Brandy A. Randall. 1995. "Clarification of the Link Between Right-Wing Authoritarianism and Religiousness: The Role of Religious Maturity." *Journal for the Scientific Study of Religion* 34:245–252.

Leege, David C. 1988. "Catholics and Civic Order: Parish Participation, Politics, and Civic Participation." *Review of Politics* 50:704–736.

———. 1989. "Toward a Mental Measure of Religiosity in Research on Religion and Politics." In *Religion and Political Behavior in the United States*, ed. Ted G. Jelen, 45–64. New York: Praeger.

Leege, David C., and Lyman A. Kellstedt, eds. 1993. *Rediscovering the Religious Factor in American Politics*. Armonk, N.Y.: M. E. Sharpe.

Leege, David C., Joel A. Lieske, and Kenneth D. Wald. 1991. "Toward Cultural Theories of American Political Behavior: Religion, Ethnicity and Race, and Class Outlook." In *Political Science: Looking to the Future*, ed. William Crotty, 193–238. Evanston, Ill.: Northwestern University Press.

Leege, David C., and Michael R. Welch. 1989. "Religious Roots of Political Orientations: Variations Among American Catholic Parishioners." *Journal of Politics* 50:137–162.

Legge, Jerome S. 1985. "Self-Interest Versus Symbolic Politics: The Formulation of Attitudes Toward Abortion Policy." Paper delivered at the annual meeting of the Southern Political Science Association, Nashville, Tennessee.

———. 1995. "Explaining Jewish Liberalism in the United States: An Exploration of Socioeconomic, Religious, and Communal Living Variables." *Social Science Quarterly* 76:124–141.

Lehr, Elizabeth, and Bernard Spilka. 1989. "Religion in the Introductory Psychology Textbook: A Comparison of Three Decades." *Journal for the Scientific Study of Religion* 28:366–371.

Lenski, Gerhard. 1963. *The Religious Factor*. Garden City, N.Y.: Doubleday-Anchor.

Le Poire, Beth A., Carol K. Sigelman, Lee Sigelman, and Henry C. Kenski. 1990. "Who Wants to Quarantine Persons With AIDS?" *Social Science Quarterly* 71:239–249.

Lerner, Robert, Althea K. Nagai, and Stanley Rothman. 1989. "Marginality and Liberalism Among Jewish Elites." *Public Opinion Quarterly* 53:330–352.

Lerner, Robert, Stanley Rothman, and S. Robert Lichter. 1989. "Christian Religious Elites." *Public Opinion* 11:54–58.

Leuchtenburg, William E. 1958. *The Perils of Prosperity, 1914–1932*. Chicago: University of Chicago Press.

Leventman, Paula Goldman, and Seymour Leventman. 1976. "Congressman Drinan, S.J., and His Jewish Constituents." *American Jewish Historical Quarterly* 66:215–248.

Levine, Lawrence W. 1975. *Defender of the Faith: William Jennings Bryan, The Last Decade, 1915–1925*. New York: Oxford University Press.

Levinson, Sanford. 1988. *Constitutional Faith*. Princeton, N.J.: Princeton University Press.

Levy, Leonard W. 1986. *The Establishment Clause: Religion and the First Amendment*. New York: Macmillan.

Lichtman, Allan J. 1979. *Prejudice and the Old Politics: The Presidential Election of 1928*. Chapel Hill: University of North Carolina Press.

Liebman, Arthur. 1979. *Jews and the Left*. New York: Wiley Interscience.

Liebman, Charles S. 1973. *The Ambivalent American Jew*. Philadelphia: Jewish Publication Society.

———. 1988. *Deceptive Images*. New Brunswick, N.J.: Transaction.

Liebman, Charles S., and Steven M. Cohen. 1990. *Two Worlds of Judaism: The Israeli and American Experiences*. New Haven, Conn.: Yale University Press.

Liebman, Robert C. 1983. "Mobilizing the Moral Majority." In *The New Christian Right*, ed. Robert C. Liebman and Robert Wuthnow, 50–73. New York: Aldine.

Lienesch, Michael. 1993. *Redeeming America: Piety and Politics in the New Christian Right*. Chapel Hill: University of North Carolina Press.

Lijphart, Arend. 1971. "Class Voting and Religious Voting in the European Democracies." Glasgow, Scotland: Survey Research Centre, University of Strathclyde.

Lincoln, Abraham. 1959a. "The Gettysburg Address." In *The Search for Democracy*. Edited by Harry W. Kirwin, 102–103. Garden City, N.Y.: Doubleday-Anchor.

———. 1959b. "Second Inaugural Address." In *The Search for Democracy*. Edited by Harry W. Kirwin, 203–205. Garden City, N.Y.: Doubleday-Anchor.

Lincoln, C. Eric, and Lawrence H. Mamiya. 1990. *The Black Church in the African American Experience*. Durham, N.C.: Duke University Press.

Lipset, Seymour Martin. 1960. *Political Man*. Garden City, N.Y.: Doubleday-Anchor.

———. 1964. "Three Decades of the Radical Right: Coughlinites, McCarthyites, and Birchers." In *The Radical Right*, ed. Daniel Bell, 373–446. Garden City, N.Y.: Doubleday-Anchor.

———. 1967. *The First New Nation*. Garden City, N.Y.: Doubleday-Anchor.

———. 1985. "Most Jews Are Still Both Democratic and Liberal." *Washington Post Weekly Edition*, 14 January, 22–23.

Lipset, Seymour Martin, and Earl Raab. 1981. "The Election and the Evangelicals." *Commentary* 71:25–31.

Lipsitz, Lewis. 1964. "Work Life and Political Attitudes: A Study of Manual Workers." *American Political Science Review* 58:951–962.

———. 1968. "If, As Verba Says, the State Functions As a Religion, What Are We to Do Then to Save Our Souls?" *American Political Science Review* 62:527–535.

Littell, Franklin H. 1970. "The Radical Reformation and Revolution." In *Marxism and Radical Religion*, ed. John C. Raines and Thomas Dean, 81–100. Philadelphia: Temple University Press.

Lorentzen, Louise J. 1980. "Evangelical Life-Style Concerns Expressed in Political Action." *Sociological Analysis* 41:144–154.

Lorinskas, Robert A., Brett W. Hawkins, and Stephen D. Edwards. 1969. "The Persistence of Ethnic Voting in Urban and Rural Areas: Results from the Controlled Elections Method." *Social Science Quarterly* 49:891–899.

Lubell, Samuel. 1965. *The Future of American Politics*. Third ed. New York: Harper and Row.

Luebke, Paul. 1985–86. "Grass-Roots Organizing: The Hidden Side of the 1984 Helms Campaign." *Election Politics* 3:30–33.

Luker, Kristin. 1984. *Abortion and the Politics of Motherhood*. Berkeley and Los Angeles: University of California Press.

Lupfer, Michael, and Kenneth D. Wald. 1985. "An Exploration of Adults' Religious Orientations and Their Philosophies of Human Nature." *Journal for the Scientific Study of Religion* 24:293–304.

Lutz, Donald S. 1984. "The Relative Influence of European Writers Upon Late 18th-Century American Political Thought." *American Political Science Review* 78:189–197.

———. 1994. "The Evolution of Covenant Form and Content As the Basis for Early American Political Culture." In *Covenant in the Nineteenth Century*, ed. Daniel J. Elazar, 31–48. Lanham, Md.: Rowman and Littlefield.

Lynd, Robert S., and Helen Merrell Lynd. 1929. *Middletown: A Study in Contemporary American Culture*. New York: Harcourt, Brace.

Macaluso, Theodore F., and John Wanat. 1979. "Voting Turnout and Religiosity." *Polity* 12:158–169.

Machovec, Milan. 1976. *A Marxist Looks at Jesus*. Philadelphia: Fortress.

MacIver, Martha Abele. 1990. "Mirror Images? Conceptions of God and Political Duty on the Left and Right of the Evangelical Spectrum." *Sociological Analysis* 51:287–295.

Maddox, William S. 1979. "Changing Electoral Coalitions from 1952 to 1976." *Social Science Quarterly* 60:309–313.

Maddox, William S., and Stuart A. Lilie. 1984. *Beyond Liberal and Conservative.* Washington, D.C.: Cato Institute.

Madison, Christopher. 1984. "Mondale Walks Tightrope to Hold Black Support Without Risking Jewish Vote." *National Journal,* 8 September, 1654–1658.

Madron, Thomas W., Hart M. Nelsen, and Raytha L. Yokeley. 1974. "Religion As a Determinant of Militancy and Political Participation Among Black Americans." *American Behavioral Scientist* 17:783–796.

Maguire, Daniel C. 1982. *The New Subversives: Anti-Americanism of the Religious Right.* New York: Continuum.

Malbin, Michael. 1986. "Jewish PACs: A New Force in Jewish Political Action." *Jerusalem Newsletter,* no. 90.

Maller, Allen S. 1977. "Class Factors in the Jewish Vote." *Jewish Social Studies* 39:159–162.

Manwaring, David R. 1962. *Render Unto Caesar: The Flag Salute Controversy.* Chicago: University of Chicago Press.

Margolis, Michael, and Kevin Neary. 1980. "Pressure Politics Revisited: The Anti-Abortion Campaign." *Policy Studies Journal* 8:698–716.

Marshall, Susan E. 1990. "Equity Issues and Black-White Differences in Women's ERA Support." *Social Science Quarterly* 71:299–314.

Martinson, Oscar B., and E. A. Wilkening. 1987. "Religious Participation and Involvement in Local Politics Throughout the Life Cycle." *Sociological Focus* 20:309–318.

Marty, Martin E. 1984. *Pilgrims in Their Own Land.* Boston: Little, Brown.

Marty, Martin E., and R. Scott Appleby. 1992. *The Glory and the Power: The Fundamentalist Challenge to the Modern World.* Boston: Beacon.

Marty, William R. 1980. "The Search for Realism in Politics and Ethics: Reflections by a Political Scientist on a Christian Perspective." *Logos* 1:93–124.

Marx, Gary T. 1967. *Protest and Prejudice: A Study of Belief in the Black Community.* New York: Harper and Row.

Mathews, Donald G., and Jane S. De Hart. 1990. *Sex, Gender, and the Politics of ERA.* New York: Oxford University Press.

Matthews, Donald R., and James W. Prothro. 1966. *Negroes and the New Southern Politics.* New York: Harcourt, Brace, and World.

May, Henry. 1976. *The Enlightenment in America.* New York: Oxford University Press.

Mazlish, Bruce, and Edward Diamond. 1979. *Jimmy Carter: A Character Portrait.* New York: Simon and Schuster.

McAneny, Leslie, and David W. Moore. 1994. "Annual Honesty and Ethics Poll." *Gallup Poll Monthly,* no. 349:2–4.

McClosky, Herbert. 1958. "Conservatism and Personality." *American Political Science Review* 52:27–45.

McClosky, Herbert, and John Zaller. 1984. *The American Ethos.* Cambridge: Harvard University Press.

McDaniel, Stephen W. 1989. "The Use of Marketing Techniques by Churches: A National Survey." *Review of Religious Research* 31:175–182.

McDonough, Peter. 1994. "On Hierarchies of Conflict and the Possibility of Civil Discourse: Variations on a Theme by John Courtney Murray." *Journal of Church and State* 36:115–142.

McDonough, Peter, Samuel H. Barnes, and Antonio Lopez Pina. 1984. "Authority and Association: Spanish Democracy in Comparative Perspective." *Journal of Politics* 46:652–688.

McIntosh, William A., Letitia T. Alston, and John P. Alston. 1979. "The Differential Impact of Religious Preference and Church Attendance on Attitudes Toward Abortion." *Review of Religious Research* 20:195–213.

McNamara, Patrick H. 1992. *Conscience First, Tradition Second: A Study of Young American Catholics.* Albany: State University of New York Press.

Mead, Sidney E. 1974. "The 'Nation With the Soul of a Church'." In *American Civil Religion,* ed. Russell Richey and Donald G. Jones, 45–75. New York: Harper and Row.

———. 1976. *The Lively Experiment: The Shaping of Christianity in America.* New York: Harper and Row.

Meconis, Charles A. 1979. *With Clumsy Grace: The American Catholic Left, 1961–1975.* New York: Seabury.

Medding, Peter Y. 1989. *The Transformation of American Jewish Politics.* New York: American Jewish Committee.

Medoff, Marshall H. 1986. "Determinants of the Political Participation of Women." *Public Choice* 48:245–253.

Meier, Kenneth J. 1994. *The Politics of Sin: Drugs, Alcohol, and Public Policy.* Armonk, N.Y.: M. E. Sharpe.

Meier, Kenneth J., and Cathy M. Johnson. 1990. "The Politics of Demon Rum: Regulating Alcohol and Its Deleterious Consequences." *American Politics Quarterly* 18:404–429.

Meier, Kenneth J., and Deborah R. McFarlane. 1993. "The Politics of Funding Abortion: State Responses to the Political Environment." *American Politics Quarterly* 21:83–101.

Menendez, Albert J. 1977. *Religion at the Polls.* Philadelphia: Westminster.

———. 1993. *The December Wars: Religious Symbols and Ceremonies in the Public Square.* Buffalo, N.Y.: Prometheus.

Mernissi, Fatima. 1992. *Islam and Democracy: Fear of the Modern World.* Reading, Mass.: Addison-Wesley.

Merton, Andrew H. 1981. *Enemies of Choice: The Right-to-Life Movement and Its Threat to Abortion.* Boston: Beacon.

Meyer, Donald B. 1961. *The Protestant Search for Political Realism, 1919–1941.* Berkeley and Los Angeles: University of California Press.

Milgram, Stanley. 1974. *Obedience to Authority.* New York: Harper and Row.

Miller, Abraham. 1974. "Ethnicity and Party Identification: Continuation of a Theoretical Dialogue." *Western Political Quarterly* 27:470–490.

Miller, Arthur H. 1993. "Social Groups As Symbols in Presidential Campaigns." In *Presidential Campaigns and American Self Images,* ed. Arthur H. Miller and Bruce E. Gronbeck, 190–213. Boulder: Westview.

Miller, Arthur H., and Martin P. Wattenberg. 1984. "Politics from the Pulpit: Religiosity and the 1980 Elections." *Public Opinion Quarterly* 48:301–317.

Miller, Perry. 1956. *Errand into the Wilderness.* Cambridge: Harvard University Press.

———. 1967. *Nature's Nation.* Cambridge: Harvard University Press.

Miller, Robert T., and Ronald B. Flowers, eds. 1987. *Toward Benevolent Neutrality: Church, State, and the Supreme Court.* Third ed. Waco, Texas: Baylor University Press.

Miller, Warren E., and Teresa E. Levitin. 1976. *Leadership and Change: Presidential Elections from 1952 to 1976.* Cambridge: Winthrop.

Miller, Warren E., Arthur H. Miller, and Edward J. Schneider. 1980. *American National Election Studies Data Sourcebook, 1952–1978*. Cambridge: Harvard University Press.

Miller, William Lee. 1961. "American Religion and American Political Attitudes." In *Religious Perspectives in American Culture,* ed. James Ward Smith and A. Leland Jamison, 81–118. Princeton, N.J.: Princeton University Press.

Mills, Samuel A. 1991. "Abortion and Religious Freedom: The Religious Coalition for Abortion Rights (RCAR) and the Pro-Choice Movement, 1973–1989." *Journal of Church and State* 33:569–594.

Moen, Matthew C. 1984. "School Prayer and the Politics of Life-Style Concern." *Social Science Quarterly* 65:1065–1071.

———. 1988. "Status Politics and the Political Agenda of the Christian Right." *Sociological Quarterly* 29:429–437.

———. 1989. *The Christian Right and Congress.* Tuscaloosa: University of Alabama Press.

———. 1995. "From Revolution to Evolution: The Changing Nature of the Christian Right." In *The Rapture of Politics,* ed. Steve Bruce, Peter Kivisto, and William H. Swatos Jr., 123–136. New Brunswick, N.J.: Transaction.

Monsma, Stephen V. 1977. "The Oval Office: Three Models for a Christian." *Christianity Today,* 21 January, 28–29.

———. 1993. *Positive Neutrality: Letting Religious Freedom Ring.* Westport, Conn.: Greenwood.

Mooney, Christopher Z., and Mei-Hsien Lee. 1995. "Legislating Morality in the American States: The Case of Pre-*Roe* Abortion Restrictions." *American Journal of Political Science* 39:599–627.

Moore, David W. 1993. "Catholics at Odds With Church Teachings." *Gallup Poll Monthly,* no. 335:21–40.

Moore, R. Laurence. 1994. *Selling God: Religion in the Marketplace of Culture.* New York: Oxford University Press.

Morgan, David R., and Kenneth J. Meier. 1980. "Politics and Morality: The Effect of Religion on Referenda Voting." *Social Science Quarterly* 61:144–148.

Morgan, David R., and Sheilah S. Watson. 1991. "Political Culture, Political System Characteristics, and Public Policies Among the American States." *Publius* 21:31–48.

Morgan, David T. 1995. *The New Crusades, The New Holy Land: Conflict in the Southern Baptist Convention, 1969–1991.* Tuscaloosa: University of Alabama Press.

Morgan, Richard E. 1968. *The Politics of Religious Conflict.* New York: Pegasus.

Morgan, Richard E. 1984. *Disabling America.* New York: Basic.

Morgenthau, Hans, and David Hein. 1983. *Essays on Lincoln's Faith and Politics.* Lanham, Md.: University Press of America.

Morris, Aldon. 1981. "Black Southern Student Sit-In Movement: An Analysis of Internal Organization." *American Sociological Review* 46:744–767.

———. 1984. *The Origins of the Civil Rights Movement.* New York: Free Press.

Mueller, Carol. 1983. "In Search of a Constituency for the 'New Religious Right'." *Public Opinion Quarterly* 47:213–229.

Mueller, Carol, and Thomas Dimieri. 1982. "The Structure of Belief Systems Among Contending ERA Activists." *Social Forces* 60:657–675.

Mueller, John E. 1973. *Wars, Presidents, and Public Opinion.* New York: Free Press.

Muir, William K., Jr. 1967. *Prayer in the Public Schools: Law and Attitude Change.* Chicago: University of Chicago Press.

Muller, Herbert J. 1963. *Religion and Freedom in the Modern World*. Chicago: University of Chicago Press.

Murchland, Bernard. 1982. *The Dream of Christian Socialism: An Essay on Its European Origins*. Washington, D.C.: American Enterprise Institute.

Murphy, Walter F., Joseph Tanenhaus, and Daniel L. Kastner. 1973. *Public Evaluations of Constitutional Courts: Alternative Explanations*. Beverly Hills: Sage.

Murrin, John M. 1990. "Religion and Politics in America from the First Settlements to the Civil War." In *Religion and American Politics*, ed. Mark A. Noll, 19–43. New York: Oxford University Press.

Myers, Ken. 1994. "Professors at Evangelist's School Sue Over Defamation, Contracts." *National Law Journal*, 24 October, 17A.

Nagel, Stuart. 1961. "Political Party Affiliation and Judges' Decisions." *American Political Science Review* 55:843–850.

———. 1962. "Ethnic Affiliations and Judicial Propensities." *Journal of Politics* 24:92–110.

National Research Council. 1982. *Diet, Nutrition, and Cancer*. Washington, D.C.: National Academy Press.

Nazario, Sonia L. 1992. "Crusader Vows to Put God Back into Schools Using Local Elections." *Wall Street Journal*, 15 July, A1, A10.

Nelsen, Hart M. 1975. "Why Do Pastors Preach on Social Issues?" *Theology Today* 32:56–73.

Nelsen, Hart M., Thomas Madron, and Raytha L. Yokeley. 1975. "Black Religion's Promethean Motif: Orthodoxy and Militancy." *American Journal of Sociology* 81:139–148.

Nemeth, Roger J., and Donald A. Luidens. 1989. "The New Christian Right and Mainline Protestantism: The Case of the Reformed Church in America." *Sociological Analysis* 49:343–352.

Nesmith, Bruce. 1994. *The New Republican Coalition: The Reagan Campaigns and White Evangelicals*. New York: Peter Lang.

Neuhaus, Richard John. 1984. *The Naked Public Square*. Grand Rapids, Mich.: Eerdman's.

Newport, Frank. 1993. "Half of Americans Believe in Creationist Origin of Man." *Gallup Poll Monthly* (September), no. 336:24–28.

Newport, Frank, and Lydia Saad. 1994. "Confidence in Institutions." *Gallup Poll Monthly* (April), no. 343:5–6.

Nice, David C. 1988. "Abortion Clinic Bombings As Political Violence." *American Journal of Political Science* 32:178–195.

Nichols, J. Bruce. 1988. *The Uneasy Alliance: Religion, Refugee Work, and U.S. Foreign Policy*. New York: Oxford University Press.

Niebuhr, H. Richard. 1959. *The Kingdom of God in America*. New York: Harper Torchbooks.

Niebuhr, Reinhold. 1944. *The Children of Light and the Children of Darkness*. New York: Scribner's.

Noll, Mark A. 1988. *One Nation Under God? Christian Faith and Political Action in America*. San Francisco: Harper and Row.

———, ed. 1990. *Religion and American Politics*. New York: Oxford University Press.

Noll, Mark A., Nathan O. Hatch, and George M. Marsden. 1983. *The Search for Christian America*. Westchester, Ill.: Crossway.

Nunn, Clyde Z., Harry J. Crockett Jr., and J. Allen Williams Jr. 1978. *Tolerance for Nonconformity*. San Francisco: Jossey-Bass.

O'Brien, David J. 1968. *American Catholics and Social Reform: The New Deal Years*. New York: Oxford University Press.

O'Grady, John F. 1982. *Models of Jesus*. New York: Image.

O'Hara, Thomas J. 1989a. "The Civil Rights Restoration Act: The Role of the Religious Lobbies." Paper delivered at the annual meeting of the American Political Science Association, Atlanta.

———. 1989b. "The Multifaceted Catholic Lobby." In *Religion in American Politics*, ed. Charles W. Dunn, 137–144. Washington, D.C.: CQ Press.

Olson, Daniel V. A., and Jackson W. Carroll. 1992. "Religiously Based Politics: Religious Elites and the Public." *Social Forces* 70:765–786.

Olson, John Kevin, and Ann C. Beck. 1990. "Religion and Political Realignment in the Rocky Mountain States." *Journal for the Scientific Study of Religion* 29:198–209.

O'Neil, Daniel J. 1970. *Church Lobbying in a Western State: A Case Study in Abortion Legislation*. Tucson: University of Arizona Press.

Ortiz, Isidro. 1984. "Chicano Urban Politics and the Politics of Reform in the Seventies." *Western Political Quarterly* 37:564–577.

Orum, Anthony M. 1970. "Religion and the Rise of the Radical White: The Case of Southern Wallace Support in 1968." *Social Science Quarterly* 51:674–688.

Page, Ann, and Donald Clelland. 1978. "The Kanawha County Textbook Controversy: A Study in Alienation and Lifestyle Concern." *Social Forces* 57:265–281.

Page, Benjamin I., Robert Y. Shapiro, Paul W. Gronke, and Robert M. Rosenberg. 1984. "Constituency, Party, and Representation in Congress." *Public Opinion Quarterly* 48:741–756.

Paige, Connie. 1983. *The Right to Lifers*. New York: Summit.

Painton, Priscilla. 1993. "Clinton's Spiritual Journey." *Time*, 5 April, 49–51.

Parenti, Michael. 1967. "Political Values and Religious Cultures: Jews, Catholics, and Protestants." *Journal for the Scientific Study of Religion* 6:259–269.

Paris, Peter J. 1978. *Black Leaders in Conflict*. New York: Pilgrim.

Pasquariello, Ronald D. 1985. *Tax Justice: Social and Moral Aspects of American Tax Policy*. Lanham, Md.: University Press of America.

Patel, Kant, Denny Pilant, and Gary L. Rose. 1982. "Born-Again Christians in the Bible Belt." *American Politics Quarterly* 10:255–272.

Pateman, Carole. 1970. *Participation and Democratic Theory*. Cambridge, Eng.: Cambridge University Press.

Patric, Gordon. 1957. "The Impact of a Court Decision: Aftermath of the *McCollum* Case." *Journal of Public Law* 6:455–464.

Penning, James. 1986. "Changing Partisanship and Issue Stands Among American Catholics." *Sociological Analysis* 47:29–49.

People for the American Way. 1989. *Press Clips*. Washington, D.C.: People for the American Way.

Perkins, H. Wesley. 1983. "Organized Religion as Opiate or Prophetic Stimulant: A Study of American and English Assessments of Social Justice in Two Urban Settings." *Review of Religious Research* 24:206–224.

———. 1985. "A Research Note on Religiosity as Opiate or Prophetic Stimulant Among Students in England and the United States." *Review of Religious Research* 26:269–280.

———. 1992. "Student Religiosity and Social Justice Concerns in England and the U.S.: Are They Still Related?" *Journal for the Scientific Study of Religion* 31:353–360.

Perry, Barbara. 1991. *A "Representative" Supreme Court? The Impact of Race, Religion, and Gender on Appointments.* Westport, Conn.: Greenwood.

Persinos, John F. 1994. "Has the Christian Right Taken Over the Republican Party?" *Campaigns and Elections* 15:20–24.

Peterson, Steven A. 1992. "Church Participation and Political Participation: The Spillover Effect." *American Politics Quarterly* 20:123–139.

Petrusak, Frank, and Steven Steinart. 1976. "The Jews of Charleston: Some Old Wine in New Bottles." *Jewish Social Studies* 38:337–346.

Pfeffer, Leo. 1967. *Church, State, and Freedom.* Rev. ed. Boston: Beacon.

Phillips, Kevin P. 1969. *The Emerging Republican Majority.* Garden City, N.Y.: Doubleday-Anchor.

———. 1982. *Post-Conservative America.* New York: Vintage.

Piazza, Thomas, and Charles Y. Glock. 1979. "Images of God and Their Social Meanings." In *The Religious Dimension: New Directions in Quantitative Research,* ed. Robert Wuthnow, 69–91. New York: Academic.

Piehl, Mel. 1982. *Breaking Bread: The Catholic Worker and the Origin of Catholic Radicalism in America.* Philadelphia: Temple University Press.

Pierard, Richard V. 1983. "From Evangelical Exclusiveness to Ecumenical Openness: Billy Graham and Socio-Political Issues." *Journal of Ecumenical Studies* 20:425–446.

Pierard, Richard V., and James L. Wright. 1984. "No Hoosier Hospitality for Humanism: The Moral Majority in Indiana." In *New Christian Politics,* ed. David G. Bromley and Anson Shupe, 195–212. Macon, Ga.: Mercer University Press.

Pomper, Gerald A. 1966. "Ethnic and Group Voting in Non-Partisan Municipal Elections." *Public Opinion Quarterly* 30:79–99.

Powell, G. Bingham, Jr. 1982. *Contemporary Democracies.* Cambridge: Harvard University Press.

Pratt, Henry J. 1972. *The Liberalization of American Protestantism.* Detroit: Wayne State University Press.

Pritchett, C. Herman. 1984. *Constitutional Civil Liberties.* Englewood Cliffs, N.J.: Prentice-Hall.

Prozesky, Martin. 1984. *Religion and Ultimate Well-Being: An Explanatory Theory.* New York: St. Martin's.

Public Opinion. 1985. "Southern Whites: The Great Conversion." *Public Opinion* 7:34.

Pyle, Ralph E. 1993. "Faith and Commitment to the Poor: Theological Orientation and Support for Government Assistance Measures." *Sociology of Religion* 54:385–401.

Quinley, Harold E. 1974. *The Prophetic Clergy: Social Activism Among Protestant Ministers.* New York: Wiley Interscience.

Quinney, Richard. 1964. "Political Conservatism, Alienation, and Fatalism: Contingencies of Social Status and Religious Fundamentalism." *Sociometry* 27:372–381.

Raden, David. 1982. "Dogmatism and Conventionality." *Psychological Reports* 50:1020–1022.

Raschke, Vernon. 1973. "Dogmatism and Committed and Consensual Religiosity." *Journal for the Scientific Study of Religion* 12:339–344.

Rawlyk, George A. 1990. "Politics, Religion, and the Canadian Experience: A Preliminary Probe." In *Religion and American Politics,* ed. Mark A. Noll, 253–277. New York: Oxford University Press.

Raymond, Paul, and Barbara Norrander. 1990. "Religion and Attitudes Toward Anti-Abortion Protest." *Review of Religious Research* 32:151–156.

Reagan, Ronald Wilson. 1981a. "Inaugural Address of President Ronald Reagan." In *Weekly Compilation of Presidential Documents*, 1–5. Washington, D.C.: GPO.

———. 1981b. "Remarks at the Annual Meeting of the International Association of Chiefs of Police." In *Weekly Compilation of Presidential Documents* 17:1039–1046.

———. 1984. "Religion and Politics Are Necessarily Related." *Church and State* 37 (October): 9–11.

Reed, Ralph, Jr. 1995. "Remarks to the Anti-Defamation League of B'nai B'rith." [http://cc.org]. 3 April.

Reichley, A. James. 1985. *Religion in American Public Life*. Washington, D.C.: Brookings.

Reid, T. R. 1987. "Robertson's Christian Soldiers Are Marching to a Political Fray." *Washington Post Weekly Edition*, 12 October, 16.

Reinhardt, Robert Melvin. 1975. "The Political Behavior of West Virginia Protestant Fundamentalist Sectarians." Ph.D. diss., University of West Virginia.

Renshon, Stanley Allen. 1975. "The Role of Personality Development in Political Socialization." In *New Directions in Political Socialization*, ed. David C. Schwartz and Sandra Kenyon Schwartz, 29–68. New York: Free Press.

Research and Forecasts Inc. 1981. *The Connecticut Mutual Life Report on American Values in the 1980s*. Hartford, Conn.: Connecticut Mutual Life Insurance Company.

Ribuffo, Leo. 1983. *The Old Christian Right*. Philadelphia: Temple University Press.

Ribuffo, Leo P. 1989. "God and Jimmy Carter." In *Transforming Faith: The Sacred and Secular in Modern American History*, ed. M. L. Bradbury and James B. Gilbert, 141–160. New York: Greenwood.

Rich, Frank. 1995. "Connect the Dots." *New York Times*, 30 April, 7.

Richards, P. Scott. 1991. "The Relation Between Conservative Religious Ideology and Principled Moral Reasoning." *Review of Religious Research* 32:359–368.

Richardson, James T. 1984. "The 'Old Right' in Action: Mormon and Catholic Involvement in an Equal Rights Amendment Referendum." In *New Christian Politics*, ed. David G. Bromley and Anson Shupe, 213–234. Macon, Ga.: Mercer University Press.

Richardson, James T., and Sandie Wightman Fox. 1972. "Religious Affiliation As a Predictor of Voting Behavior on Abortion Reform Legislation." *Journal for the Scientific Study of Religion* 11:347–359.

Richburg, Keith R. 1986. "Public Schools and the Politics of Curriculum." *Washington Post Weekly Edition*, 20 January, 14–15.

Richey, Russell E., and Donald G. Jones, eds. 1974. *American Civil Religion*. New York: Harper and Row.

Rieselbach, Leroy N. 1966. *The Roots of Isolationism: Congressional Voting and Presidential Leadership in Foreign Policy*. Indianapolis: Bobbs-Merrill.

Riley, Richard W. 1995. "Religious Expression in Public Schools." (August 17). Washington, D.C.: U.S. Department of Education.

Rischin, Moses. 1962. *The Promised City: New York's Jews, 1870–1914*. New York: Harper and Row.

Rogers, Mary Beth. 1990. *Cold Anger: A Story of Faith and Power Politics*. Denton: University of North Texas Press.

Rojek, Dean. 1973. "The Protestant Ethic and Political Preferences." *Social Forces* 52:168–177.

Rokeach, Milton. 1969. "Religious Values and Social Compassion." *Review of Religious Research* 11:24–39.

———. 1971. "Paradoxes of Religious Belief." In *Religion in Radical Transition*, ed. Jeffrey K. Hadden, 15–24. New Brunswick, N.J.: Transaction.

Roof, Wade Clark. 1974. "Religious Orthodoxy and Minority Prejudice: Causal Relationship or Reflection of Localistic World View." *American Journal of Sociology* 80:643–664.

———. 1978. *Community and Commitment: Religious Plausibility in a Liberal Protestant Church.* New York: Elsevier.

———. 1979. "Concepts and Indicators of Religious Commitment: A Critical Review." In *The Religious Dimension: New Directions in Quantitative Research*, ed. Robert Wuthnow, 17–45. New York: Academic.

Roof, Wade Clark, and William McKinney. 1987. *American Mainline Religion: Its Changing Shape and Future.* New Brunswick, N.J.: Rutgers University Press.

Roozen, David A., William McKinney, and Jackson W. Carroll. 1984. *Varieties of Religious Presence: Mission in Public Life.* New York: Pilgrim.

Rose, Richard, and Derek Urwin. 1969. "Social Cohesion, Political Parties, and Strains in Regimes." *Comparative Political Studies* 2:7–67.

Rosenberg, Morris. 1956. "Misanthropy and Political Ideology." *American Sociological Review* 21:690–695.

Rosenstone, Steven J., and John Mark Hansen. 1993. *Mobilization, Participation, and Democracy in America.* New York: Macmillan.

Rossiter, Clinton, ed. 1961. *The Federalist Papers.* New York: New American Library.

Rothenberg, Stuart, and Frank Newport. 1984. *The Evangelical Voter.* Washington, D.C.: Free Congress Research and Education Foundation.

Rothman, Stanley, and S. Robert Lichter. 1982. *Roots of Radicalism: Jews, Christians, and the New Left.* New York: Oxford University Press.

Rountree, William T., Jr. 1990. "Constitutionalism As the American Religion: The Good Portion." *Emory Law Journal* 39:203–215.

Rozell, Mark J., and Clyde Wilcox. 1995a. "Virginia: God, Guns, and Oliver North." In *God at the Grass Roots: The Christian Right in the 1994 Elections*, ed. Mark J. Rozell and Clyde Wilcox, 109–132. Lanham, Md.: Rowman and Littlefield.

———, eds. 1995b. *God at the Grass Roots: The Christian Right in the 1994 Elections.* Lanham, Md.: Rowman and Littlefield.

Rubin, Barry. 1994. "Religion and International Affairs." In *Religion, the Missing Dimension of Statecraft*, ed. Douglas Johnston and Cynthia Sampson, 20–34. New York: Oxford University Press.

Rubin, Eva R., ed. 1994. *The Abortion Controversy: A Documentary History.* Primary Documents in American History and Contemporary Issues. Westport, Conn.: Greenwood.

Ruthven, Malise. 1989. *The Divine Supermarket: Shopping for God in America.* New York: William Morrow.

Salamon, Lester M. 1973. "Leadership and Modernization: The Emerging Black Political Elite in the American South." *Journal of Politics* 35:615–646.

Salisbury, Robert H. 1983. "American Politics: Religion and the Welfare State." In *Comparative Social Research*, ed. Richard E. Tomasson, 56–65. Greenwich, Conn.: JAI.

Salisbury, Robert H., John Sprague, and Gregory Weiher. 1984. "Does Religious Pluralism Make a Difference? Interactions Among Context, Attendance, and Beliefs." Paper delivered at the annual meeting of the American Political Science Association, Washington, D.C.

Sandoz, Ellis. 1990. *A Government of Laws: Political Theory, Religion, and the American Founding.* Baton Rouge: Louisiana State University Press.

Sapp, Gary L., and Logan Jones. 1986. "Religious Orientation and Moral Judgment." *Journal for the Scientific Study of Religion* 25:208–214.

Sawyer, Darwin O. 1982. "Public Attitudes Toward Life and Death." *Public Opinion Quarterly* 46:521–533.

Schappes, Morriss U., ed. 1971. *A Documentary History of the Jews in the United States.* Third ed. New York: Schocken.

Schindeler, Fred, and David Hoffman. 1968. "Theological and Political Conservatism: Variations in Attitudes Among Clergymen of One Denomination." *Canadian Journal of Political Science* 1:429–441.

Schneider, William. 1985. "The Jewish Vote in 1984: Elements in a Controversy." *Public Opinion* 7:18–19, 58.

———. 1989. "Trouble for the GOP." *Public Opinion* 12:2, 59–60.

———. 1995. "Stealth Strategy for the Religious Right?" *National Journal,* 27 May, 1314.

Schoenfeld, Eugene. 1985. "Religion and Loyalty to the Political Elite: The Case of the Presidency." *Review of Religious Research* 27:178–188.

Schumer, Franz. 1984. "A Return to Religion." *New York Times Magazine,* 15 April, 90–98.

Schuster, William G. 1981. "Appointments." *Christianity Today,* 13 March, 58.

Scoble, Harry M., and Leon D. Epstein. 1964. "Religion and Wisconsin Voting in 1960." *Journal of Politics* 26:381–396.

Secret, Philip E., James B. Johnson, and Susan Welch. 1986. "Racial Differences in Attitudes Toward the Supreme Court's Decision on Prayer in the Public Schools." *Social Science Quarterly* 67:877–886.

Segers, Mary C. 1992. "The Loyal Opposition: Catholics for a Free Choice." In *The Catholic Church and the Politics of Abortion,* ed. Timothy A. Byrnes and Mary C. Segers, 169–184. Boulder: Westview.

Seltzer, Richard. 1993. "AIDS, Homosexuality, Public Opinion, and Changing Correlates Over Time." *Journal of Homosexuality* 26:85–97.

Sennett, Richard. 1987. "A Republic of Souls: Puritanism and the American Presidency." *Harper's Magazine* 287:41–46.

Shaiko, Ronald. 1987. "Religion, Politics, and Environmental Concern." *Social Science Quarterly* 68:244–262.

Shannon, Denise. 1993. "The Bishops' Lobby." *Humanist* 53:21–23.

Shannon, W. Wayne. 1982. "Mr. Reagan Goes to Washington: Teaching Exceptional America." *Public Opinion* 4:13–17, 55.

Sheler, Jeffrey. 1994. "Spiritual America." *U.S. News and World Report,* 4 April, 48–59.

Sherry, Suzanna. 1993. "*Lee v. Weisman*: Paradox Redux." In *The Supreme Court Review 1992,* ed. Dennis J. Hutchinson, David A. Strauss, and Geoffrey R. Stone, 123–154. Chicago: University of Chicago Press.

Shipton, Clifford K. 1947. "Puritanism and Modern Democracy." *New England Historical and Genealogical Register* 101:181–198.

Shorris, Earl. 1982. *Jews Without Mercy: A Lament.* Garden City, N.Y.: Doubleday-Anchor.

Shriver, Peggy L. 1981. *The Bible Vote.* New York: Pilgrim.

———. 1988. "Religion and Public Education: The American Context." *National Forum* 68:30–33.

Shupe, Anson, and William Stacey. 1983. "The Moral Majority Constituency." In *The New Christian Right*, ed. Robert C. Liebman and Robert Wuthnow, 104–117. New York: Aldine.

Sigelman, Lee. 1991. "If You Prick Us, Do We Not Bleed? If You Tickle Us, Do We Not Laugh?" *Journal of Politics* 53:977–992.

Sigelman, Lee, and Stanley Presser. 1988. "Measuring Public Support for the New Christian Right: The Perils of Point Estimation." *Public Opinion Quarterly* 52:325–337.

Sigelman, Lee, Clyde Wilcox, and Emmett H. Buell Jr. 1987. "An Unchanging Minority: Popular Support for the Moral Majority, 1980 and 1984." *Social Science Quarterly* 68:876–884.

Silk, Mark. 1988. *Spiritual Politics: Religion and America Since World War II*. New York: Simon and Schuster.

Simmons, Paul D. 1990. "Religious Liberty and the Abortion Debate." *Journal of Church and State* 32:567–584.

Simon, Paul. 1984. *The Glass House*. New York: Continuum.

Simon Wiesenthal Center. 1986. "The Farrakhan Phenomenon." *Response* 13:2–3.

Simonds, Robert L. 1985. *How to Elect Christians to Public Office*. Costa Mesa, Calif.: NACE/CEE.

Simpson, Alan. 1955. *Puritanism in Old and New England*. Chicago: University of Chicago Press.

Simpson, John H. 1983. "Moral Issues and Status Politics." In *The New Christian Right*, ed. Robert C. Liebman and Robert Wuthnow, 188–207. New York: Aldine.

Singer, David. 1987. *American Jews As Voters: The 1986 Elections*. New York: American Jewish Committee.

Skill, Thomas, James D. Robinson, John S. Lyons, and David Larson. 1994. "The Portrayal of Religion and Spirituality on Fictional Network Television." *Review of Religious Research* 35:251–267.

Sklare, Marshall, and Joseph Greenblum. 1967. *Jewish Identity on the Suburban Frontier*. New York: Basic Books.

Smidt, Corwin. 1980. "Civil Religious Orientation Among Elementary School Children." *Sociological Analysis* 41:25–40.

———. 1982. "Civil Religious Orientations and Children's Perception of Political Authority." *Political Behavior* 4:147–162.

———. 1983. "Born-Again Politics: The Political Behavior of Christians in the South and Non-South." In *Religion and Politics in the South*, ed. Tod A. Baker, Robert P. Steed, and Laurence W. Moreland, 27–56. New York: Praeger.

———. 1988. "Evangelicals Within Contemporary American Politics: Differentiating Between Fundamentalist and Non-Fundamentalist Evangelicals." *Western Political Quarterly* 41:601–620.

———. 1989a. "Evangelicals and the New Christian Right: Coherence Versus Diversity in the Issue Stands of Evangelicals." In *Contemporary Evangelical Political Involvement: An Analysis and Assessment*, ed. Corwin E. Smidt, 75–98. Lanham, Md.: University Press of America.

———. 1989b. "Identifying Evangelical Respondents: An Analysis of 'Born-Again' and Bible Questions Used Across Different Surveys." In *Religion and Political Behavior in the United States*, ed. Ted G. Jelen, 23–44. New York: Praeger.

———. 1989c. "'Praise the Lord' Politics: A Comparative Analysis of the Social Characteristics and Political Views of American Evangelical and Charismatic Christians." *Sociological Analysis* 50:53–72.

———. 1993. "Evangelical Voting Patterns: 1976–1988." In *No Longer Exiles: The Religious New Right in American Politics*, ed. Michael Cromartie, 85–117. Washington, D.C.: Ethics and Public Policy Center.

Smidt, Corwin, and Paul Kellstedt. 1992. "Evangelicals in the Post-Reagan Era: An Analysis of Evangelical Voters in the 1988 Presidential Election." *Journal for the Scientific Study of Religion* 31:330–338.

Smidt, Corwin E., and James M. Penning. 1982. "Religious Commitment, Political Conservatism, and Political and Social Tolerance in the United States: A Longitudinal Analysis." *Sociological Analysis* 43:231–246.

———. 1988. "A Party Divided? A Comparison of Robertson and Bush Delegates to the 1988 Michigan Republican State Convention." *Polity* 23:127–138.

———. 1991. "Religious Self-Identification and Support for Robertson: An Analysis of Delegates to the 1988 Michigan Republican State Convention." *Review of Religious Research* 32:321–336.

Smith, Donald Eugene. 1970. *Religion and Political Development*. Boston: Little, Brown.

Smith, Robert C. 1981. "The Black Congressional Delegation." *Western Political Quarterly* 34:203–221.

Smith, Robert C., and Robert Seltzer. 1992. *Race, Class, and Culture: A Study in Afro-American Mass Opinion*. Albany: State University of New York Press.

Smith, Timothy L. 1965. *Revivalism and Social Reform: American Protestantism on the Eve of the Civil War*. New York: Harper and Row.

Smith, Tom W. 1982. "General Liberalism and Social Change in Post–World War II America: A Summary of Trends." *Social Indicators Research* 10:1–28.

Solomon, Burt. 1993. "Inside the Yuppie from Yale . . . Is a Southern Baptist's Soul." *National Journal*, 18 December, 3014–3015.

Sorauf, Frank J. 1959. "*Zorach v. Clauson*: The Impact of a Supreme Court Decision." *American Political Science Review* 53:777–791.

———. 1976. *The Wall of Separation: The Constitutional Politics of Church and State*. Princeton, N.J.: Princeton University Press.

Spiegel, Stephen. 1985. *The Other Arab-Israeli Conflict*. Chicago: University of Chicago Press.

Spitzer, Robert J. 1987. *The Right to Life Movement and Third Party Politics*. New York: Greenwood.

Spring, Beth. 1984. "Some Christian Leaders Want Further Political Activism." *Christianity Today* 28:46–49.

Stanfield, Rochelle L. 1994. "The V-Word." *National Journal*, May 28, 1235–1238.

Stark, Rodney. 1964. "Class, Radicalism, and Religious Involvement in Great Britain." *American Sociological Review* 29:698–706.

Stark, Rodney, and William Sims Bainbridge. 1985. *The Future of Religion*. Berkeley and Los Angeles: University of California Press.

Stark, Rodney, Bruce D. Foster, Charles Y. Glock, and Harold E. Quinley. 1971. *Wayward Shepherds*. New York: Harper and Row.

Starr, Jerrold. 1975. "Religious Preference, Religiosity, and Opposition to War." *Sociological Analysis* 36:323–334.

Steiber, Steven R. 1980. "The Influence of the Religious Factor on Civil and Sacred Tolerance." *Social Forces* 58:811–832.

Steiner, Gilbert Y., ed. 1983. *The Abortion Dispute and the American System*. Washington, D.C.: Brookings.

Stellway, Richard J. 1973. "The Correspondence Between Religious Orientation and Socio-Political Liberalism and Conservatism." *Sociological Quarterly* 14:430–439.

Stewart, Thomas A. 1989. "Turning Around the Lord's Business." *Fortune*, September 25, 78–84.

Stockton, Ron R. 1989. "The Evangelical Phenomenon: A Falwell-Graham Typology." In *Contemporary Evangelical Political Involvement: An Analysis and Assessment*, ed. Corwin E. Smidt, 45–74. Lanham, Md.: University Press of America.

Stone, Walter J. 1991. "On Party Switching Among Presidential Activists: What Do We Know?" *American Journal of Political Science* 35:598–607.

Stouffer, Samuel. 1966. *Communism, Conformity, and Civil Liberties*. New York: John Wiley.

Strand, Douglas Alan, and Kenneth Sherrill. 1993. "Electoral Bugaboos? The Impact of Attitudes Towards Gay Rights and Feminism on the 1992 Presidential Vote." Paper delivered at the annual meeting of the American Political Science Association, Washington, D.C.

Strate, J., C. J. Parrish, C. D. Elder, and C. Ford. 1989. "Life Span Civic Development and Voting Participation." *American Political Science Review* 83:443–464.

Strout, Cushing. 1974. *The New Heavens and the New Earth*. New York: Harper and Row.

Sullivan, John L., James Piereson, and George E. Marcus. 1982. *Political Tolerance and American Democracy*. Chicago: University of Chicago Press.

Sullivan, John L., Pat Walsh, Michal Shamir, David G. Barnum, and James L. Gibson. 1993. "Why Politicians Are More Tolerant: Selective Recruitment and Socialization Among Political Elites in Britain, Israel, New Zealand, and the United States." *British Journal of Political Science* 23:51–76.

Summers, Gene F., Richard L. Hough, Doyle P. Johnson, and Kathryn A. Veatch. 1970. "Ascetic Protestantism and Political Preference: A Reexamination." *Review of Religious Research* 12:17–25.

Surrey, David S. 1982. *Choice of Conscience: Vietnam Era Military and Draft Resisters in Canada*. New York: Praeger.

Swanson, Wayne R. 1990. *The Christ Child Goes to Court*. Philadelphia: Temple University Press.

Swatos, William H., Jr. 1988. "Picketing Satan Enfleshed at 7-Eleven: A Research Note." *Review of Religious Research* 30:73–82.

Swierenga, Robert P. 1990. "Ethnoreligious Political Behavior in the Mid-Nineteenth Century: Voting, Values, Culture." In *Religion and American Politics*, ed. Mark A. Noll, 146–171. New York: Oxford University Press.

Szajkowski, Bogdan. 1983. *Next to God . . . Poland: Politics and Religion in Contemporary Poland*. New York: St. Martin's.

Tabor, James D., and Eugene V. Gallagher. 1995. *Why Waco? Cults and the Battle for Religious Freedom in America*. Berkeley and Los Angeles: University of California Press.

Tamney, Joseph B., Ronald Burton, and Stephen Johnson. 1988. "Christianity, Social Class, and the Catholic Bishops' Economic Policy." *Sociological Analysis* 49:78–96.

Tamney, Joseph, and Stephen D. Johnson. 1983. "The Moral Majority in Middletown." *Journal for the Scientific Study of Religion* 22:145–157.

Tamney, Joseph B., and Stephen D. Johnson. 1985. "Christianity and the Nuclear Issue." *Sociological Analysis* 46:321–328.

Tatalovich, Raymond, and Byron W. Daynes. 1988. "What Is Social Regulatory Policy?" In *Social Regulatory Policy: Moral Controversies in American Politics*, ed. Raymond Tatalovich and Byron W. Daynes, 1–4. Boulder: Westview.

Tatalovich, Raymond, and David Schier. 1993. "The Persistence of Ideological Cleavage in Voting on Abortion Legislation in the House of Representatives, 1973–1988." *American Politics Quarterly* 21:125–139.

Taylor, Paul. 1985. "He Went Out for Pizza and Came Back the Definitive Campaigner." *Washington Post Weekly Edition*, 30 September, 12.

Tedin, Kent L. 1978. "Religious Preference and Pro/Anti-Activism on the Equal Rights Amendment Issue." *Pacific Sociological Review* 21:55–66.

Tedin, Kent L., et al. 1977. "Social Background and Political Differences Between Pro- and Anti-ERA Activists." *American Politics Quarterly* 5:395–408.

Tesh, Sylvia. 1984. "In Support of 'Single-Issue' Politics." *Political Science Quarterly* 99:27–44.

Thomas, J. Mark. 1984. "Reagan in the State of Nature." *Christianity and Crisis*, 17 September, 321–325.

Thomas, Michael C., and Charles C. Flippen. 1972. "American Civil Religion: An Empirical Study." *Social Forces* 51:218–225.

Tiryakian, Edward A. 1982. "Puritan America in the Modern World: Mission Impossible?" *Sociological Analysis* 43:351–368.

Tocqueville, Alexis de. 1945. *Democracy in America*. New York: Vintage.

Toner, Robin. 1993. "The Catholic Hierarchy and Clinton: Already a Complicated Relationship." *New York Times*, 3 February, 10A.

Tong, Xiaoxi. 1992. "Market and Political Explanations of Religious Vitality: Comments on Chaves and Cann." *Rationality and Society* 4:474–476.

Toolin, Cynthia. 1983. "American Civil Religion from 1789 to 1981: A Content Analysis of Presidential Inaugural Addresses." *Review of Religious Research* 25:39–48.

Tracy, David. 1973. "The Religious Dimension of Science." In *The Persistence of Religion*, ed. Andrew Greeley and Gregory Baum, 128–135. New York: Herder and Herder.

Traugott, Michael W., and Maris A. Vinovskis. 1980. "Abortion and the 1978 Congressional Elections." *Family Planning Perspectives* 12:238–246.

Truman, David. 1962. *The Governmental Process*. New York: Knopf.

Tygart, Clarence E. 1977. "The Role of Theology Among Other 'Belief' Variables for Clergy Civil Rights Activism." *Review of Religious Research* 18:271–278.

Ulmer, S. Sidney. 1973. "Social Background As an Indicator to the Votes of Supreme Court Justices in Criminal Cases: 1947–1956 Terms." *American Journal of Political Science* 17:622–630.

U.S. Bureau of the Census. 1994. *Statistical Abstract of the United States*. Washington, D.C.: GPO.

Vedlitz, Arnold, Jon P. Alston, and Carl Pinkele. 1980. "Politics and the Black Church in a Southern Community." *Journal of Black Studies* 10:367–375.

Verba, Sidney. 1965. "The Kennedy Assassination and the Nature of Political Commitment." In *The Kennedy Assassination and the American Public*, ed. Bradley S. Greenberg and Edward S. Parker, 348–360. Stanford, Calif.: Stanford University Press.

Verba, Sidney, Kay Lehman Schlozman, Henry Brady, and Norman H. Nie. 1993. "Race, Ethnicity and Political Resources: Participation in the United States." *British Journal of Political Science* 23:453–497.

Vines, Kenneth. 1964. "Federal District Judges and Race Relations Cases in the South." *Journal of Politics* 26:337–357.

Vinovskis, Maris A. 1979. "Abortion and the Presidential Election of 1976: A Multivariate Analysis of Voting Behavior." *Michigan Law Review* 7:1750–1771.

Wagenaar, Theodore C., and Patricia E. Bartos. 1977. "Orthodoxy and Attitudes of Clergymen Toward Homosexuality and Abortion." *Review of Religious Research* 18:114–125.

Wald, Kenneth D. 1983. *Crosses on the Ballot: Patterns of British Voter Alignment Since 1885*. Princeton, N.J.: Princeton University Press.

———. 1989. "Assessing the Religious Factor in Electoral Behavior." In *Religion in American Politics*, ed. Charles W. Dunn, 105–122. Washington, D.C.: CQ Press.

———. 1991. "Ministering to the Nation: The Campaigns of Jesse Jackson and Pat Robertson." In *Nominating the President*, ed. Emmett H. Buell Jr. and Lee S. Sigelman, 119–149. Knoxville: University of Tennessee Press.

———. 1992. "Religious Elites and Public Opinion: The Impact of the Bishops' Peace Pastoral." *Review of Politics* 54:112–143.

———. 1994. "The Religious Dimension of American Anti-Communism." *Journal of Church and State* 36:483–507.

Wald, Kenneth D., James W. Button, and Barbara A. Rienzo. 1996. "The Politics of Gay Rights in American Communities: Explaining Antidiscrimination Ordinances and Policies." *American Journal of Political Science*, forthcoming.

Wald, Kenneth D., Lyman Kellstedt, and David C. Leege. 1993. "Church Involvement and Political Behavior." In *Rediscovering the Religious Factor in American Politics*, ed. David C. Leege and Lyman A. Kellstedt, 121–139. Armonk, N.Y.: M. E. Sharpe.

Wald, Kenneth D., and Michael B. Lupfer. 1983. "Religion and Political Attitudes in the Urban South." In *Religion and Politics in the South: Mass and Elite Perspectives*, ed. Tod A. Baker, Robert B. Steed, and Laurence W. Moreland, 84–100. New York: Praeger Special Studies.

Wald, Kenneth D., Dennis E. Owen, and Samuel S. Hill Jr. 1988. "Churches as Political Communities." *American Political Science Review* 82:531–548.

———. 1989a. "Evangelical Politics and Status Issues." *Journal for the Scientific Study of Religion* 28:1–16.

———. 1989b. "Habits of the Mind? The Problem of Authority in the New Christian Right." In *Religion and Political Behavior in the United States*, ed. Ted G. Jelen, 93–108. New York: Greenwood.

———. 1990. "Political Cohesion in Churches." *Journal of Politics* 52:197–215.

Wald, Kenneth D., and Corwin E. Smidt. 1993. "Measurement Strategies in the Study of Religion and Politics." In *Rediscovering the Religious Factor in American Politics*, ed. David C. Leege and Lyman A. Kellstedt, 26–49. Armonk, N.Y.: M. E. Sharpe.

Wallis, Roy, and Steve Bruce. 1992. "Secularization: The Orthodox Model." In *Religion and Modernization*, ed. Steve Bruce, 8–30. Oxford: Oxford University Press.

Walton, Hanes, Jr. 1985. *Invisible Politics: Black Political Behavior*. Albany: State University of New York Press.

Walzer, Michael. 1985. *Exodus and Revolution*. New York: Basic Books.

Warner, John B., Jr. 1968. "Religious Affiliation as a Factor in the Voting Records of Members of the Eighty-ninth Congress." Ph.D. diss., Boston University.

Warner, R. Stephen. 1979. "Theoretical Barriers to the Understanding of Evangelical Christianity." *Sociological Analysis* 40:1–9.

————. 1988. *New Wine in Old Wineskins: Evangelicals and Liberals in a Small-Town Church*. Berkeley and Los Angeles: University of California Press.

Wasserman, Ira M. 1989. "Prohibition and Ethnocultural Conflict: The Missouri Prohibition Referendum of 1918." *Social Science Quarterly* 70:886–901.

Wattenberg, Ben J. 1995. *Values Matter Most*. New York: Free Press.

Way, H. Frank, Jr. 1968. "Survey Research on Judicial Decisions: The Prayer and Bible-Reading Cases." *Western Political Quarterly* 21:189–205.

Way, Frank, and Barbara J. Burt. 1983. "Religious Marginality and the Free Exercise Clause." *American Political Science Review* 77:652–665.

Weber, Mary Cahill. 1983. "Religion and Conservative Social Attitudes." In *Views from the Pews: Christian Beliefs and Attitudes*, ed. Roger A. Johnson, 103–122. Philadelphia: Fortress.

Weber, Max. 1958. *The Protestant Ethic and the Spirit of Capitalism*. Translated by Talcott Parsons. New York: Charles Scribner's.

Weber, Paul J. 1982a. "Examining the Religious Lobbies." *This World* 1:97–107.

————. 1982b. "James Madison and Religious Equality: The Perfect Separation." *Review of Politics* 44:163–186.

Weber, Paul J., and W. Landis Jones. 1994. *U.S. Religious Interest Groups: Institutional Profiles*. Westport, Conn.: Greenwood.

Weber, Paul J., and T. L. Stanley. 1984. "The Power and Performance of Religious Interest Groups." *Quarterly Review* 4:28–43.

Welch, Michael R., and David C. Leege. 1988. "Religious Predictors of Catholic Parishioners' Sociopolitical Attitudes: Devotional Style, Closeness to God, Imagery, and Agentic/Communal Religious Identity." *Journal for the Scientific Study of Religion* 27:536–552.

————. 1991. "Dual Reference Groups and Political Orientations: An Examination of Evangelically Oriented Catholics." *American Journal of Political Science* 35:28–56.

Welch, Michael R., David C. Leege, Kenneth D. Wald, and Lyman A. Kellstedt. 1993. "Are the Sheep Hearing the Shepherds? Cue Perceptions, Congregational Responses, and Political Communication Processes." In *Rediscovering the Religious Factor in American Politics*, ed. David C. Leege and Lyman A. Kellstedt, 235–254. Armonk, N.Y.: M. E. Sharpe.

Wells, Robert M. 1995. "Prayer Amendment Unlikely Despite Push from Right." *Congressional Quarterly Weekly Report*, 8 July, 1998–2000.

Wenz, Peter. 1992. *Abortion Rights As Religious Freedom*. Philadelphia: Temple University Press.

White, John Kenneth. 1990. *The New Politics of Old Values*. Second ed. Hanover, N.H.: University Press of New England.

White, Lynn, Jr. 1967. "The Historical Roots of Our Ecological Crisis." *Science* 155:1203–1207.

White, O. Kendall, Jr. 1984. "Overt and Covert Politics: The Mormon Church's Anti-ERA Campaign in Virginia." *Virginia Social Science Journal* 19:11–16.

Whyte, John H. 1981. *Catholics in Western Democracies: A Study in Political Behavior*. New York: St. Martin's.

Wilcox, Clyde. 1986. "Fundamentalists and Politics: An Analysis of the Effects of Differing Operational Definitions." *Journal of Politics* 48:1041–1051.

————. 1989a. "Evangelicals and the Moral Majority." *Journal for the Scientific Study of Religion* 28:400–414.

————. 1989b. "The New Christian Right and the Mobilization of the Evangelicals." In *Religion and Political Behavior in the United States*, ed. Ted G. Jelen, 139–156. New York: Praeger.

————. 1990. "Religious Sources of Politicization Among Blacks in Washington, D.C." *Journal for the Scientific Study of Religion* 29:387–394.

————. 1992a. *God's Warriors: The Christian Right in Twentieth-Century America*. Baltimore: The Johns Hopkins University Press.

————. 1992b. "Race, Religion, Region, and Abortion Attitudes." *Sociological Analysis* 53:97–105.

————. 1992c. "Religion and the Preacher Vote in the South: Sources of Support for Jackson and Robertson in Southern Primaries." *Sociological Analysis* 53:323–331.

Wilcox, Clyde, and Leopoldo Gomez. 1990a. "The Christian Right and the Pro-Life Movement: An Analysis of the Sources of Political Support." *Review of Religious Research* 31:380–389.

————. 1990b. "Religion, Group Identification and Politics Among American Blacks." *Sociological Analysis* 51:271–285.

Wilcox, Clyde, and Ted Jelen. 1990. "Evangelicals and Political Tolerance." *American Politics Quarterly* 18:25–46.

Wilcox, Clyde, Ted G. Jelen, and David C. Leege. 1993. "Religious Group Identifications: Toward a Cognitive Theory of Religious Mobilization." In *Rediscovering the Religious Factor in American Politics*, ed. David C. Leege and Lyman A. Kellstedt, 72–99. Armonk, N.Y.: M. E. Sharpe.

Will, George F. 1983. *Statecraft As Soulcraft*. New York: Simon and Schuster.

Williams, Rhys H., and Susan M. Alexander. 1994. "Religious Rhetoric in American Populism: Civil Religion as Movement Ideology." *Journal for the Scientific Study of Religion* 33:1–15.

Williamsburg Charter Foundation. 1988. *The Williamsburg Charter Survey on Religion and Public Life*. Washington, D.C.: Williamsburg Charter Foundation.

Wilson, Andrew J. 1995. *Irish America and the Ulster Conflict, 1968–1995*. Washington, D.C.: Catholic University of America Press.

Wilson, Bryan. 1966. *Religion in Secular Society*. Baltimore: Penguin.

Wilson, Glenn D., and Christopher Bagley. 1973. "Religion, Racism, and Conservatism." In *The Psychology of Conservatism*, ed. Glenn Wilson, 117–128. New York: Academic.

Wilson, John F. 1978. *Religion in American Society: The Effective Presence*. Englewood Cliffs, N.J.: Prentice-Hall.

Wilson, John F., and Donald L. Drakeman, eds. 1987. *Church and State in American History*. Second ed. Boston: Beacon.

Wilson, James Q. 1965. *Negro Politics: The Search for Leadership*. New York: Free Press.

Wilson, Thomas. 1990. "Introduction." In *The Northern Ireland Economy*, ed. Richard Harris, Clifford Jefferson, and John E. Spencer, 1–12. London: Longman.

Wimberly, Ronald C. 1976. "Testing the Civil Religion Hypothesis." *Sociological Analysis* 37:341–352.

————. 1979. "Continuity in the Measurement of Civil Religion." *Sociological Analysis* 40:59–62.

Wise, William. 1976. *Massacre at Mountain Meadows*. New York: Crowell.

Witt, Stephanie L., and Gary Moncrief. 1993. "Religion and Roll Call Voting in Idaho: The 1990 Abortion Controversy." *American Politics Quarterly* 21:140–149.

Witte, John, Jr. 1990. "How to Govern a City on a Hill: The Early Puritan Contribution to American Constitutionalism." *Emory Law Journal* 39:41–64.

————. 1991. "The Theology and Politics of the First Amendment Religion Clauses: A Bicentennial Essay." *Emory Law Journal* 40:489–507.

Witten, Marsha G. 1993. *All Is Forgiven: The Secular Message in American Protestantism*. Princeton, N.J.: Princeton University Press.

Wohlenberg, Ernest H. 1980. "Correlates of Equal Rights Amendment Ratification." *Social Science Quarterly* 60:676–684.

Wolf, Donald J., S.J. 1968. *Toward Consensus: Catholic-Protestant Interpretations of Church and State*. Garden City, N.Y.: Doubleday-Anchor.

Wolin, Sheldon. 1956. "Politics and Religion: Luther's Simplistic Imperative." *American Political Science Review* 50:24–42.

Wolkomir, Michelle, Michael Futreal, Eric Woodrum, and Thomas Hoban. 1995. "Conceptualizing Substantive Religious Beliefs and Environmentalism." Paper delivered at the annual meeting of the Southern Sociological Society, Atlanta.

Wood, James R. 1981. *Leadership in Voluntary Organizations: The Controversy Over Social Action in Protestant Churches*. New Brunswick, N.J.: Rutgers University Press.

Wood, Michael, and Michael Hughes. 1984. "The Moral Basis of Moral Reform: Status Discontent vs. Cultural Socialization As Explanations of Anti-Pornography Social Movement Adherence." *American Sociological Review* 49:86–99.

Wood, Richard L. 1994. "Faith in Action: Religious Resources for Political Success in Three Congregations." *Sociology of Religion* 55:397–417.

Woodrum, Eric, and Arnold Bell. 1989. "Race, Politics, and Religion in Civil Religion Among Blacks." *Sociological Analysis* 4:353–367.

Woodrum, Eric, and Beth L. Davison. 1992a. "Images of God and Environmentalism." Paper delivered at the annual meeting of the Society for the Scientific Study of Religion, Washington, D.C..

————. 1992b. "Reexamination of Religious Influences on Abortion Attitudes." *Review of Religious Research* 33:229–243.

Woodrum, Eric, and Thomas Hoban. 1992. "Support for Prayer in School and Creationism." *Sociological Analysis* 92:309–321.

————. 1994. "Theology and Religiosity Effects on Environmentalism." *Review of Religious Research* 35:193–206.

Woodward, Kenneth L. 1993. "Dead End for the Mainline?" *Newsweek*, 9 August, 46–48.

World Bank. 1994. *World Tables 1994*. Baltimore: The Johns Hopkins University Press.

Wright, Benjamin F. 1949. "The Federalist on the Nature of Political Man." *Ethics* 59:1–31.

Wuthnow, Robert. 1973. "Religious Commitment and Conservatism: In Search of an Elusive Relationship." In *Religion in Sociological Perspective*, ed. Charles Y. Glock, 117–132. Belmont, Calif.: Wadsworth.

————. 1983. "The Political Rebirth of American Evangelicals." In *The New Christian Right*, ed. Robert C. Liebman and Robert Wuthnow, 168–187. New York: Aldine.

————. 1988. *The Restructuring of American Religion*. Princeton, N.J.: Princeton University Press.

Yankelovich, Daniel. 1981. "Stepchildren of the Moral Majority." *Psychology Today* 15:5–10.

Young, Robert L. 1992. "Religious Orientation, Race, and Support for the Death Penalty." *Journal for the Scientific Study of Religion* 31:76–87.

Zlatos, Bill. 1984. "When Faith Lets Children Die." *Washington Post Weekly Edition,* 15 October, 31–32.

Zwier, Robert. 1988. "The World and Worldview of Religious Lobbyists." Paper delivered at the annual meeting of the Midwest Political Science Association, Chicago.

Index

Abington School District v. Schempp, 98-99, 112, 114

abolitionist crusade, 25-26. *See also* slavery

abortion, 125
  Bible on, 212
  Canada versus United States, 33-35
  as Catholic issue, 285-293
  Catholic response to, 281-285
  congressional voting and, 147-148
  democracy and, 333-334
  government action on, 158
  judicial appointments and, 138
  political activism and, 332-334
  Republican party and, 259-260
  Right-to-Life party and, 135
  Roe v. Wade, 33-34, 128, 261, 282, 284, 286-287
  as social issue, 184-185
  violence and, 128
  Webster decision, 261, 284

Abraham, 46

accommodation doctrine, 79-81, 87, 115-118

ACLU. *See* American Civil Liberties Union

activism, 166-167
  abortion and, 332-334
  of churches, 166-167
  of clergy, 293-297
  of Protestants, 31, 297-299

Adams, John, 55-56, 84, 85

Adams, Samuel, 88

affirmative action, 130, 312-313

African Americans
  black-Jewish relations, 311-315
  infrastructure of black politics, 303-310
  opinions on race relations, 181-183
  Protestants, 171-172, 301-303
  religious activity as social group, 30
  role of clergy, 40, 134, 303-307
  social status of black Protestants, 196-197
  voter registration, 159, 306-307

"Age of Reason," 69

Aguilar v. Felton, 101

Ahlstrom, Sydney, 52

AIDS (acquired immunodeficiency syndrome), 187-188

Allport, Gordon, 329

American Association of Humanists, 112

American Baptist Association, 128

American Bible Society, 89

American Civil Liberties Union (ACLU), 104, 112, 235, 328

American Family Association, 39-40, 127, 234

American National Election Studies (ANES), 170-176

Americans for Democratic Action (ADA), 148

Americans United for Separation of Church and State, 112, 235

Amish, 109

Ammerman, Nancy, 297

Andersen, Kristi, 211

Anderson, John, 228

animal sacrifice, 118

Anti-Defamation League (ADL), 130, 316-317

appointments, political, 137-138

Aristotle, 58

Assemblies of God, 226, 251

Atwood, Thomas, 231

authority, challenging, 341-342

Baptist Bible Fellowship, 242
Baptist Joint Committee, 112, 255
Baptists, 44, 87, 173, 299. *See also*
  Southern Baptists
Batson, C. Daniel, 330
Bauer, Gary, 234
Beck, Paul Allen, 36
Bellah, Robert, 61
benevolent neutrality. *See* accommoda-
  tion doctrine
Bennett, William, 189, 269
Benson, Peter L., 149
Bergmann, Allyson, 75-76
Bernardin, Joseph Cardinal, 291
Berrigan, Daniel, 274
Berrigan, Phillip, 274
Bible
  on abortion, 212
  authority of, 44-45, 172,
    203
  reading in schools, 113, 116
Billings, Bob, 227
Birkby, Robert, 113
birth control, 197, 282, 285-286
Black, Hugo, 79
Black Muslims, 304, 315
black power movement, 304-305
Blau, Peter, 270
blue laws, 110
Board of Education v. Allen, 100
Bond, Jon R., 158
boundary problem, 74, 76-77
boycotts, 127, 223
Branch Davidians, 26, 119-120
Bridenbaugh, Carl, 51-52
broadcasting, 241-243
Brown, John, 129
Bryan, William Jennings, 26-27, 202,
  218, 221
Bryant, Anita, 224
Buber, Martin, 322
Buchanan, Patrick, 1, 230, 260,
  269
Burger, Warren, 101
Bush, George (Bush administration)
  abortion issues, 284
  Christian Right support of, 229-230,
    259
  Gulf War, 3
  judicial appointments, 116
  voter preference for, 178

Call to Action, 142
campaigns. *See* political campaigns
Canada, antiabortion movement, 33-35
Cantwell v. Connecticut, 106
capitalism, 195
Carroll, Jackson, 190
Carter, Jimmy (Carter administration),
  218
  civil religion and, 66
  evangelical Protestantism and, 222,
    244
  Jewish support for, 314
  personal religiosity of, 154-155
case law
  on free-exercise, 106-108
  on separationism, 93-97
Catholic Alliance, 292
Catholic Charities, 10
Catholic League for Religious and Civil
  Rights, 112
Catholic Worker movement, 271
Catholicism
  abortion and, 127, 143, 158, 184-185,
    281-293
  birth control and, 197, 282, 285-286
  Catholic immigrants, 270-271
  conservative political heritage of, 268-
    272
  Democratic party and, 31, 175, 195,
    209
  economic policy, 279-281
  Irish-American Catholics, 25, 26, 164-
    165
  liberation theology and, 274
  lobbying and, 130, 138-139
  military policy, 269-270, 274-279, 281
  nuclear disarmament policy, 26, 276-
    279
  organization of, 141-142
  parochial schools, 31, 100, 102, 111-
    112, 206-208
  political campaigns and, 134
  political involvement, 30-32, 125,
    140-141
  poverty and, 21, 31-32
  race relations and, 159
  redemption doctrine, 54
  religious affiliation of, 171-176
  Sanctuary movement and, 128, 211
  transformation of attitudes, 272-281
  voting patterns, 136-137

Catholics for Free Choice, 142, 285
Caucus for Soviet Jewry, 136
Challenge of Peace, The (Catholic bishops'
  letter on nuclear weapons), 276-279
charismatics, 250-251
Chavez, Cesar, 280
Chesterton, G. K., 60
chosen people, 46, 60
Christian Bill of Rights, 227
Christian Broadcasting Network, 229,
  243
Christian Coalition, 233, 234, 236-237
Christian Reconstructionist movement,
  323
Christian Right. *See* New Christian Right
Christian Scientists, 75
Christian Voice, 140, 226-228, 231-232,
  243
Christianity
  class conflict theory and, 7
  endorsement of core assumptions, 13
Christmas displays, 104
church and state, 73-74, 120-121. *See
  also* government
  conflict between, 74-77
  establishment clause, 101-105, 115-
    118
  Founders and religion, 82-87
  free-exercise clause, 74-76, 105-111,
    118-120
  limits on government, 87-92
  church-state relations, 111-115
  principles of church-state relations,
    77-82
  public opinion on, 81
  religious expression in public schools,
    97-101
  separationism and, 87-97
church burnings, 197
Church of England, 43-44, 51
Church of Jesus Christ of Latter-day
  Saints. *See* Mormons
Church of Scientology, 127
church planting, 241
church schools, 29, 93, 206-208. *See also*
  parochial schools
  bus transportation for students, 100,
    101-102
  state-aid laws and, 111-112
churches
  activism of, 166-167

affiliation patterns, 170-176
  attendance, 11-12, 15, 37-38
  broadcasting and, 241-243
  commitment to, 213-214, 328-331,
    340-341
  contributions to, 10
  government structure and political
    action of, 32-35
  as institutions, 9-10, 28-32, 206-210,
    241-243, 339
  membership, 9, 12, 22
  as political organizations, 37
  practices of, 11-12
  property taxes on, 102-103
  representation of members' views,
    143-144
  social integration role, 210-215
  as social system, 37-38
Citizens for Educational Freedom, 112
Citizens for Excellence in Education, 234
civil disobedience, 127-128
civil liberties, 325
civil peace, 289-290
civil religion, 59-66
  balance between priestly and prophet-
    ic functions, 66-68
  conservative version, 68
  liberal version, 68
  personal virtue of candidates and, 62-
    63
  presidency and, 61-62, 66
  priestly function, 63, 65-66, 302
  prophetic function, 64-66
  standards provided by, 63-65, 67
Civil Rights Act of 1964, 132-133, 140
civil rights issues, 140, 181-182, 297,
  311-312
Civil Rights Restoration Act, 140, 291
class conflict theory, 5-9, 17-19
Cleaver, Eldridge, 19
clergy
  African American, 40, 134, 303-307
  evangelical Protestant, 241
  ideology of, 201
  political activism of, 293-297
  political campaigning and, 134
  public policy and, 124
  respect for, 10
Clinton, Bill (Clinton administration),
  263
  abortion issues, 284-285

gay rights and, 186-187
health care, 291-292
1992 presidential campaign, 1-2, 50, 63, 178
1996 presidential campaign, 261
religion of, 156
Cochran, Clarke E., 319
Coles, Robert, 329
colonial period
Founders and religion, 82-87
Puritanism, 43-46
Colson, Charles, 19
Commentary, 314
commitment, 213-214, 328-331, 340-341
Committee for Public Education v. Nyquist, 100
communism, 2, 18-19, 67, 183, 270
compacts, 47
Concerned Women of America, 234
Conference of Presidents of Major Jewish Organizations, 142
Congregationalists, 44, 173
Congress, U. S.
elections, 2, 256-257, 262
religious values of members, 204-205
roll call votes and religious influences, 146-149
conscience, free exercise of, 108-111
conscientious objection, 79, 107, 108
Conservative Caucus, 226
Constitution, U. S.
amendments to, 114, 117
as covenant, 49-50
establishment clause, 77-79, 97-105, 115-118
free-exercise clause, 74-76, 78, 105-111, 118-120
human sinfulness concept and, 53-59
ratification of, 57
Continental Congress, 48-49, 89
Contract with America, 233-236, 262
County of Allegheny v. ACLU, 104
covenant theology, 46-50
Crawford, Alan, 223
creationism, 102
creed, 28-32, 60, 61
cults, 26, 119-120
cultural compatibility, and secularization, 19-20

culture war, 188-191
Cuomo, Mario, 263, 269, 289-290

Dade County, Fla., 223-225
Danforth, John, 114
Day, Dorothy, 271
deaf students, 100
December Wars, 104
Declaration of Independence, 48-49
democracy
abortion and, 333-334
essential beliefs, 335-336
Puritanism and, 50-53
religious values and, 335-343
Democratic party
Catholicism and, 31, 175, 195, 209
evangelical Protestantism and, 221-222
Judaism and, 209, 315-316
religious alliances of, 209
demonstrations, 126-127
denominations, 171. diversity of, 21-22, 86
political action and, 139-140
desacralization process, 4, 15
differentiation process, 4
Disciples of Christ, 156, 299
Dobson, James, 235
Dolan, John "Terry," 226
Dole, Robert, 229, 260
Douglas, William O., 79-80, 107
Drinan, Robert, 275
Duke, David, 324
Dutch Reformed church, 44

Eagle Forum, 234
East Brooklyn Churches (EBC), 306
economic advantage
political culture and, 69-70
social status and, 195
economic policy of Catholic church, 279-281
Ecumenical Council, 273
Education Department, U.S., 99-100, 137, 227, 261-262
educational achievement, 192-194
Edwards v. Aguillard, 99
Einstein, Albert, 17
Elazar, Daniel, 160-162
Employment Division v. Smith, 118
Engel v. Vitale, 98-99, 112, 114

Engels, Friedrich, 6
Enlightenment movement, 69, 86
environmentalism, 2, 203-204
Episcopalians, 173, 293, 299
Epperson v. Arkansas, 99
"equal access" law, 114-115, 132, 263
Equal Rights Amendment (ERA), 153, 198, 224-225, 263
Erastian model, 78
establishment clause, 77-79, 101-105
  broadening meaning of, 115-118
  religious expression in public schools and, 97-101
Etzioni, Amitai, 190
evangelical Protestants, 197, 198, 203, 217-218. *See also* New Christian Right
  Democratic party and, 221-222
  diversity among, 249-251
  evangelical mobilization theories, 237-244
  institutional influences, 241-243
  membership of, 247-248
  national movement of, 225-228
  in 1980s, 228-230
  in 1990s, 230-237
  political background, 218-222
  public opinion on, 245-249
  public policy and, 261-263
  Republican party and, 225-226, 228-230, 253-254, 257-261
  social influences and, 238-240
  in the South, 220-222
  values and, 243-244
Everson v. Board of Education, 97-98, 100
evolution, teaching of, 99
executive branch, 153-157. *See also* presidency

Faith Assembly Church, 75-76
Falwell, Jerry, 241, 243, 251, 256, 341
  Christian Bill of Rights, 227
  civil rights issues, 140
  Jewish voters and, 316
  Moral Majority and, 226, 229, 236, 246, 248
Family Research Council, 234
family values. *See* values, family
farm workers, 298
Farrakhan, Louis, 315
Fauntroy, Walter, 305

Federal Communications Commission (FCC), 242
Federalist Papers, The, 55-56
feminism, 292
Fenton, John, 146
Ferraro, Geraldine, 289
Festinger, Leon, 136
First Amendment, 77-78. *See also* Constitution, U. S.
flag, U. S., 107-108, 262
Flake, Floyd, 305
Florida Catholic Conference, 130
Focus on the Family, 235
Ford, Gerald, 131, 155
foreign policy, 67-68, 163-165, 183
Founders, and religion, 82-87
Fourteenth Amendment, 106
Fowler, Robert Booth, 20, 251
Frankfurter, Felix, 153
free-exercise clause, 74-76, 78, 105-111
  case law on, 106-108
  extending claims of, 105-108
  rise and fall of, 118-120
  standard for, 108-111
Friedman, Milton, 203
Frum, David, 261
fundamentalists, 161, 250-251

"gag" rule, 284-285
Garn, Jake, 332
gay rights, 3, 186-187, 223-225. *See also* homosexuals, discrimination against
George III (King of England), 48-49
Girouard v. United States, 107
Glasser, Ira, 235
God
  belief in, 9, 13, 21, 78-79
  image of, 16, 199, 201, 293
  will of, 293
Goldwater, Barry, 114, 221
government. *See also* church and state
  as covenant, 46-50
  decentralization of, 32-33
  foreign policy of, 67-68, 163-165, 183
  institutional restraint and, 53-59
  limits on, 87-92
  negative view of, 57-58
  popular sovereignty, 33-35
  power of, 54-56
  religious values and government activities, 157-162

right to revolt, 46-50
structure of, 32-35, 55-56
Graham, Billy, 251
Grand Rapids v. Ball, 101
Great Britain, 46, 48-49. *See also* colonial
period
Greeley, Andrew, 199, 277
Green, John, 148
Greenawalt, Kent, 344
Griffith, Ernest, 335
Gulf War, 3, 68, 183
Gusfield, Joseph, 239
Guth, James, 148

Hall, Joel David, 75-76
Hamilton, Alexander, 54-55
Hamilton, Howard, 145
*Hamilton v. Regents of the University of
California,* 106-107
Hanna, Mary, 148, 273
Hansen, Susan B. 158
Hatch, Orrin, 114
Hatfield, Mark, 114, 332
Helms, Jesse, 114, 256
Hertzke, Allen, 144
Himmelfarb, Gertrude, 203
Hirsch, H. N., 153
Hofrenning, Daniel, 144
Holtzmann, Marc, 136
home schooling, 207, 263
homosexuals, discrimination against, 3,
186-187, 223-225
Hoover, Herbert, 208
Horwitz, Robert, 59
housing laws, 145, 295, 298
Howe, Daniel Walker, 45
human rights, 3, 155, 335
Humphrey, Hubert, 222
Hunter, James Davison, 188-189
Hyde, Henry, 269

Indiana, 14-15
infiltration, 135-139
Institute for First Amendment Studies,
235
institutional religion, 9-10, 16, 28-32,
206-210, 241-243, 339
intellectualism, 69
interest groups, 111
direct action, 126-129
infiltration, 135-159

lobbying, 129-133, 165-166
political campaigning, 133-135
public policy and, 125-139
Interfaith Alliance, 235
intolerance, and religiosity, 325-334
Irish nationalism, 164-165
Islamic fundamentalism, 2

Jackson, Jesse, 135, 203, 302, 307-308,
314-315
Jackson, Robert, 106
Jay, John, 54-55, 89
Jefferson, Thomas, 20, 84, 85, 88, 90
Jehovah's Witnesses, 105-106, 107
Jelen, Ted, 213
Jewish Defense League (JDL), 312
Jewish National Fund, 136
John Birch Society, 269
Johnson, Charles A., 158, 161
Johnson, Lyndon B., 163, 222
Johnston, Michael, 161-162
Jones, W. Landis, 129
Judaism, 83, 89-90, 101
black-Jewish relations, 311-315
Conservative, 128
Democratic party and, 209, 315-316
holiday displays, 104
as liberal faith, 199-203, 310-316
lobbying, 131
Middle East policy and, 163-165, 313-
314
military dress, 119
organization of, 141-143
Orthodox, 110
political trends and, 310-317
religious affiliations of, 171-176
social standing and Jewish liberalism,
196
state aid laws and, 112
voting patterns, 137
judicial branch
appointments, 137-138
public opinion of, 116
public policy and, 149-153
race relations and, 151-152
JustLife, 291

Kahane, Meier, 312
Kanawha County (West Virginia) Board
of Education, 223-225
Kelley, Dean, 300

Kemp, Jack, 229
Kennan, George, 67
Kennedy, Edward, 269, 289
Kennedy, John F., 20, 61-62, 155
Kersten, Lawrence, K., 200
King, Martin Luther, Jr., 64-65, 76, 303, 304
Kirchwey, Freda, 219
Kiryas Joel v. Grumet, 101
Klatch, Rebecca E., 258-259
Knights of Columbus, 112
Koresh, David, 26, 119
Kristol, Irving, 203, 314
Kristol, William, 203
Ku Klux Klan, 104, 208, 236

LaHaye, Beverly, 234
Lee v. Weisman, 99
Lemon v. Kurtzman, 100, 101, 103-105, 108, 117
Levitt v. Committee for Public Education, 100
Levy, Leonard, 88
Lewis, John, 305
liberalism, 188-191, 301-303
liberalization process, 4
liberation theology, 274
Liberty University, 341-342
Lincoln, Abraham, 65-66
Lipset, Seymour Martin, 316
lobbying, 129-133, 138-139, 165-166
Luker, Kristin, 287-288
Luther, Martin, 200
Lutherans, 173, 199-200
Lutz, Donald, 45
Lynch v. Donnelly, 104
Lynn, Barry, 235

Madison, James, 54-56, 73, 79, 84, 88, 89
Malone, James, 289, 290
Marshall, Susan, 302
Marx, Karl, 6-7, 20-21
Marxism, 6-9, 17-19
Mayflower Compact, 47
McAteer, Ed, 226
McCollum v. Board of Education, 98
McDonough, Peter, 321
Medding, Peter, 141
medical care, withholding, 75-76
medical technology, 18
Meek v. Pittenger, 100

Mennonites, 28, 132
Methodists, 44, 87, 128, 173
Middle East policy, 163-165, 313-314
Middletown study, 14-15
Milgram, Stanley, 340
military
    ban on homosexuals, 3, 186-187
    Catholic policy, 269-270, 274-279, 281
    conscientious objection to service, 79, 107, 108
    training in college, 106-107
    uniforms, 119
militia movement, 18, 129
Miller, William Lee, 42
Million Man March, 315
ministers. *See* clergy
minority religions, 22, 89, 105-108, 110, 118, 170-171
modernization theory, 5-9, 17-19, 299
Moen, Matthew C., 263
moment of silence. *See* prayer in schools
Mondale, Walter, 316
Moral Majority, 198, 218, 242, 248-249
    civil rights and, 140
    disbanding of, 217
    founding of, 226
    membership of, 246
    political appointments of, 137
Morgan, David, 161
Mormons
    abortion and, 147-148, 158
    Equal Rights Amendment and, 153, 198, 224
    origins of, 25, 26
    political activism of, 31
    polygamy practice of, 93
Morris, Aldon, 303
Mueller v. Allen, 102
Muncie, Ind., 14-15
Murray, John Courtney, 289-290

Nagel, Stuart, 150-151
Nation of Islam, 315
National Abortion Rights Action League, 138
National Association for Hebrew Day Schools, 112
National Association for the Advancement of Colored People (NAACP), 305, 309-310

National Catholic Educational Association, 112
National Catholic News Service, 270
National Christian Action Coalition (NCAC), 227-228, 232
National Committee for a Human Life Amendment, 282
National Committee for the Survival of a Free Congress, 226
National Conference of Catholic Bishops, 138
National Conservative Political Action Committee (NCPAC), 226
National Council of Churches (NCC), 112, 130, 132, 300
National Education Association, 248
National Endowment for the Arts, 263
National Jewish Commission on Law and Public Affairs, 112
National Jewish Community Relations Advisory Council (NJCRAC), 141-142
National Organization for Women (NOW), 248, 287
Native American religions, 118, 119
nativity displays, 104
Nazis, 328
Nelsen, Hart, 296-297
Netanyahu, Benjamin, 143
Neuhaus, Richard J., 337
New Christian Right (NCR), 29-30, 227. *See also* evangelical Protestants
    as electoral movement, 252-257
    as mass movement, 244-249
    in 1980s, 228-230
    opponents of, 235-236
    organizations of, 234-235
    roots of, 223-225
New Deal politics, 208-209, 221, 272, 280
New Religious Right. *See* New Christian Right
Newsweek, 172
Nixon, Richard, 63, 116, 155
nonpreferentialism. *See* accommodation doctrine
North, Oliver, 259
Notes on the State of Virginia (Jefferson), 90
Notre Dame Study of Catholic Parish Life, 205
nuclear disarmament, 26, 128, 276-279

O'Connor, John Cardinal, 289
O'Hara, Thomas, 140
Oklahoma City bombing, 129, 324
Olson, Daniel, 190
Opportunities Industrialization Commission (OIC), 305
original sin, 53-59, 199, 339

pacifism, 26-27, 107
PACs. *See* political action committees
Paine, Tom, 86
Palestine Liberation Organization (PLO), 314
Parenti, Michael, 198
Parker, Suzanne, 36
parochial schools, 31, 100, 102, 111-112, 206-208. *See also* church schools
Pennock, J. Roland, 335
People for the American Way, 236
People United to Save Humanity (PUSH), 305
Perkins, H. Wesley, 330
Perot, Ross, 178
peyote (drug), 118
Phillips, Howard, 226
Pilgrims. *See* Puritans
Plamenatz, John, 335
Planned Parenthood, 138, 142, 287
Pledge of Allegiance, 37, 60
pluralism, 21-22
Plymouth Compact, 47
political action committees (PACs), 331-332
political behavior, 169-170
    appointments, 137-138
    "culture war" thesis, 188-191
    group interests and religion, 206-210
    identity, 176-179
    issues, 179-183
    religious affiliation patterns, 170-176
    social integration and, 210-215
    social issues and, 184-188
    social standing and religious differences, 191-197
    values and religion, 197-206
political campaigns
    Catholic involvement, 134
    contributions to, 331-332
    interest groups and, 133-135
    moral behavior of candidates, 62-63
    religious techniques of, 45

political culture, 42-43
  civil religion and, 59-68
  covenant theology and, 46-50
  economic advantage and, 69-70
  influences on, 68-70
  inherent sinfulness and, 53-59
  institutional restraint and, 53-59
  intellectualism and, 69
  Puritanism and colonial thought, 43-46
  Puritanism and democracy, 50-53
  right to revolt and, 46-50
  traditionalist view of, 160-161
political identity, 176-179
political independence, and secularization, 20-21
political life in America, 319-320
  case against religious in politics, 320-327
  case for religion in politics, 334-344
  religiosity and intolerance, 325-334
political office, religious tests for, 83
political party preferences, 176-177
political socialization, 209
politics
  ancient view of, 58
  case against religious influence in politics, 320-327
  case for religion in politics, 334-344
  causes of religious intervention in, 27-32
  of church-state relations, 111-115
  defined, 169
  government structure and political action by churches, 32-35
  image of, 58-59
  limits on religious influence in, 38-41
  moralistic approach, 161-162
  religious activism in, 166-167
  status politics, 239-240, 271, 298
  as substitute for religion, 18-19
polygamy, 93, 106
popular sovereignty, 33-35
Porteous, Skipp, 235
Post Office, U. S., 90-92
poverty, 21, 31-32
Powell, Colin, 257
prayer in schools, 81, 98-99, 102, 112-117
Presbyterians, 44, 128, 173, 293, 299
presidency

civil religion and, 61-62, 66
  inaugural ceremony, 66, 78-79
  religion of the president, 153-157
presidential elections
  1928, 208
  1948, 221
  1976, 154, 244
  1980, 228, 253-254
  1984, 229, 254
  1988, 62-63, 135, 229-230, 247, 254
  1992, 1-2, 50, 63, 170-176, 178, 230, 254
  1996, 259-260, 261
private schools. See church schools; parochial schools
privatization process, 4
profamily agenda, 2, 125, 188-191, 227-228, 233-236, 246-247
property taxes, 102-103
Protestant Ethic and the Spirit of Capitalism, The (Weber), 195
Protestants. See also evangelical Protestants; Puritans
  abortion attitudes, 213
  African American, 171-172, 301-303
  ethic of, 195
  evangelical, 172-176
  mainline, 172-176, 293-299
  political activism of, 31, 297-299
  political traditions of, 293-297
  religious affiliation of, 171-176
  retrenchment, 300-301
Proxmire, William, 114
Public Health Act, 284
Public Interest, 314
public policy, 124-125
  evangelical Protestants and, 261-263
  influences on, 145-149
  interest group activities, 125-139
  judiciary and, 149-153
  limitations on religious influence, 162-166
  on Middle East, 163-165
  political action, 139-143
  president's religion and, 153-157
  religious activism in politics, 166-167
  religious values and government activities, 157-162
  religiously based value systems and, 160-161
  representation, 143-144

public relations techniques, 127
public schools, 97-101
Puritans
  chosen people concept, 46, 60
  civil religion and, 59-66
  covenant theology and, 46-50
  democracy and, 50-53
  effect on colonial thought, 43-46
  inherent sinfulness and, 53-59
  moralistic approach to politics, 160

Quakers, 44, 83, 89, 128
Quayle, Dan, 230
Quayle, Marilyn, 230
Quinley, Harold, 295-296, 297

race relations
  judicial branch and, 151-152
  government action on, 158-159
  segregation, 64-65, 197-198
Reagan, Ronald (Reagan administra-
    tion), 1
  civil religion and, 66
  New Christian Right and, 228-229,
    259
  nuclear weapons and, 276-277
  political appointments, 116, 137,
    227
  religion of, 155-156
redemption doctrine, 54, 199
Reeb, James, 295
Reed, Ralph, 234, 236, 237
Reformation, Protestant, 43, 44, 82
religion. *See also* civil religion; minority
  religions
  aspects of, 28-32
  behaviors, 12-13
  commitment, 213-214, 328-331, 340-
    341
  communal approach, 204-206
  conservative versus liberal, 198-203
  decline of influence, 3-16
  establishment of, 82-86
  Founders on role of religion, 82-87
  as government control, 337-338
  group interests and, 206-210
  human need for, 17
  as institution, 9-10, 16, 28-32, 206-
    210, 241-243, 339
  limitations on religious influence,
    162-166

persistence of, 8-16
pluralism, 21-22, 237
political intervention of, 27-32
as political factor, 1-3
as political resource, 35-38
political values and, 197-206
politics as substitute for, 18-19
science as substitute for, 17-18
Supreme Court definition of, 108
traditions, 171
Religious Coalition for Reproductive
  Choice, 287
Religious Freedom Restoration Act, 119,
  132, 263
Religious Right, 26
Religious Roundtable, 226, 243
Republican party
  abortion and, 259-260
  evangelical Protestants and, 225-226,
    228-230, 253-254, 257-261
  1994 elections, 2, 217-218
  traditional values and, 189-190
resource mobilization theory, 242
revolt, right to, 46-50
Revolutionary War, 45-46, 88
Reynolds v. U.S., 93, 106
Richardson, James, 147
Rieselbach, Leroy, 146
Right-to-Life party, 135
Robb, Chuck, 259
Robertson, Pat, 203, 243, 341
  as charismatic, 250-251
  Christian Coalition and, 233, 237
  presidential bid, 135, 217, 229-230,
    246-247, 249, 302
Robison, James, 229, 243
Roe v. Wade, 33-34, 128, 261, 282, 284,
  286-287
Rokeach, Milton, 326
Roman Catholics. *See* Catholicism
Roof, Wade Clark, 267, 299
Roosevelt, Franklin D., 208-209, 272,
  280

Sabbatarians, 109
Sanctuary movement, 127-128, 211
Santeria religion, 118
Save Our Children, 223-224
Schanberg, Sidney, 64
Schlafly, Phyllis, 64-65, 224, 234, 269
school prayer. *See* prayer in schools

schools. *See* church schools; parochial schools; public schools
science, as substitute for religion, 17-18
Scriptures, 44-45
secular humanism, 225, 240, 248, 258, 260-262
secularization, 3-16, 247
  cultural compatibility and, 19-20
  defined, 4
  explanations for, 17-19
  internal secularization, 4
  naive secularization theory, 8
  persistence of religion, 8-16
  political independence and, 20-21
  religious pluralism and, 21-22
  social identity and, 20
  in United States, 19-23
segregation, 64-65, 197-198
separation of church and state, 20, 74, 79-87. *See also* church and state
  case law on, 93-97
  development of, 92-97
Seventh-Day Adventists, 105, 107
Sheldon, Lou, 235
Sherbert v. Verner, 108-111, 118-120
Shiloh Baptist Church, 305-306
Sicurella v. U.S., 107
Sijlander, Mark, 231
Simon, Paul, 165-166
Simonds, Robert, 234
sinfulness of humans, 53-59, 199, 339
slavery, 25-26, 65-66, 129
Smith, Alfred E., 208, 271
Smith, Larry, 135-136
social change theory, 5-8
Social Gospel, 251, 293-294
social groups, 30-32, 37-38, 238-240
social identity, and secularization, 20
social integration, 210-215
social issues, 184-188, 263
social standing, and religious differences, 191-197
Sojourners, 251
Solzhenitsyn, Alexander, 73
Southern Baptist Convention, 226, 254-255
Southern Baptists, 154-155, 156, 221. *See also* evangelical Protestants
Southern Christian Leadership Conference (SCLC), 303, 308
sovereignty, 33-35

Soviet Union, 67, 155
Specter, Arlen, 257
Spellman, Francis Cardinal, 269-270, 275
status politics, 239-240, 271, 298
Stone, Ann, 190
Stone v. Graham, 99
Street, Nicholas, 45-46
Sullivan, Leon, 305
Supreme Court, U. S.
  appointments, 137-138
  establishment clause and, 116-117
  lobbying and, 129-130
  public opinion of, 116
  voting patterns on criminal cases, 151
Swaggart Ministries v. California, 103
Swierenga, Robert, 42

tax issues, 28-29, 32, 102-103, 125, 133
textbooks, 99, 100, 102, 223-225
theocracy, 78
Thomas Road Baptist Church, 241
Time, 217
tobacco exports, 165-166
Tocqueville, Alexis de, 44, 51, 169
Toolin, Cynthia, 66
"total depravity" concept, 53-59
totalitarianism, 78, 337-338
traditional values, 188-191, 245, 247
Traditional Values Coalition, 235
Truman, Harry S., 155, 163
Twain, Mark, 8

Ulmer, S. Sidney, 151
unemployment discrimination, 109
Unitarians, 128
United States
  antiabortion movement, 33-35
  divine purpose of, 61, 65
  secularization in, 19-23
United States Catholic Conference, 112, 138, 140-141, 142, 273
United States v. Seeger, 108
University of Virginia, 76-77, 88, 121

Valentine, Herbert, 235
values
  of congressional members, 204-205
  democracy and, 335-343
  evangelical Protestants and, 243-244

family, 2, 125, 188-191, 227-228,
    233-236, 246-247
  government activities and, 157-162
  liberal, 188-192
  political, and religion, 197-206
  traditional, 189-190
Vatican II, 273
Verba, Sidney, 61-62
Vietnam War, 198, 270, 274-275
Viguerie, Richard, 226
Vines, Kenneth, 151
violence, as public action, 128-129, 323
voter participation
  church attendance and, 37-38
  evangelical Protestants and, 252-257
voting patterns, 178
  of Catholics, 136-137
  of Jews, 137
  political issues and, 179-183

Wagner, Robert F., 271
wall of separation, 20, 74, 76-77
Wallace, George, 222, 311
Wallace v. Jaffree, 113
Walton, Hanes, 304
*Walz v. Tax Commissioner of the City of New
  York*, 103
Warner, John, Jr., 146
Warner, R. Stephen, 172
Washington, George, 85, 86, 88, 89-90
Washington, Harold, 307
Washington Post, 127
Watson, Sheilah, 161
weapons development, 18, 26, 128, 276-
    279

Weber, Max, 195
Weber, Paul, 129, 139
Webster v. Reproductive Health Services, 261,
    284
Weekly Standard, 203
Weicker, Lowell P., Jr., 1
welfare spending, 181
*West Virginia State Board of Education v.
  Barnette*, 107
Weyrich, Paul, 226
White, Lynn, 203-204
Wide Awake Productions, 76-77
Wightman, Sandie, 147
Wildmon, Donald, 234
Williams, Dorothy L, 149
Wilmore, Gayraud, 309-310
Wilson, Pete, 257
Wimberly, Ronald, 61
Wisconsin v. Yoder, 109
women, roles in society, 185-186, 258-
    259
Wood, Richard L., 212
World Values Survey, 21
Wuthnow, Robert, 68, 201, 243-244,
    327

Yom Kippur War, 142
Young, Andrew, 314
Young Women's Christian Association,
    130

Zionism, 26, 163, 313-314, 323-
    324
Zorach v. Clausen, 98
Zorinsky, Edward, 114